REVISIONING TRANSPERSONAL THEORY

SUNY series in Transpersonal and Humanistic Psychology

RICHARD D. MANN, editor

JORGE N. FERRER

FOREWORD BY RICHARD TARNAS

REVISIONING TRANSPERSONAL THEORY

A Participatory Vision of Human Spirituality

STATE UNIVERSITY OF NEW YORK PRESS

Published by
STATE UNIVERSITY OF NEW YORK PRESS
ALBANY

For information, address
State University of New York Press,
90 State Street, Suite 700, Albany, NY 12207

Production and book design, Laurie Searl
Marketing, Mike Campochiaro

Library of Congress Cataloging-in-Publication Data

Ferrer, Jorge Noguera, 1968–
    Revisioning transpersonal theory : a participatory vision of human
spirituality / Jorge Noguera Ferrer ; with a foreword by Richard Tarnas.
        p. cm.—(SUNY series in transpersonal and humanistic psychology)
Includes bibliographical references and index.
ISBN 0-7914-5167-4 (alk. paper)—ISBN 0-7914-5168-2 (pbk. : alk. paper)
    1. Sprituality—Psychology. 2. Transpersonal psychology. 3. Psychology,
Religious. I.
Title. II. Series.

BL624.F455 2001
291.4—dc21
                                                                2001042013

10   9   8   7   6   5   4   3   2   1

CONTENTS

Foreword by Richard Tarnas   vii

Preface   xvii

Acknowledgments   xxiii

1   TRANSPERSONAL THEORY—NOW AND THEN   1

PART I   DECONSTRUCTION

2   THE EXPERIENTIAL VISION OF HUMAN SPIRITUALITY   15

3   THE EMPIRICIST COLONIZATION OF SPIRITUALITY   41

4   TROUBLE IN PARADISE:
THE PERENNIAL PHILOSOPHY REVISITED   71

PART II   RECONSTRUCTION

5   THE PARTICIPATORY NATURE OF SPIRITUAL KNOWING   115

6   AN OCEAN WITH MANY SHORES:
THE CHALLENGE OF SPIRITUAL PLURALISM   133

7   AFTER THE PARTICIPATORY TURN   159

8   A MORE RELAXED SPIRITUAL UNIVERSALISM   183

Notes   193

References   227

Index   257

FOREWORD

Revolutions in human thought seldom take place in a single clean sweep. Whether in science or philosophy, religion or art, major advances always emerge in a particular context and with a specific historical background that deeply shape and even constrain the way they unfold. A paradigm shift will often be initiated by a distinct, extraordinary break from the past—a kind of declaration of independence—yet this initial breakthrough will retain from the old paradigmatic structure certain essential and usually unexamined assumptions that limit the success of the new vision.

These limiting assumptions held over from the past are, to use Erich Voegelin's term, like a mortgage imposed on the new paradigm by the historical circumstances of its origin. On the one hand, the retained principles make possible the paradigm revolution in the first place, since the intellectual climate and presuppositions of the time could not have successfully supported a more radical break all at once. Yet on the other hand, the unconscious holdover often weakens the power of the new paradigm, and can even threaten to destroy it. Eventually, a crisis is reached. It may then happen that a second intervention will take place, a second conceptual breakthrough virtually as essential as the first, which will emancipate the original revolution from its unconscious limitations and allow the full paradigm shift to be realized.

We see this dramatic sequence in the classic case of the Copernican revolution. Copernicus's fundamental insight, that a more elegant and compelling cosmology could be conceived around a planetary Earth and a central Sun, was deeply constrained by his retaining the long-established ancient Greek assumption that the planets must move with uniform circular motion. This unquestioned principle forced Copernicus's system to have as much mathematical complexity as Ptolemy's, requiring the retention of various ad hoc epicyclic constructions in order to approximate the observed planetary positions. Even with these elaborate corrections the heliocentric theory proved no more accurate than the old geocentric model in matching the empirical data. This was the situation for more than half a century until the

arrival of Kepler, fully committed to the Copernican hypothesis, yet willing
to confront squarely the stubborn anomalies and ad hoc epicyclic complexities
that undermined the theory's viability. Having arduously attempted to fit the
most recent planetary observations into every possible hypothetical system of
circles and epicycles he could devise, he was finally obliged to conclude that
some other geometrical figure must be the true form of planetary orbits. By
daring to step outside the ancient framework of assumptions about what could
possibly be true, Kepler discovered that the observations precisely matched
orbits that were not circular in shape but elliptical, sweeping out equal areas in
equal time. Kepler thereby dispensed with all the inadequate epicyclic correc-
tive devices of the Ptolemaic system and brilliantly solved the ancient "problem of the planets" that had driven and riddled astronomical theory for two
thousand years. By so doing, Kepler liberated the Copernican hypothesis from
its unconscious fetters. Within a few months of the publication of Kepler's discovery, Galileo turned his telescope to the heavens, and the Copernican revolution proceeded on to its epochal triumph in the modern age.

We can now recognize a similar situation with respect to the paradigm
shift initiated by transpersonal psychology. From its birth in the late 1960s
with the seminal work of Abraham Maslow and Stanislav Grof, the transpersonal movement represented a profoundly liberating impulse, and in certain
respects a revolutionary break from the past, within the field of psychology.
Compared with the positivism and reductionism that had long dominated the
field, transpersonal psychology's inclusion and validation of the spiritual
dimension of human experience opened the modern psychological vision to
a radically expanded universe of realities—Eastern and Western, ancient and
contemporary, esoteric and mystical, shamanic and therapeutic, ordinary and
non-ordinary, human and cosmic. Spirituality was now recognized as not
only an important focus of psychological theory and research but an essential
foundation of psychological health and healing. Developing ideas and directions pioneered by William James and C.G. Jung, transpersonal psychology
and theory began to address the great schism between religion and science
that so deeply divided the modern sensibility.

But as the work of Jorge Ferrer now illuminates, the very circumstances of
transpersonal psychology's origins, born as it was out of a modern science with
philosophical roots in the Enlightenment, compelled the field to build its theoretical structures and foundations on inherited principles that—while crucial
for its immediate success—gradually revealed themselves to be acutely prob-

lematic in the long term. With modernity's focus on the individual Cartesian subject as the starting point and foundation for any understanding of reality, with its pervasive assertion of the knowing subject's epistemic separation from an independent objective reality, and finally with the modern disenchantment of the external world of nature and the cosmos, it was virtually inevitable that transpersonal psychology would emerge in the form that it did: namely, with an overriding commitment to legitimate the spiritual dimension of existence by defending the empirical status of private, individual intrasubjective experiences of an independent universal spiritual reality. With modern cosmology's voiding of any intrinsic spiritual meaning or structure in the publicly accessible external universe, empirical validation of a spiritual reality had to be via private and intrasubjective experience. And since experience of the ultimate spiritual reality was regarded as one shared by mystics of all ages, it was, like scientific truth, independent of human interpretations and projections, and empirically replicable by anyone properly prepared to engage in the appropriate practices. In turn, this consensually validated supreme reality was seen as constituting a single absolute Truth which subsumed the diverse plurality of all possible cultural and spiritual perspectives within its ultimate unity. This was the essential transcendent Truth in which all religions at their mystical core ultimately converged.

Transpersonal psychology's commitment to such an epistemology and ontology certainly also reflected the powerful legacy of modern humanism and the longer Western humanistic tradition dating back to the Renaissance and earlier to ancient Greece, which exalted the sovereign value of the individual—of individual human experience, human potential, and self-actualization. Moreover, the expansive and intense private subjectivity of much psychedelic experience, a key factor in the philosophical transformation of a generation of transpersonal thinkers, played a critical role in strengthening transpersonal psychology's commitment to an inner empiricism.

Less obvious, though no less influential, was the great underlying drama of the modern Western self as it strove to emerge from its historical religious matrix, that is, to define itself autonomously and thus in some sense to disengage itself from Christianity, the dominant vessel of the West's spiritual impulse for the better part of two millennia. The leading figures in transpersonal psychology were all working within and reacting against a Western cultural tradition whose religious imagination had been deeply informed, and problematically dominated, by Christianity. The reasons for this tension were many and complex, but an antagonistic response—sometimes subtle, other times explicit—to the Judaeo-Christian legacy in the West was generally shared by the entire transpersonal community and the larger counterculture of which it was part, and this in turn influenced and encouraged its immense attraction to the spiritual riches of the East. But beyond the explicitly spiritual and religious dimension of this attitude, all the leaders of the transpersonal movement shared the larger background of the Enlightenment's historical struggle with the Christian religion for dominance in the modern world view.

The Enlightenment impulse to privilege the universal truth of an objective reality—an unambiguous independent truth that could be reliably confirmed by direct experience and the appropriate experimental procedures, that transcended the diversity of various cultural and personal perspectives, that cleansed the mind of all subjective distortions and superstitious delusions, that demystified reality of all mythological baggage and anthropomorphic projections—this overriding impulse had effectively served the modern project of freeing modern thought from the perceived constrictions of a dogmatic Christianity.

But transpersonal psychology was now motivated by the same impulse in a new quest, focused this time not on the nature of the material world but on the nature of spirituality: namely, to free spirituality from its previous obligatory association with the now increasingly relativized Christian religion, yet also to free spirituality from its negation by modern science while remaining true to scientific principles of empiricist testing and validation. In turn, this quest was deeply affected by the widespread encounter with various Asian mystical practices and perspectives, usually removed from their complex cultural contexts and emphasizing a contemplative goal of nondual transcendence. The combined result of these several factors was transpersonal theory's commitment to a "perennial philosophy" which in essence privileged the same kind of truth in the psychospiritual world that the rationalist Enlightenment had privileged with respect to the physical world: a pregiven, impersonal, universal truth that was independent of all subjective and cultural interpretations and that could be empirically verified with appropriate methodologies employed by an appropriate community of investigators. This perennialist Truth was the highest truth, superior to all others. It was a Truth exclusively capable of including and defining all other truths.

In a sense, the pioneers and leading theorists of transpersonal psychology had two aims. They wished to legitimate their new discipline and the ontological status of spirituality in the eyes of empirical science, the dominant force in the modern world view. Yet they equally sought to legitimate spirituality and their discipline in their own eyes, which required them to satisfy those standards and assumptions of empirical science that they themselves had internalized in the course of their own intellectual development.

The belief in a pregiven objective reality—whether spiritual or material—that could be empirically validated; the further conviction that this reality was ultimately single and universal, independent of the diversity of human interpretations, and that its deep structures could be described by progressively more accurate representations as the history of thought advanced; the corollary belief that on this basis, sharply bivalent assessments, either affirmative or rejecting, could be made of all "competing" spiritual and psychological perspectives, and that hierarchical rankings of religious traditions and mystical experiences as more or less evolved could thereby be established according to their relative accuracy in representing this independent reality: all these principles, derived from the scientific ideology of modernity, were carried forth into the transpersonal paradigm. And in being carried forth, they at once helped legitimate the paradigm and yet increasingly began to engender internal tensions, theoretical incoherencies, and even internecine conflicts.

In practice—on the ground level, as it were, in its lived reality—the transpersonal tent from the beginning was an extraordinarily embracing, tolerant, richly pluralistic community of seekers and scholars, students and teachers. The periodic large gatherings around the world of the International Transpersonal Association, founded by Grof in the 1970s, were exceptionally encompassing events, each one a combination of wide-ranging psychology conference, new age cultural festival, and something resembling the World Parliament of Religions. Few gatherings could have been more fertilely dialogical. A similar ethos pervaded the ongoing seminars, symposia, and workshops at Esalen Institute, for many years an epicenter of the transpersonal world.

But at the theoretical level, in books, journals, and graduate classrooms, the most energetic and widely discussed conceptual frameworks in transpersonal theory were marked by an increasingly intense commitment to a single absolute universal truth, stringent bivalent logic, and the construction of all-subsuming metasystems that confidently rejected or affirmed particular spiritual traditions and philosophical perspectives according to specific abstract criteria and ranked them in ascending evolutionary sequences. This in turn brought forth increasingly heated controversies and conflicts, as representatives of an enormous range of diverse traditions and perspectives—indigenous and shamanic, esoteric and gnostic, Romantic and Neo-Romantic, Jungian and archetypal, feminist and ecofeminist, as well as Wiccan and Goddess spirituality, Buddhism, nature mysticism, Christian and Jewish and Islamic mysticism, anthroposophy, American Transcendentalism, deep ecology, systems theory, evolutionary cosmology, Whiteheadian process theology, Bohmian physics, and many others—all asserted the intrinsic worth of their positions against theoretical superstructures by which they felt marginalized, devalued, and misrepresented. The situation was further complicated by the fact that transpersonal psychology's own data—the findings of modern consciousness research, experiential therapies, psychedelic reports, spiritual emergencies, research in non-ordinary states of consciousness, field anthropology, thanatology, the reports of mystics across diverse cultures and eras—suggested a far more complex picture than the leading theoretical systems could accommodate. By the 1990s, a kind of civil war had emerged, engulfing the field in controversy and schism.

It is this immensely complex and conflicted situation, in all its conceptual intricacy, that Jorge Ferrer's *Revisioning Transpersonal Theory* brilliantly confronts, diagnoses, and recontextualizes. This is a profoundly liberating book. Ferrer has assimilated all the major works and ideas of the field, and thought through the difficult issues at stake. He has integrated the most recent developments in fields that had heretofore been inadequately engaged by transpersonal theory—crosscultural philosophy of religion, comparative mysticism, interreligious dialogue, hermeneutics and poststructuralism, post-Kuhnian philosophy of science—fields acutely relevant to the current debates. And perhaps especially important, he has explored deeply a range of transformative practices, spiritual paths, and spiritually informed social action that have brought crucial dimensions of embodiment to the intellectual and spiritual issues.

I will leave it to the reader to enjoy the unfolding drama of Ferrer's masterful analysis as he lays the groundwork for resolving the crisis of transpersonal theory. In essence, Ferrer has comprehended the most valuable insights of the postmodern mind and integrated them into the transpersonal vision, while fully transcending the dogmatic relativism and compulsively fragmenting skepticism that afflicted some earlier postmodern perspectives (limitations rooted in that hidden secular reductionism which served as postmodernity's own unconscious mortgage to the modern). The underlying project of the leading transpersonal metatheories has explicitly been to integrate modern science with premodern religion. To achieve this, numerous ad hoc theoretical modifications were required to explain the many resulting anomalies and incoherencies, blunt the diverse criticisms, and patch up the attempted supersynthesis. These modifications usually drew on various postmodern ideas that were helpful for meeting the specific problems at issue, but in the long run proved to be essentially epicyclic corrections for an overall strategy that could not do justice to the complex reality it sought to explain.

Ferrer, by contrast, has absorbed the full meaning of the postmodern turn at its deepest and irreplaceable core: He has articulated a radically *participatory* and *pluralistic* understanding of spiritual realities, spiritual practices, and spiritual knowledge. He critiques the intrasubjective empiricism imported from empiricist science that has dominated the field and colonized it with inapt and self-defeating requirements for replication, testing, and falsification. And he affirms the validity of a multiplicity of spiritual liberations, in which various spiritual traditions and practices cultivate and "enact," bring forth, through cocreative participation in a dynamic and indeterminate spiritual power, a plurality of authentic spiritual ultimates.

With this crucial insight into the participatory, enactive, and pluralistic nature of spiritual truth, the transpersonal field frees itself to enter into a new world of openness to the Mystery of being that is its ground, accompanied by a newly respectful and fruitful dialogue between diverse religions, metaphysical perspectives, and spiritual practices. By cutting the Gordian knot that has invisibly bound transpersonal theory to the Enlightenment like an outlived umbilical cord, the transpersonal field can open to new horizons, its vision no longer so riven by futile and too often intolerant, undialogical debate.

I salute Ferrer's emphatic affirmation of the Mystery with which all transpersonal and spiritual inquiry is concerned, the boundless creative freedom of the ultimate ground, its liberating defiance of all intellectual schemas that claim to theorize the whole of reality. And this affirmation is achieved, not simply by apodictic declaration, but by rigorous epistemological analysis of the relevant transpersonal theories, an equally meticulous comparison of crosscultural religious and mystical reports, and an incisive critique of contemporary spiritual practice. It is a pleasure to see here a powerful mind employed fully in service of opening to the Mystery of existence, rather than attempting to contain, categorize, and rank, in service of the needs of an overarching system.

This is in many ways a very simple book. It certainly is extremely clear, written with an intelligent and patient care to make every point transparent to the reader, with every position at issue represented with conscientious accuracy, and with each possible objection or alternative lucidly addressed. Each successive chapter brings greater penetration into the field's central problems and greater freedom from their constraints. One finishes this book with a clearer mind and a more spacious vision than one begins it.

To engage transpersonal discourse at the level required to write this book, one must have done an incalculable amount of close reading and deep thinking, on an extremely broad range of topics and in a wide range of disciplines. And because it is this particular field—involving not only philosophy and psychology but spirituality and religion—there is an even greater potential in the process of such an accomplishment for spiritual inflation.

But Ferrer demonstrates in this book the very qualities of scholarship and dialogue that best reflect the character of his spiritual vision—the care with which he describes both his own positions and those of others, the openness to being corrected, the ability to be critical without sarcasm or rancor, the setting forth of opposing ideas in a manner that scrupulously reflects how their exponents themselves would articulate them. The consistent priority is clearly to seek and serve truth, rather than advance or preserve one's own position and reputation at others' expense.

Transpersonal realities can never be adequately or accurately described by intellectually confident assessments and rankings of the multiplicity of humanity's spiritual paths and perspectives measured against a single pre-given universal Reality. They can be approached, rather, only by a much more subtly intelligent and more heartful dialogical engagement with the Mystery that is source of all—hence, by a dialogical engagement with each other in respectful openness to the diversity of wisdom's self-disclosures, and a dialogical engagement with one's interior being and with the cosmos itself, in reverent openness to the irreducible depths of its mystery, intelligence, and power. Such knowledge is an act of the heart as much as it is an act of the mind, the two inextricably united.

We can perhaps now recognize that great temptation to which our field temporarily succumbed, seen in certain stages of the spiritual and intellectual quest, a temptation that any brilliant spiritually informed mind may encounter: to attempt intellectually to master the Mystery, to overpower its power, to overcome its free spontaneity, to show how everything fits one's system, to avoid the psychological fears and anxieties of confronting the larger Unknown, that which can never be mastered. This book provides the theoretical matrix for honoring this recognition. It honors that Spirit which blows like the wind, "where it wills."

As the transpersonal field moves to an understanding of human spirituality as more profoundly encompassing and participatory, many have begun to see the very word "transpersonal" as needing to be addressed, and perhaps fundamentally redefined. For as we integrate more fully the amplitude and immanence of the sacred, we better discern that spiritual power moving in and through the human person in all her and his living, embodied, situated specificity: psychological and physical, gendered, relational, communal, cultural and historical, ecological and cosmic. In this understanding, "trans" recovers its original Latin larger range of meanings—signifying not only *beyond* but also *across, through, pervading; so as to change, transform; occurring by way of.* Here "transpersonal" multivalently acknowledges the sacred dimension of life dynamically moving beyond as well as within, through, and by way of the human person in a manner that is mutually transformative, complexly creative, opening to a fuller participation in the divine creativity that *is* the human person and the ever unfolding cosmos. It is precisely this spiritual dynamism in the human person embedded in a spiritually alive cosmos that empowers, and challenges, the human community's participatory cocreation of spiritual realities, including new realities still to unfold.

If the founding works of transpersonal psychology by Maslow and Grof constituted its declaration of independence, then this book may well be seen as its emancipation proclamation, its "new birth in freedom." For here transpersonal theory is liberated from that mortgage to the past, those constraining assumptions and principles inherited from its Enlightenment and modern scientific origins. As revolutionary and profound a force as transpersonal theory has been over the past three decades, it has in a fundamental way been working inside a conceptual box. It has been subtly constrained by epistemological and metaphysical blinders that have unconsciously restricted its vision, thereby engendering numerous seemingly irresolvable problems, distortions, and conflicts. Only with the recognition of these inhibiting assumptions could the full emancipatory potential of the original transpersonal breakthrough finally be fulfilled.

If I may draw again on the Copernican analogy, transpersonal theory in its first thirty years, after freeing itself from a kind of geocentric/egocentric materialist reductionism dominant in mainstream psychology, tended to constellate itself around the transcendent Sun of perennialism as the absolute and single fixed center of the spiritual universe. Only with time has it become apparent that we live in a much vaster, more interesting, radically pluralistic world, an omnicentered cosmos with innumerable suns and stars around which are constellated multiple universes of meaning. These meanings are not pregiven and objective but rather are participatively and cocreatively brought forth out of an indeterminate and dynamic matrix of spiritual mystery.

We owe a debt of gratitude to Ferrer for his courage in bringing forth this work, though in a sense it reflects the maturation of the entire field, of the wider transpersonal community. I stand in admiration before the magnitude and depth of thought and experience, dialogue and reflection that has taken place within the transpersonal field to permit the possibility of this work being written at the present time. For at a deep level, the transpersonal community itself has brought forth this book: As Ferrer would himself be the first and most enthusiastic to declare, it is not the work of one person— though we owe so much to the person who articulated it.

RICHARD TARNAS

PREFACE

We live in times of extreme confusion about spiritual matters. With the decline of Christianity and the increasing interest in indigenous and Eastern traditions, many Westerners have involved themselves in a continuing and often seemingly endless exploration of spiritual paths and practices. Some have rejected their religious roots, traveled to India or South America, and embraced philosophies and ways of life that they feel are more harmonious with their essential nature, more effective in bringing balance and well-being to their lives, and more sensitive to contemporary problems and concerns. Others have adopted some kind of spiritual eclecticism or syncretism, importing and mixing from a variety of religious traditions those beliefs and practices they consider to be vital at certain times and for certain purposes. And others, often in dialogue with other traditions, have launched a modern reconstruction of their root religions, proposing this as the remedy for the individual and collective alienation characteristic of our modern times. All three movements are essential components of what may be called the Spiritual Renaissance of the Western world.

For several decades, in the midst of this confusing flux, a number of theorists have been developing conceptual frameworks and understandings that attempt not only to legitimize spirituality in the secularized West, but also to bring order to the prevailing religious chaos and apparent anarchy. This, I believe, is the original impetus of the transpersonal movement: to present cogent visions of human nature and reality that honor the increasing interest and hunger for a deeper spiritual connection in the context of the philosophical and scientific discourse of modernity.

I have chosen transpersonal theory as the context of this book not only because of my familiarity with this field, but also, and most importantly, because many transpersonal thinkers have decisively affected the ways in which an increasing number of individuals in our culture understand and live their spirituality in modern times. Transpersonal authors, for example, have unpacked many of the complex dynamics of psychospiritual growth and offered a variety of orienting maps to more skillfully navigate the some-times turbulent spiritual waters. Transpersonal authors have also developed influential models to understand interreligious relations, comprehensive classi-fications of spiritual experiences, and a variety of compelling arguments sug-gesting the epistemic value of spirituality and its connection to optimal psy-chological health.

Given its origins in twentieth century Western culture, however, the transpersonal enterprise has been for the most part a rather *modern* project. The birth of transpersonal psychology can be seen as emerging from the encounter of the modern self with the sacred dimensions of life and exis-tence. At a time when personal identity was primarily experienced as an iso-lated Cartesian ego, and spirituality mainly understood in terms of individual subjective experience, it was probably inevitable that the modern reconnec-tion with the sacred had to be launched through a trans-personal psychology, with "trans" understood essentially as "beyond." On the one hand, it is natu-ral that in a culture that confined spirituality to the innermost depths of indi-vidual subjectivity, the reunion of the modern self and the sacred had to begin within the discipline that most directly studies human experience, that is, psychology. On the other hand, it is understandable that a Cartesian men-tal ego that lives essentially dissociated from its body, the depths of its heart, and the very vital energies that would naturally connect it with the spiritual dimensions of life, had to experience and understand the sacred as something beyond itself, beyond its sense of personhood, or, in this sense, trans-personal.

It should not be surprising, then, that as the Cartesian ego dissolves its grip on the contemporary self, as human beings become more whole or intuitively foresee their wider and deeper identity, a narrow understanding of the term transpersonal as "beyond the personal" may become increasingly unsatisfactory. As human beings reconnect with their heart, their body, and the vital energies that enliven them, the sacred is no longer experienced as a *transpersonal* "hierophany"—an irruption of the sacred in a profane self or world (Eliade, 1959)—but as a fundamental dimension of both personhood and reality. In other words, as we become more aware of our intrinsic vital connection with the sacred, the transpersonal gradually reveals itself to us as more and more personal. In short, this is the shift from a Cartesian ego that experiences the sacred as "other" to a complete human being that naturally and spontaneously participates in the deeper, sacred dimensions of life. Likewise, as the presence of Spirit is recognized not only in our interior

depths, but also in the rich texture of our relationships and the very substance of the world, a transpersonal psychology had to pave the way to a
transpersonal theory (Washburn, 1995), a variety of transpersonal disciplines
such as transpersonal anthropology, transpersonal sociology, and transpersonal ecology (Walsh & Vaughan, 1993), or, more recently, a multidisciplinary
transpersonal orientation that encompasses social work, ecology, art, literature, acting, law, and business and entrepreneurship (Bocouvulas, 1999).

But the modern spell upon our spiritual endeavors is not yet fully exor-
cised. It breathes with ease, for example, in the still prevailing understanding
of spirituality as individual inner experience, the defense of spiritual knowledge as empirical, and the reductionistic nature of most universalist accounts
of spiritual diversity. One of the theses of this book is that these proposals,
although once salutary and probably inevitable, have become increasingly
problematic, and that a fresh approach to spirituality is called for.

This was the prevalent intellectual climate existing when I first came to
the United States eight years ago, and it continues to be so. I arrived in the
Bay Area of California with a fairly basic universalist scheme of spirituality
and the desire to expand my own spiritual growth and understanding. Despite
their supposedly inclusivist stance, I soon realized that most of the proposed
universalist visions in the modern West are reductionistic in that they tend to
privilege certain human potentials and spiritual paths over others, subverting
their explicit intentions of honoring all truths and often resulting in an oversimplification, distortion, or limitation of the vast and rich possibilities for
human spiritual flourishing. Furthermore, I gradually became aware that these
universalist visions are neither sensitive enough to the diversity of individual
archetypal and spiritual needs, dispositions, and developmental dynamics, nor
generous enough to the infinite creative potential of Spirit. More often than
not, contemporary seekers struggle to make their lives conform to a pregiven
spiritual ideas or pathway that their minds have adopted from either a tradition, teacher, or universalist scheme. Too often, spiritual seekers are involved in
a self-absorbed search for certain inner experiences that those models or teachers
present as more enlightened or spiritually evolved, thereby unconsciously
sabotaging the natural process of their own unique spiritual unfolding and
constraining the creative potential of the spiritual power that can manifest
through them. Although fruits can be obtained from a commitment to
almost any spiritual practice, the final outcome of these endeavors is often a
spiritual life that is devitalized, stagnated, dissociated, or conflicted.

We want to be free and happy. We want to be free from unnecessary suffering, from alienating self-preoccupation, from unwholesome conditionings, from limiting illusions and debilitating self-deceptions. We want to feel fully alive, to be in harmony with other human beings, to feel connected with the rich sources of life, to be attuned to Nature and the Cosmos. There is nothing wrong with these desires. To be free and happy is perhaps our true heritage, our natural condition, our most essential nature. But whenever we find a specific pathway that provides us with some freedom and happiness, our minds tend to subtly devalue other paths, even those that seem to be working quite well for others. Our minds start constructing and imposing compelling rational schemes that situate our spiritual choices in a privileged place, thus automatically prejudging other options as inferior. Hierarchical arrangements of traditions and practices follow: Nondual traditions are closer to the source of Being than dual ones. Buddhist meditation is a more evolved spiritual practice than shamanism. Working with a guru is more spiritually effective than working without one. And so forth. The tendency to value as better or higher what has been liberating for us is understandable. But given the number of personal, academic, and religious conflicts that stem from such attitudes, I find this tendency not only unnecessary but also problematic and misleading. One of my aims in this work is to suggest directions to start thinking about spirituality in a different and, I believe, more fruitful light.

As to how this work should be approached, I need to appeal straight away to the patience of the reader when reading some of the passages of this book. Some of the discussions are dense and technical in nature. This is because many of the epistemological presuppositions of the transpersonal project have become the unconscious lenses through which we approach our spiritual lives and the world at large, and, as I argue in this book, they have an impoverishing effect on how we live and interact with others. In other words, I believe that many assumptions that secretly guide our spiritual choices and judgments are rooted in a very arid epistemological terrain. To reveal and deconstruct these assumptions effectively, we need to address them in their own terms.

My goal in this book, however, is not only to increase awareness about the desolate state of the soil in which we have too often planted our "spiritual trees," but also to work alternative epistemological and metaphysical grounds that I believe are conducive to a richer spiritual harvest. To foster the growth of newly invigorated stems, branches, and fruits in our spiritual trees, we need to transplant their roots to more fertile grounds: Grounds that allow us to expand the range of valid spiritual choices and root them in our unique psychospiritual dispositions; grounds that allow us to appreciate a rich variety of spiritual pathways as potential skillful means to develop and express love and wisdom; grounds that, I believe, naturally foster more optimal conditions for a fuller manifestation of the endless creativity of Spirit on Earth. In a later book, I will address the ramifications of these new grounds for individual and collective psychospiritual growth. Here my efforts are directed at preparing the terrain. In any event, if you find that the discussion gets too complex at times, I encourage you to skip over it and move to the next sections or chapters. And if you read patiently through the entire book, my hope is that at the end of the journey you may be able to look at your spiritual life with new eyes.

ACKNOWLEDGMENTS

My greatest joy in concluding this book is not to offer it to the world. My greatest joy is to have the opportunity to thank all the truly exceptional beings who generously offered me the time, support, love, insight, and critical perspectives so necessary to complete it.

I owe thanks above all to Richard Tarnas for his continuous support and meticulous critical reading of earlier versions of this book, as well as for kindly agreeing to write its Foreword. Our numerous dialogues during the writing of this work have always been rich sources of inspiration, and some of the original ideas advanced in his writings have profoundly impacted central aspects of my thinking. His caring advice and seasoned insight are precious jewels that shine through each one of the sentences of this book.

I want also to thank Larry Spiro and Michael Washburn for their continued encouragement, constructive criticism, and, especially, for their friendship. In particular I would like to thank Larry Spiro for his gentle guidance of the general direction of my early efforts, and for his recognition of the spiritual value of this revision of transpersonal theory. A gesture of gratitude to Michael Washburn, who not only offered me critical feedback that helped me to balance and qualify my perspective in important ways, but also modeled the spirit of inquiry and openness so central to the present project.

Kenneth Ring and Jenny Wade appeared in my life like angels from the sky. I have no doubt that without their enthusiastic encouragement, penetrating minds, and, especially, loving presence, this work would not be the same. I want also to thank Kenneth Ring for his constructive comments on earlier versions of this book.

I am also grateful to John Heron, whose original work and critical views have enriched and complemented my perspective in fundamental ways. Our ongoing dialogue has helped me to articulate many of the ideas of this book with greater precision than I would have been able to do on my own.

Donald Rothberg has been a decisive influence in the development of this work. His pioneering critique of some aspects of an experiential account of spirituality is clearly one of the foundations upon which this work is built. Also, my debt to his inspiring example in attempting to develop a spiritually informed scholarship is incalculable.

Ken Wilber's thinking has also been a rich source of stimulation and challenge in the development of my ideas, and although this book contains sections critical of some aspects of his work, they should be seen in the context of my deep appreciation for his person and singular brilliance.

Special thanks to Steve Dinan, who patiently and carefully read an earlier version of this manuscript, offering me priceless suggestions of content and style that significantly improved my presentation.

I owe special gratitude to Brendan Collins for his early encouragement and supportive presence, and to Brant Cortright, Sean Kelly, and Jürgen Kremer for their friendship and discerning feedback.

I have also been enriched by numerous dialogues with Daniel Chapman, who not only taught me about the spirit of the in-between, but also provided me with a number of references that have been pivotal for the growth of my vision.

Conversations and exchanges with many other friends and colleagues helped me to bring greater clarity to this work, including Rosemarie Anderson, Chris Bache, John Buchanan, Mariana Caplan, Robert Fisher, Michael Fosler, Octavio García, Ray Grasse, Will Keepin, James Mitchell, III, Peter Nelson, Kaisa Puhakka, Fernando Rodriguez Bornaetxea, David Welty, and the anonymous SUNY Press reviewers.

Thanks to the initiative of Kenneth Ring, Donald Rothberg, and Kaisa Puhakka, a number of individuals combined their efforts to provide me with the support necessary to continue my work in the United States. Without their care and generosity, this book would not have been possible. In this regard, I would like to make special mention of Chris Bache, Seymour Boorstein, Jim Fadiman, Tobin Hart, John Heron, Jürgen Kremer, Jeanne Loveless-Green, Ralph Metzner, Stan Quinn, Stuart Sovatsky, Larry Spiro, Richard Tarnas, Jenny Wade, Michael Washburn, Ken Wilber, and, most especially, my students at the Institute of Transpersonal Psychology, Palo Alto, California, who happened to became aware of my situation and anonymously added their help.

I also owe special gratitude to Rob Lehman for the granting a Fetzer Presidential Award that allowed me to conclude this book in much briefer time than it would have been otherwise possible, and to Richard Tarnas and Wink Franklin for their invaluable support in obtaining the award.

I want to thank "La Caixa" Cultural Foundation, Barcelona, Spain, for granting me a fellowship that supported my research in the United States during 1993–1995, and the California Institute of Integral Studies, San Francisco, for an International Scholarship that helped me to finance the completion of my studies.

In addition, I want to thank Jane Bunker, Laurie Searl, and the editorial staff at SUNY Press for their kind and extremely helpful assistance throughout this project.

A few portions of this book are based on or derived from material published elsewhere, as follows: parts of chapters 2 and 5 are excerpted by permission of the publisher from "Transpersonal Knowledge: A Participatory Approach to Transpersonal Phenomena" in *Transpersonal Knowing: Exploring the Horizon of Consciousness*, edited Tobin Hart, Peter Nelson, and Kaisa Puhakka (Albany, NY: SUNY Press, 2000); parts of chapter 3 appeared in "Speak Now or Forever Hold Your Peace. An Essay Review of Ken Wilber's *The Marriage of Sense and Soul: Integrating Science and Religion,*" *The Journal of Transpersonal Psychology, 30*(1), 1999; parts of chapters 4 and 6 are from "The Perennial Philosophy Revisited," *The Journal of Transpersonal Psychology, 32*(1), 2000, used with permission from the Institute of Transpersonal Psychology; and parts of the preface, chapters 6 and 7 are from "New Horizons in Contemporary Spirituality: An Introduction" and "Towards a Participatory Vision of Human Spirituality," *ReVision*, 24(2), 2001, used with permission from Heldref Publications.

Finally, I would like to dedicate this work with love and appreciation to a number of individuals, communities, and presences that have deeply touched my life and affected the nature of this work: My mother, who was always there; my father, whose poet's heart I carry within me wherever I go; my grandparents, my brother and my extended family; Veronica Balseiro, Mariana Caplan, Rosa Castrejón, Octavio García, Joan Halifax, Suraya Keating, Helena Martinez, Elizabeth Shaver, Vernice Solimar, and Christopher Titmus; my colleagues and students at the California Institute of Integral Studies and the Institute of Transpersonal Psychology; the brave Latino women of the center Arriba Juntos; the members of the Buddhist Peace Fellowship and the Buddhist Alliance for Social Engagement; the members of the Holistic Sexuality network; Stanislav Grof and the members of the Holotropic Breathwork community; various spiritual presences and teacher plants; and, of course, the whispering voices of the trees, the breeze, and the water.

I cannot conclude these acknowledgments without mentioning that the seeds of many of the ideas contained in this work germinated in intimate contact with two extraordinary human beings and modern-day *boddhisattvas*: Ramon V. Albareda and Marina T. Romero. Their presence in my life, as well as the profoundly innovative and transforming work they created, are solid roots out of which this work grows. My love and gratitude for them is boundless: Thanks to Life, Gracias a la Vida!

Needless to say, although this work is to large degree a collaborative effort, I alone am responsible for any errors it may contain.

TRANSPERSONAL THEORY

<hr>

NOW AND THEN

We live in a culture in which spirituality is at best regarded as edifying subjective experiences without real cognitive value about the world. In this chapter, I introduce the project of this book and suggest that the glue of the transpersonal vision is its commitment to the epistemic value of spirituality, that is, the conviction that a complete understanding of reality and human nature needs to include spiritual insights and perspectives. I also offer a personal narrative of the origins of the participatory vision of human spirituality I present in this book.

THIS BOOK IS A REVISION of transpersonal theory from a participatory perspective of knowledge and reality. The revision begins with a critical appraisal of some of the main philosophical foundations of the field, and then introduces an alternative participatory vision to understand and live transpersonal and spiritual phenomena. This book is, then, a deconstruction and a reconstruction of the entire transpersonal project aimed at the articulation of what I believe it is a more sophisticated, pluralistic, and spiritually grounded transpersonal theory.

Part I of the book (Deconstruction) uncovers and challenges three interrelated presuppositions of the conceptual framework prevalent in most transpersonal scholarship so far: *experientialism*, the assumption that transpersonal and spiritual phenomena are fundamentally individual inner experiences;

inner empiricism, the assumption that transpersonal inquiry needs to be empirically grounded; and *perennialism,* the assumption that spiritual knowledge, spiritual liberation, and spiritual ultimates are most basically universal. These beliefs about transpersonal phenomena allude respectively to their nature (intrasubjective experiences), the method and epistemology for their study and justification (empiricist), and the wider metaphysical framework within which they are understood (universalist). One of the main theses of this book is that these assumptions, although once probably inevitable and even salutary, have become today increasingly limiting and problematic, and their value should therefore be restricted to certain aspects or stages of transpersonal inquiry.

Let me briefly introduce here the nature of these problems and some of the directions towards their resolution advanced in Part II of the book (Reconstruction). First, by experientialism I mean the prevalent understanding of transpersonal and spiritual phenomena in terms of individual inner experiences. In questioning this view, I am not denying that there is an intrasubjective dimension in the human participation in these phenomena. Rather, my claim is that this dimension, although important, is not the fundamental one for understanding their nature, and that this kind of transpersonal experientialism is therefore both distorting and reductionistic. What is more, I argue that this experiential understanding not only afflicts transpersonal theory with unnecessary Cartesian anxieties and pseudoproblems, but also has pernicious consequences for the ways in which transpersonal and spiritual phenomena are engaged and integrated in everyday life (chapter 2). On the one hand, experientialism structures these phenomena in terms of a "subject" having experiences of transpersonal or spiritual "objects," making transpersonal theory vulnerable to the myths of subjectivism and objectivism, the aporias (unresolvable puzzles) of absolutism and relativism, and the riddles of epistemic mediation. On the other hand, spiritual events in which I participate become *my* experiences, and this interpretation effectively paves the way for their egoic and narcissistic appropriation.

As an antidote, I delineate an alternative conceptual framework, a *participatory vision,* which I believe enables us to understand and live transpersonal phenomena more harmoniously with their nature and the aims of spiritual life. Briefly, the kernel of this participatory vision is a *turn from intrasubjective experiences to participatory events in our understanding of transpersonal and spiritual phenomena.* Transpersonal phenomena, I argue, can be more adequately conceived not as individual inner experiences, but as participatory events that can emerge in the locus of an individual, a relationship, a collective identity, or a place. The intrasubjective dimension of transpersonal phenomena, then, should be regarded as the participation of an individual consciousness in a multilocal transpersonal event, and not as their essential nature. This participation engages human beings in the activity I call *participatory knowing*, that is, a multidimensional access to reality that can involve not only the creative power of the mind, but also of the body, the heart, and the soul (chapter 5).

Second, inner empiricism refers to the study of transpersonal and spiritual phenomena through the language, methods, and standards of empiricist science. Central to inner empiricism is the belief that transpersonal and spiritual claims are valid because they can be replicated and tested through disciplined introspection, and can be therefore intersubjectively verified or falsified. In challenging inner empiricism, it is not my intention to devalue the scientific and empirical study of transpersonal experiences, which I consider both important and necessary. In contrast, my claim is that importing scientific standards into transpersonal studies often results in an *empiricist colonization of spirituality* that not only distorts the nature of spiritual inquiry, but also has self-defeating consequences for the contemporary legitimization of spirituality (chapter 3).

What is needed, I claim, is not to burden spirituality with the concerns and demands of empiricist science (replicability, falsifiability, verifiability, etc.), but to discern the logic of spiritual inquiry and establish its own standards of validity. The validity of spiritual knowledge, I argue, has more to do with its emancipatory power for self, relationships, and world (i.e., its capability to free individuals, communities, and societies from egocentric understandings of reality and associated ways of life) than with any particular spiritual referent or picture of reality disclosed (chapter 7). I should say straight off that this aspect of the project is by far the least developed. Although I offer some suggestions throughout these pages about what a logic of and standards of validity for spiritual inquiry may look, a more systematic presentation awaits a future work.

Finally, perennialism refers to the universalistic vision of a common core of spirituality generally assumed and endorsed in transpersonal works. More concretely, by perennialism I mean the view that the various spiritual traditions and insights correspond to different interpretations, dimensions, or levels of a single spiritual ultimate that is both pregiven and universal. My objections to this view should not be taken as implying that there are no common elements among religious traditions, or that any type of spiritual universalism is necessarily mistaken. Actually, I believe that the search for interreligious parallels is a crucial enterprise, and in the concluding chapter I suggest how a more relaxed, permissive, and fertile universalism can be consistently maintained. However, I do claim that the kind of perennialism presupposed in most transpersonal works is an a priori position that has been uncritically taken for granted, that it is contingent upon questionable Cartesian presuppositions, and that it raises important obstacles for interreligious dialogue and spiritual inquiry. For example, traditions that do not accept the perennialist vision are regarded as inauthentic, lower, or merely "exoteric" (chapter 4).

As a gesture of balance, this work shows that transpersonal theory does not need the perennial philosophy as its foundational metaphysical framework. To this end, I provide a more pluralistic understanding of spiritual knowledge and liberation that seeks not only to free us from the shortcomings of perennialism, but also to better honor the diversity of ways in which the sense of the sacred can be cultivated, embodied, and lived. Roughly, I argue that there are different spiritual liberations (i.e., different ways to overcome limiting self-centeredness and fully participate in the Mystery from which everything arises), and that spiritual traditions cultivate, enact, and express, in interaction with a *dynamic and indeterminate spiritual power*, potentially overlapping but independent spiritual ultimates. Or put in metaphorical terms, the Ocean of Emancipation has many shores (chapter 6). Furthermore, although higher and lower spiritual insights may exist both within and between religious traditions, I claim that these qualitative distinctions need to be elucidated through spiritual inquiry, interreligious dialogue, and the assessment of their emancipatory power for self, community, and world, and not determined from any overarching metaphysical scheme that tells us, in an a priori and doctrinal manner, which insights and traditions are superior or inferior (chapter 7).

Before proceeding further, I should clarify that I do not think that experientialism, inner empiricism, and perennialism are ubiquitous in transpersonal theory. There are important exceptions to these trends and by no means do I want to suggest that every transpersonal author endorses all of them. However, I do believe that these assumptions have strongly configured the basic contours of transpersonal scholarship so far. In other words, my claim is that experientialism, inner empiricism, and perennialism have been the prevalent interpretive lenses for the study of transpersonal and spiritual phenomena since the very birth of the field. Although I offer no comprehensive review of the literature to substantiate this claim, I refer to a number of influential transpersonal works throughout the book, and direct the reader to extra references in the footnotes when necessary. In proceeding this way, I am assuming that readers acquainted with the transpersonal literature will easily recognize the pervasiveness of these assumptions in the field, so that we can move to the more fruitful and challenging task of analyzing their pitfalls and suggesting some tentative solutions.

But before starting this analysis, and in order to offer some very general coordinates for the present inquiry, it may be helpful to briefly introduce here the historical origins, spiritual import, and epistemological challenge of the transpersonal vision. To conclude this chapter, then, I offer some reflections on the personal roots of the participatory vision introduced in this book.

THE BIRTH OF THE TRANSPERSONAL MOVEMENT

Transpersonal theory is concerned with the study of the transpersonal and spiritual dimensions of human nature and existence. Etymologically, the term *transpersonal* means beyond or through (trans-) the personal, and is generally used in the transpersonal literature to reflect concerns, motivations, experiences, developmental stages (cognitive, moral, emotional, interpersonal, etc.), modes of being, and other phenomena that include but transcend the sphere of the individual personality, self, or ego.[1]

The historical origins of the transpersonal orientation have been eloquently narrated elsewhere and need not be repeated here (see Sutich, 1969, 1976; Vich, 1990; Walsh, 1993a). Suffice it to say that the transpersonal orientation originated in the mid-1960s out of the interest of a group of psychologists and psychiatrists (Anthony Sutich, Abraham Maslow, Stanislav Grof, Miles Vich, etc.) in expanding the field of humanistic psychology beyond its focus on the individual self and towards the creation of "a still 'higher' Fourth Psychology, transpersonal, transhuman, centered in the cosmos rather than in human needs and interests, going beyond humanness, identity, self-actualization, and the like" (Maslow, 1968, pp. iii–iv).

Historically, the transpersonal orientation emerged out of the encounter between Western psychology—psychoanalytic, Jungian, humanistic, and existentialist schools in particular—Eastern contemplative traditions—especially Zen, Advaita Vedanta, and Taoism—and the psychedelic counterculture of

California in the 1960s. The roots of the transpersonal perspective in the Western psychological tradition can be traced to Brentano's psychology of consciousness and emphasis on lived experience; William James's radical empiricism and studies in mysticism; Freud's formulation of the unconscious and concern with the oceanic feeling and evenly suspended attention; Jung's notions of the collective unconscious, the archetypes, and the individuation process, as well as his studies in Asian religions and Western esoteric traditions; Fromm's interest in Zen Buddhism and Vedanta; Assagioli's psychosynthesis; Maslow's studies on metamotivations, peak-experiences, and self-actualization; and Grof's pioneering psychedelic research.[2] The transpersonal perspective also finds precedents in Western philosophies such as Plato's metaphysics, contemplative ideals, and theory of recollection (*anamnesis*); Husserl's transcendental phenomenology; Hegel's dialectic of Spirit; nineteenth century European Romanticism; American Transcendentalism; Heidegger's inquiries into Being; and a plethora of spiritual traditions such as Neoplatonism, Gnosticism, Hermeticism, Christian mysticism, Kabbalah, and the various schools usually amalgamated under the name of Western esotericism.[3]

The Eastern influence upon the nascent transpersonal movement came mainly by the hand of thinkers such as D. T. Suzuki, who popularized Zen philosophy in the West; Alan Watts, whose interpretation of Taoist, Buddhist, and Hindu thinking had a major impact on the counterculture of the 1960s; and Haridas Chaudhuri, who brought to America the integral vision of the Neo-Hindu mystic Sri-Aurobindo. Other Hindu influences include Maharishi Mahesh Yogi, Bagwan Rajneesh, Paramahansa Yogananda, and Swami Mutkananda. Another important catalyst of the transpersonal movement was the introduction of Tibetan Buddhism to the West by teachers such as Chögyam Trungpa, founder of the Naropa Institute in Boulder, Colorado, or Tarthang Tulku, prime mover of the translation of numerous Tibetan works into English. Somewhat later, transpersonalism was strongly influenced by the Theravada *vipassana* movement, originally extended to America by Western teachers trained in South Asia such as Jack Kornfield and Joseph Goldstein.[4] The coming to the West of these and other Eastern traditions, together with the interest in consciousness and altered states triggered by the widespread use of psychedelics, paved the way for the birth of the transpersonal movement in the California of the late 1960s.

THE SPIRITUAL IMPORT OF THE TRANSPERSONAL VISION

Although a strict correspondence between transpersonality and spirituality cannot be maintained, the study of transpersonal phenomena led most authors to delve into the spiritual depths of human existence.[5] Actually, the focus on the experiential and cognitive dimensions of spirituality is one of the main factors that distinguishes transpersonal theory from most other scientific and humanistic disciplines.

Transpersonal theory, however, is not merely another academic discipline. The transpersonal vision is a way of thinking *and* living self, other, and world that can be *diversely* manifested not only in transpersonal states, but also in relationships, community, society, ethics, education, politics, philosophy, religion, cosmology, and almost any other area of human thinking, feeling, and action.[6] Transpersonal theory, that is, can shed new light and transform virtually any phenomenon in which human beings participate. When I say that the transpersonal vision can transform the world, I am not talking in poetic or metaphoric terms. What I am suggesting is that the final intention of any genuine transpersonal vision is not the elaboration of theoretical models to understand transpersonal phenomena, but to midwife an intersubjectively shared reality, a transpersonal reality. The ultimate aim of the transpersonal vision is to bring forth a transpersonal world.[7]

When I talk of transpersonal theory as a vision, I do not mean to suggest that there is a unified transpersonal paradigm. There is not. Disagreements among transpersonalists are the norm rather than the exception. And these divergences are not merely about minor theoretical issues, but often about the central philosophical and metaphysical foundations of the field, for example, the understanding of transpersonal phenomena, the meaning of spirituality, or the very nature of reality (e.g., see Funk, 1994; Rothberg & Kelly, 1998). The lack of consensus on fundamental matters in the transpersonal movement is so pronounced that rather than talk about a transpersonal paradigm, it may be more accurate to talk about different transpersonal paradigms under the roof of one transpersonal vision.

But, what then is the unifying tissue of the transpersonal vision? Ever since its inception, transpersonal theory has given spirituality a central place in our understanding of human nature and the cosmos (Sutich, 1969). Transpersonal theorists have typically regarded Spirit not only as the essence of human nature, but also as the ground, pull, and goal of cosmic evolution. In spite of its internal divergences, then, I believe that it is still possible to distinguish the transpersonal vision from other world views by its conviction that a comprehensive understanding of human beings and the cosmos requires the inclusion of spiritual phenomena. The conviction that, as William James (1902/1961) puts it in allusion to mystical states, "no account of the universe in its totality can be final which leaves these other forms of consciousness quite disregarded" (p. 305). As I elaborate below, the different transpersonal paradigms converge in their commitment to the epistemic import of spirituality.

THE TRANSPERSONAL EPISTEMOLOGICAL CHALLENGE

Particularly relevant for our present inquiry is the assertion, common in the transpersonal literature, that both the source and justification of spiritual claims should be sought in the intrasubjective experiential dimension of transpersonal and spiritual phenomena. Put somewhat differently, transpersonal knowledge claims have been generally understood and justified within an inner empiricist framework. This intrasubjective empiricism is one of the main targets of this book. As I mentioned above, I believe that this account has formidable conceptual and practical problems that ultimately sabotage the transpersonal perspective from within. Later on I will explore in some detail both the nature of these shortcomings and how they can be overcome through a participatory turn in our understanding of transpersonal phenomena. Here, in order to highlight the heart of the transpersonal challenge to the modern world view, I would like to portray the transpersonal vision not in experiential, but in epistemic terms.

Although with different emphases, every transpersonal theorist has maintained that transpersonal and spiritual phenomena provide important and valid knowledge about human beings and the world. This commitment situates the transpersonal vision in sharp contrast with scientist, materialist, positivist, analytical, and reductionistic paradigms, which have consistently regarded spirituality as wishful thinking, infantile illusions, mere ideology, psychotic hallucinations, pseudoscience, language games with no reference to the real world, or, at best, edifying private, subjective experiences without public, objective cognitive value.[8] The thread common to all these approaches is their assessment of spirituality as epistemologically sterile. Spiritual and transpersonal phenomena, we are told, do not provide any form of valid, reliable, or real knowledge about human beings or the world. The transpersonal vision, in contrast, holds that transpersonal and spiritual phenomena do have epistemic value. And this conviction is, I believe, the unifying glue that connects the different transpersonal paradigms: The unifying feature of the transpersonal vision is its commitment to the epistemic value of transpersonal and spiritual phenomena.

THE ORIGINS OF THE PARTICIPATORY VISION

It was several years ago that I became aware of the centrality of knowledge in transpersonal studies. The epistemic dimension of transpersonal phenomena seemed to me fundamental for understanding their nature and emancipatory power: What makes transpersonal phenomena distinctly "transpersonal" (as well as interesting, provocative, and transforming) is not their nonordinary or occasional ecstatic character, but the character of the knowledge they provide during an expansion of individual consciousness.

Despite the centrality of knowledge in transpersonal phenomena, discussions about its nature and justification were virtually absent in the literature. And with a few exceptions, the discussions I found struck me as unsatisfactory. On the one hand, there was much confusion about the epistemological framework within which transpersonal knowledge claims were to be understood and evaluated. The lack of criteria for determining what could be considered valid transpersonal knowledge was rendering transpersonal theory a free-for-all open to any form of metaphysical speculation. On the other hand, most transpersonal authors were working upon unexamined and outdated objectivist epistemological assumptions which, I gradually came to see, severely undermined the very transpersonal orientation they championed.

What is more, this conceptual confusion regarding the nature of transpersonal knowledge had practical ramifications in the transpersonal community. In some of the transpersonal circles with which I was acquainted, for example, I often witnessed the pronouncement of strong knowledge claims about the ultimate nature of the self and the world—about "things as they really are"—on the basis of the transpersonal experiences some very thoughtful and well-intended individuals had gone through. Two elements were particularly striking about these claims: The first was the uncritical, and sometimes dogmatic, tone that usually accompanied them. When challenged with the epistemic duty of justifying such claims, for example, the empirical—meaning here experiential—nature of this knowledge was frequently purported as the unquestionable evidence for their objective validity or even status as universal truths. The second was the many contradictions existing between the different transpersonal revelations. It was simply fascinating to notice how modern Western individuals appeared to be accessing spiritual insights belonging to a rich variety of traditional cosmologies. Over and over again, I witnessed with perplexity how the clash between different religious world views was coming alive in the transpersonal community. In the middle of such turmoil, of course, the temptations to fall into one or another form of perennialism to honor all those truths were tremendous. For the reasons that I expound in this book, however, I could not find the seductions of the perennialist vision either alluring or satisfying.

After years of study, dialogue, and spiritual inquiry, I resolved that this nebulousness around the nature of transpersonal knowledge was deeply detrimental for the legitimization of spirituality in academic and social milieus, a legitimization that was sorely needed. Transpersonal theory lacked an adequate epistemology, and the consequences were disastrous.

This realization led me to focus my research initially on the study of the nature and justification of transpersonal knowledge. The regulative goal of my original project was the development of a transpersonal epistemology, that is, an epistemological framework that would provide (1) an understanding of the nature and possibilities of transpersonal knowledge (descriptive component), and (2) criteria for the acceptance and rejection of transpersonal knowledge claims (normative component). By that time, I defined transpersonal knowledge as the knowledge claimed to be accessed during transpersonal experiences, and my general plan was to analyze the nature of this knowledge along four interrelated axes: Objective/constructed, immediate/mediate, universal/contextual, and absolute/relative. To this end, I would rely on several bodies of knowledge, with particular emphasis on the field of comparative mysticism, the epistemologies of several contemplative traditions, the literature on interreligious dialogue, and relevant works on contemporary Western epistemology, philosophy of science, and religious epistemology. My hope was that these interdisciplinary explorations would illuminate the way transpersonal knowledge claims had to be understood, and suggest adequate guidelines for their justification.

Although I frankly believed in the relevance of searching for a transpersonal epistemology, a vague but insidious feeling of dissatisfaction with the project soon grew in me. At first, I thought that its source was the very ambitious nature of the project and the associated self-doubts about my knowledge and skill to undertake it successfully. As my discontent increased, however, I began to consider the possibility that its roots were somewhere else. Whatever the source of this feeling, it was undermining most of my creative efforts. The more I struggled to develop my thinking along the lines envisioned in my original project, the more stuck and frustrated I felt. This feeling of dissatisfaction culminated in a period of intellectual stagnation in which I could not write directly on the project for almost a year. Painfully aware of my inability to advance the research in any satisfactory way, I decided to set it aside for some time and focus my energies on other projects. During this time, however, the project was continuously present in the back of my mind—sometimes as if it were mischievously mocking me!

Looking in part for a deeper understanding of this intellectual impasse, I explored my thoughts, feelings, and sensations around the subject during meditation and while in different states of expanded awareness. At some point during this inquiry, I started to suspect that there was "something" terribly wrong in the very nature of the project. As I looked more deeply, the real face of my frustration showed itself in my consciousness. My discontent was not rooted in lacking the answers to my questions, but in the very questions I was asking. Joanna Macy once said that "if we were lucky enough, we would find the right question, rather than the right answer" (Macy & Rothberg, 1994, p. 25). How I appreciated this insight at that time!

As I see it now, standard questions about knowledge claims and epistemic justification are associated with modes of discourse characteristic of the Cartesian ego. On the one hand, I realized, these epistemological concerns were parasitic of a Cartesian model of knowledge concerned with explaining and justifying the gap between subject and object. On the other hand, I repeatedly observed, these problems collapsed when approached through contemplative modes of cognition. Issues of epistemic normativity, that is, strike me now as contingent on Cartesian modes of consciousness. In light of this new awareness, I reconsidered the direction of my efforts, and decided to let go of the normative aims of my research—if not of the entire project itself. And yet, a deeper voice was whispering to me, gently but breathlessly, that there was still something truly crucial in exploring the epistemic dimension of transpersonal experiences.

An important shift of direction in my research occurred when, unsatisfied with the current definitions of transpersonal experience, I tried to elaborate my own. It was then when I became aware not only of the difficulties of defining transpersonal phenomena as individual inner experiences, but also of the serious conceptual and practical limitations of such experiential understanding.[9] Clearly, if I wanted to make any substantial advance in my inquiries into transpersonal knowledge, I had to start from scratch and find a different voice to talk about transpersonal phenomena. To my surprise, I then realized that this alternative voice, although dormant, had been present in my project ever since my early insight into the centrality of knowledge in transpersonal phenomena: Transpersonal phenomena, I thought, are not individual inner experiences, but epistemic events.

This epistemic approach, as I called it, essentially proposed the need for an epistemic turn, a radical shift from experience to knowledge in our understanding of human spirituality that would free transpersonal studies from their limiting Cartesian moorings. The epistemic turn led the way out of Cartesianism, as well as from its associated epistemological dilemmas, by conceiving human spirituality not as intrasubjective experiences, but as multilocal epistemic events that can emerge not only in the locus of an individual, but also in a relationship, a community, a collective identity, or a place.[10]

The final turn in my exploration happened when I realized that the distinction between experiential and epistemic I had pragmatically constructed to free transpersonal studies from Cartesianism was ultimately artificial and arbitrary.[11] Since both experience and knowledge can be conceptualized in Cartesian and non-Cartesian terms, it became gradually obvious that the revision I was proposing could be more accurately conveyed not so much in terms of an epistemic turn, a shift from experience to knowledge, but of a participatory turn, a shift from intrasubjective experiences to participatory events which can be equally understood in both experiential and epistemic terms. Human participation in transpersonal and spiritual phenomena is a creative, multidimensional event that can involve every aspect of human nature, from somatic transfiguration to the awakening of the heart, from erotic communion to visionary cocreation, and from contemplative knowing to moral insight.[12]

This book tells the story of where this insight has led me so far.

PART I

DECONSTRUCTION

Part I of this book examines the conceptual framework that has guided most transpersonal scholarship so far. Chapter 2 (The Experiential Vision of Human Spirituality) describes the nature and origins of the experiential vision of transpersonal phenomena, as well as identifies some of its main conceptual and practical limitations. Chapter 3 (The Empiricist Colonization of Spirituality) uncovers some of the fundamental problems of inner empiricism, the prevalent method and epistemology of the experiential vision. Chapter 4 (Trouble in Paradise: The Perennial Philosophy Revisited) questions the type of universalist vision of spirituality that has usually provided the metaphysical foundations of the experiential vision.

2

THE EXPERIENTIAL VISION
OF HUMAN SPIRITUALITY

The two greatest challenges faced today by many spiritual seekers are arguably the danger of spiritual narcissism and the failure to integrate spiritual experiences into their everyday life. An inadequate assimilation of spiritual energies often leads to subtle forms of self-absorption and inflation, as well as to an increased, and often insatiable, thirst for spiritual experiences. In this chapter, I suggest that these two interrelated problems are fueled by the modern understanding of spirituality as individual inner experience. Also, I argue that this understanding both is inconsistent with the nature of spiritual knowing and perpetuates the disenchanted world view characteristic of the modern West.

MY PRIMARY AIM in this chapter is to present some of the main conceptual and practical limitations of what I call the experiential vision (i.e., the modern understanding of transpersonal and spiritual phenomena in terms of individual inner experiences). First, I explain the nature and origins of the experiential vision, and then I identify its main problematic implications for our understanding and participation in spiritual states.

THE NATURE OF THE EXPERIENTIAL VISION

Transpersonal theory conceptualizes transpersonal and spiritual phenomena in experiential terms.[1] In other words, transpersonal and spiritual phenomena are generally understood and defined as *intrasubjective experiences* or *states of consciousness.* The basic idea underlying this experiential vision is that individuals have transpersonal experiences, and then, during these states of expanded awareness, access sources of knowledge that lie beyond their biographical histories and ordinary time-space limitations. Implicit in this view is the assumption that transpersonal experiences provide individuals with transpersonal insights. In the experiential vision, the experiential dimension of transpersonal phenomena is regarded as primary and results in the epistemic one. Transpersonal experiences, it is commonly believed, lead to transpersonal knowledge.

A couple of influential definitions should serve to illustrate the fundamental nature of the experiential vision. According to Grof (1988), "transpersonal experiences can be defined as experiential expansion or extension of consciousness beyond the usual boundaries of the body-ego and beyond the limitations of time and space" (p. 38). In a similar vein, Walsh and Vaughan (1993) define transpersonal phenomena as "experiences in which the sense of identity or self extends beyond (trans) the individual or personal to encompass wider aspects of humankind, life, psyche or cosmos" (p. 203).[2]

Readers acquainted with the transpersonal literature will recognize that this experiential understanding has guided transpersonal studies since the early configuration of the field in the late 1960s. Actually, the past thirty years of transpersonal research have been primarily devoted to the description, classification, and interpretation—developmental, cognitive, phenomenological, systemic, evolutionary, ontological, metaphysical, and so on—of transpersonal experiences or states of consciousness (e.g., Grof, 1972, 1988, 1998; Hunt, 1984, 1985, 1995a, 1995b; Hunt, Gervais, Shearing-Johns, & Travis, 1992; Levin, 1988b; Miller & Cook-Greuter, 1994; Tart, 1971, 1977, 1983; Valle, 1995; Wilber, 1996b, 1996c).

As should be obvious, this experiential vision continues to be the prevailing framework for understanding transpersonal phenomena. Recently, for example, Walsh and Vaughan (1993) defined the transpersonal disciplines as "those disciplines that focus on the study of transpersonal experiences and related phenomena. These phenomena include the causes, effects and correlates of transpersonal experiences and development, as well as the disciplines and practices inspired by them" (p. 202). Likewise, Lajoie and Shapiro (1992), after surveying more than two hundred definitions of transpersonal psychology, conclude that this field "is concerned with the study of humanity's highest potential, and with the recognition, understanding, and realization of unitive, spiritual, and transcendent states of consciousness" (p. 91). Let us briefly look now at the origins of such an experiential account.

THE ORIGINS OF THE EXPERIENTIAL VISION

The origins of the experiential vision are manifold. To offer an exhaustive analysis of them here is not possible, so I will merely indicate the three interrelated sources I consider most significant: the historical, the philosophical, and the methodological.

   1. *Historically, the experiential vision is rooted in the modern conceptualization of spirituality in the West.* According to Max Weber (1978) and Jürgen Habermas (1984, 1987a, 1987b), one of the main features of modernity was the breaking down of the unified metaphysical-religious world view characteristic of the premodern era into three different domains or worlds: The objective or natural world (realm of empirical science, approached by an instrumental-technical rationality), the intersubjective or social world (realm of politics and ethics, approached by a moral-pragmatic rationality), and the subjective or individual world (realm of arts, religion, and psychotherapy, approached by an aesthetic-expressive rationality). In this context, as Rothberg (1993) points out, all religious and spiritual phenomena were automatically relegated to the individual subjective world and invariably regarded as not meeting the standards of valid, objective knowledge characteristic of natural science (e.g., public nature of observation, repeatability, verifiability, etc.). Although not a typical modern thinker and open to the cognitive value of religious experiences, Whitehead's (1926) words capture this individualistic understanding of spirituality: "Religion is what the individual does with his own solitariness" (p. 26). In short, in the modern West, spirituality came to be basically understood in terms of (1) individual inner experiences which are (2) epistemically empty, or not providing any form of valid knowledge.[3]

   Contrary to popular belief, then, the notion of religious or spiritual "experience" is relatively recent. In Western religious studies, for example, the idea of religion as inner experience can be traced to Schleiermacher's *On Religion*, originally published in 1799, and whose explicit aim was to protect religious doctrines from the Enlightenment critique of metaphysics (Proudfoot, 1985). Likewise, in Buddhist studies, the focus on spiritual experiences stems in large part from the new Japanese Zen movements such as the Kyoto school (Nishida Kitaro, D. T. Suzuki, etc.), and the so-called *vipassana* revival of South Asia, both of which, deeply influenced by modern Western notions of religion, developed at the end of the nineteenth century as an attempt to ground Buddhism in a universal experience immune to emerging relativistic threats (Sharf, 1995a, 1995b). Similarly, the experiential emphasis in Hindu studies primarily derives from the works of nineteenth century Neo-Hindu thinkers (e.g., Rammohan Roy, Rabindranath Tagore, and especially Sarvepalli Radhakrishnan), who attempted to reconcile Hinduism and the empiricism of Western science (Halbfass, 1988b).[4]

As I see it, the wide acceptance of the experiential vision in transpersonal studies suggests that, in spite of reclaiming the epistemic status of spiritual phenomena, transpersonal theorists have uncritically accepted the modern conception of spirituality as mere inner experience. Already at the dawn of the transpersonal orientation, we find extremely eloquent articulations of a vision of spirituality in terms of private, individual experiences. Consider, for example, Abraham Maslow's words on religion and peak-experiences: "What I have been saying is that the evidence from the peak-experiences permits us to talk about the essential, the intrinsic, the basic, the most fundamental religious or transcendent experience as a totally private and personal one which can hardly be shared" (1970, pp. 27–28). Since its beginnings, then, transpersonal theory conceptualized spiritual phenomena as individual inner experiences.

The experiential account of spirituality articulated by Maslow and other founders of the transpersonal orientation—such as Anthony Sutich or Stanislav Grof—was prophetic of the direction taken during the following thirty years of transpersonal research. In this treatment of transpersonal and spiritual phenomena as individual inner experiences—and, consequently, of transpersonal knowledge as empirical—it becomes evident that transpersonal theory's emancipation from the disenchanted world of modernity, to paraphrase Max Weber, is still partial and, as I will argue, problematic and unsatisfactory.

2. *Philosophically, the experiential vision stems from the essentially humanistic origins of the transpersonal orientation.* Transpersonal studies were born at the very heart of the Western humanist tradition, primarily concerned with the affirmation of the intrinsic ontological and epistemological value of individual human experience (Bullock, 1985; Davidson, 1994).[5] It should not be surprising, therefore, that the emphasis on individual experience—on its potentials, its creative nature, its peak moments, and so on—emblematic of humanistic psychology was naturally incorporated into the root metaphors, philosophical assumptions, and research programs of the transpersonal disciplines.

As is well known, among the direct humanistic sources of early transpersonal studies are Maslow's (1968, 1970) groundbreaking studies on self-actualization and peak-experiences. In his seminal studies on positive psychological health, Maslow (1968) explains that self-actualized individuals—those people who had attained a high level of maturation, health, and self-fulfillment—frequently report the transient episodes he called peak-experiences. According to Maslow (1968, 1970), peak-experiences are the most fulfilling, joyous, and blissful moments in one's life. During these moments, an individual could experience, among other phenomena, a sense of self-transcendence, wholeness, and undeserved grace; a resolution of the polarities of ordinary life; a variety of creative and spiritual insights; a complete loss of anxiety and fear; and a compelling certainty of the intrinsically benevolent nature of the world.

Crucial for the emergence of the transpersonal orientation was Maslow's (1970) equation of the peak-experience with what he called the "core-religious experience," that is, the essential, intrinsic, and fundamental transcendent experience that he believed could be found at the heart of all religious traditions.[6] It was this connection between psychological health and religious experience that impelled Maslow to move beyond the mostly secular and existential concerns of humanistic psychology, and towards the articulation of a new psychology: A psychology that, in contrast to the humanistic orientation, would be "transpersonal, transhuman, centered in the cosmos rather than in human needs and interests, going beyond humanness, identity, self-actualization, and the like" (1968, pp. iii–iv).

Of course, with the twilight of the Western metaphysical traditions in the modern era, the search for confirmation and legitimization of Maslow's germinal insights had basically two options: Jung or the East.[7] On the one hand, Jungian psychology incorporated, although camouflaged in psychological language, many of the insights of esotericism, thereby carrying into modernity the legacy of Western metaphysical traditions (Hanegraaff, 1998; Noll, 1994). On the other hand, in the East, the early transpersonalists found living traditions which offered not only nonpathological perspectives on transpersonal phenomena, but also extensive evidence supporting the connection between spirituality and optimal psychological health. Virtually all transpersonal theorists followed one of these two paths and some of the modern transpersonal debates, such as the discrepancies between Wilber and Washburn on the nature of transpersonal development, are a reflection of this historical disjunction (Washburn, 1990, 1995, 1996a, 1996b; Wilber, 1990c, 1996d, 1997a).

To conclude, if one adds to the individualistic character of humanistic psychology and Maslow's account of spirituality, the highly "experientalist" climate of the California of the late 1960s—the widespread experimentation with psychedelics, meditation, isolation tanks, and other technologies of consciousness alteration; the proliferation of experiential approaches to psychotherapy and self-growth; and so forth—the experiential nature of the emerging field of transpersonal psychology is not only comprehensible but also probably inevitable.

3. *Methodologically, the experiential vision emerged as an epistemic strategy to bolster the validity of transpersonal knowledge claims.* What I am suggesting here is that one of the principal reasons for the turn to inner experience in transpersonal studies was the attempt to appear empirical, and therefore scientific, in the eyes of the wider academic and social communities.

In my opinion, there are three main factors behind the quasi-obsessive preoccupation of transpersonalists with establishing the empirical foundations of the field: (1) the vast technological success and social prestige of empirical science in the twentieth century, (2) the historical association between religion and dogmatism in the Western world, and (3) the modern marginalization of spirituality to the status of subjective experiences. Naturally, the combination of these factors made the empirical justification of transpersonal studies nearly imperative: If spirituality was essentially a subjective experience, and if the only valid knowledge was the empirical one, then the epistemic legitimacy of transpersonal studies had to be defended in terms of a "science of human experience," an "inner empiricism," a "Taoist science," a "subjective epistemology," a "science of consciousness" or, more recently, a "science of spiritual experience." Although these proposals in support of the empirical bases (meaning here anchored in inner experience) of transpersonal and spiritual claims had different emphases, they all had an unequivocally identical purpose: the legitimization of transpersonal studies as empirical, and therefore epistemically valid, disciplines of knowledge.

We will return to these methodological issues in the next chapter. Before concluding this section, however, I should say some words about my choice of Maslow's work to illustrate the main sources of the experiential vision. The primary reason for selecting Maslow is that he was a pivotal figure in the emergence of transpersonal studies, and the influence of his ideas on later developments of the field is probably unparalleled. I should clarify here, however, that my intention has not been to criticize Maslow's pathbreaking studies.[8] On the contrary, I believe that, at the time of the emergence of the transpersonal orientation, an experiential account of transpersonal phenomena was not only historically inevitable, but also methodologically crucial. That is, the legitimization of transpersonal studies in the intellectual climate of the late 1960s and 1970s (and even 1980s) *had* to be empirical. What I will argue, however, is that this experiential account, although once indispensable and perhaps even salutary, has become unnecessary, limiting, and counterproductive.

This should not be surprising. There are abundant examples in human history—as well as in the psychological and spiritual literature—of insights that were once crucially emancipatory, but that as time passed became troublesome burdens that needed to be abandoned. Consider, for instance, the case of Descartes's separation of the world into two different realities—a *res cogitans* (a thinking substance: the subjective experience, the mind, etc.) and a *res extensa* (an extended substance: the objective world, the body, etc.). In the sixteenth century, Cartesian dualism had profound emancipatory effects, such as the liberation of human reason and empirical science from the clutches of a dogmatic Catholic Church. Today, however, Cartesianism has been associated with all types of philosophical, ecological, social, and existential maladies—such as the double bind imposed by objectivist-relativist dilemmas, and the worries derived from the so-called Cartesian Anxiety (i.e., the failure to find ultimate foundations for human knowledge and morality) (Bernstein, 1985); the "disenchantment of the world" and the exploitation of nature (Berman, 1981; Capra, 1982); the repression of the feminine and the dissociation from our bodily existence (Bordo, 1987; Leder, 1990); and the ontological estrangement and spiritual alienation characteristic of our times (Grof, 1985; Tarnas, 1991). For these and other reasons, an increasingly large number of contemporary critical thinkers have urged its demise (see also, e.g., Damasio, 1995; Levin, 1988a; Marsh, 1988; O'Donovan-Anderson, 1996; Varela, Thompson, & Rosch, 1991). For the reasons that I present in this book, I believe that the experiential vision deserves a parallel treatment.

THE FUNDAMENTAL PROBLEMS
OF THE EXPERIENTIAL VISION

In this section, I want to present several important limitations of the experiential vision. Conceptually, I argue that the experiential vision (1) perpetuates

the modern restrictive understanding of spirituality as individual inner experience (*intrasubjective reductionism*), and (2) follows a Cartesian epistemology that
is inconsistent with the nature of most transpersonal and spiritual phenomena
(*subtle Cartesianism*). Practically, I suggest that this experiential account (1) fosters all types of spiritual distortions such as ego-inflation, self-absorption, and
spiritual materialism (*spiritual narcissism*); and (2) hinders the integration of
transpersonal phenomena into everyday life *(integrative arrestment)*.

THE CONCEPTUAL BETRAYAL

Once transpersonal phenomena are understood as individual inner experiences, transpersonal theory tends to fall into the two interrelated traps of
intrasubjective reductionism and subtle Cartesianism.[9] Let us have a closer
look at these pitfalls.

Intrasubjective Reductionism

Up to this point, we have seen how the experiential vision conceives transpersonal and spiritual phenomena as individual inner experiences, and how
this account is in large part rooted in the uncritical acceptance of one of the
premises of the structure of modernity, that is, the confinement of spirituality to the subjective world of the individual. In this section I want to explain
in more detail (1) how the experiential vision perpetuates this modern interpretation of spirituality, and (2) why this understanding of transpersonal and
spiritual phenomena is reductionistic, and should therefore be expanded.

As we have seen, the beginning of the modern era was characterized by
the breaking down of the unified religious–metaphysical world view of premodern times into three different spheres of knowledge and reality: the
objective or natural world (realm of empirical science, approached by instrumental-technical rationality), the intersubjective or social world (realm of
politics and ethics, approached by moral-pragmatic rationality), and the subjective or individual world (realm of arts, religion, and psychotherapy,
approached by aesthetic-expressive rationality) (Habermas, 1984; Rothberg,
1993). According to Habermas (1984), the validity claims in each one of
these worlds are evaluated through different criteria: "objective truth" in the
natural world, "normative rightness" in the social world, and "sincerity" in
the individual world. In this scheme, spiritual phenomena fall naturally into
the category of individual, subjective experiences, edifying in the best of

cases, but always epistemically sterile, that is, not meeting the objective standards for valid knowledge of empirical science.[10]

In this context, the emergence of transpersonal theory can be seen as an attempt to free spirituality from the constraints imposed upon it by the modern conception of the world. The transpersonal commitment to the cognitive import of spiritual experiences, for example, radically challenges the modern epistemic devaluation of spirituality. To be sure, in the context of the philosophical discourse of modernity, transpersonal theory's rescue of the epistemic status of spirituality was, and indeed continues to be, radically revolutionary.

Nevertheless, transpersonal theory's emancipation from the restrictions imposed by the structure of modernity is still an *incomplete project*. Essentially, the strategy followed by most transpersonal theorists to redeem spiritual knowledge has been the exaltation of the epistemic value of individual inner experiences. As we will see in chapter 3, transpersonal theory has traditionally anchored the validity of its knowledge claims in the experiential dimension of transpersonal and spiritual phenomena. However, it should be obvious that, in its focus on individual inner experiences, transpersonal theory perpetuates the modern marginalization of spirituality to the realm of the private and subjective. With these experiential premises, transpersonal theory falls into what I call *intrasubjective reductionism* (i.e., *the reduction of spiritual and transpersonal phenomena to individual inner experiences*).

What the previous analysis suggests is that the task of emancipation of spirituality set forth by the transpersonal project will be incomplete as long as transpersonalists remain committed to the experiential vision. The agenda, therefore, is clear: We need to free transpersonal theory from its modern experiential prejudices and expand the reach of spirituality out of its confinement to subjective space to the other two worlds, that is, the objective and the intersubjective.

The need for this expanded understanding of spirituality, as well as some of the dangers and limitations of intrasubjective reductionism, have been already observed by transpersonal authors Donald Rothberg and Ken Wilber. In a series of articles, Rothberg (1993, 1994, 1996b, 1999) not only identifies several serious problems associated with this experiential account of spirituality, but also offers specific practical guidelines towards their resolution. In an important essay, Rothberg (1993) points out that:

Much of the recent renewal of spirituality in North America and Western Europe in the last thirty years has taken the shape of an intense individual quest to explore more deeply the nature and depths of individual human experience, understanding something like self-actualization as a pathway to the sacred. (p. 109)

However, Rothberg adds, this vision of spirituality as an individual and experiential affair may be not only limiting but also one-sided and selective. Traditionally, most contemplative religions have regarded individual experiences and practices such as meditation as an important but partial element of a larger system that also comprises communal life, strong ethical commitments, relationships with teachers, and the study of sacred scriptures.

As a practical remedy for the narcissism and fragmentation inherent in both the modern era and the subjective quest for meaning, Rothberg (1993) prescribes a "socially engaged spirituality." In Rothberg's eyes, the explicit intention of a socially engaged spirituality is "simultaneously to inquire into and to transform self *and* society, self *and* world, not to have to choose to transform only self or only world" (p. 112). What Rothberg is suggesting is that the active engagement of spiritually motivated individuals in the social, political, and ecological problems of our times has the potential of not only integrating the presently dissociated natural, social, and individual worlds, but also emancipating spirituality from its limiting inner and individualistic constraints.

Another author who is struggling to free transpersonal studies from the conceptual straitjacket of modernity is Ken Wilber. In recent works, Wilber (1995, 1996a, 1997a) introduces the Four Quadrant Model, a framework devised, among other things, to carry forward what he considers to be the most crucial task of our present predicament: the integration of the three worlds—the subjective, the intersubjective, and the objective—or, in his own terms, the Big Three (i.e., I, we, and it).

Following Habermas's (1984, 1987a, 1987b) analysis of the modern era, Wilber (1995) considers the differentiation of the Big Three a tremendous cognitive and cultural achievement that allowed the autonomous development of the spheres of arts (I), morals (we), and science (it).[11] The downside of modernity, however, is that the increasing hegemony of instrumental-technological reason in all three worlds has led to a "hyper-differentiation" or dissociation of these spheres. And this state of fragmentation is, for Wilber, behind most of the maladies besetting our postmodern times, such as the ecological crisis, ethnocentric imperialism, or egocentric narcissism (see, e.g., 1995, pp. 148–149, 390–396; 1996a, p. 337). It is fundamental to stress that neither Habermas nor Wilber is advocating a return to undifferentiated premodern worlds. On the contrary, the diagnosis for the symptoms of our present era is not differentiation but dissociation, and therefore the cure is not undifferentiation but integration, an integration that transcends but preserves the decentration of the three worlds.

According to Wilber (1995), the solution for such a state of affairs—and this is his original proposal to remedy the problems of modernity—lies in the emergence of vision-logic, a novel form of cognition beyond Piaget's formal operations which is able to hold and integrate all perspectives, contradictions, and opposites in a dialectical and nonlinear fashion. Only this form of cognition, which for Wilber can be facilitated by the practice of meditation or simply by "thinking globally," can successfully accomplish the tasks of integrating the Big Three and situating humankind "on the brink of the transpersonal" (1995, p. 264).[12]

It is in this context, I believe, that we can grasp the import of the Four Quadrant Model. Briefly, the Four Quadrant Model maps reality (the Kosmos, in Wilber's terms) in four interrelated dimensions or quadrants: the Upper Left (the interior of the individual: prehension, subjective experience, intentionality, etc.), the Upper Right (the exterior of the individual: atoms, behavior, etc.), the Lower Left (the interior of the collective: cultural worldviews, etc.), and, finally, the Lower Right (the exterior of the collective: social systems, etc.). Wilber argues that all phenomena of existence partake in these four quadrants, that is, they have individual (intentional and behavioral) and collective (cultural and social) dimensions, and all types of problems and contradictions emerge whenever we ignore or try to reduce any of them. The Four Quadrant Model, Wilber tells us, is a framework that makes it possible to think globally about whatever situation, problem, or phenomenon we are facing. Seen this way, the Four Quadrant Model becomes a modern mandala that invites us to take many perspectives into account, to hold in mind possible contradictions, to enter the space of vision-logic, and, arguably, to integrate the Big Three (I, We, It).

I say "arguably" because, despite the obvious fact that the interior/individual quadrant corresponds to the I (subjective world), the interior/collective quadrant to the We (intersubjective world), and the exterior/individual and collective quadrants to the It (objective world), the practical ways in which these conceptual equivalencies can actually help us to integrate the

Big Three in our culture and lived experience remain, in my opinion, obscure in Wilber's work.

But, what is the place that spirituality occupies in this modern mandala? Against this background, Wilber (1995) advances that an integral approach to spirituality can no longer be focused only on individual experiences, but should take into account all four quadrants:

> As Spirit manifests, it manifests in and as the four quadrants, or simply the Big Three—I, it, we. As Spirit/Consciousness evolves into the transpersonal domain, the Big Three appear as Buddha (the ultimate I), Dharma (the ulti- mate it), and Sangha (the ultimate We). Many mystics have an understandable tendency to emphasize the I-strand, where one's mind and Buddha Mind become, or are realized to be, one Self (which is no-self individually) . . .
>
> But by recognizing that all manifestation is in the form of the four quad- rants, this tendency to a certain solipsism is carefully guarded against. At the same time, the timeless and eternal nature of Spirit can nonetheless be intu- ited in (or through) any of the four quadrants (I, it, or we). (1995, p. 606)

Again, what Wilber is suggesting is that all human phenomena, including spiritual ones, have both individual (intentional and behavioral) and collec- tive (cultural and social) dimensions. Therefore, the interpretive and transfor- mative intentions of both transpersonal studies and spiritual practices should be focused not only on the self-body, but also on human relationships, com- munities, cultural forms, and social-political structures. In Wilber's (1996a) own words: "Since Spirit-in-action manifests as all four quadrants, then an adequate interpretation of a spiritual experience ought to take all four quad- rants into account" (p. 104).

Using Wilber's Four Quadrant Model as a lens to examine the experi- ential vision is useful to perceive one of its most fundamental flaws. In its focus on individual inner experiences, the experiential vision can be rightly charged with the most subtle of reductionisms made in the name of spiritu- ality: an intrasubjective reductionism, that is, the reduction of spiritual and transpersonal phenomena to the Upper Left Quadrant, the realm of the inte- rior and individual. To recognize the presence of Spirit only in the interior depths of the individual not only perpetuates the disenchanted world of modernity, but also forces the individual to search for meaning and spiritual realization essentially within, putting a tremendous pressure on the structures of human subjectivity that can lead to a variety of excesses and distortions (see Rothberg, 1993).

It is certainly one of Wilber's accomplishments to have offered a modern conceptual framework that extends our understanding of spirituality out of the merely interior and individual. More recently, Wilber (1998a) attempts to overcome intrasubjective reductionism through an "expanded empiricism," which extends the notion of experience beyond sensory realms to all levels of reality and human existence (including spiritual). Although clearly aware of many of its shortcomings, however, Wilber still appears to be committed in some respects to the experiential vision. As we will see in chapter 3, for example, his proposal for the justification of spiritual claims is not only clothed in empiricist language, but also attempts to meet the standards for valid knowledge of empirical science such as verifiability and falsifiability. A crucial point to discern here, however, is that once spirituality is conceived as a four-quadrant affair, these empiricist principles are probably inadequate.

To the arguments of these two authors, I would like to add that, in most traditions—such as Advaita Vedanta, many Buddhist schools, and some forms of Christian monasticism—a period (usually lasting several years) of rigorous study of religious scriptures and "right views" is often regarded as a prerequisite for meditative practice and the experiential enactment of the teachings (see, e.g., Klein, 1986; McGinn, 1996a; Rambachan, 1991). The immersion in experiential practices without an appropriate understanding of the teachings is generally considered not only premature but also potentially problematic. Likewise, in the Yoga system of Patañjali (1977), a very demanding ethical preparation (yama, niyama)—that includes the practice of non-violence, truthfulness, self-discipline, right speech, devotion, and so forth—is considered a necessary foundation for the practice of meditation (dharana) and contemplation (dhyana), as well as for the attainment of unitive states (samadhi) and liberation (moksa).

All this strongly suggests that the modern Western search for spiritual experiences, usually divorced from serious religious study and deep ethical commitments, may be profoundly misleading. As I will argue, for example, once inner spiritual experiences are segregated from ethical and/or traditional contexts, they tend to lose their sacred and transformative quality and become merely peak-experiences—temporary gratifications for an ego hungry for subjective spiritual heights, but often leading to further self-absorption and narcissism—the antithesis of what any authentic spiritual path strives for.

Finally, from a traditional perspective, intrasubjective reductionism is profoundly misleading because spiritual phenomena are seen as resulting from the participation in spheres of being and awareness that transcend the merely human. As virtually all mystical traditions maintain, spiritual events are not to be understood merely in phenomenological terms, but rather as emerging from the participation in spiritual realities that exist beyond the realm of human experience. From this angle, to view human intrasubjective experience as the fundamental lens through which to understand the nature and essence of spiritual phenomena cannot be but another product of modern anthropocentrism. In Part II of this book, I suggest that this intrasubjective dimension can be better understood as how spiritual phenomena are lived from the perspective of a participating individual consciousness. To infer from this participation that transpersonal and spiritual phenomena are merely inner experiences is both distorting and egocentric.

In sum, although redeeming the epistemic value of spirituality, transpersonal theory accounts for transpersonal and spiritual phenomena in terms of individual inner experiences. Hence, transpersonal theory is still committed, at least in this fundamental respect, to the intrasubjective reductionism characteristic of the modern understanding of spirituality. In this commitment, transpersonal theory perpetuates an extremely partial and marginal view of spirituality, and acts in complicity with the very way of thinking that it is attempting to dethrone. Because of its inherent reduction of spirituality to the subjective world of the individual, I suggest that the experiential vision is an inadequate framework to meet the challenges that transpersonal studies face today. What is needed, I will argue, is to free transpersonal theory from these experiential prejudices—and thereby from its implicit commitment to modernity—and extend our vision of Spirit to the entire cosmos.

Subtle Cartesianism

Briefly, *subtle Cartesianism is the understanding of spiritual and transpersonal phenomena according to a subject-object model of knowledge and cognition.* In this section, I want to suggest that although (1) it is widely recognized that this Cartesian framework is inappropriate in accounting for most transpersonal phenomena, (2) the experiential vision structures transpersonal phenomena in terms of a subject having experiences of different transpersonal or spiritual objects.

Ever since Maslow's (1969) reflections on a Taoist science, Cartesianism—and its associated subject-object model of cognition—has been one of the main targets of transpersonal studies. Since its very beginnings, transpersonal theory has been explicitly anti- or post-Cartesian and searched for alternatives to objectivist and subjectivist accounts of transpersonal phenomena (Capra, 1982; Grof, 1985; Harman, 1988). Let us briefly look at some of the reasons for the inadequacy of a Cartesian model of knowledge to account for transpersonal phenomena.

To begin with, the Cartesian philosophy of consciousness is at the heart of all representational paradigms of cognition, which envision human knowledge as the inner, subjective representation of an externally independent and objective world—as Rorty (1979) nicely portrayed with his metaphor of the "mind as the mirror of nature." This representational view underlies all the objectivist demands for valid knowledge of traditional empiricism, positivism, and realism. For these epistemologies, our knowledge claims about the world, even if imperfect and approximate, need to be justified by matching them against a pregiven world that exists out there independently of human cognition.

Today, however, Cartesianism—and its associated representational paradigms of cognition and foundationalist epistemologies—has been seriously challenged in virtually all disciplines of knowledge, from phenomenology (e.g., Ihde, 1986; Marsh, 1988) to cognitive science (e.g., Shanon, 1993; Thompson, 1996; Varela, Thompson, & Rosch, 1991), and from linguistics (e.g., Lakoff, 1987; Lakoff & Johnson, 1980) to feminist critical thinking (e.g., Bordo, 1987), among many others (e.g., O'Donovan-Anderson, 1996). Giving voice to this increasingly pervasive post-Cartesian *Zeitgeist*, philosopher Richard Bernstein (1985) contends that the most insidious problems of postempiricist philosophies—such as those arising from the bogus dichotomy between objectivism and relativism—are "parasitic upon the acceptance of the Cartesian persuasion that needs to be questioned, exposed, and overcome" (p. 19). What is needed, Bernstein (1985) continues, is "to exorcise the Cartesian Anxiety and liberate ourselves from its seductive appeal" (p. 19).[13] In this post-Cartesian turn of contemporary thinking, the transpersonal eye may see a movement auguring the dawn of postformal and transpersonal modes of cognition. From a transpersonal perspective, contemporary philosophy seems to be going nondual in certain epistemological respects.

And yet, it is in transpersonal studies where the limitations of Cartesianism are exposed at their best. As soon became evident, Cartesianism was an inadequate epistemology for transpersonal studies because transpersonal phenomena collapse the distinction between subject and object, and accordingly between what has been traditionally regarded as subjective and objective. In other words, during transpersonal events, the subjective-objective structuration of phenomena suffers such drastic inversions that these categories lose their descriptive and explanatory value. In transpersonal phenomena, it became strikingly obvious, *not only what is subjective can become objective, but also what is objective can become subjective.* Let us look at these two singular inversions in some detail.

On the one hand, what is subjective can become objective insofar as elements belonging to human subjectivity can become potential objects for the emerging transpersonal self. This subjective-objective fluidity has been noted, for example, in the dynamics of personal and transpersonal development, in which the self disidentifies from structures with which it was previously identified and can act upon them as objects of consciousness (Wilber, 1996b, 1997a). In early childhood, for example, the self is identified with the body until the emergence of the mind, the time in which the self identifies with the mind and can potentially operate with the body as an object. Similarly, in ordinary adulthood, the self is usually identified with the mind until the emergence of witness-consciousness, the time in which the self identifies with witness-consciousness and can potentially operate with the mind as an object. In both cases, elements belonging to the structures of subjectivity with which the self was identified become potential objects for the new self.

This process of transition from subjective to objective can also be observed during mindfulness practices such as *vipassana* or some types of Zen meditation. In these forms of Buddhist meditation, practitioners develop the detached attitude of a witness towards any content that emerges in the field of their consciousness (e.g., Nyanaponika, 1973). Through these practices, meditators learn to disidentify themselves from these contents, and many aspects that ordinarily pertain to the subjective structures through which they experience themselves and the world—such as desires, feelings, thoughts, sensations, and so forth—become objects for their consciousness.

Another example of this subjective-objective fluidity can be found in the mystical phenomenon Hollenback (1996) calls empowerment (*enthymesis*). According to Hollenback, one of the main effects of many recollective and meditative practices is the empowerment (*enthymesis*) of the mystic's conscious and unconscious thoughts and desires. Hollenback (1996) argues that this process of *enthymesis* transforms the imagination of the mystic into an organ of supranormal perception and knowledge capable not only of obtaining paranormally veridical information, but also, and this is especially relevant for us here, of objectifying the contents of the mystic's subjective space. It is through this empowerment, Hollenback claims, that the mystic's imagination shapes the different spiritual landscapes according to the metaphysics, anthropology, and soteriology of his or her tradition.[14] During this process, Hollenback tells us, "the ordinary solid boundaries between the subjective and objective domains of experience begin to blur" (p. 156). Again, what is subjective can become objective.

Up to this point, we have seen several examples of how what is subjective can become objective in the inner or intrapyschic world. However, a parallel case can be made in relation to what is experienced in the outer or extrapsychic world.[15] In other words, aspects belonging to the structures of subjectivity can reach out and become, in a way, objects for consciousness in the external world. Of course, the defense mechanism of projection comes rapidly to mind in this regard. However, psychodynamic accounts of projection are not helpful in explaining the idea to be grasped here, because they depict this external objectification of the subjective as an intrapsychic phenomenon: The projection of our repressed feelings or unconscious personality traits upon people or events does not really transform them; what changes is only our experience of them. By contrast, in transpersonal and spiritual development, as Wilber (1995) conveys with his notion of *worldspace*, new worlds of corresponding objects and meanings *actually* emerge as consciousness evolves and identifies itself with new structures of subjectivity. This idea receives support from many contemplative traditions such as Vajrayana Buddhism or Kabbalah, which maintain that inner spiritual practices are not merely aimed at changing the self, but at the actual transformation of the world. For example, according to Kukai, founder of Shingon Buddhism, the world is a manifestation of the cosmic Buddha that, depending on the state of mind of the viewer, "actually takes form not only as different world views, but also as different worlds" (Kasulis, 1988, p. 269). A more detailed explanation of this mystical transformation of the world will have to await until Part II of this book, when I present the epistemology and metaphysics of the participatory vision.

On the other hand, what is objective can become subjective because in transpersonal phenomenology what once were objects of knowledge can be incorporated, temporarily or permanently, into the very identity of the self. Intrapsychically, for example, archetypes which were first experienced as distinct from oneself can become, in transpersonal development, structures with which the self identifies (Wilber, 1996b). Extrapsychically, the self can also become identified with previous objects of the external world, as in nature mysticism, where the subjectivity of an individual can encompass aspects of the environment or even the entire natural world. As Grof's (1985, 1988) research has widely documented, human consciousness can become identified with a rich variety of biological, social, cultural, planetary, and cosmic phenomena. After all, is it not the most fundamental claim of transpersonal theory that self-identity can expand and encompass other aspects of the psyche, life, and cosmos (Walsh & Vaughan, 1993a, 1993b)?

The ontological (versus merely phenomenological) nature of this subject-object identification is carefully emphasized by Puhakka (2000) in her discussion on spiritual knowing:

> The coming together of subject and object, or the knower and the known, in the act of knowing obliterates their distinction in the moment of contact. . . . To the degree that contact occurs, it involves an *ontological shift*—it is not a matter of the subject "viewing" the object but rather the subject is now "being" the object. But note: the subject is not being the object "in" his or her subjective experience or viewpoint. By "ontological shift" I mean a shift not just from one viewpoint to another (by the "same" subject) but a shift in the constitution of the viewing subject. In other words, a transformation of the subject takes place. . . . Knowing is not merely a subjective experience of assimilating the object. (p. 18)

In addition to this subjective-objective fluidity, it should be obvious that Cartesian epistemic categories such as objectivism or subjectivism can be highly confusing when talking about the philosophical stance of many transpersonal thinkers. As we will see in chapter 4, for example, many transpersonalists support a Neo-Advaitin version of the perennial philosophy, according to which "at the highest levels, world and self, outer reality and inner reality, coincide as the 'ground' of all that is" (Rothberg, 1986b, p. 3). Or, in Wilber's (1993a) words: "The core insight of the psychologia perennis is that our 'innermost' consciousness is identical to the absolute and ultimate reality of the universe" (p. 22). But then, to talk about transpersonal perennialists as objectivists or subjectivists becomes seriously misleading insofar as they maintain the essential identity between the deepest human subjectivity and the ultimate nature of the objective reality.

In transpersonal studies, then, it is not clear how to coherently demarcate between what is objective and what is subjective. As I see it, all these subjective-objective and objective-subjective transpositions, rather than merely indicating the fluidity of these epistemic categories, strongly suggest that the Cartesian model of cognition is inadequate to account for transpersonal phenomena. The transpersonal dismantlement of the subject-object organization of phenomena shows that these epistemic categories have lost their descriptive and explanatory value in relation to transpersonal events—and, arguably, to human knowledge in general.

In spite of these apparent limitations, however, many transpersonal authors often conceptualize transpersonal knowledge following a Cartesian model of discourse, for example, making objectivist claims (cf. Levin, 1988b).[16] Here I want to suggest that this subtle Cartesianism is largely rooted in the experiential understanding of transpersonal phenomena. The experiential vision is foundational for this self-betrayal because it structures transpersonal phenomena in terms of a subject having experiences of transpersonal objects. The intentional structure connoted by the modern notion of *experience* linguistically manifests in the constitution of a grammatical subject (a "who") and grammatical object (a "what"). Ever since Brentano, Husserl, Sartre, and others, all experience and states of consciousness are said to be always "of something" and usually "by someone." As a result, whenever we hear the word *experience*, we immediately want to know who had what experience.

In the context of transpersonal studies, then, the expression *transpersonal experience* automatically configures transpersonal phenomena in terms of an experiencing subject in relation to objects of experience. In other words, the experiential talk reifies both a Cartesian subject and a Cartesian object with respect to transpersonal and spiritual phenomena. On the one hand, it consolidates a subject of the experience with which the ego eagerly identifies itself.[17] As we will see, this has pernicious consequences for how transpersonal and spiritual phenomena are lived. On the other hand, it objectifies whatever transpersonal cognition is said to reveal, even in those cases in which what is disclosed is said to be "emptiness," "nothingness," or "pure consciousness." In this subtle perpetuation of Cartesianism, the experiential vision betrays some of the fundamental premises and aims of the transpersonal orientation.

To conclude this section, I would like to stress that these two problems can be seen as the result of two consecutive dissociative moves. First, intrasubjective reductionism isolates transpersonal and spiritual phenomena from the world and confines them into the limited realm of individual inner experience. Second, already in inner space, subtle Cartesianism creates a further division, this time between an experiencing subject and experienced objects of transpersonal cognition. With these two moves, the experiential vision not only betrays the transpersonal orientation, but also becomes vulnerable to all the anxieties and dilemmas of Cartesian modes of consciousness, such as the myths of subjectivism and objectivism, the false dichotomy of absolutism and relativism, the riddles of epistemic mediation and construction, and, as we will see in the next section, the seductions of spiritual materialism.[18]

THE PRACTICAL BETRAYAL

In the previous pages, we have seen how the experiential vision is incoherent with the nature of transpersonal phenomena and perpetuates a reductionistic account of spirituality. As Lakoff and Johnson (1980) explain, however, the way we conceptualize any phenomenon has a profound impact on how we live it. It should not come as a surprise, then, that the problematic ramifications of the experiential vision are not limited to conceptual mapping, but extend to the territory of spiritual practice. Here I want to suggest that the experiential vision has problematic implications for how transpersonal phenomena are engaged in everyday life. More precisely, I want to propose that the experiential vision breeds two potential pitfalls of the spiritual path: spiritual narcissism and integrative arrestment.

Spiritual Narcissism

There are many ways to understand spirituality. Different approaches emphasize diverse aspects of the spiritual life, the spiritual path, or one or another spiritual tradition. For our present purposes, I will adopt the definition offered by Evans (1993) in his superb *Spirituality and Human Nature*. According to Evans, "spirituality consists primarily of a basic transformative process in which we uncover and let go of our narcissism so as to surrender into the Mystery out of which everything continually arises" (p. 4). Even though the means and goals of mystical paths are diverse, Evans explains, mystics tend to agree that any authentic spiritual transformation "involves a shedding of narcissism, self-centeredness, self-separation, self-preoccupation, and so on" (p. 158).

In his influential work, *The Culture of Narcissism*, sociologist Christopher Lasch (1978) argues that the logic of competitive individualism, consumer capitalism, and hopelessness in the teeth of the global disasters of our modern times has culminated in the dead end of an extreme narcissistic self-preoccupation. In this context, and as critical thinkers such as Jacoby (1975/1997) warned more than twenty years ago, the immersion in self-growth and spiritual work can easily become strategies of narcissistic survival. Spirituality, rather than transforming the self through a decrease or eradication of narcissism, can become one more egoic scheme at the service of self-centered ways of being.[19]

By *spiritual narcissism* I understand a set of related distortions of the spiritual path, such as ego-inflation (the aggrandizement of the ego fueled by spiritual energies), self-absorption (the over-preoccupation with one's spiritual status and achievements), and spiritual materialism (the appropriation of spirituality to strengthen egoic ways of life). As I see it, the thread common to all these pitfalls is what I call *spiritual narcissism* (i.e., *the misuse of spiritual practices, energies, or experiences to bolster self-centered ways of being*). The main symptoms of spiritual narcissism are, among others, a fragile sense of empowerment and self-importance; a preoccupation with one's comparative spiritual status; a constant and repetitious chattering about one's spiritual experiences and achievements; a strong need for being positively reinforced and praised; a preoccupation with the sense of being special, chosen for some distinguished spiritual purpose, or preferred by spiritual teachers; an extreme idealization or demonization of spiritual teachers; serious difficulties in working with authority figures; and finally, an exaggerated susceptibility and defensiveness towards any sort of criticism (cf. Almaas, 1996).

The phenomenon of spiritual narcissism is well documented in the world religious literature, and has been invariably regarded as one of the most serious hazards of the spiritual path. One of the most lucid expositions of this danger is by Chögyam Trungpa (1987), who coined the term *spiritual materialism* to refer to an "ego-centered version of spirituality [in which] we can deceive ourselves into thinking we are developing spiritually when instead we are strengthening our egocentricity through spiritual techniques" (p. 3). Once we have learned the new language and rules of the spiritual "game," Trungpa (1987) points out, we can become attached to these ideals and use them in ways that bolster our ego and new self-image, rather than as skillful means towards liberation. Apart from the traditional accounts, several modern authors have also eloquently discussed the narcissistic tribulations of the ego in search of spiritual realization (see Almaas, 1996; Caplan, 1999; Evans, 1993; Wilber, 1986).[20]

In short, narcissism can be seen as diametrically opposed to spirituality. Both traditional and modern spiritual thinkers coincide in that the more we participate in Spirit, the more we move naturally away from self-centered ways of being. And conversely, the more we preoccupy ourselves with self-gratification and self-grandiosity, the more we alienate ourselves from Spirit.[21]

There are two main reasons, I believe, why the experiential vision nourishes the different varieties of spiritual narcissism. First, its intrasubjective reductionism paves the way for the egoic appropriation of spiritual phenomena because it confines spirituality to the very domain where the ego believes itself sovereign and continuously struggles to dominate: the realm of inner experience. As Wilber (1996a) observes, an exclusive experiential understanding makes individuals prone to engage narcissistically spiritual insights:

> Many people interpret these spiritual experiences basically in terms of only the Upper Left quadrant—they see the experience in terms of a higher Self, or higher consciousness, or archetypal forms. They tend to completely ignore the cultural and social and behavioral components. So their insights are crippled in terms of how to relate this higher Self to the other quadrants, which are all interpreted rather narcissistically as mere extensions of their Self. The new age movement is full of this type of Self-only interpretation. (p. 103)

Second, its subtle Cartesianism effectively expedites the narcissistic appropriation of spiritual objects by a reified egoic subject. Spiritual events in which I participate, that is, become *my* experiences. The association between Cartesianism and narcissism is also noted by Evans (1993). For this author, both subjectivism and objectivism are complementary epistemological stances of narcissistic modes of consciousness that preclude a genuine availability to others, and a real participation in the world and spiritual energies.[22] While in subjectivism the world becomes my experience of the world, in objectivism, by contrast, I retreat to a position of a detached observer and the world appears as entirely outside me. However, Evans points out, "whether I include everything [subjectivism] or exclude everything [objectivism] I am like a god in my aloneness, my self-sufficiency, and my domination of the universe. In the one case I dominate by devouring and assimilating into my experience. In the other case I dominate by subjecting to my intellect and will" (p. 44).

Integrative Arrestement

The integration of transpersonal phenomena in everyday life is arguably one of the most urgent tasks of modern transpersonal psychology. A failure to adequately integrate spiritual openings, for example, is widely regarded as a potential source of psychological disorders and spiritual pathologies (e.g., Bragdon, 1990; Grof & Grof, 1989, 1990; Wilber, 1986). In addition, while access to transpersonal states has become more widespread, their stabilization into enduring traits—a hallmark of genuine transpersonal development—continues to be a fundamental challenge for transpersonal psychologists. This awareness was already present in Maslow (1971), who towards the end of his life shifted the emphasis of his work from the study of peak-experiences to what he called plateau-experiences—the latter being a more serene, stable, and noetic response to the sacred than the former.

A basic issue here is that, as it has often been stressed in the religious literature, the goal of the spiritual quest is not to have spiritual experiences, but to stabilize spiritual consciousness, live a spiritual life, and transform the world accordingly. And it cannot be repeated too often that, *regardless of the quantity, spiritual experiences do not produce a spiritual life.* A crucial task for transpersonal studies, then, is to develop both conceptual frameworks and practical injunctions that support the translation of transient spiritual states into the stable transformation of self, relationships, and world.

In this regard, I believe that the experiential vision, rather than fostering this integration, raises several obstacles that crystallize in what I call *integrative arrestment.* By integrative arrestment I mean *the hindrance of the natural integrative process that translates spiritual realizations into everyday life towards the transformation of self, relationships, and world.*

There are at least two features of the experiential vision that contribute to this sequestration of the natural integrative power of spiritual phenomena. The first is the emphasis placed on individual inner experiences (intrasubjective reductionism), which comes usually accompanied by a disregard towards other elements of traditional spiritual paths, such as ethical commitments, community life, relationships with teachers, serious study of scriptures, and so forth (Rothberg, 1993). However, many of these non-experiential elements are traditionally regarded as essential to the integration of spiritual insights and the effective navigation of the spiritual journey. A correct understanding of spiritual doctrines, for example, is considered in most spiritual traditions a prerequisite for the practice of meditation and the transconceptual access to the ultimate.[23]

Spiritual systems offer an integrated understanding of the totality of reality and the role of humanity therein. The integrative power of spiritual realizations depends to a large extent on the meaning that such events possess in the larger scheme of things. Without such an integrated understanding, the serious difficulties of the modern Western self in integrating spiritual insights in everyday life should not be surprising. Divested from the cosmological meaning provided by spiritual traditions, these "experiences" not only often promote spiritual narcissism, but also tend to lose their natural transformative quality. Likewise, once spiritual openings are divorced from wider ethical and social contexts, their sacred and transformative quality substantially diminish. As a result, spiritual realizations become merely peak-experiences. From this viewpoint, peak-experiences may be seen, at their best, as *secularized spiritual phenomena*, and, at their worst, as temporary gratifications for an always hungry-for-heights Cartesian ego.

The second reason lies in the structuring of spiritual phenomena as objects experienced by a subject (subtle Cartesianism). One of the consequences of subtle Cartesianism is a conception of spiritual phenomena as transient experiential episodes that have a clear-cut beginning and end—in contrast, for example, to realizations or insights that, once learned, change the way one sees life and guide one's future actions in the world. This experiential understanding, then, precipitates the pitfall known popularly in spiritual circles as the *collection of experiences* (i.e., the search for a periodic access to spiritual highs outside the context of a genuine transformative process).

To conclude this section, I would like to stress that I am not suggesting that everybody in the transpersonal community is prey to these pitfalls of the spiritual path (spiritual narcissism and integrative arrestment), or that the experiential vision *inevitably* results in these distortions.[24] There are many transpersonalists, as well as some naturally gifted individuals who, even operating in the context of the experiential vision, are sharply aware of these issues and clearly are involved in genuine processes of spiritual transformation: moving away from spiritual narcissism and integrating spiritual insights into their everyday lives towards the emancipation of self, community, and world. Rather, what I am suggesting here—perhaps in a somewhat exaggerated fashion to highlight what I see as an increasing trend—is that many transpersonalists overlook or are ineffective in dealing with these issues, and that these gifted individuals seem to be the exception to the rule.

SUMMARY AND CONCLUSIONS

Since its very origins, transpersonal theory conceived transpersonal and spiritual phenomena in terms of individual inner experiences. When one looks at the intellectual and cultural *Zeitgeist* of the California of the late 1960s, the tendency of the early transpersonalists to focus on individual experiences and to defend the empirical foundations of the field is certainly comprehensible. In this chapter, however, I have sought to show that this experiential vision, although once salutary and probably inevitable, is today both unnecessary and problematic.

In particular, I have suggested that the experiential vision betrays on both conceptual and pragmatic grounds some of the central aims of the transpersonal orientation. Conceptually, the experiential vision falls into intrasubjective reductionism (the reduction of spirituality to the status of individual inner experiences) and subtle Cartesianism (the structuration of transpersonal and spiritual phenomena according to a subject-object model of cognition). Pragmatically, the experiential vision fosters spiritual narcissism (the egoic appropriation of spirituality at the service of a narcissistic motivation) and integrative arrestment (the sequestration of the natural integrative process of spiritual phenomena towards the transformation of self, relationships, and world). Some of the most insidious practical problems repeatedly reported by transpersonalists, then, may be to some degree symptomatic of an experiential understanding of spirituality.

Taken together, these conceptual and practical shortcomings strongly suggest, I believe, that the experiential vision has become inadequate to meet the challenges that transpersonal studies face today. What is needed, then, is to go beyond the experiential talk in transpersonal studies and explore alternative frameworks to understand and live transpersonal and spiritual phenomena. But before attempting to articulate an alternative vision, it is necessary first to examine the methodological, epistemological, and metaphysical underpinnings of the experiential vision. This is the task of the next two chapters.

3

THE EMPIRICIST COLONIZATION

OF SPIRITUALITY

Spiritual knowledge is not the fruit of psychological imagination or patho-
logical delusion. Anyone who has seriously engaged in a spiritual life
knows that essential information about human nature and reality can be
revealed through spiritual states. The wholesome impulse to legitimize
spiritual knowledge in our modern times, however, has often taken the
form of defending its scientific or empirical status. Parallels between the
spiritual path and the scientific method are established and the birth of a
new science of spiritual experience is triumphantly announced. In this
chapter, I suggest that the similarities between spirituality and science are
more apparent than real, and therefore that the efforts to legitimate spiri-
tual knowledge by appealing to its scientific status may be both mislead-
ing and counterproductive.

IN THE LAST CHAPTER I proposed that the experiential emphasis of transpersonal studies is in part rooted in the attempt to establish the empirical,
and therefore scientific, foundations of the field. In this chapter, I want to
spell out the main ways in which these empirical foundations have been
sought, and explain why I believe that these efforts, although valuable, are
ultimately misguided and counterproductive.

My main intention in this chapter, then, is to show that the importation
of empiricist language, methods, and standards of validity to account for the
logic of transpersonal inquiry and justify its knowledge claims is not only
misleading, but also unnecessary and often self-defeating. To this end, the
first part of the chapter reviews a number of early as well as more recent

proposals for the empiricist study of spirituality in transpersonal theory and related fields. The second part of the chapter illustrates some of the fundamental problems with this empiricist colonization of spirituality, taking as a paradigmatic case Wilber's (1998a) recent attempt, in *The Marriage of Sense and Soul*, to marry science and religion under the roof of a broad empiricism. After summarizing the main arguments and merits of this project, I argue that Wilber's nuptial arrangement results in several unexpected marital conflicts. First, Wilber's proposal of empiricist standards (replicability, verifiability, falsifiability, etc.) for all ways of knowing perpetuates the fragmentation of the modern era that he is rightfully trying to overcome. Second, his resuscitation of Popper's principle of falsifiability as the hallmark of genuine knowledge is not only misguided in the natural sciences, but also inimical to the nature of spiritual inquiry. Finally, serious questions can also be raised about the identity of the science and the religion whose marriage Wilber arranges and, I believe, prematurely celebrates.

THE NATURE AND ORIGINS OF INNER EMPIRICISM

In the first issue of the *Journal of Transpersonal Psychology*, Sutich (1969) writes:

> The emerging Transpersonal Psychology ("fourth force") is concerned specifically with the *empirical,* scientific study of, and responsible implementation of the findings relevant to, becoming, individual and species-wide meta-needs, ultimate values, unitive consciousness, peak experiences. (p. 16)

Although scientific studies of transpersonal experiences abound in the literature, it would be a mistake to read this statement as suggesting that transpersonal research has strictly followed the empiricism of the natural sciences. After all, to endorse the scientific demand for the public (meaning here perceptible through the senses) nature of observation would raise a truly formidable obstacle for a field primarily concerned with the study of transpersonal, spiritual, and mystical "inner" experiences.[1] It should not come as a surprise, then, that the starting point of most transpersonal epistemological programs is a direct challenge to the sensory reductionism of traditional empiricism. But then, what is understood by empiricism in transpersonal studies?

I would like to point out here that the prevalent method and epistemology proposed for transpersonal studies corresponds to what Weber (1986, p. 7) calls *inner empiricism*. Briefly, the main idea behind this term is that *transpersonal and spiritual knowledge claims are valid because they can be replicated and tested through disciplined introspection, and can therefore be intersubjectively verified or falsified.* Central to inner empiricism, then, is an expansion of the meaning of "public" observation from the merely perceptible through the senses to any potentially intersubjective meaning or referent. This is a welcome extension in total harmony with the interpretative turn of contemporary philosophy, and its recognition of the intrinsically dialogical and intersubjective character of human understanding. As we will see, however, this salutary development comes quickly to a standstill because it occurs in the context of a transpersonal theory that is not fully emancipated from the Cartesianism of the natural sciences. But before analyzing some of these objectivist problems, it may be helpful to explore the origins and widespread influence of inner empiricism in transpersonal studies and related fields.

To my knowledge, the first explicit allusion to inner empiricism in the transpersonal conversation took place in a symposium on "Consciousness and Cosmos" organized by Welwood at the University of Santa Barbara, California (see Welwood et al., 1978). In a panel discussing the relationship between science and spirituality, Needleman points out that:

> It is a question of inner empiricism as well as outer empiricism: How to have a lens or whatever you want to call it, an awareness, an empirical attitude toward oneself that is as tough-minded as the one that empirical science has given us toward the outer data. We need to look at the inner data with as much care, tough-mindedness, experimental method and verification as possible. Now you cannot get public verification in the way you can of a scientific hypothesis, but there is such a thing as private verification which is shared and is communicable among people who have gone through a particular discipline. A form of yoga may be just as scientific, communicable, shareable, and in a certain strange sense even quantifiable, as the outer things. (Welwood et al., 1978. p. 97)

In the same panel, Capra explains how spiritual insights attained through inner empiricism can be verified:

> The verification occurs when you go to a Zen master and he tells you how to sit and breathe, and gives you a puzzle (koan) and says, Go away for five years and come back again. You'll have verified my experiment. (Welwood et al., 1978, p. 104)

This inner empiricist approach to the study of transpersonal and spiritual experiences defined the contours of most methodological proposals in the field during the following decades. In her early outline of the field of transpersonal psychology, Boucouvalas (1980) already emphasizes the widespread use of inner or experiential empiricism as a method of inquiry in transpersonal psychology. To mention a typical example, this empiricist impetus is obvious in articles such as Nelson's (1990) "The Technology of the Praeternatural: An Empirically Based Model of Transpersonal Experiences," published in The *Journal of Transpersonal Psychology*. After defending an ontologically neutral return to an empiricism of direct experience, Nelson (1990) concludes his essay endorsing John Stuart Mill's claim that the "backward state of the (psychological) sciences can only be remedied by applying to them the methods of physical science, duly extended and generalized" (p. 45).

As should be obvious, inner empiricism is alive and well in contemporary transpersonal theory. In a recent review of the literature, Rothberg (1994) critically notes the allegedly inner and empirical nature and testability of most transpersonal accounts of spiritual inquiry. For example, Baruss (1996) recently defended a spiritual empiricism based on inner personal replication and testing. From a psychodynamic perspective, Washburn (1995) maintains a similar view concerning the potential inner verification of spiritual energies: "Admittedly, then, the foregoing account of the power of the Ground, although empirically meaningful, is not presently empirically verifiable except in a subjective and introspective way, and even then, only by those for whom the power of the Ground has become active as spirit" (p. 130). Likewise, in their *Transpersonal Research Methods for the Social Sciences*, Braud and Anderson (1998) stress the need to expand our definition of empiricism so that transpersonal studies can "honor human experience." The goal of the transpersonal research programs they present is unequivocal: To study "human experiences that are *personal, subjective, significant,* and *relevant*" (p. 19). "These events [transpersonal, spiritual]," they add, "typically have been private, subjective, and inwardly experiential" (p. 19).[2]

VARIETIES OF INNER EMPIRICISM

Having indicated the scope of inner empiricism in transpersonal theory, I would like to briefly review now the main forms in which it has been articulated in transpersonal and related disciplines.

JUNG'S EXPERIENTIAL EPISTEMOLOGY

An important precedent to an inner empiricist approach to spirituality can be found in C. G. Jung's conviction of the epistemological import of inner experiences, as well as in his consensual theory of truth regarding experiential knowledge (see, e.g., Nagy, 1991, pp. 23–36, 145–55). According to Jung, interior experience reveals genuine knowledge of psychological and archetypal realities which are phenomenologically testable by adequate observers. Since the Jungian psyche is *naturaliter religiosa* [naturally religious] an analogous argument has been often extrapolated to spiritual realities, at least in relation to how these realities are imprinted in the human psyche, as Jung believed. Furthermore, Jung's consensual theory of truth regarding psycho-spiritual truths, evident in his *Consensus Gentium* argument for the existence of the God archetype, also anticipates the intersubjective justification maintained by the advocates of transpersonal empiricism.[3]

It should be noted that, in contrast to many transpersonal empiricists, Jung frequently stressed the strictly psychological nature of his approach, and his consequent agnosticism regarding the extrapsychic status of religious and metaphysical claims. In Jung's (1992) words: "Psychology . . . treats all metaphysical claims as mental phenomena, and regards them as statements about the mind and its structure that derive ultimately from certain unconscious dispositions" (pp. 48–49). Operating within the boundaries of a Neo-Kantian epistemology, he generally rejected mystical claims about direct knowledge of extramental spiritual realities. Rather, for Jung (1935), "mystics are people who have a particularly vivid experience of the processes of the collective unconscious. Mystical experience is experience of the archetypes" (p. 218). In Jung's eyes, then, mystical epistemologies were pre-Kantian and therefore naïve and dubious: "Epistemological criticism proves the impossibility of knowing God" (quoted in Clarke, 1992, p. 33).[4]

In his late works, however, Jung seems to have emancipated himself to some extent from these Neo-Kantian commitments through his intuition of a deep interconnection of psychological and physical realms. This move is apparent, for example, in his discussions of the Renaissance idea of *unus mundus*, his notion of the psychoid nature of the archetypes, and his postulation of the principle of synchronicity. Furthermore, in certain statements—admittedly anomalous in the overall corpus of his work—Jung suggests that ordinary epistemological constraints can be overcome in certain spiritual states of consciousness. In *Aion*, for example, after one of his typically Neo-Kantian pronouncements claiming that "the fact that metaphysical ideas exist and are believed in does nothing to prove the actual existence of their content or of the object they refer to," he admits that "the coincidence of idea and reality in the form of a special psychic state, a state of grace, should not be deemed impossible, even if the subject cannot bring it about by an act of will" (Jung, 1968, p. 34). To be sure, Jung's epistemological views about the nature of spiritual knowledge are ambiguous, but in them we can surely find seeds for the growth of an inner empiricist orientation in transpersonal studies.

MASLOW'S SELF-VALIDATING PEAK-EXPERIENCES

Although rudimentary, the earliest version of inner empiricism in transpersonal studies is due to Abraham Maslow. In his pioneering studies on self-actualization, Maslow (1968, 1970) stresses that peak-experiences were not merely emotional and ecstatic states, but frequently possessed a cognitive or noetic element. For example, in his essay, "What is the Validity of Knowledge Gained in Peak-Experiences?" Maslow (1970) maintains that the knowledge accessed during peak-experiences is both empirical and self-validating. By empirical, Maslow means grounded in human experience. And by self-validating he means that the experiences themselves provide the justification for the insights they provide.

It should be added, however, that Maslow also points out that "peak-knowledge *does* need external, independent validation" (1970, p. 77), and that some of the "revelations" gained in these experiences may be mistaken (1971, p. 333). In spite of these caveats, Maslow neither explains the nature of this external validation, nor offers specific criteria to distinguish between erroneous and accurate "revelations." The issue of the justification of peak-knowledge claims, then, is a tension never completely resolved in Maslow's work. In any event, for Maslow (1971), the new transpersonal psychology "would have to be experiential (phenomenological), at least in its foundation. It would have to be holistic rather than dissecting. And it would have to be empirical rather than a priori" (p. 337). Clearly, then, Maslow's work was another influential impulse for the development of inner empiricism in transpersonal theory.

TART'S STATE-SPECIFIC SCIENCES

The first actual inner empiricist research program in transpersonal studies was Charles Tart's proposal of state-specific sciences. According to Tart (1971, 1977, 1983), knowledge gained in altered states of consciousness (such as meditative, mystical, hypnotic, psychedelic, etc.) can be tested and verified by trained researchers following the essential principles of the scientific method: (1) good observation, (2) public nature of observation, (3) logical theorizing, and (4) testing of the theory by observable consequences (inner or outer). These observable consequences, Tart (1971, 1977) emphasizes, can be inner and experiential, and constitute the central element for the verification of state-specific knowledge claims. The validity of state-specific knowledge is anchored in the intersubjective agreement of adequately trained observers: "In principle," he tells us, "consensual validation of internal phenomena by a trained observer is possible" (1983, p. 213).

In addition, Tart (1983) suggests the need to subject traditional religious and mystical systems to the test of these new state-specific sciences: "Practically all the religions we know can mainly be defined as state-specific *technologies*, operated in the service of a priori belief systems" (p. 218). And he adds:

> I have nothing against religious and mystical groups. Yet I suspect that the vast majority of them have developed compelling belief systems rather than state-specific sciences. Will scientific method be extended to the development of state-specific sciences to improve our human condition? Or will the immense power of d-ASCs [discrete altered state of consciousness] be left in the hands of many cults and sects? (pp. 227–228)

For Tart, then, an inner empiricist epistemology is not only adequate for the study of spirituality, but also authoritative upon traditional religious claims.

WILBER'S BROAD EMPIRICISM

The most detailed account of inner empiricism in transpersonal theory is due to Ken Wilber (1990a). Given its profound impact on the field, the second section of this chapter analyzes in some detail its most recent articulation. Here it should suffice to say that Wilber (1990a) originally argued that the apparent lack of empirical verifiability and falsifiability of spiritual claims is rooted in the scientific reduction of the term empirical to refer only to sensory experience. However, Wilber (1990a) claims, all human knowledge (sensory, mental, and spiritual) can be tested through specific verification procedures having in common three basic components: (1) instrumental injunction ("If you want to know this, do this"), (2) intuitive apprehension (the experience itself), and (3) communal confirmation (consensus about the knowledge gained). The last stage, communal confirmation, is the key point of the validation procedure. The knowledge gained in any intuitive apprehension is considered valid only if it is confirmed by other individuals who have gone through the injunction and apprehension stages in each specific domain of experience. And vice versa, if these claims are not consensually established, they can be regarded as empirically falsified and refuted.

According to Wilber (1990a, 1990b), then, traditional metaphysical claims such as reincarnation, ontological idealism (reality as consciousness), Hindu *mahavakyas* such as "Thou art That," or the existence of God should be considered valid empirical hypotheses, or at least as valid as any other scientific statement. In short, the argument runs as follows: These features of reality, although beyond human senses and rational understanding (empirical and mental knowledge, respectively), can be apprehended, tested, and verified or falsified through direct contemplation (transcendental knowledge).

MODERN RELIGIOUS STUDIES

Interestingly enough, some modern interpreters of Eastern religions claim that this inner empiricist orientation can be found at the core of many contemplative traditions. At the dawn of the twentieth century, Sir John Woodroffe (1919) already had suggested the experimental nature of Hindu Tantrism and Vedantic thought and its subsequent conformity with the canons of modern science. The empirical foundations of Hinduism were also defended by Western Neo-Vedantists such as Aldous Huxley, Christopher Isherwood, or Gerald Heard (Clarke, 1997). More recently, Paranjpe (1984, 1988) argued that Advaita Vedanta epistemology is both empirical and scientific because it offers an open experiential training that allows the testing and verification of its claims:

> Claims pertaining to the nature of the Atman experienced in such states are therefore in principle falsifiable. It is the verifiability of its most important propositions that gives Vedanta a scientific character. (1988, p. 202)

In the same vein, Nuernberger (1994) proposes that the Hindu Tantric tradition of Shaktism is an inner science whose view of reality can be empirically and experimentally verified and validated only through personal practice and experience, and a parallel argument is advanced by Mishra (1993) in relation to Kashmir Śaivism. Furthermore, Phillips (1986) describes Neo-Vedantic thinker Sri-Aurobindo as a "mystic empiricist in that he would count particular extraordinary experiences as providing important data for his metaphysical theory-building" (p. 3). And Chaudhuri (1977), a student of Sri-Aurobindo,

coined the terms *integral experientalism* and *total empiricism* to refer to a methodology that would combine objective investigation and subjective experience.

In modern Buddhist studies, Thurman (1991) characterizes Tibetan psychology as an inner science, and Klein (1987) claims that certain ontological
truths such as the empty nature of the self (*anatman*) are available only in
particular subjective states. In the same vein, Hayward (1987) proposes that
Buddhist meditation can be regarded as scientific because its claims can be
validated through intersubjective experiential verification or refutation.
Similarly, Fontana (1997) argues that the authority of Buddhist claims rests
upon experience, upon "the very empirical methodology indeed to which
Western science professes allegiance" (p. 46). And in her discussion of the
validation of knowledge in science and Buddhism, Valentine (1997) even
points out that "it is important that science does not lose its authority. . . .
Buddhism, like phenomenology, can provide data but its methods cannot
replace the experimental and theoretical analysis of science" (p. 215).

A more general manifesto of this type of contention can be found in
Murphy (1993):

> Virtually all contemplative traditions have claimed that objects of mystical
> insight such as Buddha Nature, God or Brahman are realities that exist inde-
> pendently of any human experience; they have also held that these objective
> realities can be apprehended through particular experiences (or data) that can
> be confirmed by the contemplative's mentor or fellow seekers. In this they
> are, broadly speaking, empirical. (p. 11)

To be sure, there are many other empiricist reconstructions of these and
other Eastern spiritual paths that cannot be mentioned here. The central
question, however, is whether inner empiricism actually depicts, and legitimately represents, the type of epistemic justification at work in these contemplative traditions. Although I cannot discuss this issue at length here, I
would like at least to suggest that this empiricist interpretation of Eastern
spiritual teachings (i.e., as experientially originated and verifiable) has more
to do with the apologetic attempt of some Western-influenced scholars to
show their scientific validity than with the nature of Eastern contemplative
paths and epistemologies.

In Advaita Vedanta, for example, this experientialist emphasis can be
traced to Neo-Advaitin thinkers such as Radhakrishnan (1923/1971), a Hindu
educated in the West who had considerable impact upon many modern scholars

like Paranjpe (1984, 1988), Sharma (1993, 1995), and Smart (1964/1992).
For Radhakrishnan (1929/1957), "if philosophy of religion is to become
scientific, it must become empirical and found itself on religious experience" (p. 84). As a number of historical commentators point out, however,
the projection of empiricist concerns and foundations to the system of
Vedanta is not consistent with the traditional teachings, whose emphasis was
always placed on knowledge (*jñana*) and revelation (*sruti*) (Fort, 1996;
Halbfass, 1988a, 1991; Rambachan, 1991, 1994). Halbfass (1988b) shows, for
example, that in contrast to the cautious and skeptical attitude of classical
Hinduism towards personal experience, Neo-Hinduism sees in experience
both the quintessence and foundation of all religion. A parallel case has been
made in relation to the traditional and modern interpretations of the
Sankhya-Yoga school, and particularly to the textual tradition based on
Patañjali's *Yogasutras* (Grinshpon, 1997).

The situation is analogous in Buddhist studies, where scholars such as
Jayatilleke (1963) and his pupil Kalupahana (1975, 1986) argue that Buddhist
liberation is attained and confirmed by experiences gained during meditative practice. Jayatilleke (1963), for example, even talks about a Buddhist
"stretched empiricism" that includes paranormal experiences. It is highly
questionable, however, that these empiricist interpretations can account for
the nature of Buddhist doctrines, epistemologies, and liberation. In his
analysis of Dharmakirti's theory of knowledge, for example, Hayes (1997)
concludes that "the doctrine of radical empiricism may have its virtues, but
it is clear that the virtue of being easily reconciled with classical Buddhist
doctrine is not one of them. Each of the three classical formulations of the
Buddha's awakening . . . involves the use of the intellect to arrive at a correct
interpretation of the world of experience" (pp. 116–117). Although I cannot
specify here the arguments offered, the so-called Buddhist empiricist thesis
has also been challenged and refuted on both conceptual and historical
grounds in the works of Halbfass (1988b), Hoffman (1982), Kalansuriya
(1981, 1987), and Sharf (1995a). In sum, what these and other analyses
strongly suggest is that empiricist readings of Eastern spiritual endeavors are
an apologetic response to the impact and prestige of Western empirical science that has little or nothing to do with Hindu and Buddhist contemplative
paths. In the words of Halbfass (1988b):

> The Neo-Hindu appeal to religious or mystical experience often involves the
> claim that religion can and should be scientific, and that Hinduism, and

Vedanta in particular, has a scientific and experimental basis. The concept of experience has thus become one of the most significant devices for presenting and interpreting the Hindu tradition to a world dominated by science and technology. (pp. 398–399)

Finally, in the field of Western religious studies, a number of scholars have also suggested the viability of grounding spiritual knowledge claims, such as the existence of God, on direct experiences (J. E. Smith, 1968), experiential awareness (Alston, 1991), or numinous experiences (Yandell, 1993a).[5] In this vein, William James's radical empiricism has been frequently proposed as an adequate epistemological framework for the justification of theistic beliefs (e.g., Frakenberry, 1987) and for the exploration of consciousness (e.g., Harman, 1994; Laughin & McManus, 1995; Nelson, 1998; Taylor, 1996). Some feminist theologians have also defended this inner empiricist orientation regarding spiritual and metaphysical claims. Daly (1984), for example, claims that feminine experience provides women with a privileged vision of "things as they really are" because a natural correspondence exists between the female mind and the structure of reality.[6]

THE FUNDAMENTAL PROBLEMS OF INNER EMPIRICISM

Despite the pervasiveness of inner empiricism in transpersonal studies, few articulations have been so widely accepted as Ken Wilber's (1990a, 1995, 1997a, 1998a). In light of Wilber's proposal, for example, A. P. Smith (1984) suggests that the metaphysical notion of "involution" can be accepted on the grounds of transcendental experiences. Similarly, Doore (1990) follows Wilber in believing that reincarnation is a spiritual hypothesis about which "we may eventually acquire the type of 'contemplative evidence' . . . which will give us final certainty" (p. 279). Other authors that have endorsed Wilber's expanded epistemology for the justification of spiritual knowledge claims include Laughlin, McManus, and D'Aquili (1990), Murphy (1993), Olds (1992), von Brück (1991), Walsh (1992), and Walsh and Vaughan (1994).

If I have settled on Wilber as a paradigmatic example, however, it is not only because his presentation is the most influential and sophisticated, but also because it clearly reflects some of the fundamental problems of inner empiricism. In the remainder of this chapter, then, I illustrate some of the problems typically arising from the importation of empiricist standards to transpersonal and spiritual studies through a critical appraisal of Wilber's (1998a) recent work, *The Marriage of Sense and Soul*, in which he tries to integrate science and religion under the roof of a broad empiricism. Let us begin with a brief summary of this popular book.

Briefly, the primary aim of *The Marriage of Sense and Soul* is "to integrate premodern religion with modern science" (p. 10). By premodern religion Wilber means the Great Chain of Being, a hierarchy of levels of reality (matter, body, mind, soul, and spirit) which he believes lies at the core of most world religious traditions and constitutes the basis for a universal perennial philosophy (i.e., a contemplative consensus about the nature of reality). By modern science he understands, following Max Weber and Jürgen Habermas, the type of autonomous scientific research that emerged in the sixteenth and seventeenth centuries in the West after the breakdown of the unified religious-metaphysical world view of the Middle Ages into the cultural value spheres of science, art, and morality. As Wilber points out, these differentiations allowed scientific, artistic, and moral-political practices to develop their own logic and standards of validity free from the dogmatic clutches of the Church. For Wilber, then, "to integrate religion and science, we need to *integrate the Great Chain with the differentiations of modernity*" (p. 14). In addition, as we will see, Wilber identifies the structure of modern scientific inquiry with certain aspects of the philosophies of empiricism, Thomas Kuhn, and Karl Popper.

According to Wilber, to marry science and religion is important not only to legitimize the cognitive value of spiritual experiences, but also to foster the integration of the currently fragmented cultural spheres of morality, art, and science—or, as he puts it, the Big Three: the We, the I, and the It, or the Good, the Beautiful, and the True. On the one hand, Wilber claims, this union can emancipate religion from both its problematic commitment to mythical and dogmatic claims, and its modern marginalization as mere subjective experience that cannot provide any form of valid, objective knowledge. On the other hand, it can help to integrate the Big Three, whose healthy differentiation defined the dignities of the modern era—such as democracy, individual rights, and the abolition of slavery—but whose present state of dissociation is, for Wilber, lurking behind most of the maladies besetting our present predicament—such as the ecological crisis, ethnocentric imperialism, and the culture of narcissism.

Following Habermas (1984, 1987a, 1987b), Wilber identifies the main cause of this dissociation as the colonization of the I and the We by the It, that is, the dominance of all value spheres by the instrumental-technical rationality typical of the natural sciences. This form of reason aims at prediction and control and only admits as source of valid knowledge public, replicable, and verifiable sensory experiences. As a result of this colonization, Wilber observes, all genuine human knowledge has been reduced to sensory evidence, and the interiority of the Kosmos thereby collapsed into a flatland without depth where no qualitative distinctions can be consistently made. Only by redeeming the epistemic status of inner experiences and other ways of knowing, then, can the flatland be overcome, the Big Three integrated, and the cognitive value of spirituality regained.

Before offering his own proposal for reconciliation, Wilber (1998a) critically reviews several previous attempts to integrate the Big Three. First, he charges romanticism with having confused dedifferentiation with integration and consequently devaluing rationality and falling prey to regressive agendas. Then he examines German idealism, whose glorious vision was undermined by not having a yoga, that is, for not developing practical injunctions or "interior experiments" that would allow the experiential reproduction and testing of its extraordinary insights. Finally, he accuses postmodernism of having taken too far the interpretive element of human knowledge and degenerated into narcissistic egocentrism, self-contradictory relativism, and a nihilistic "aperspectival madness" that denies all depth and celebrates the view that "no belief is better than any other" (p. 136).[7]

As a radical cure for the flatness and fragmentation of our times, Wilber proposes a *broad empiricism* that embraces not only sensory experience (approached by the natural sciences), but also mental experience (approached by logic, mathematics, semiotics, phenomenology, and hermeneutics) and spiritual experience (approached by experiential mysticism). This common epistemological framework for all human knowledge—which, he states, corresponds to some aspects of the philosophies of empiricism, of Kuhn, and of Popper—rests on a unified methodology which incorporates what Wilber believes are the "essential aspects" of the scientific method. According to Wilber, any genuine human inquiry (sensory, mental, or spiritual) follows the same "three strands of all valid knowledge": (1) an instrumental injunction, or a paradigm, practice, ordinance, or procedure (e.g., histological instructions, learning geometry, meditation), (2) a direct apprehension of the data disclosed by the injunction (e.g., seeing that the cell has a nucleus, mentally recognizing the truth of the Pythagorean theorem, spiritually realizing God), and (3) a communal confirmation, a verification or refutation of the apprehension by others who have adequately completed the injunctive and apprehensive strands (e.g., by scientists, mathematicians, and mystics who have followed similar procedures).

Central to Wilber's proposal is a defense of Popper's principle of falsifiability as the criterion for both anchoring the validity of knowledge claims and demarcating between genuine and dogmatic knowledge in every domain: sensory, mental, and spiritual. In the sense Wilber uses it, the principle of falsifiability holds that genuine knowledge must be potentially refutable by experiential evidence, and that this falsifiability allows us to demarcate between science and pseudoscience: "The falsifiability principle," he tells us, "becomes an important aspect of the knowledge quest in all domains, sensory to mental to spiritual. And in each of those domains, it does indeed help us to separate the true from the false, the demonstrable from the dogmatic" (p. 160).

As in all genuine marriages, of course, some form of compromise is required to warrant a fruitful and enduring union, and these distinguished consorts are not exempt from having to take serious vows. Science needs to let go of its narrow reductionism and accept a broad empiricism which accepts not only sensory, but also mental and spiritual experiences as valid sources of knowledge. And religion must bracket its bogus mythical beliefs, accept scientific notions such as evolution, focus on its experiential and universal mystical core, and subject its claims to the falsificationist challenge. (Arguably, such vows would be more costly for religion and, as I will contend, misguided and ultimately undermining its own integrity.) Once this covenant is consummated, Wilber assures us, we can happily realize that the conflict is not between "real science" and "real religion," which now become "fraternal twins" following the three strands of valid knowledge accumulation (injunction, apprehension, falsification), but between bogus science (reductionistic scientism) and bogus religion (unfalsifiable myth and dogma). In fact, Wilber contends, "real science and real religion are actually *allied* against the bogus and the dogmatic and the nonverifiable and the nonfalsifiable in their respective spheres" (p. 169).

To recapitulate, Wilber's nuptial arrangement between religion and science is actually a marriage between the Great Chain of Being and an empiricist-Kuhnian-Popperian account of science.[8] This ceremony entails their mutual commitment to a broad empiricism and a unified methodology (the "three strands of all valid knowledge") that anchors the validity of sensory, mental, and spiritual claims on their falsifiability. To ensure a happy future together, both consorts need to take important vows: Science will adopt a broad empiricism that embraces sensory, mental, and spiritual experiences, and religion will drop its mythical beliefs and focus on its alleged empirical (experiential), universal, and falsifiable mystical core. The promised fruits of this union are the recovery of the depths of the Kosmos, the legitimization of spirituality, and the integration of the Big Three.

The Marriage of Sense and Soul contains many valuable and important insights. Some of them are not new but still worth repeating, like the critique of the contradictions of scientism and the pitfalls of dogmatic religion. As usual in his scholarship, Wilber should be credited for having synthesized vast amounts of complex information with extraordinary clarity. Another of his attainments is to have expanded the Great Chain of Being by incorporating the differentiations of modernity, giving thereby the perennial vision greater contemporary relevance and explanatory power than any other traditional account. Furthermore, as we have seen, by stressing the fourfold intrinsic nature of all phenomena—intentional, behavioral, cultural, and social—Wilber paves the way for extending our understanding of spirituality out of the merely inner and individual to other corners of reality, redeeming spirituality from its modern marginalization as subjective individual experience while conserving the fundamental differentiations of modernity. In my opinion, however, the main merit of the book is to have shown with unparalleled force that contemporary forms of spirituality (in the West, I would qualify) need to embrace the differentiations of modernity if they want to avoid a calamitous regression to premodern religious dogmatism and imperialism. Finally, Wilber's suggestion that the integration of the value spheres of art, morality, and science calls for both a recovery of the interiors and, perhaps more originally, a reevaluation of the epistemic status of spirituality needs to be, in my opinion, seriously considered by modern critical thinkers.

In spite of these achievements, however, I believe that Wilber's remedies tragically prescribe the illness for the cure: *Wilber's marriage not only perpetuates the dissociations of the modern era, but also renders the legitimation of spiritual knowledge hopeless.* In the remainder of this chapter, then, I focus on three interrelated points. First, I argue that Wilber's proposal of empiricist standards of knowledge as paradigmatic for all ways of knowing fosters, rather than heals, the fragmentation of the modern era. Second, I show that to resuscitate Popperian falsifiability to characterize all genuine knowledge and demarcate between science and dogma is not only misguided and unpracticable in the natural and social sciences, but also inimical to the nature of spiritual inquiry. Finally, I raise some questions about the identity of *the* science and *the* religion whose marriage Wilber arranges and prematurely celebrates. Let us have a more detailed look at the reasons for these unexpected conflicts.

THE EMPIRICIST COLONIZATION OF SPIRITUALITY

According to Wilber (1998a), "the real problem of our modern fragmentation . . . is that *all higher modes of knowing have been brutally collapsed into monological and empirical science. . . . it is the reduction of all knowledge to monological modes that constitutes the disaster of modernity*" (p. 38).[9] Wilber rightly points out that this positivist prejudice results in the reduction of all valid knowledge to sensory evidence and the consequent devaluation of spirituality to subjective experiences that now cannot meet the objective standards of valid knowledge characteristic of the natural sciences.

Although accurate, I believe that this is only half of the story. In addition to sensory reductionism, positivism holds both that there exists a single method for all valid knowledge (methodological monism), and that the natural sciences represent this methodological ideal for all other sciences (scientism) (Chalmers, 1990; Sorell, 1991; von Wright, 1971). The problem with positivism, then, is not only the reduction of valid knowledge to sensory evidence, but also the assimilation of all human inquiry (aesthetic, historical, social, spiritual, etc.) to the methods and aims of the natural sciences (experimentation, replication, testing, verification, falsification, etc.). Accordingly, the empiricist colonization responsible for many of the maladies of modernity stems not only from sensory reductionism, but also, and perhaps more fatally, from *the understanding of all human disciplines and practices according to the language, methods, and standards of validity of empirical knowledge.* And this, alas, is *precisely* the heart of Wilber's integration of science and religion!

Let us have a closer look at the nature of this move. In spite of talking about different types of inquiry and truth (empirical, phenomenological, spiritual, etc.), Wilber consistently uses the language and principles of empirical science as the universal standards for genuine knowledge in all domains. Echoing the positivist aspirations, Wilber (1998a) suggests that "the Big Three—art, objective science, and morals—can be brought together under one roof using the core methodology of deep empiricism and deep science (the three strands of all valid knowledge)" (p. 176). The "three strands of all valid knowledge" (injunction, apprehension, and confirmation/falsification), let us remember here, correspond to certain aspects of the philosophies of empiricism, Kuhn, and Popper, all of which emerged from the study of the natural sciences (of physics, to be more exact). Wilber celebrates that the use of this "same general methodology . . . brings broad science to the interior domains of direct mental and spiritual experience" (p. 176). For example, Wilber (1998a) claims that a genuine spiritual science should be based on inner experiments that generate replicable and falsifiable experiential data: "In the spiritual sciences the exemplar, the injunction, the paradigm, the practice is meditation or contemplation. It too has its injunctions, its illuminations, and its confirmations, all of which are repeatable—verifiable or falsifiable—and all of which therefore constitute a perfectly valid mode of knowledge acquisition" (p. 170). "With this move," he adds, "science is . . . *satisfied* that its central method is still the epistemological cornerstone of all inquiry" (p. 176). There are no ambiguities here; this is in fact the positivist dream made true in the service of spiritual legitimization.

As should be evident, Wilber's attempt to overcome the colonization of all value spheres by instrumental reason and to validate other forms of inquiry actually leads to the opposite outcome he wants to achieve. Ignoring the attainments of decades of human and social science (Gadamer, 1990; Polkinghorne, 1983; Rabinow & Sullivan, 1987), Wilber tries to persuade us that the method of the natural sciences (of physics, to be more exact) constitutes the paradigm of good science that all human inquiry must adopt. And rather than trying to unpack the validity claims of spiritual inquiry, Wilber suggests that a genuine spiritual science must meet such imported empiricist standards as replicability or falsifiability. As we will see, these unnecessary constraints confine spiritual inquiry within an epistemic straitjacket that sabotages the validation of its knowledge claims.

The pitfalls of this move have already been eloquently explained by others. According to Habermas (1971, 1987b, 1988), for example, one of the main difficulties of modernity is the understanding of all spheres of knowledge according to the structure of natural science. For Habermas, it is this extension of the instrumental reason characteristic of the natural sciences to other domains of life, and not merely sensory reductionism, that is lurking behind the empiricist colonization of the life-world and the fragmentation of modernity. Extending this critique to the realm of spiritual inquiry, Rothberg (1994) points out that:

> to interpret spiritual approaches through categories like "data," "evidence," "verification," "method," "confirmation," and "intersubjectivity" may be to enthrone these categories as somehow the hallmarks of knowledge as such,

even if these categories are expanded in meaning from their current Western usage. But might not a profound encounter with practices of spiritual inquiry lead to considering carefully the meaning of other comparable categories (e.g. *dhyana, vichara, theoria, gnosis,* or *contemplatio*) and perhaps to developing understandings of inquiry in which such spiritual categories are primary or central when we speak of knowledge? To assume that the categories of current Western epistemology are adequate for interpreting spiritual approaches is to prejudge the results of such an encounter. (p. 8)

What Habermas, Gadamer, Chalmers, Polkinghorne, Rothberg, and many others have convincingly shown is that it is highly questionable to import the language and epistemic categories emerging from the study of the natural world to account for the validity of knowledge in all domains of human reality (arts, literature, economics, politics, spirituality, etc.). Most artistic, social, and spiritual endeavors are aimed not so much at describing human nature and the world, but at *engaging them in creative, participatory, and transformative ways,* and therefore have different goals, methods, and standards of validity. According to Gadamer (1990), for example, hermeneutics "is not concerned primarily with amassing verified knowledge, such as would satisfy the methodological ideal of science" (p. xxi) but with "the experience of truth that transcends the domain of scientific method wherever that experience is to be found" (p. xxii). To burden these alternative ways of knowing with demands of experimental evidence, replicability, and falsifiability may be equivalent to trying to test the flavor of a savory soup with a very rusty fork.

Interestingly enough, Wilber admits the validity of an epistemological pluralism and says he has taken a different path to integrate science and religion simply because such a notion is not accepted in our times. This is an odd claim. Epistemological pluralism is widely embraced today not only between but also within the natural and human sciences (Chalmers, 1990; Habermas, 1971; Heron, 1996a; Polkinghorne, 1983; Reason, 1994). The positivist myth of a single epistemology and unified methodology for all human knowledge is only alive in the minds of a few recalcitrant scientists. As Habermas (1984) puts it, "the empiricist theory of science has defended the concept of the unity of scientific method that was already developed in the Neo-Positivism of Vienna. This discussion can be regarded as over, the few remaining echoes notwithstanding" (p. 109). Furthermore, although Wilber describes his own account as pluralistic, his broad empiricism is not pluralistic enough. His proposal of three eyes of knowledge, although radically overcoming sensory reductionism, still restricts sensory, mental, and spiritual inquiries within his reconstruction of the method of natural science (the "three strands of all human knowledge"). This is not epistemological pluralism, but a positivist extension of the canons of instrumental reason to all areas of human life.

The inconsistency of trying to legitimize other ways of knowing by imposing the logic of natural science naturally engenders a number of important tensions in Wilber's work. For instance, it leads him to accept certain objectivist assumptions that have been strongly challenged today, if not refuted, even in relation to natural science. I will just mention two examples: First, it is not clear how one can reject the representational paradigm of cognition and still defend the adequacy of a correspondence theory of truth for natural science. Even accepting that some of the features of the empirical-sensoriomotor world are intrinsic, as I believe they are, a correspondence theory of truth does not necessarily follow from this premise. In any case, he should at least address the fatal assaults that the correspondence theory of truth has suffered in the last half of the twentieth century at the hands of philosophers like Davidson (1984), Goodman (1978), Kuhn (1970a), Putnam (1979), Quine (1953, 1990), or Rorty (1979). Second, in spite of more than twenty-five years of feminist science showing the inescapable presence and essential role of emotions in all human inquiry (Jaggar, 1990; Keller & Longino, 1996; Shepherd, 1993), Wilber still endorses the objectivist illusion that objective truth is "the truth according to dispassionate standards" (p. 49). Actually, although Wilber carefully avoids identifying which is the bride and which is the groom of this marriage, the assimilation of spiritual inquiry to the methods and aims of a masculinized science may even make us wonder if these nuptials are fated to result in patriarchal domination, rather than in dialogical partnership.

Taken together, these empiricist tensions and demands strongly suggest that Wilber has not taken his critique of scientism far *enough*. After denouncing the colonization of all cultural spheres by empirical monological science, he surprisingly, and inconsistently, proclaims the language, method, and standards of natural science as paradigmatic for all ways of knowing. The elevation of the logic of natural science as the model for all human inquiry (aesthetic, hermeneutic, spiritual, etc.) obviously perpetuates the colonization of the I and the We by the It that he is rightfully trying to overcome. This relapse into positivism effectively short-circuits his noble attempt to articulate an expanded account of human knowledge and traps him into the very cul-de-sac from which he claims to have escaped. In the next section, we will see how the retention of these positivist prejudices sacrifices the integrity of spirituality and leaves us with a self-defeating account of spiritual inquiry.

KNOWLEDGE, FALSIFIABILITY, AND SPIRITUALITY

One of the unfortunate consequences of this residual positivism is the resuscitation and extension of Popperian falsifiability as the hallmark of genuine knowledge in all domains of inquiry, sensory to mental to spiritual. As we have seen, Wilber claims that falsifiability helps us to anchor the validity of all knowledge claims and to demarcate between science and pseudoscience, genuine and bogus knowledge, authentic spirituality and dogma. In this section I show that the falsifiability principle not only is implausible in the natural and social sciences, but also that its application to spiritual matters is deeply self-defeating.

Falsifiability in Science

It is general knowledge that falsifiability is regarded in contemporary philosophy of science as both a naive account of scientific practice and an unreliable guideline to demarcate between science and pseudoscience (Curd & Cover, 1998; Klee, 1997). The standard objections to Popperian falsifiability are well known and need not to be repeated here in detail. The history of science, for example, does not support a falsificationist view of scientific practice, as the writings of Paul Feyerabend (1975), Thomas Kuhn (1970a), and Richard Swinburne (1964) showed decades ago. In spite of his several exaggerations, Feyerabend (1995) was correct when he pointed out that "the doctrine of falsifiability would wipe out science as we know it. There are few episodes that seem to conform to the falsifiability pattern" (p. 90).

Ever since the 1960s and 1970s, it has become obvious that a fundamental shortcoming of this doctrine is that, because theories are not single entities but sets of interrelated initial conditions, assumptions, and hypotheses, they can always be saved from seemingly falsifying data through the introduction or modification of auxiliary hypotheses. These ad hoc procedures, historians of science observed, rather than being rare or inimical to good science, were actually everyday scientific practice and essential for scientific progress (Kuhn 1970b; O'Hear, 1980). To mention a classic example, irregularities in Uranus's orbit did not lead to the refutation of Newton's gravitational theory, but to the postulation of a new planet that eventually resulted in the discovery of Neptune (Bamford, 1996). Furthermore, falsifying evidence is not normally taken as refuting a given theory, but is put aside as an unexplained anomaly to be answered in the future. In practice, a theory is regarded as refuted not when it is falsified, but only when a better one comes along (Lakatos, 1970). In addition, what counts as the standards of falsification is open to interpretation and ultimately depends on conventional decisions taken by the different scientific communities (Bernstein 1985; Kuhn 1970b): There are no pure falsifying data floating "out there," nor are there crucial experiments providing a conclusive refutation of a theory (Pinch, 1985), as Popper himself admitted (1959, p. 50). But then, as Kuhn (1970b) asked in a well-known passage, "what is falsification if it is not conclusive disproof? . . . Rather than a logic, Sir Karl has provided an ideology; rather than methodological rules, he has supplied procedural maxims" (p. 15).

Another fatal stroke to falsificationism was provided by the Duhem-Quine principle of underdetermination of theory by evidence, which revealed not only that logically incompatible theories may fit all possible evidence, but also that theories can accommodate virtually any disconfirming evidence by making the adequate adjustments in the system (Duhem, 1953; Quine 1953, 1990). Of course, this principle made the entire falsificationist logic flawed, and this is why contemporary textbooks in philosophy of science consider that falsificationism was "killed" by the underdetermination of theory (Klee, 1997). Needless to say, these and other formidable problems have made falsificationism inapplicable today in virtually all natural and human science disciplines, from mathematics (Kitcher, 1984) to economics (Caldwell, 1984; Hausman, 1985), from astronomy (Bamford, 1996) to hermeneutics (Gadamer, 1990), from evolutionary biology (Ruse, 1988; Stamos, 1996; Van Der Steen, 1993) to social sciences (Fay, 1996; Hollis, 1994; Outhwaite, 1996), from cognitive science (Bechtel, 1988) to psychoanalysis (Ahumada, 1997; Cioffi, 1985; Orange, 1995), and from science teaching (Lawson, 1993) to evolutionary epistemology (Gatens-Robinson, 1993), to mention a few.

As for falsificationism as a demarcation criterion between science and pseudoscience, it soon became apparent that it was simultaneously too strong and too weak, too restrictive and too permissive. Actually, the application of falsifiability seems to lead exactly to the opposite picture that Wilber paints. On the one hand, falsificationism would make nonscientific most well accepted scientific notions and disciplines of human knowledge. For example, the idea of evolution, one of Wilber's favorite scientific notions, is not falsifiable according to Popper himself, but this of course has never been a problem for evolutionary biologists (Kitcher, 1982; Sanders & Ho, 1982; Stamos, 1996). On the other hand, falsificationism would make us accept as scientific any potentially falsifiable claim that no one has yet refuted, including irrationalities such as that three flying elephants will land on the dark side of the moon this morning. As philosopher of science Laudan (1996) puts it, falsificationism renders:

> "scientific" every crank claim which makes ascertainably false assertions. Thus flat Earthers, biblical creationists, proponents of laetrile or orgone boxes, Uri Geller devotees, Bermuda Triangulators, circle squarers, Lysenkoists, charioteers of the Gods, *perpetuum mobile* builders, Big Foot searchers, Loch Nessians, faith healers, polywater dabblers . . . all turn out to be scientific on Popper's criterion—just as long as they are prepared to indicate some observation, however improbable, which (if it came to pass) would cause them to change their minds. (p. 219)

Wilber's claim that falsifiability allows us to differentiate between genuine and dogmatic knowledge is an empiricist myth that has already been laid to rest.

Falsifiability in Religion

In addition to dubiously resurrecting falsifiability in the natural and human sciences, Wilber extends its scope to spiritual matters. Briefly, Wilber (1998a) proposes that "authentic spirituality . . . must be based on falsifiable evidence" (p. 166), and that this falsifiability helps us to discriminate between genuine and dogmatic spiritual claims:

> The three strands of deep science (injunction, apprehension, confirmation; or paradigm, data, falsifiability) apply not only to exterior experience; they are the means whereby we decide if a particular interior experience carries genuine knowledge and cognitive content, or whether it is merely hallucinatory, dogmatic, bogus, idiosyncratic, or personal preference. (p. 202)

By using this demarcation principle, Wilber wants to discriminate between mythical and dogmatic religious beliefs (which are unfalsifiable) and genuine contemplative insights (which are falsifiable). What is more, Wilber believes that these falsifiable insights will make the Great Chain of Being the well-founded spiritual ontology upon which all religions will rest: "*Submitted to the tests of deep science*, the Great Chain of Being and its newfound validity ought to be enough foundation for any religion" (p. 204).

In what follows, I argue that, contrary to Wilber's assertion, most contemplative claims are *not* falsifiable and that to ground the validity of spiritual knowledge on this principle is therefore a well-intentioned but ultimately self-defeating exercise in apologetics. Perhaps the best way to illustrate this claim is to invite the reader to make the following thought experiment: Imagine, for example, that you are in a Theravada Buddhist retreat and report to your teacher the unmistakable direct spiritual insight you had during meditation into the eternal, indestructible, independent, absolute, and substantial nature of the Self (as Advaita Vedanta claims)—or into the existence of the soul (as Christian mysticism claims), or into the reality of a personal and loving God (as most Semitic mystics claim). Will these "experiential data" be taken as falsifying or refuting the Buddhist doctrine of no-self (*anatman*)? Will the teacher even consider that doctrine's potential fallibility? Hardly so. As any Buddhist practitioner well knows, these data will be regarded as an obvious sign of delusion, wrong view, attachment to permanent existence, or even of egoic resistance. And you will probably be told by your teacher, with more or less gentleness, to go back to your meditation cushion and keep practicing until you overcome delusion and see "things as they really are," that is, marked by no-self and impermanence as the Theravada canons maintain.[10] Needless to say, a similar parable can be told, *mutatis mutandis*, in the case of any other contemplative tradition.[11] The reader is invited to try to make a solid case for the falsifiability of the central claims of any mystical tradition: Which "experiential evidence" would count as falsifying the ultimate identity of Atman-Brahman in an Advaitin community? Which "experiential data" would falsify the claim of the existence of a personal and loving God in a community of Christian contemplatives? So much for the falsifiability of direct spiritual experiences in communities of the adequate.[12]

Of course, this parable raises many interesting questions about the nature of spiritual knowledge which I cannot adequately address in this chapter. For our present purposes, it should suffice to say that, in any contemplative community, no single spiritual experience will count as falsifying evidence against the sacred knowledge of their tradition. Furthermore, as our parable suggests, what in one tradition is seen as a crucial spiritual insight, in another can be regarded as the most deceptive of delusions. In their corresponding communities, we need to conclude, *spiritual claims can be corroborated, but not falsified. And the validity of this corroboration is not universal or absolute (as it is traditionally claimed) but contextual and relative.*

An alternative for avoiding the contextuality of such a corroboration is to assume, erroneously I believe, that there are pregiven spiritual data existing out there, independently from the spiritual traditions and practices that enact them, against which we can clash our spiritual claims. As I elaborate in Part II of this book, this objectivist assumption represents a serious distortion of the nature of the spiritual knowing and the logic of spiritual inquiry. What most mystical traditions offer are not so much *descriptions* of reality to be confirmed or falsified by experiential evidence, but *prescriptions* of ways of "being-*and*-the-world" to be intentionally cultivated and lived. To put it another way, spiritual cosmologies are not primarily descriptive systems in need of experiential testing, but prescriptive systems that invite us to radically transform ourselves and the world. In the same vein, the aim of most contemplative practices is not to have experiences, but rather to bring forth and participate in special states of discernment (involving somatic as well as affective, cognitive, and intuitive dimensions) that have a transforming and emancipatory power. Meditative practices are not replicable experiments designed to provide data that verify or falsify spiritual claims, but the embodiment and lived expression of the teachings of a given tradition. The role of spiritual experiences on the spiritual path is not to test the teachings of a spiritual tradition, but to provide one with signposts of being on the right track in the specific soteriological path laid down by that tradition. And this is not to say, as some radical constructivists wrongly claim, that novel insights do not occur or are never incorporated by spiritual traditions. They actually are, and this is why religious traditions are not closed, self-encapsulated systems, but "living hermeneutic processes" (Vroom, 1989, p. 328) which grow and renew themselves out of the interaction among doctrines, interpretations, and new experiences. Finally, if I may dare to say, from a contemplative perspective, it could be argued that *what makes a spiritual claim dogmatic is not that it cannot be experientially falsified, but that it is held with attachment, with clinging, as an Absolute Truth*, and so forth. This, and not the unfalsifiability of its claims, is the real dead end of any genuine spiritual inquiry.

In spite of Wilber's salutary intentions, then, to posit falsifiability as the principle to anchor the validity of genuine spiritual claims and distinguish them from dogma would undermine the central insights of the very contemplative traditions he champions. Once again, this strongly suggests that what is needed is not to artificially force spirituality to meet the standards of natural science, but to challenge the hegemony of these canons and articulate standards of validity emerging from the logic of spiritual inquiry. As I argue in chapter 7, what is needed is to ground the validity of spiritual knowledge not on replicable spiritual experiments that bring falsifiable experiential data, but on its emancipatory and transformative power for self, relationships, and world.

WHICH SCIENCE? WHICH RELIGION?

Serious questions can also be raised about the identity of the consorts whose marriage Wilber seeks to arrange. What I am asking here is not whether or not Wilber's religion and science can be married (he shows that they can), but rather which religion and which science need to be brought to the altar today. As we have seen, Wilber marries premodern religion (i.e., a perennialist version of the Great Chain of Being) and modern science (i.e., an empiricist account of the method of natural science). But, we may rightfully ask: Why *premodern* religion? Why *modern* science? Even accepting that premodern religion could be equated with the Great Chain of Being, how well does the Great Chain represent contemporary spiritual consciousness? How adequately does Wilber's amalgam of classical empiricism and his not necessarily accurate accounts of the philosophies of science of Thomas Kuhn and Karl Popper depict the current natural, social, and human sciences? In short, is this the ceremony we really need to bear witness to today?

I have serious doubts. Perhaps the science that needs to be married today is not an artificial reconstruction of exhausted philosophies of science, but the pluralistic view of valid knowledge that has gradually arisen during the last decades of postempiricist philosophy of science, hermeneutics, feminist scholarship, and human science research, among other disciplines. And perhaps the religion that is waiting to be espoused is not a universalist Great Chain of Being—a hybrid of Neoplatonism and Neovedanta—but forms of spiritual awareness emerging, for example, from the living interreligious dialogue, which, incidentally, started with universalist assumptions and aspirations but gradually moved to more dialogical, hermeneutic, and pluralistic understandings (Clarke, 1997; Corless, 1993; Griffiths, 1991; Heim, 1995; Prabhu, 1996; Vroom, 1989). Listen to the Dalai Lama (1996):

> In order to develop a genuine spirit of harmony from a sound foundation of knowledge, I believe it is very important to know the fundamental differences

between religious traditions. . . . Some people believe that the most reasonable way to attain harmony and solve problems relating to religious intolerance is to establish one universal religion. However, I have always felt that we should have different religious traditions because human beings possess so many different mental dispositions. . . . If we try to unify the faiths of the world into one religion, we will also lose many of the qualities and richness of each particular tradition. Therefore, I feel it is better, in spite of the many quarrels in the name of religion, to maintain a variety of religious traditions. (p. 41)

This is the spirit that was cultivated, for example, in the recent Gethsemani encounter between Buddhist and Christian monastics, where, in spite of the acknowledgment of important differences in their spiritual lives (on God, on grace, on anger, on intuition, etc.), a profound sense of mutual enrichment and communion emerged in the midst of this rich diversity (Mitchell & Wiseman, 1997, p. xxii).

Do not misunderstand me here. I am not advocating a vulgar relativist (and ultimately dogmatic and intolerant) celebration of religious pluralism per se. On the contrary, as I argue in chapter 6, I firmly believe not only that the ecumenical search for common grounds is a crucial enterprise, but also that qualitative distinctions can be made among spiritual teachings and traditions. However, I do claim that to regard the Great Chain of Being as the universal foundation for all traditional and contemporary religions may be highly problematic. But this is a subject for our next chapter, in which I critically revise the very idea of a perennial philosophy and its relation to transpersonal theory.

A REJOINDER TO WILBER

In response to an earlier version of this critique of his epistemology (Ferrer, 1998b), Wilber (1998b) claims, first, that I underestimate his commitment to epistemological pluralism, a "unity-in-diversity of methods" that embraces a variety of modes of knowing (sensory, hermeneutic, analytical, aesthetic, etc.) that nonetheless share a commitment to what he considers to be the three strands characteristic of all valid knowledge (injunction, direct apprehension, confirmation/falsification). Second, he points out that I misread his extended use of the categories of sensory empiricism, and claims that, on those precarious grounds, I accuse him of sensory reductionism and scientism. For example, he tells us that "every time I use the word 'data' . . . [Ferrer] tends to see it as evidence that I am using it in the sensory, positivistic, or scientific fashion" (1998b, p. 70). Third, Wilber says that he uses the term falsifiability, not so much in a strict Popperian fashion, but simply to mean that "we hold all our experiences open to further refinement" (1998b, p. 71). Finally, he provides an example of a Buddhist-Vedanta interreligious parallel in support of the idea of a perennial philosophy (i.e., between the Buddhist Dharmakaya, Sambhogakaya, and Nirmanakaya and the Vedantic causal body, subtle body, and gross body, which can be, according to both traditions, respectively experienced in deep dreamless sleep, dream state, and waking state), and concludes his essay by stating that he considers the perennial philosophy "a good place to start—but not end—one's spiritual dialog" (1998b, p. 72).

In response, I would like to make the following points. First, Wilber's admitted defense of the three strands as paradigmatic for all valid human knowing is precisely the main target of my critique. There are many forms of human inquiry and truth that do not need to follow the three strands to gain validity—and this is one of Gadamer's (1990) main points in his *Truth and Method*. Wilber's three-stranded methodological monism—however variably applied to nonsensory ways of knowing—is still based on the methodology of physical science, and this is why I talked about the presence of a "residual" positivism (not scientism, not sensory reductionism) in some aspects of his theorizing, and concluded by saying that he "has not taken his critique of scientism far *enough*" (1998b, p. 59).

Second, Wilber misrepresents my presentation by implying that I include in it a charge of sensory reductionism, and then he uses this misrepresentation to throw away my critique of his methodological monism and not deal with the problematic issues derived from it. In my paper, however, I drew a *very clear distinction between sensory reductionism and methodological monism,* and pressed the critical implications of the latter without mixing it with the former. In this regard, for example, I stated that: "His proposal of the three eyes of knowledge, although radically overcoming sensory reductionism, still restricts sensory, mental, and spiritual inquiries within his reconstruction of the method of natural sciences (the "three strands of all human knowledge") (p. 59). Much of Wilber's response, then, rather than addressing the issues I raised, is a defense against charges I never made.

Third, as for the falsifiability principle, it seems to me that the issue was simply begged. Wilber (1990a, 1995, 1997a, 1998a) has spent more than a decade insisting on the need to import Popperian falsifiability to test the validity of spiritual knowledge claims. In one of his most recent books, for example, he writes:

> As it is now, the Popperian falsifiability principle has one widespread and altogether perverted use: it is implicitly restricted *only* to *sensibilia*, which, in an incredibly hidden and sneaky fashion, *automatically bars all mental and spiritual experience from the status of genuine knowledge*. (1997a, p. 87)

And he adds:

> When we free the falsifiability principle from its restriction to sensibilia, and set it free to police the domains of intelligibilia and transcendelia as well, then it most definitively becomes an important aspect of the knowledge quest in all domains, sensory to mental to spiritual. And in each of these domains, it does indeed help us to separate the true from the false, the demonstrable from the dogmatic, the dependable from the bogus. (1997a, p. 88)

After this unequivocal defense of the need to use Popperian falsifiability to police spiritual territories, however, he surprisingly tells us in his response to my paper that by falsifiability he simply meant that "we hold all our experiences open to further refinement" (1998b, p. 71). The tentativeness of human knowledge, however, is not an accurate description of the falsifiability principle in any accepted sense in the philosophy of science. That knowledge is always tentative and approximate does not refer to falsifiability, but to *fallibilism*, something that everybody (even the hard scientists) accept today as a feature of all human knowledge, but not as a principle of epistemic justification or of demarcation between genuine and dogmatic knowledge (as Wilber uses his third strand).

Finally, as for Wilber's example supporting a perennial philosophy, I should say that, as we will see in Part II of this book, a participatory vision embraces and can explain a number of interreligious parallels without endorsing the hard claims of perennialism (e.g., about the universality of spiritual ultimates and spiritual liberations). Although I agree with Wilber that a perennialist position is one of the many possible starting points to initiate dialogue about spiritual matters, in our next chapter I argue that, quite frequently, it is not a very fertile one.

I should add here that even if something like Wilber's three strands would eventually result in an adequate model of spiritual inquiry, it would have to be limited to what, paraphrasing Kuhn, we could call, in the context of *a single tradition*, periods of *normal spiritual inquiry,* in which already existing spiritual insights are never fully questioned, and spiritual practice is conservatively managed and controlled by the prevailing spiritual paradigm of a given tradition.

However, it should be obvious that the validity of Wilber's model cannot be consistently maintained either *across traditions* or in periods of what we may call *revolutionary spiritual inquiry*, in which anomalies in relation to accepted doctrines arise and new paradigms of spiritual understanding are developed. On the one hand, as my parable shows, well accepted spiritual insights of one tradition are neither confirmed in other traditions nor are they potentially falsifiable in their own. On the other hand, Wilber's three strand model of spiritual inquiry cannot account for the validity of new, revolutionary spiritual insights. Take, for example, the Buddha's enlightenment (or many of the claims of the so-called heretic Christian mystics): There was simply no community of the adequate to confirm or falsify the Buddha's creative spiritual insights, but this does not automatically invalidate them, as we would be forced to do if we were to follow Wilber's criteria. As I see it, these limitations render Wilber's model of spiritual inquiry impoverished and, at the most, limited to very conservative stages of spiritual inquiry within a single tradition. Overall, these limitations strongly suggest, I believe, the need to explore different avenues to legitimize spiritual knowledge.

SUMMARY AND CONCLUSIONS

In their search for an adequate method and epistemology for the field, transpersonalists have repeatedly suggested that the study of transpersonal phenomena needs to conform to the principles and demands of empiricist science. On the one hand, some transpersonal authors claimed that transpersonal studies can and should follow, although in an expanded way that includes not only outer but also inner experience, the essential principles of the empirical method. Transpersonal and spiritual phenomena, that is, need to be empirically studied. On the other hand, they told us that, in contrast to the dogmatic nature of most traditional religious claims, transpersonal knowledge is valid because it can be grounded in experience.[13] Transpersonal and spiritual knowledge claims, that is, can and should be empirically justified. Accordingly, the methodological and epistemic validity of transpersonal studies has been generally maintained in terms of scientific empiricism (e.g., as an "inner empiricism," a "science of human experience," a "Taoist science," a "subjective epistemology," a "science of consciousness," or, more recently, a "science of spiritual experience.")[14]

Before concluding this chapter, I should reemphasize here that my intention has not been to discredit these pioneering epistemological efforts.

On the contrary, I believe that during the first two decades of transpersonal scholarship, the attempt to justify transpersonal phenomena through an appeal to experience was not only historically inevitable, but also methodologically crucial. At a time when spirituality was confined to the merely subjective and individual, it should be obvious that inner empiricism was not only a legitimate response, but also an adequate means to argue for the validity of spiritual knowledge. The legitimization of transpersonal studies in the intellectual climate of the late 1960s and 1970s (and even 1980s) *had* to be empirical.

Although once valuable and indispensable, however, this empiricist approach to transpersonal and spiritual phenomena has become today problematic and detrimental. On the one hand, the extension of empiricist canons to human spirituality perpetuates the instrumental colonization of value spheres responsible in part for the fragmentation of the modern era. On the other hand, the application of empiricist validity standards to spiritual knowledge is hostile to the nature of spiritual inquiry and often has self-defeating consequences. On these grounds, I want to suggest that transpersonal studies need to let go of empiricist prejudices about what counts as valid knowledge and search for more appropriate epistemologies to account for the nature and validity of transpersonal and spiritual knowing. In Part II of this book, I suggest that a more adequate justification of transpersonal and spiritual knowledge can be drawn from the very nature of spiritual inquiry.

4

TROUBLE IN PARADISE

THE PERENNIAL PHILOSOPHY REVISITED

We live in a world of rich spiritual diversity and innovation. Spiritual traditions offer disparate and often conflicting visions of reality and human nature. To the modern mind, this is profoundly perplexing: How to account for these important differences when most of these traditions are supposedly depicting universal and ultimate truths? In the wake of this predicament, it is both tempting and comforting to embrace universalist visions that, in their claim to honor all truths, seem to bring order to such apparent religious chaos. In this chapter, I argue that despite their professed inclusivist stance, most universalist visions distort the essential message of the various religious traditions, covertly favor certain spiritual paths over others, and raise serious obstacles for spiritual dialogue and inquiry.

IF I HAD TO IDENTIFY the most implicit belief, the most unexamined presupposition, the most tacitly extended metaphysical doctrine of contemporary transpersonal theory, it would doubtless be the so-called perennial philosophy (*philosophia perennis*).[1]

Transpersonal studies are generally characterized as disciplines independent of any particular religious tradition, philosophical school, or world view (e.g., Walsh & Vaughan, 1993a). However, the philosophical foundations of transpersonal theory have generally been associated with the perennial philosophy (e.g., Hutchins, 1987; Rothberg, 1986b; Valle, 1989; Wilber, 1990a, 1995), and the spiritual universalism typical of perennialism pervades both early and contemporary transpersonal scholarship (e.g., Grof, 1988, 1998; Grof & Bennet, 1993; Harman, 1988; Maslow, 1970; Nelson, 1994; Vaughan, 1982, 1986; Wilber, 1975, 1977, 1995; Wittine, 1989).

According to Wilber (1994), for example, "the aim of transpersonal psychology . . . is to give a psychological presentation of the perennial philosophy and the Great Chain of Being" (p. x). Vaughan (1982), one of the leaders of the transpersonal movement, also asserts that the transpersonal perspective "has its roots in the ancient perennial philosophy" (p. 38), and "recognizes the transcendental unity of all religions and sees the unity in the mystical core of every spiritual tradition" (p. 37). In the same vein, Hutchins (1987) presents transpersonal psychology as a contemporary exploration of the perennial philosophy, and Wittine (1989) defines transpersonal psychotherapy as "an approach to healing/growth that aims to bridge the Western psychological tradition . . . and the world's perennial philosophy" (p. 269). Somewhat more cautiously, Walsh (1993a), after a review of the achievements of the transpersonal movement during its first twenty-five years, concludes that: "We have even begun to suspect that the most profound and radical claims of the perennial philosophy may be correct" (p. 135). And one of the main aims of a recent work by Grof (1998) is to show that "modern consciousness research has generated important data that support the basic tenets of the perennial philosophy" (p. 3). As any reader acquainted with the transpersonal literature will easily recognize, these examples could be multiplied almost indefinitely.

Only in recent years have a few transpersonal authors begun to recognize this tacit association between transpersonal theory and the perennial philosophy. Discussing some of the assumptions of current transpersonal definitions, for example, Walsh and Vaughan (1993a) write: "Exploring the precise relationship between transpersonal psychology and the perennial philosophy is an important task for future research, but assuming the nature of the relationship in current definitions may be premature" (p. 201).

In this spirit, the main objective of this chapter is to critically examine the adhesion of transpersonal theory to a perennialist metaphysics. First, I offer a historical overview of the idea of a perennial philosophy and a typology of the main varieties of perennialism. Second, I present the two versions of perennialism most widely accepted in transpersonal scholarship: Grof's Neo-Advaitin perennial philosophy and Wilber's structuralist neoperennialism. Third, I discuss a number of fundamental problems of the perennial vision in general, and of Wilber's neoperennialism in particular. Finally, I explore why transpersonalists have searched for philosophical and metaphysical foundations in the perennial philosophy, and suggest, in light of previous discussions, that the commitment of transpersonal theory to the perennial vision may have been not only premature, but also misleading and counterproductive. In Part II of this book, then, I present an alternative participatory vision of human spirituality that will enable us to free transpersonal studies from their a priori perennialist assumptions and pave the way for the emergence of a more dialogical, pluralistic, and sophisticated transpersonal theory.

THE IDEA OF A PERENNIAL PHILOSOPHY

The idea of a perennial philosophy (*philosophia perennis*) has received different articulations throughout the history of Western philosophy. The search for a universal, permanent, and all-encompassing philosophy can be traced to the Neoplatonism of Philo of Alexandria or the Platonic-Christian synthesis of St. Augustine. However, it is not until the Renaissance that we find the term *perennial philosophy* explicitly used in philosophical circles (Loemker, 1973). More precisely, it was Agostino Steuco (1497–1546), bishop of Kisamos and librarian of the Vatican, who coined this term to refer to the *prisca theologia* or *philosophia priscorium* of Marsilio Ficino, a unifying philosophical system based on a synthesis of Platonic principles and Christian doctrines. Thus, the modern notion of a perennial philosophy should be regarded as a product of the ecumenical interest of the Christian tradition in the Neoplatonic Renaissance (Marsilio Ficino, Giovanni Pico della Mirandola, Nicolas de Cusa, Agostino Steuco, etc.) in finding unity and harmony amidst a multiplicity of conflicting world views (Schmitt, 1966).[2]

Throughout the history of philosophy, the term perennial philosophy or *philosophia perennis* was also used as a synonym for Scholasticism and Thomism; as the final goal of philosophy by Leibniz; as the regulative ideal of philosophical practice by Jaspers; and as a world philosophy, synthesis of East and West, by Radhakrishnan (Collins, 1962; Loemker, 1973). Common to all these conceptions, however, is the idea that a philosophical current exists that has endured through centuries, and that is able to integrate harmoniously all traditions in terms of a single Truth which underlies the apparent plurality of world views. According to the defenders of the perennial philosophy, this unity in human knowledge stems from the existence of a single ultimate reality which can be apprehended by the human intellect under certain special conditions.

Although already reintroduced in the West first by Madame Blavatsky and the Theosophical Society founded in 1875, and later by Swami Vivekananda in his influential address to the World's Parliament of Religions held in Chicago in 1893 (Clarke, 1997; Faivre, 1994), it was not until the publication of Aldous Huxley's (1945) *The Perennial Philosophy* that perennialist ideas reached the masses and became popular beyond esoteric and academic elites.[3] As is well known, Huxley (1945) described the perennial philosophy as "the metaphysics that recognizes a divine Reality substantial to the world of things and lives and minds; the psychology that finds in the soul something similar to, or even identical with, divine Reality; the ethic that places man's final end in the knowledge of the immanent and transcendent Ground of all being" (p. vii).

What characterizes Huxley's perennialism, as well as the one of the so-called traditionalists such as René Guénon, Ananda K. Coomaraswamy, or Frithjof Schuon (see Borella, 1995; Quinn, 1997), is the conviction that the single Truth of the perennial philosophy can be found at the heart of the mystical teachings of the world religious traditions. Although with different emphases, all these authors claim that whereas the exoteric beliefs of the religious traditions are assorted and at times even incompatible, their esoteric or mystical dimension reveals an essential unity that transcends this doctrinal pluralism. This is so, traditionalists argue, because mystics of all ages and places can transcend the different conceptual schemes provided by their cultures, languages, and doctrines, and consequently access a direct, intuitive understanding of reality (*gnosis*). Therefore, perennialists generally distinguish between mystical experience, which is universal and timeless, and its interpretation, which is culturally and historically determined. According to this view, the same mystical experience of the nondual Ground of Being would be interpreted as emptiness (*sunyata*) by a Mahayana Buddhist, as Brahman by an Advaita Vedantin, as the union with God by a Christian, or as an objectless absorption (*asamprajñata samadhi*) by a practitioner of Patañjali's yoga. In all cases, the experience is the same, the interpretation different.

In sum, modern perennialists maintain not only the existence of an experiential contemplative consensus about the ultimate nature of reality, but also the objective truth of such a vision (i.e., that it depicts "things as they really are" once divested of individual and cultural projections).[4] In its most general form, then, the perennialist thesis entails two different knowledge claims: a descriptive claim that affirms the homogeneity of the message of the contemplative traditions and a normative or epistemological claim that maintains the absolute truth of that message (cf. Griffiths, 1991). Although I cannot develop this point here, it is important to note that the assessment of these two claims probably requires different methods and skills. The examination of the first claim, for example, may involve hermeneutic comparative studies of different mystical texts, as well as interviews with and dialogues among representatives of the living traditions. In contrast, the evaluation of the second claim may need to include epistemological analyses of the cognitive value of mysticism, personal involvement in one or another form of spiritual inquiry (e.g., see Rothberg, 1994), and probably participation in interreligious dialogues.

But what is this single Truth about which all contemplative traditions supposedly converge? According to modern defenders of the mystical version of the perennial philosophy, such as Nasr (1989, 1993), Schuon (1984a), and Smith (1976, 1987, 1989), the doctrinal core of the perennial philosophy is the belief that Spirit, Pure Consciousness, or the Universal Mind, is the fundamental essence of both human nature and the totality of reality. Although there may be some descriptive or interpretive divergences, all contemplative traditions regard reality as originated by, and ontologically the same as, a simultaneously immanent and transcending Spirit which is identical in essence to human innermost consciousness. This Spirit constitutes the ultimate referent for what can be regarded as real, true, and valuable. In the perennialist view, then, Spirit is the primary ontological, epistemological, and axiological foundation of the cosmos.

Other major principles frequently derived from this primordial Truth include involutionary cosmology, hierarchical ontology and axiology, and hierarchical epistemology (see, e.g., Nasr, 1989, 1993; Quinn, 1997; Rothberg, 1986b; H. Smith, 1976; 1989; Wilber, 1977, 1990a, 1993a). Let us briefly look at them one by one:

1. *Involutionary cosmology* is the postulate that the physical universe is the result of a process of emanation, restriction, or involution of Spirit. In other words, Spirit is prior to matter, and matter has evolved from It.

2. *Hierarchical ontology and axiology* refer to the vision of reality as composed by different layers or levels of being that are hierarchically organized (e.g., matter, mind, and spirit)—the so-called Great Chain of Being. In this hierarchy, the higher levels are those closer to Spirit, and are regarded as more real, more causally effective, and more valuable than the lower.

3. Hierarchical epistemology is the theory of knowledge according to which knowledge of the higher realms of the hierarchical ontology is more essential, reveals more about reality, and is therefore authoritative concerning knowledge of the lower ones. That is, knowledge of Spirit (contemplation, *gnosis*) is more true and valuable than knowledge of the mental and physical levels (rational and empirical knowledge, respectively).

As we will see, this is the version of the perennial philosophy that Ken Wilber expanded and popularized in transpersonal circles.

VARIETIES OF PERENNIALISM

For the sake of clarity, I have been talking about mystical perennialism as a monolithic approach. However, I would like to suggest here that it should be more accurately regarded as a family of interpretative models. In this section, I briefly review the main perennialist interpretative models developed in the fields of comparative mysticism, cross-cultural philosophy of religion, and transpersonal studies: Basic, Esotericist, Structuralist, Perspectivist, and Typological.[5]

I. BASIC

The first, and most simple form of perennialism, maintains that there is only *one path* and *one goal* for spiritual development. According to this model, spiritual paths and goals are everywhere the same, and descriptive differences either reflect an underlying similarity or are the result of the different languages, religious doctrines, and cultural backgrounds. The point here is, then, that although mysticism is phenomenologically the same, non-experiential variables may affect its interpretation and description (e.g., Huxley, 1945; Smart, 1980).

2. ESOTERICIST

The second form of perennialism, while admitting *many paths*, holds that there is only *one goal* common to all spiritual traditions. As in the previous model, this goal, although universal, may have been differently interpreted and described according to the specific doctrines of the various mystical traditions. Although not exclusive to this school, this view is usually associated with traditionalists such as Schuon (1984a) or Smith (1976, 1989), who claim that the spiritual unity of humankind can only be found in the eso-

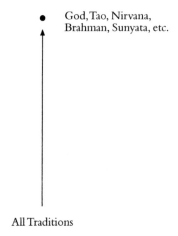

God, Tao, Nirvana,
Brahman, Sunyata, etc.

All Traditions

FIG. 1. BASIC

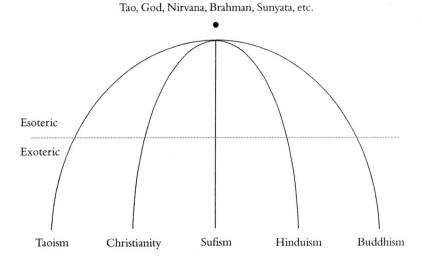

Tao, God, Nirvana, Brahman, Sunyata, etc.

Esoteric

Exoteric

Taoism   Christianity   Sufism   Hinduism   Buddhism

FIG. 2. ESOTERICIST

teric or mystical core of religious traditions, and not in their exoteric or
doctrinal forms. The guiding root metaphors of this model are the images of
different rivers reaching the same ocean, different pathways leading to the
peak of the same mountain, or different cascades of water issuing from a single spring.

3. STRUCTURALIST

This model understands the many mystical paths and goals as contextual manifestations (surface structures) of underlying universal patterns (deep structures) which ultimately constitute *one path* and *one goal* paradigmatic for all spiritual traditions. Already implicit in Jung's distinction between noumenal and phenomenal archetypes, and in Eliade's studies on myth, a two-level structuralist account of universal religion and mysticism was first explicitly proposed by Anthony and Robbins (Anthony, 1982; Anthony & Robbins, 1975). The structuralist approach to perennialism took a developmental and evolutionary turn in transpersonal studies in the hands of Wilber. According to Wilber (1984, 1995, 1996b, 1996c), although historical and cultural factors determine the surface manifestations of spiritual forms, human spirituality is ultimately universal, as constituted by an evolutionary hierarchy of invariant deep structures or levels of spiritual insight: psychic, subtle, causal, and nondual. A metaphor used by Wilber to depict this model is a ladder whose rungs correspond to the different spiritual levels. Given the considerable influence of Wilber's ideas on transpersonal scholarship, a section of this chapter examines this model in more depth. Another structuralist account of transpersonal and spiritual experiences is the biogenetic structuralism proposed by Laughlin, McManus, and d'Aquili (1990).

4. PERSPECTIVIST

The fourth form of perennialism, although conceding the existence of both *many paths* and *many goals* in mysticism, conceives these goals as different perspectives, dimensions, or manifestations of the same Ground of Being or ultimate Reality. As we will see, for example, Grof (1998) explains the diversity of spiritual ultimates (a personal God, an impersonal Brahman, sunyata, the Void, the Tao, Pure Consciousness, etc.) as different ways to experience the same supreme cosmic principle (p. 26ff). The title of the essay, "One Is the Spirit and Many Its Human Reflections," by Nasr (1993), is characteristic of this approach. This position may take the form of suggesting the complementarity of Eastern and Western traditions, as did some of the early Western orientalists like Müller in comparative religion, Northrop in philosophy, or Edmunds in theology (Clarke, 1997). Or it may take a Kantian outlook, as in the case of Hick (1992), who suggests that conflicting spiritual knowledge claims and world views result from different historically shaped

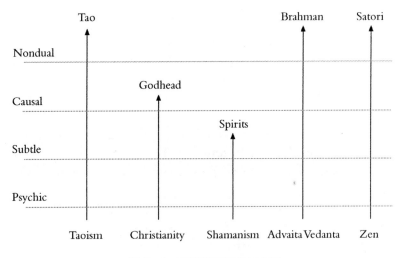

FIG. 3. STRUCTURALIST

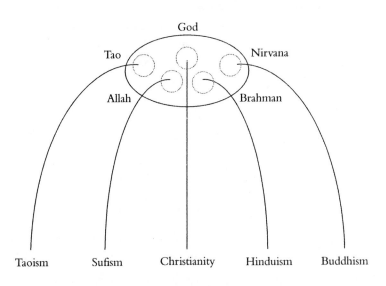

FIG. 4. PERSPECTIVIST

phenomenal awarenesses of the same Noumenal reality. The guiding root metaphor here is the popular Sufi story of the several blind men touching different parts of the same elephant, each insisting that their description accurately depicts the whole.

5. TYPOLOGICAL

Closely related to universal perspectivism is the postulation of a *limited number of types of paths and goals* that run across the different mystical traditions, for example, Otto's (1932) outward and inward, Stace's (1960) extrovertive and introvertive, or Zaehner's (1970) nature, monistic, and theistic.[6] This model is also perennialist insofar as these types of mysticism are claimed to be independent of time, place, culture, and religion. Typological universalism often takes a perspectivist stance and affirms that the different types of mysticism are diverse expressions or manifestations of a single ultimate spiritual reality.

While considering the previous classification, the reader should bear in mind that there is a substantial degree of overlap between models, and that some of the authors quoted as representatives of a particular model could also have been situated in support of others. This is because, in some cases, the thinking of an author contains elements that apply to different models, and, in others, different works by a single author may emphasize one or another perennialist model. Also, it is important to notice that there may be important differences between authors grouped under the same roof. In model #5, for example, in contrast to Otto's universalism of the numinous, Zaehner, a Catholic theologian, was firmly skeptical about the idea of a unity underlying all religious traditions. Both scholars, however, posit the existence of different types of mystical experience that occur across the traditions and can therefore be classified as typological perennialists. In spite of the admittedly somewhat artificial character of this classification, I believe that it can help to clarify the variety of ways in which a perennialist view of spirituality can be articulated.

GROF'S NEO-ADVAITIN PERENNIAL PHILOSOPHY

Grof's (1998) recent book, *The Cosmic Game*, is an exploration of the metaphysical implications of his forty-year long groundbreaking research into special states of consciousness. In the introduction, Grof suggests that the experiential data he has gathered support the basic tenets of the perennial philosophy:

> This research . . . shows that, in its farther reaches, the psyche of each of us is essentially commensurate with all of existence and ultimately identical with the cosmic creative principle itself. This conclusion . . . is in far-reaching

agreement with the image of reality found in the great spiritual and mystical traditions of the world, which the Anglo-American writer and philosopher Aldous Huxley referred to as the "perennial philosophy." (p. 3)

In this spirit, he adds, "the claims of the various schools of perennial philosophy can now be supported by data from modern consciousness research" (p. 4). In chapter 6, I argue that Grof's experiential data can also be consistently explained without appealing to a perennialist metaphysics, but for our present purposes it may suffice to identify here the specific version of perennialism endorsed by Grof.

First, Grof shares with esotericist perennialists the belief that true spirituality needs to be sought in an esoteric core common to all religious traditions. In support of this idea, for example, he writes: "Genuine religion is universal, all-inclusive, and all-encompassing. It has to transcend specific culture-bound archetypal images and focus on the ultimate source of all forms" (1998, p. 24). Grof's (1988, 2000) distinction between spirituality and (exoteric) religion is also indicative of this stance: "The spirituality that emerges spontaneously at a certain stage of experiential self-exploration should not be confused with the mainstream religions and their beliefs, doctrines, dogmas, and rituals" (1988, p. 269). And echoing the voice of esotericists such as Frithjof Schuon or Huston Smith, he adds: "The really important division in the world of spirituality is not the line that separates the individual mainstream religions from each other, but the one that separates all of them from their mystical branches" (p. 270).

Second, Grof's perennialism is perspectivist in that it explains the diversity of spiritual ultimates—a personal God, an impersonal Brahman, emptiness (*sunyata*), the Void, the Tao, Pure Consciousness, etc.—as different ways to experience the same supreme cosmic principle (1998, p. 26ff). Perspectival perennialism, let us remember here, is the view according to which the variety of experiences and visions of ultimate reality should be understood as different perspectives, dimensions, or levels of the very same Ground of Being. In this spirit, Grof and Bennet (1993) tell us, "The ultimate creative principle has been known by many names—Brahman in Hinduism, Dharmakaya in Mahayana Buddhism, the Tao in Taoism, Pneuma in Christian mysticism, Allah in Sufism, and Kether in Kabbalah" (p. 164).

Third, Grof (1998) describes this esoteric core, supreme cosmic principle, and ultimate source of all religious systems in terms of *Absolute Consciousness*.

This Absolute Consciousness is both the ultimate ground of all that exists (monism) and essentially identical to the individual human soul (nondual). Talking about the nondual relationship between Absolute Consciousness and the individual soul, for example, Grof (1998) states that:

> When we reach experiential identification with Absolute Consciousness, we realize that our own being is ultimately commensurate with the entire cosmic network. The recognition of our own divine nature, our identity with the cosmic source, is the most important discovery we can make during the process of deep self-exploration. (p. 38)

For Grof (1998), this recognition confirms the truth of the essential message of the Hindu Upanishads: "*Tat tvam asi*" or "Thou are that," that is, the essential unity between the individual soul and the divine.

Fourth, Grof (1998) reads some of his experiential data as supporting Sri-Aurobindo's notion of involution, according to which the material world is the product of a process of restriction, partition, or self-limitation of Absolute Consciousness. From a state of undifferentiated unity, Grof points out, Absolute Consciousness splits and forgets itself to create infinite experiential realities. Although a variety of reasons for this self-forgetting is suggested, Grof tends to use Hindu terminology to explain it and repeatedly suggests that the entire creation is *lila* or a cosmic drama ultimately played out by only one actor: Absolute Consciousness. Talking about the dimensions of the process of creation, for example, Grof (2000) tells us:

> These are elements that have best been described in ancient Hindu texts which talk about the universe and existence as *lila*, or Divine Play. According to this view, creation is an intricate, infinitely complex cosmic game that the godhead, Brahman, creates himself and within himself. (p. 278)

Fifth, although Grof (1998) quotes Sri-Aurobindo's view that evolution is not merely a return to the One, but "the gradual emergence of higher powers of consciousness in the material universe leading to an even greater manifestation of the divine Consciousness Force within its creation" (p. 79), Grof states that the ultimate zenith and goal of spiritual evolution is the self-identification with Absolute Consciousness: "In its farthest reaches, this process [evolution] dissolves all the boundaries and brings about a reunion with Absolute Consciousness" (p. 79).

Finally, we find in Grof's cosmology repeated examples of a subtle devaluation of the material world as illusory, imperfect, or even defiled. Summarizing the conclusions of his research, for example, he tells us that:

In the light of these insights, the material world of our everyday life, including our own body, is an intricate tissue of misperceptions and misreadings. It
is a playful and somewhat arbitrary product of the cosmic creative principle,
infinitely sophisticated "virtual reality," a divine play created by Absolute
Consciousness and the Cosmic Void. (1998, p. 39)

A similar tendency can be observed in his description of involution, which,
for Grof, implies an increasing loss of contact with the pristine nature of the
original unity (p. 50). To illustrate this process, Grof draws on Jain cosmology, according to which "the world of creation is an infinitely complex system of deluded units of consciousness . . . trapped in different aspects and
stages of the cosmic process. Their pristine nature is contaminated by their
entanglement in material reality and, particularly, in biological processes" (p.
52). Finally, repeatedly throughout the book we find Grof suggesting that his
research supports the Hindu view that "the material reality as we perceive it
in our everyday life is a product of a fundamental cosmic illusion called
maya" (p. 66). Or, as he puts it some pages later: "all boundaries in the material world are illusory and the entire universe as we know it, in both its spa-
tial and temporal aspects, is a unified web of events in consciousness" (p. 85).

To sum up, Grof interprets his findings as supporting a *Neo-Advaitin eso-
tericist-perspectivist version of the perennial philosophy.* The variety of spiritual
ultimates are understood as different ways to experience the same universal
ground, which can only be found, beyond all archetypal forms, in the esoteric
universal heart of all religious traditions. This universal core is described as a
monistic Absolute Consciousness, its relationship with human individual
consciousness is understood in nondual terms, and the creation of an ultimately illusory material world is explained through the Neo-Hindu notion
of involution.

KEN WILBER'S NEOPERENNIALISM

Through his many works, Ken Wilber has identified himself as a modern
translator of the perennial philosophy, and has championed the perennial
doctrines in the transpersonal arena for more than two decades (e.g., 1977,
1982, 1984, 1990a, 1993a, 1995, 1996a, 1997a). As Wilber (1997a) recently
stressed, however, there is a fundamental difference between his neoperennialism and the traditional versions of the perennial philosophy. In contrast to
the merely involutionary accounts of the traditions, Wilber (1997a) claims
that a more adequate description of the perennial Truth today should necessarily incorporate the notion of evolution.[7] As Walsh (1995) points out, the

aim of Wilber's recent work "is to trace evolution—physical, biological, and human—and to set it within the context of the perennial philosophy" (p. 18). Following thinkers like Hegel, Sri-Aurobindo, or Teilhard de Chardin, then, Wilber (1997a) proposes an *evolutionary perennialism* that holds that:

> There is still That One, or the timeless and absolute Spirit of which the entire universe is but a manifestation, but that world of manifestation is not now devolving away from Spirit, it is evolving toward Spirit. God does not lie in our collective past, God lies in our collective future; the Garden of Eden is tomorrow, not yesterday; the Golden Age lies down the road, not up to it. (p. 63)

What Wilber is claiming is that the involutionary cosmology of the traditional perennial philosophy should be complemented with a special type of *teleological evolutionism*. Teleological evolutionism is the view that cosmological, phylogenetic, and ontogenetic processes are ultimately directed towards a predetermined goal. In the classic evolutionary perennialist view, this pre-given goal is generally equated with Spirit itself. For traditional evolutionary perennialists like Teilhard de Chardin or Sri-Aurobindo, Spirit is not only the beginning, but also the end point of evolution. Spirit is both the Alpha and the Omega of all cosmological and evolutionary processes. It is important to stress here that, in contrast to these philosophers, Wilber (1995, 1997a) does not believe that this Omega point (Spirit) towards which the evolutionary process is directed will ever be reached in the world of time and space and form. Since Spirit is timeless and formless, Wilber (1997a) argues, It will never be reached at any point in time, but can only be realized "by stepping off the cycle of time and evolution altogether" (p. 280). Still, it should be noted here that Wilber (1995) regards Spirit as the final cause, pull, and telos of the entire cosmic and human evolutionary process.

It is certainly one of Wilber's achievements to have given the perennial vision greater contemporary finesse and explanatory power than most traditional or modern accounts. In my opinion, this is due not only to the incorporation of the notion of evolution, but also to the adoption of two conceptual frameworks: one modern, structuralism; the other postmodern, constructivism. Against an evolutionary background, these two frameworks allow Wilber to accommodate, somewhat artificially I believe, both the plurality of human spiritual forms and some modern epistemological insights within the universalist vision of the perennial philosophy. On the one hand, the application of structuralist logic permits him to house cultural differences within a universalist view of consciousness and reality. For example, defending a perennialist view of spirituality, Wilber (1995) proposes that the diversity of experiences, symbols, doctrines, and cultural forms found in the various contemplative traditions stems from the existence of surface structures, culturally and historically situated manifestations of an underlying universal hierarchy of deep structures which ultimately constitute one path and one goal for human spiritual evolution. Talking about mysticism, he writes: "Common deep structures with culturally situated surface structures seem to me to steer a course between 'no similarities at all' and 'mostly or only one common core'" (1995, p. 604, note 16).

Accordingly, Wilber (1995) plots the transpersonal territory into four types of hierarchically laddered realms or deep structures. The psychic (or nature mysticism: the realm of out-of-body experiences [OBEs], vibrations, Kundalini, chakras, etc.), the subtle (or deity mysticism: the realm of luminosity and archetypal forms, of God, etc.), the causal (or formless mysticism: the realm of pure consciousness, emptiness, nothingness, the Void, etc.), and, finally, the nondual (nondual mysticism: beyond being and nonbeing, where "emptiness is form, and form is emptiness," the world as expression of Spirit, etc.). According to Wilber (1995), these four types of mysticism "can most definitely be found cross-culturally. Nobody is denying that a Buddhist will interpret the luminosity as the Sambhogakaya, the Christian will interpret it perhaps as an angel or Christ himself, a Jungian will interpret it as an archetypal emergence, and so on" (p. 621, note 58). In other words, although very specific archetypal visions and deities (different surface structures) can be observed in different traditions, all of them belong to the same level of spiritual development, that is, the subtle level, the realm of the archetypal manifestations (the same deep structure). In sum, *human spirituality is ultimately universal, as constituted by an evolutionary hierarchy of deep structures. Contextual factors only shape and determine the situated manifestations and interpretations of these deep structures, as well as the level of spiritual evolution attainable in each tradition.*

On the other hand, Wilber (1995) adds to the perennial vision several constructivist principles inspired by Varela, Thompson, and Rosch's (1991) enactive paradigm, such as the rejection of the representation paradigm, the emancipation from the constraints of a pregiven reality, or the idea of "enacted worldspaces" (i.e., intersubjectively shared worlds of referents that are disclosed in the process of the mutually codetermined evolution of consciousness and the world). Wilber should certainly be credited for having extended the application of the enactive paradigm from its original confinement in the monological sensoriomotor world to the dialogical mental and the translogical spiritual realms. I should point out here, however, that Wilber's inclusion of these modern epistemological insights occurs under the shadow of an objectivist/universalist scheme that sabotages the very nature of the enactive paradigm. According to Wilber (1995), although the different worldspaces are not pregiven but enacted, their unfolding follows a still pregiven evolutionary pattern governed by a spiritual telos: "The deep structures are given, but the surface are not" (Wilber, 1996a, p. 212).

In sum, Wilber has softened and actualized the perennial vision, thereby allowing for much more diversity, variety, and creative novelty than most traditional accounts. However, by retaining an objectivist/universalist core in his notion of deep structure, Wilber still runs the risk of falling prey to the several dangers intrinsic to traditional perennialism. In the next sections, we will examine in more detail the nature of these pitfalls. Here, what should be clear is that, for Wilber, underlying all apparent contextual diversity and undeterminism, there exists a pregiven and universal evolutionary process that determines the deep structure of world views, social structures, and human psychospiritual evolution. This evolutionary process is driven by a dynamic telos-Spirit that, although never reachable in the world of time and form, is the ultimate origin, end, and ground of all that exists.

THE FUNDAMENTAL PROBLEMS
OF THE PERENNIAL PHILOSOPHY

Up to this point, I have presented the perennialist vision as neutrally and accurately as I have been able. We have seen both the evolution of the idea of a perennial philosophy and the various ways in which a perennialist vision of spirituality can be articulated. It is now time to shift to a more critical mode of discourse and discuss certain fundamental problems and assumptions shared by all types of perennialism. First, I focus on the perennial vision in general, and then more particularly on Wilber's neoperennialism. Before starting our discussion, however, the reader should be warned that the philosophical questions involved in the following discussion are too large to be dealt with adequately here, so in the next few pages I merely offer several critical points in a somewhat abbreviated and simplistic manner, and leave a more exhaustive treatment for another occasion.

TRADITIONAL PERENNIALISM

Briefly, I want to point out that perennialism: (1) is an a priori philosophical stance, (2) privileges a nondual monistic metaphysic, (3) is geared to an objectivist epistemology, (4) leans towards essentialism, and, consequently, (5) tends to fall into religious dogmatism and intolerance in spite of its avowed inclusivist stance.

Perennialism Is an A Priori Philosophical Stance

What I am suggesting here is that the common core of spirituality espoused by the perennial philosophy is not the conclusion of cross-cultural research or interreligious dialogue, but an inference deduced from the premise that there is a transcendent unity of reality, a single Absolute that underlies the multiplicity of phenomena and towards which all spiritual traditions are directed.

The evidence provided by perennialists to support their claim of a common goal for all spiritual traditions is both striking and revealing. Perennialists generally claim that the transcendent unity of religions can only be intuitively apprehended and confirmed by an organ or faculty known as the Intellect (also called Eye of the Heart or Eye of the Soul). According to perennialist thinkers, the Intellect participates in the Divine reality and, being therefore universal and unaffected by historical constraints, is able to objectively see "things as they really are" through direct metaphysical intuition (*gnosis*) (see, e.g., Cutsinger, 1997; Schuon, 1997; H. Smith, 1987, 1993). To be sure, to postulate intuitive forms of knowing beyond the structures of ordinary subject-centered and communicative reason is a bold and salutary step for which perennialists should be commended. However, to claim that this intuitive knowledge necessarily reveals a perennialist metaphysic is a self-serving move that cannot escape its own circularity. To be genuine, we are told, metaphysical intuitions must be universal. And this is so, we are assured, because universality is the distinctive mark of what is True. In Schuon's (1984a) words: "The [perennial] truths just expressed are not the exclusive possession of any school or individual; were it otherwise they would not be truths, for these cannot be invented, but must necessarily be known in every integral traditional civilization" (p. xxxiii). And he adds: "Intelligence is either individual or universal; it is either reason or Intellect" (p. 152). But then, the perennialist discourse boils down to saying that either your metaphysical intuition confirms the Primordial Truth, or it is false, partial, or belonging to a lower level of spiritual insight. By means of its own circular logic, the perennial philosophy has made itself invulnerable to criticism (cf. Dean, 1984).

In the wake of these circularities, a more cogent explanation for the insight into the transcendent unity of religions is that it stems from an a priori commitment to the perennial truth, a commitment that, after years of traditionally oriented study and spiritual practice, is gradually transformed into a direct metaphysical intuition which grants the believer a sense of unquestionable certitude. According to Nasr (1996), for example, the goal of perennialist hermeneutics is not to study what the diverse spiritual traditions say about themselves, but "to see beyond the veil of multiplicity . . . that unity which is the origin of all sacred forms" (p. 18), and to discover "the truth that shines forth within each authentic religious universe manifesting the Absolute" (p. 18). This task can only be accomplished, Nasr (1996) asserts, by focusing on the esoteric dimension of the religious traditions, the hierarchy of levels of reality, the distinction between phenomenon and noumenon, and other perennialist postulates. In other words, perennialist hermeneutics assumes what it is supposed to discover and prove. This circularity is apparent in Quinn's (1997) description of the hermeneutic of the tradition: "Thus, for Guénon and Coomaraswamy, it was an absolute and indispensable requisite to believe a profound religious or metaphysical doctrine or principle in order to understand it" (p. 25). And this is probably why perennialist thinkers usually characterize faith as a faculty ontologically situated between ordinary reason and the Intellect (e.g., Schuon, 1984b). Needless to say, for perennialist thinkers, "faith is a profound and total 'yes' to the One, which is both absolute and infinite, transcendent and immanent" (Schuon, 1981, p. 238).

Space does not allow me to discuss in detail here the question of whether the superiority of perennialism (or of any other metaphysical system) can be established by appealing to the phenomenological content of spiritual experiences, as Grof (1998) suggests. As we have seen, the position of traditional perennialism is that the truth of the perennial philosophy can only be accessed and validated, not by mystical experiences, but through a special type of abstract metaphysical intuition. As Huston Smith (1987) points out, for example, to justify the perennial philosophy, we should "not appeal to experience at all" but rather focus on "doctrines [that] derive from metaphysical intuitions . . . that the perennial philosophy appeals [to]. To discern the truth of a metaphysical axiom one need not have an experience" (p. 554).

Furthermore, it would seem that, in the same way that alternative or even logically incompatible theories can fit all possible evidence—as the Duhem-Quine principle of underdetermination of theory by evidence shows (Duhem, 1953; Quine, 1953, 1990)—alternative metaphysical systems can fit all possible spiritual experiences. As we will see in chapter 6, for example, Grof's experiential data can be consistently explained by a non-perennialist metaphysics. If this is the case, the prospects for demonstrating the privileged truth of the perennial philosophy through an appeal to experience are, I think, quite poor.[8]

Perennialism Privileges a Nondual Monistic Metaphysic

As we have seen, perennialist models typically assume the existence of a universal spiritual reality which is the Ground of all that is, and of which the contemplative traditions are an expression. In spite of their insistence on the ineffable and unqualifiable nature of this Ground, perennialists consistently characterize it as Nondual, the One, or the Absolute. The perennialist Ground of Being, that is, strikingly resembles the Neoplatonic Godhead or the Advaitin Brahman. As Schuon (1981) states, "the perspective of Sankara is one of the most adequate expressions possible of the *philosophia perennis* or sapiential esoterism" (p. 21). In other words, the Absolute of the perennial philosophy, far from being a neutral and truly unqualifiable ground, is represented as supporting a nondual monistic metaphysics.

In transpersonal studies, both Grof's and Wilber's defense of a perennial philosophy closely follows this trend. Whereas Wilber (1995, 1996c, 1997a) consistently situates an impersonal nondual ground as the zenith of spiritual evolution, Grof (1998) describes the common core of all religious traditions as an Absolute Consciousness that, being identical in essence to human individual consciousness, creates an ultimately illusory material world through a process of involution. For both authors, this recognition confirms the truth of the essential message of the Hindu Upanishads: "*Tat tvam asi*" or "Thou are that," that is, the essential unity between the individual soul and the divine.[9]

Apart from the aforementioned exclusive intuitionism, the arguments offered by perennial thinkers for this single Absolute are both a priori and circular. For example, perennialists often assert that, since multiplicity implies relativity, a plurality of absolutes is both a logical and a metaphysical absurdity: "The absolute must of necessity be One and, in fact, *the* One as asserted

by so many metaphysicians over the ages" (Nasr, 1996, p. 19). This commitment to a monistic metaphysic is closely related to the perennialist defense of
the universality of mysticism. As Perovich (1985a), a perennialist philosopher,
puts it: "The point [of the perennial philosophers] in insisting on the identity
of mystical experiences was, after all, to bolster the claim that the most varied
mystics have established contact with 'the one ultimate truth'" (p. 75).

Perennialism is Geared to an Objectivist Epistemology

Admittedly, to charge the perennial philosophy with objectivism may sound
at first surprising. After all, certain perennialist doctrines represent a serious
challenge for objectivist standards, and perennialists writers have often con-
tested the scientistic view of valid knowledge as one anchored in an objective and detached rationality. On the one hand, the affirmation of a fundamental identity between human innermost subjectivity and the ultimate
nature of objective reality obviously represents a formidable objection to
the Cartesianism of natural science. On the other hand, perennialists have
repeatedly stressed not only the existence of intuitive knowing (the Eye of
the Heart), but also the centrality of the moral and affective dimensions of
knowledge. Most of these challenges to scientism are well grounded, and
perennialist philosophers should be credited for having anticipated them
even decades before objectivism was exhausted in mainstream science and
philosophy.

   Nonetheless, the perennialist vision falls back into objectivism with its
insistence that there is a pregiven ultimate reality that can be objectively
known by the human Intellect (intuitive knowing). As Schuon (1981) states:
"The prerogative of the human state is objectivity, the essential content of
which is the Absolute" (p. 15). Although objectivity should not be understood as limited to the empirical and external, Schuon (1981) tells us that
"knowledge is 'objective' when it is capable of grasping the object as it is and
not as it may be deformed by the subject" (p. 15).

   Of course, these assumptions make the perennial philosophy subject to
all the anxieties and aporias of Cartesian consciousness, such as the false
dichotomies between absolutism and relativism, or between objectivism and
subjectivism. This relapse leads perennialists to demonize and combat what
now have become in their eyes the horrors of relativism and subjectivism
(e.g., Schuon, 1984b; H. Smith, 1989). In the introduction to a contemporary perennialist anthology, for example, Stoddart (1994) writes: "The only

antidote to the relative and the subjective is the absolute and the objective, and it is precisely these that are the contents of traditional philosophy or 'perennial wisdom' (*Sophia perennis*)" (p. 11). Or, in Schuon's (1984b) words:

> We have to take our choice: either objective knowledge, absolute therefore in its own order, is possible, proving thereby that existentialism [subjectivism] is false; or else existentialism is true, but then its own promulgation is impossible, since in the existentialist universe there is no room for any intellection that is objective and stable. (p. 10)

Paradoxically, these rigid dichotomies between the absolute and the relative, between the objective and the subjective, only emerge in the context of the very Cartesian epistemology that the perennial vision rightfully challenges.[10]

With these premises, perennialists claim that the spiritual path leads simultaneously to both objective knowledge of "things as they really are," and the realization of the true, essential nature of humankind. Against a background of objectivist assumptions, that is, the spiritual path is regarded as a process of deconstruction or *de*conditioning of certain conceptual schemes, cognitive functions, and psychophysical structures that constitute a deluded vision of selfhood and reality, an illusion that is in turn the primordial cause of human alienation. The key words of the perennialist discourse are, then, realization, awareness, or recognition of what is "already there," that is, the essential and objective nature of both reality and human beings.

Perennialism Leans toward Essentialism

The perennialist attribution of a greater explanatory power or ontological status to what is common among religious traditions is problematic. The nature of this problem can be illustrated by the popular story of the woman who, observing her neighbor entering into an altered state of consciousness three consecutive days first with rum and water, then through fast breathing and water, and finally with nitrous oxide and water, concludes that the reason for his bizarre behaviors was the ingestion of water. The moral of the story, of course, is that what is essential or more explanatory in a set of phenomena is not necessarily what is most obviously common to them.

Furthermore, even if we could find an essential substratum to the different types of mystical awareness (for example, pure experience, suchness, or one taste), it does not necessarily follow that this common ground is the goal of all traditions, the most spiritually valuable aim, or the zenith of our spiritual efforts. Although it is certainly possible to find parallels across religious traditions, the key to the spiritually transforming power of a given tradition may lie in its own distinctive practices and understandings. The limitations of the following image notwithstanding, the perennialist agenda could be compared to the desire of an individual who enters a rustic Parisian bakery and, observing the variety of delicious croissants, baguettes, and coffee-cakes displayed, insists that he wants to savor what is essential and common to all them, that is, flour. Like the many succulent flavors we can sample in a French bakery, however, I will argue that the fundamental spiritual value and beauty of the various traditions derives precisely from their unique creative solution to the transformation of the human condition. As Wittgenstein (1968) puts it, to taste the real artichoke we do not need to divest it from its leaves.

Perennialism Tends Toward Dogmatism and Intolerance

These universalist and objectivist assumptions generally lead perennial philosophers to recede into dogmatism and intolerance towards different spiritual world views. As we have seen, the perennial philosophy conceives the different religious traditions as pathways directed to a single Absolute reality. In spite of the different metaphysical universes espoused by the contemplative traditions, perennialists insist that "there is only one metaphysic but many traditional languages through which it is expressed" (Nasr, 1985, p. 89).

But, what about spiritual traditions which do not posit a metaphysical Absolute or transcendent ultimate Reality? What about spiritual traditions that refuse to fit into the perennialist scheme? The perennialist solution to conflicting spiritual traditions is well known: Religious traditions and doctrines that do not accept the perennial vision are inauthentic, merely exoteric, or represent lower levels of insight in a hierarchy of spiritual revelations whose culmination is the perennial Truth (cf. Hanegraaff, 1998). For example, Schuon (1984b) frequently distinguishes between the Absolute in Itself, which is beyond any form, and the relatively absolute posited by each religion. In this scheme, the different spiritual ultimates, although absolute within their own specific religious universe, are merely relative in relation to the single Absolute that perennialism champions.

And since this single Absolute, far from being neutral or unqualifiable, is best depicted by a nondual monistic metaphysics, perennialists generally rank as lower those traditions that do not conform to nondualism or impersonal monism: Sankara's impersonal nondualism is closer to the Absolute than

Ramanuja and Semitic personalistic monotheisms (Schuon, 1981), nondual traditions closer than theistic ones (Wilber, 1995), and so forth.

As we have seen, perennialists justify these rankings on the basis of metaphysical intuitions about the ultimate nature of the Absolute. We have already pointed out the inescapable circularity involved in this line of argumentation. Here I would like to add that the problems with this claim become even more apparent when we look at the spiritual history of humankind. As is well known, mystics from the most diverse times and places have reported metaphysical intuitions that not only did not conform to the perennialist cosmology, but also were fundamentally at odds with each other. Actually, generations of mystics from different traditions, and often from a single tradition, have debated metaphysical issues for centuries without substantial signs of agreement—the everlasting quarrels between Buddhist and Hindu contemplatives about the ultimate nature of the self and reality are well known in this regard (see, e.g., Chinchore, 1995). In addition, it is important to stress that these differences did not arise only among the exoteric representatives of the traditions (as perennialists often maintain), but among the contemplatives themselves. As any student of the history of religions well knows, for every ecumenically oriented mystic (actually the exception to the rule), there are dozens of notably exclusivist figures. To quote one paradigmatic example, witness Ramanuja's views on Sankara's Advaita Vedanta:

> This entire theory rests on a fictitious foundation of altogether hollow and vicious arguments, incapable of being stated in definite logical alternatives, and devised by men who are destitute of these particular qualities which cause individuals to be chosen by the Supreme Person revealed in the Upaniṣads; whose intellects are darkened by the impressions of beginningless evil; and who thus have no insight into the nature of words and sentences, into the real purport conveyed by them, and into the procedure of sound argumentation, with all its methods depending on perception and the other means of knowledge—assisted by sound reasoning—have an insight into the true nature of things. (Thibaut, 1904, p. 39)

And this is just the prelude to more than one hundred pages of attacks on the followers of Sankara (in the Thibaut translation).

The esotericist claim that mystics of all ages and places converge about metaphysical matters is a dogma that cannot be sustained by the evidence. In contrast to the perennialist view, what the spiritual history of humankind suggests is that *spiritual doctrines and intuitions affected, shaped, and transformed each other, and that this mutual influence led to the unfolding of a variety of meta-physical worlds—rather than to one metaphysic and different languages.*[11]

One of the central problems with the rigid universalism of the perennial philosophy is that once one believes oneself to be in possession of a picture of "things as they really are," dialogue with traditions maintaining different spiritual visions often becomes an uninteresting and sterile monologue. At its worst, the conflicting viewpoints are regarded as less evolved, incoherent, or simply false. At best, the challenges presented are assimilated within the all-encompassing perennialist scheme. In both cases the perennialist philosopher appears not to able to listen to what other people are saying, because all new or conflicting information is screened, processed, or assimilated in terms of the perennialist framework. Therefore, a genuine or symmetrical encounter with the other in which opposing spiritual visions are regarded as real options is rendered unlikely.

In the name of ecumenism and universal harmony, then, perennialists overlook the essential message and unique soteriological solution offered by the various spiritual traditions. By equating all spiritual goals with the insight into an Advaitin-like nonduality, the multiplicity of revelations is rendered accidental and the creative richness of each way of salvation is considered a historical and cultural artifact. Even though perennialists, to their credit, reject both the exclusivism of exoteric believers and the inclusivism of sentimental ecumenism (Cutsinger, 1997), their commitment to a nondual monistic metaphysic that is supposed to be Absolute, universal, and paradigmatic for all traditions is ultimately a return to dogmatic exclusivism and intolerance. At the heart of this exclusivism is the claim that the perennial Truth is the superior view (i.e., the only one capable of including all others). The associated intolerance does not lie in the perennialists' belief that other approaches, such as pluralist or theistic, are wrong, but in their conviction that the others are less right. As historian of religions Hanegraaff (1998) eloquently puts it, talking about contemporary perennialism:

> New Age "perennialism" suffers from the same inner conflict which haunts universalist schemes generally. It is meant to be tolerant and inclusive because it encompasses all religious traditions, claiming that they all contain at least a core of truth; but it qualifies the actual diversity of faiths by pointing out that, whatever the believers may say, there is only *one* fundamental spiritual truth. Only those religious expressions which accept the perennialist premises can be regarded as "genuine." All this can be reduced to two brief and paradoxical formulations: New Age "perennialism" (like perennialism in general) cannot

tolerate religious intolerance; and it sharply excludes all exclusivism from its own spirituality. . . . Religious tolerance on a relativistic basis, which accepts other religious perspectives in their full "otherness," is unacceptable because it sacrifices the very idea that there is a fundamental "truth." (pp. 329–330)

WILBER'S NEOPERENNIALISM

In this section, I want to analyze some of the problems with Wilber's structuralist version of the perennial philosophy. Before proceeding, however, I should clarify that by no means am I suggesting that Wilber's integral theory as a whole belongs to the structuralist tradition. Wilber's overall theorizing integrates so many different approaches that any traditional label would be inaccurate to describe it—except perhaps the one he sometimes uses, integral. What we can rightfully say, I believe, is that his theory contains important structuralist elements, and that his approach to interreligious relations, and particularly his defense of a perennial philosophy, clearly follow a structuralist logic.

As we have seen, Wilber's defense of the perennial philosophy heavily rests on the distinction between surface and deep structures.[12] While accepting substantial differences among spiritual traditions, Wilber (1995) claims that these variations should be regarded as the surface manifestations of a universal hierarchy of deep structures that is paradigmatic for past, present, and future spiritual evolution:

The deep structures of worldspaces (archaic, magic, mythic, rational, and transpersonal) show cross-cultural and largely invariant features at a deep level of abstraction, whereas the surface structures (the actual subjects and objects in the various worldspaces) are naturally and appropriately quite different from culture to culture. (p. 276)

In other words, although surface structures are indeterminate and culture-bound, deep structures are pregiven and universal, and it is in this deep structural universality where Wilber thinks he can find good grounds to believe in the perennial wisdom.

In my opinion, an adequate understanding of the pregiven and universal nature of deep structures in Wilber's transpersonal theory must discern the relationship between the deep structures, the idea of involution, and the Great Chain of Being.[13] On the one hand, the deep structures are pregiven because they existed prior to evolution itself. That is, since evolution (the movement from matter to Spirit) is essentially a recapitulation of involution (the movement from Spirit to matter), the stages of the evolutionary process *must* necessarily follow an already preordained route. And this is why, Wilber (1995) believes, the structural potentials of these future spiritual worldspaces (psychic, subtle, causal, and nondual) are already available to all of us today.[14] On the other hand, the deep structures are universal because they represent the ontological links of the Great Chain of Being, a hierarchy of levels of reality which, for Wilber, is central to the perennial philosophy: "*The basic structures of consciousness are essentially the traditional Great Holoarchy of Being*" (1997a, p. 140; see also 1993b).[15] As we will see, it is precisely this supposed correspondence that allows Wilber to compare and assess levels of development, stages of evolution, world views, and spiritual traditions.

In what follows I present some of the main fundamental problems and assumptions of this structuralist account of spirituality. Before proceeding, however, it may be helpful to say some words about structuralism in itself.[16] Structuralism is a method and philosophy developed in the 1940s in France after Ferdinand de Saussure's pioneering studies on linguistics at the beginning of the century—more specifically, after his description of the linguistic sign as the combination of a signifier (sound-image) and a signified (concept). Coined as a method by linguist Roman Jakobson in 1929, structuralism was applied not only to linguistics (Chomsky), but also to anthropology (Radcliffe-Brown, Lévi-Strauss), psychoanalysis (Lacan), literary theory (Barthes), philosophy (early Foucault), and religious studies (Ricoeur) (Caws, 1973, 1997; Leach, 1987; Stiver, 1996).[17]

Essentially, structuralist approaches seek to uncover abstract patterns or regularities that exist behind the empirical, observable variety of human behaviors (languages, rituals, etc.), mental capabilities (cognitive, moral, etc.), or cultural forms (myths, kinship rules, etc.). At the heart of structuralism, then, is the search for universal invariant structures that organize all mental, social, and cultural phenomena. A central assumption of the structuralist method is that these invariant structures are more important, more essential, and more explanatory than the variable forms, which are regarded as contingent cultural artifacts. And this is so, structuralists maintain, because all human phenomena are ultimately a reflection of the fundamental structure of the human mind. As is well known, the structuralist program was guided in many fundamental respects by the Kantian aim of discerning the universal, transcendental, and innate structure of the human mind (Gardner, 1981; R. L. Zimmerman, 1987).

Even at its height, however, structuralism never offered a satisfactory solution to existentialist, methodological, and philosophical critiques from

inside and outside the movement. To begin with, some structuralists themselves considered highly questionable that their methods could be legitimately applied beyond the field of linguistics (Chomsky, 1968), and even
more dubiously to grand-scale cross-cultural comparisons à la Lévi-Strauss
(Leach, 1987). Central to these critiques was the challenge to the structuralist assumption that all symbolic forms such as cultures or religions were types
of language (Caws, 1973). In addition, structuralism was charged with arbitrariness and intuitionism on the assignation of deep structures; lack of verifiability and falsifiability; lack of consensus among structural analyses of same
materials; serious methodological flaws in the selection, reporting, and analyses of data; begging the truth question of its findings; and underestimation of
human freedom and intentionality in favor of anonymous structures as determinants of human expressions (see, e.g., Barrett, 1997; Gardner, 1981; Leach,
1987; Stiver, 1996). Finally, after the poststructuralist reintroduction of the
subject (Derrida), the rise of incredulity towards grand theories (Lyotard),
the self-critical embarrassments of structuralism (Foucault), the emergence
of dialogical paradigms of mutual understanding (Habermas), and the discredit of universalist and objectivist claims (Bernstein), structuralism is generally regarded today as exhausted and misleading, its methods flawed, and its
claims and assumptions unsupported. This is probably why, as Barrett (1997)
puts it, "today the number of prominent anthropologists who continue to
follow structuralism probably could be counted on the fingers of one hand"
(p. 149). The same can be said of the fate of structuralism in almost any other
discipline of knowledge.

However, the fact that structuralism is surely *passé* in contemporary
thought does not automatically invalidate Wilber's approach. To be sure, the
unresolved philosophical and methodological tensions of structuralism suggest that the foundations of Wilber's neoperennialism may be extremely
fragile. But although I think it is important to point out the problematic
assumptions and the obsolete status of the structuralist program, I also believe
that it is necessary to address Wilber's proposal on its own terms. What follows are some of the main problems of Wilber's structuralist account of spiritual development and evolution.[18]

Reification and Elevation of Deep Structures

As we have seen, Wilber claims that the deep structures disclosed by his
structuralist analyses correspond to the metaphysical links of the Great
Chain of Being.[19] By doing so, however, he is not only reifying the results of

a method of analysis, but also elevating them to cosmic and transcendental status. The deep structures are granted not only ontological value, but also supraordinate powers over human affairs (evolutionary stages, developmental levels, religious world views, etc.). Indeed, Wilber claims that the hierarchy of deep structures constitutes a privileged explanatory framework that allows us to understand, assess, and even rank as more or less evolved the diverse spiritual cosmologies and experiences.

Nonetheless, any method of analysis constructs as much as discovers, imposes as much as reveals. Different methods, that is, bring forth different aspects or potential meanings of a given phenomenon: While traditional phenomenology seeks and finds the essences of particular experiences, semantic or critical analyses may reveal important differences in their meaning and function. While structuralism discloses deep commonalities among a diverse set of phenomena, hermeneutics may highlight their culturally and historically situated meaning, and so forth. Depending on the lens we use to look at the religious traditions, we can find either striking parallels or drastic differences among their spiritual paths and goals. But to use an approach that emphasizes similarities is one thing; it is another to insist, as Wilber does, that these similarities not only are more essential than the differences, but also correspond to the ontological levels of the Great Chain of Being and therefore warrant the application of hierarchical rankings and the configuration of a perennial philosophy. This is speculative elevationism of a highly problematic kind.

Notice that I am not saying that it is not possible or valuable to establish structural parallels among spiritual traditions. Actually, I do believe not only that it is possible (spiritual traditions are not incommensurable in any strict form), but also that it can be a feasible starting point for interreligious dialogue and inquiry. However, I do not understand how and why these structural parallels can be reified into a privileged framework that allows us to rank the various spiritual traditions. As I see it, structuralism, like any other method, is not *the* key to the universe, but one of the many avenues from which we can approach, engage, and participate in the inexhaustible Mystery out of which everything arises.

Subtle Objectivism

Closely allied to the above charge is the objectivism implicit in Wilber's claim that deep structures are pregiven: "In my opinion," he tells us, "surface structures are learned, conditioned, historically contingent, and culturally molded, whereas deep structures are cross-cultural, given, transcontingent, and invariant" (1982, p. 87). Or, as he puts it more succinctly, "the deep structures are given, but the surface are not" (Wilber, 1996a, p. 212). This claim should not be surprising. After all, structuralists are heirs of the Cartesian-Kantian legacy and, as Harland (1987) points out, "their stance is still the traditional scientific stance of Objectivity, their goal the traditional scientific goal of Truth" (p. 2).

Interestingly, Wilber (1995) recently adopted several constructivist insights inspired by Varela, Thompson, and Rosch's (1991) enactive paradigm—such as the rejection of the representation paradigm, the challenge to the idea of a pregiven reality, and the notion of enacted worldspaces—that could have potentially emancipated his model from objectivist premises. However, this salutary undertaking immediately comes to a standstill. This becomes clear in his unnecessary subordination of the enactive paradigm to a universal sequence of pregiven evolutionary deep structures. On the one hand, this move obviously betrays the very essence of the enactive paradigm, which was not only devised to provide a "middle way or entre-deux between the extremes of absolutism and nihilism" (Varela, Thompson, & Rosch, 1991, p. 238), but also developed in the context of a view of "evolution by natural drift" that is undeterministic and inimical to any pregiven evolutionary path. On the other hand, this action naturally leads Wilber straightway back to objectivist dungeons and makes him captive of a host of Cartesian tensions and anxieties, such as the perpetuation of false dichotomies between universalism and vulgar relativism (Ferrer, 1998a).

As I see it, it is probable that Wilber's residual objectivism is associated with the universalist vision of spirituality that inspires his thinking. In one of his recent works, for example, he (1995) tells us:

> But to the extent that the contemplative endeavor discloses universal aspects of the Kosmos, then the deep structures of the contemplative traditions (but not their surface structures) would be expected to show cross-cultural similarities at the various levels of depth created/disclosed by the meditative injunctions and paradigms." (p. 276)

This statement is highly revealing. Clearly, it boils down to saying that the deep structures of the different traditions must be common because reality has a single universal structure that can be deciphered through a particular mode of meditative training and spiritual practice.

Essentialism

Once reified into anonymous existents with supraordinate powers, the deep structures are accordingly considered more essential than their surface manifestations. As we have seen, this is one of the central assumptions of the structuralist method, which has been defined in this account as

> the view that structure in this sense is a more fundamental characteristic of the objects it studies (all, it must be noted, products of the human mind or of human culture), than are their physical components, their genetic origins, their historical development, their function or purpose, and so on. (Caws, 1973, p. 322)

Nevertheless, we have already seen, to attribute greater causal, explanatory, or ontological status to what is common upon what is different in a set of phenomena is problematic. As Habermas (1992) puts it speaking about de Saussure's linguistic structuralism: "But structuralism also gets caught in the snare of abstractive fallacies. By elevating anonymous forms of language to a transcendental status, it downgrades the subjects and their speech to something merely accidental" (p. 47).

Self-Refuting Fallacies

Since Foucault's (1970) concluding chapter of his *The Order of Things,* virtually all poststructuralist authors have pointed out that structuralism is self-refuting (see, e.g., Habermas, 1987a, lectures IX and X). If all human expressions (epistemes, behaviors, ideas, etc.) are determined by anonymous deep structures, then the validity of the structuralist approach is relative to the deep structure operating in a specific historical moment—or, if we were to follow here Wilber's logic for a moment, relative to the developmental level of the structuralist thinker in question. In the latter case, unless Wilber claims to be speaking from the highest spiritual structure, the universalist and objectivist truth claims of his integral vision are severely undermined.

Lack of Structuralist Validity

This is a more technical criticism, but an important one whenever one has to assess the validity of any structuralist approach. Essentially, the validity of structural analysis is anchored in the identification of a formal system of rules of transformations (Chomsky's generative grammar, for example) that enable us to operationally establish relations between surface and deep structures (Chomsky, 1965; Lane, 1970). Although apparently aware of this issue (1984, pp. 45–54), Wilber has not yet offered the rules of transformation by means of which he assigns apparently disparate surface structures (e.g., kundalini awakening, nature mysticism) to a single deep structure (e.g., psychic level).[20] If he does operate with any rules at all, he should tell us which ones they are; otherwise his entire structuralist approach rests precariously on his personal preferences and intuitions, which, even if accurate, would not meet structuralist standards of validity and therefore render his perennialist model suspect by his very own terms.

Constraints upon Spiritual Evolution

Since Wilber's deep structures correspond to the immutable levels of the Great Chain of Being, they exist unaffected by historical or existential contingencies. Like the Platonic ideas, the deep structures are eternal, unchanging, and transcendental. But then, the creative power of evolution, although unlimited and unpredictable in terms of novelty and number of different forms (surface structures), is confined by the possibilities of the specific deep structure characteristic of each evolutionary moment. This view results in unnecessary constraints for both spiritual evolution and human spiritual choices. As Heron (1997) puts it: "A theory which tells us that we have surface novelty and also tells us what will deeply and serially constrain it, is taking away much more than it gives. . . . True human novelty is not mere superficial flexibility; it is rooted in creative choice *at depth*, at the level of deep structures themselves" (p. 4). The assumption that deep structures both have a fundamental center and cannot therefore be essentially transformed while operative, has been seriously undermined by most poststructuralist thinkers (see, e.g., Derrida, 1978; Frank, 1989).

Homogenization of Traditions and Resultant "Bad" Hermeneutics

According to Stiver (1996), structuralist methods "cannot easily convey the uniqueness of a particular message, in part because they are geared to the stable and universal structures that are used to state particular messages" (p. 172). In the case of insisting upon the deep structural equivalence of the message of the diverse spiritual traditions, I must add that structuralist analyses not only do not convey the uniqueness of their messages, but also frequently lead to severe distortions of these messages.

As I argue in more detail elsewhere (Ferrer, 1998a), for example, Wilber's treatment of the celebrated Buddhist philosopher Nagarjuna is an outstanding example of how objectivist and universalist premises often hinder an adequate hermeneutic understanding. Briefly, Wilber (1995) equates Nagarjuna's emptiness (*sunyata*) with pure Consciousness (p. 539, note 2); with Absolute reality (pp. 693–694, note 1); with the Suchness of all Forms (p. 693, note 1); with pure Presence (p. 696, note 1); and even suggests that, once the Madhyamaka via negativa is relaxed, Nagarjuna's emptiness can be metaphorically matched with the Hindu Brahman (p. 698, note 1). Furthermore, Wilber (1995) adds, the Buddhist no-self doctrine cannot be literally applied to the Absolute, because both self and nonself "are equally manifestations of the Primordial State, self-cognizing Emptiness and spontaneous luminosity" (p. 706, note 1).

The problem with this interpretation, apart from exclusively relying in Murti's (1955) work, whose Kantian absolutist account of Madhyamaka Buddhism is unanimously regarded today as a paradigmatic example of the projection of Western philosophical notions on Eastern thinking (Hayes, 1994; Huntinchon, 1989; Streng, 1967; Tuck, 1990), is that modern interpreters of Nagarjuna find any form of absolutist account of emptiness (*sunyata*) unacceptable, and in no way grounded on textual evidence. According to Richards (1978), for example, "it is a mistake to subsume the Madhyamika philosophy of Nagarjuna in Advaita Vedanta and thereby to change a dialectical philosophy into an ontology. Equally it would be a mistake to translate *sunyata* into a transcendental absolute such as *Tathagata*" (p. 259). Central to the critiques of this absolutist interpretation is that emptiness (*sunyata*) was explicitly devised to be a via media between absolutism and nihilism, and the reification of any of these extremes is the worst service one can offer to Nagarjuna's intentions. It is in the middle way, between absolutism and nihilism, where the soteriological and transformative power of emptiness (*sunyata*) resides: Suffering results from the reifying tendencies of the mind towards positions and beliefs, and liberation is attained by the avoidance of all views, including the transformation of emptiness (*sunyata*) into another theory or view of reality. In Nagarjuna's own words:

> The Victorious Ones have announced that emptiness is the relinquishing of all views. Those who are possessed of the view of emptiness are said to be incorrigible. (*Mulamadhyamakarikas* 13:8; in Kalupahana, 1986, p. 223)

In sum, emptiness (*sunyata*) is used by Nagarjuna as an antidote to all absolutist and nihilist metaphysical speculation about the ultimate nature of reality. Emptiness (*sunyata*) is neither referring to the ultimate, universal, or
absolute nature of reality nor standing for any philosophical position, dogma,
or view; its ultimate value is not descriptive or explanatory, but pragmatic
and soteriologic (cf., Barnhart, 1994; Garfield, 1994). Therefore, Nagarjuna's
philosophy cannot be consistently interpreted or quoted to support any
absolutist or universalist view of spirituality, least of all one equating emptiness (*sunyata*) with Pure Consciousness, Absolute reality, and the like.

Doctrinal Ranking of Traditions

While claiming to honor all truths, Wilber's neoperennialism arranges the
insights of the various religious traditions according to levels of spiritual
achievement relative to a universal sequence of deep structures: psychic, subtle, causal, and nondual. As we have seen, in Wilber's eyes, this ranking is war-
ranted because these deep structures correspond to the levels of the Great
Chain of Being, levels that consecutively disclose increasing degrees of Being,
Truth, and Value as they approach nondual Spirit. Wilber (1995, 1997a)
believes that different religious traditions are directed to different levels of
the Great Chain of Being, and therefore that we can legitimately compare
them and assess their absolute evolutionary value.

A few examples will help to clarify the nature and implications of these
assumptions. According to Wilber, the highest stages of spiritual development are mainly represented by the nondual insights of Eastern traditions
such as Advaita Vedanta's Atman-Brahman realization (*Brahmajñana*), Mahayana
Buddhism's emptiness (*sunyata*), or Zen's satori. The Neoplatonic, Sufi, and
Christian *unio mystica* with an impersonal One or Godhead is interpreted as
a less complete spiritual attainment corresponding to the causal level. Likewise, Platonic mysticism of the archetypal forms, the Christian *gnosis* (vision
of God), or the kabbalistic *devekut* ("cleaving to God") are manifestations of
a lower subtle level. And the mystical ecstasy characteristic of the Mystery
religions, as well as many indigenous forms of spirituality, belong to an even
inferior psychic level of spiritual insight.

One of the obvious problems of approaching interreligious relations
from a developmental or hierarchical perspective is the justification of criteria
for the ranking of spiritual traditions, teachings, and experiences. According

to Wilber (1993b), a level can be said to be higher or more valuable than another not in a moralistic way, but only in the sense of being more holistic, inclusive, and encompassing (i.e., including the features of the previous level and then adding new ones). In his own words, "as used by the perennial philosophy . . . hierarchy is simply a ranking of orders of events *according to their holistic capacity*" (Wilber, 1993b, p. 215). More precisely, Wilber (1982) offers three criteria for the hierarchical arrangement of deep structures: (1) access: a higher level has access to the lower level and its capacities; (2) development: a higher level emerges later than the lower ones; and (3) Chinese box: a higher level has extra capacities than the previous levels.

To be sure, these criteria are problematic in themselves, especially when offered, as they are by Wilber, as absolute and universal axioms. Even accepting for a moment these criteria, however, we might ask: Does Wilber actually follow them in his arrangement of spiritual traditions? Let us take a brief look, for example, at his judgment of Mahayana Buddhism as higher than theistic forms of Christian mysticism. As we have seen, Wilber regards the realization of Buddhist emptiness (*sunyata*) as spiritually more evolved than visions (low subtle level) or even unions with a personal God (high subtle level). Upon careful examination, however, we find that this ranking does not conform to any of Wilber's own hierarchical criteria. First, Buddhist contemplatives in general do not seem to have ever accessed or reported visions or unions with a personal God, or with any deep structural equivalent (failure of the access criterion). Second, Buddhists' nondual insight does not emerge after having seen or gone through a *unio mystica* with a personal God (failure of the development criterion). And third, Buddhist emptiness (*sunyata*) has no "extra" capacities than the Christian *unio mystica*, or at least no more than the Christian *unio mystica* has in relation to Buddhist emptiness (*sunyata*). But all this should not come as a surprise: After all, there is not room for a creature like a personal God in the Buddhist cosmology. An analogous case can be made, *mutatis mutandis*, for most of Wilber's interreligious assessments.

These problems become heightened when we look at different spiritual biographies. Even the most preliminary study of the biographies of mystics who claim to have participated in both dual and nondual states reveals serious anomalies in Wilber's presumably universal sequence. On the one hand, there are cases which actually do conform to Wilber's scheme. For example, contemporary Christian mystic Bernadette Roberts (1984) claims to have gone from dualistic events to an ultimate nondual insight. On the other hand, however, there is also the testimony of Hindu-oriented mystics such as Swami Abhishiktananda (1974), who claims to have transcended the Advaitic state of nonduality to enter into a more dualistic state of participation in the Holy Trinity.[21] As Comans (1998) puts it: "According to Abhishiktananda, the Christian jñani *goes through* the advaita experience of the non-dual to again recover his own uniqueness in relation to the personal Lord and the world" (p. 114). What the spiritual literature suggests, then, is that neither the order of emergence of dual and nondual insights is preordained nor is their spiritual value universal or pregiven. As Cortright (1997) rightly sums up this issue: "In the spiritual domain a single invariant sequence of development does not appear to exist" (p. 73).

In the light of these anomalies, we can conclude that there are serious problems not only with Wilber's structuralist arrangement of traditions, but also with the very idea of ranking spiritual traditions. On the one hand, it is highly questionable that Wilber's arrangement of these deep structures actually emerges from an impartial analysis of mystical texts and biographies. Like most traditionalist models, Wilber's neoperennialism privileges a nondual spirituality, of which he himself is a practitioner (Wilber, 1999a). This bias leads him ipso facto to prejudge as spiritually less evolved any mystic or tradition that does not seek the attainment of nondual states. On the other hand, the fact that the various mystical traditions consider different insights as the highest, purest, or most complete, suggests that the ranking of mystical experiences may be a doctrinal matter.

We will revisit the very idea of ranking of traditions in chapter 7, when we explore the implications of the participatory turn for spiritual studies. Here, I would like to conclude this chapter exploring the relationship between the perennial philosophy, transpersonal theory, and the experiential vision.

TRANSPERSONAL THEORY AND THE PERENNIAL PHILOSOPHY

As we have seen, a significant number of transpersonal scholars have taken for granted the universalist account of spirituality espoused by the perennial philosophy. But, one might rightfully ask, given the obvious problems inherent in its tenets and assumptions, why have transpersonal theorists embraced so uncritically the perennial vision? In the remainder of this chapter, I attempt to answer this fundamental question. When considering the relationship between transpersonal theory and the perennial philosophy, however, it should be evident that any monocausal explanation would surely be too simple to explain fully such a complex phenomenon. Therefore, I would like first to discuss several contextual factors that contributed in important ways to this association, and then suggest what I believe is the main conceptual reason for the persistence of perennialism in transpersonal scholarship.

MASLOW, WILBER, AND TRANSPERSONAL SCHOLARSHIP

The first contextual factor has to do with the historical roots of the transpersonal movement. As I suggested in chapter 2, the perennialist dispositions of transpersonal psychology can be traced to the very birthplace of the transpersonal orientation: Maslow's seminal works on self-actualization and peak-experiences. Maslow (1970) equated peak-experiences with what he called the "core-religious experience" (i.e., the essential, intrinsic, and fundamental transcendent experience that he believed could be found at the heart of all religious traditions). Maslow's most clear perennialist manifesto can be read in chapter 3 of his *Religions, Values, and Peak-Experiences* (1970), aptly entitled "The 'Core-Religious,' or 'Transcendent,' Experience." In this influential essay, he writes: "To the extent that all mystical or peak-experiences are the same in their essence and have always been the same, all religions are the same in their essence and always have been the same" (p. 20). And he adds: "This private religious experience [the peak-experience] is shared by all great religions including the atheistic ones like Buddhism, Taoism, Humanism, or Confucianism" (p. 28). In Maslow's views about the nature of peak-experiences, then, we find not only the seeds of the experiential vision, but also the origins of the continuing relation between transpersonal theory and a universalist view of spirituality. Transpersonal theory was born in a perennialist world.

A second factor behind the perennialist flavor of transpersonal scholarship may be found in the strong influence of Wilber's thinking in transpersonal circles (see, e.g., Rothberg & Kelly, 1998; Rowan, 1993; Walsh & Vaughan, 1994). As we have seen, for Wilber (1994), "the aim of transpersonal psychology . . . is to give a psychological presentation of the perennial philosophy and the Great Chain of Being, fully updated and grounded in modern research and scientific developments" (p. x). The impact of Wilber's ideas upon transpersonal studies is general knowledge and does not need further justification. Only to quote a recent example, three issues of the journal

ReVision—one of the most important forums of transpersonal scholarship—have been exclusively devoted to discussing one of his latest works (for a compilation of these issues, see Rothberg & Kelly, 1998). Wilber's contemporary articulation of the perennial vision is broad and logically compelling, and it is not surprising that it has gained many followers in transpersonal circles.

I believe that a third factor can be found in the rather isolated manner in which the transpersonal field has developed until very recently. To be sure, many transpersonalists have been in dialogue (and sometimes fierce debate) with other psychological schools, and have studied, with more or less depth, some Western, Eastern, and indigenous spiritual traditions. However, transpersonal scholars have generally overlooked important developments in related fields such as comparative mysticism, cross-cultural philosophy of religion, East-West hermeneutics, or interreligious dialogue, all of which started with universalistic assumptions and aspirations, but gradually moved to more dialogical, hermeneutic, and pluralist approaches (see, e.g., Byrne, 1995; Clarke, 1997; Dean, 1995; Deutsch, 1991; Heim, 1995; Knitter, 1985; Min, 1997; Vroom, 1989; Wiggins, 1996). The following statement by Knitter illustrates the increasing awareness of a plurality of spiritual worlds emerging in the contemporary interreligious dialogue:

> Like a newly married couple growing out of the first stages of infatuation into real living together, partners in religious sharing, as they get to know each other, soon arrive at the existential realization of how bewilderingly different they are. What had been initially experienced as similarities now become differing, even opposing, faces. . . . One gradually becomes aware of the naivete and the downright danger of proclaiming a "common essence" or a "common core" within all the religions of the world . . . but right now, in the dust and dirt of the real world, we have to deal with the manyness, the differences, among the religions before we can ever contemplate, much less realize, their possible unity or oneness. (In Wiggins, 1996, p. 86)

Had the transpersonal orientation been more in touch with these disciplines, it is probable that perennialism would have been questioned before and that transpersonalists would have felt more encouraged to explore alternative visions for understanding interreligious relations and the nature of spiritual phenomena.

Although important, however, I believe that these factors represent only part, and by no means the whole, of the story. These factors may help to explain, for example, why early transpersonal psychology inherited a universalist agenda, and how these perennialist dispositions were subsequently reinforced throughout the history of the transpersonal movement. But I do not think that the fact that perennialism has been so easily, so uncritically, and so eagerly maintained and defended by so many transpersonal authors for more than thirty years of research and scholarship can be satisfactorily explained by appealing merely to historical reasons. There is something truly perplexing about it, and to find the missing central piece of the puzzle we have to go back, I believe, to the experiential vision.

THE PERENNIAL PHILOSOPHY AND THE EXPERIENTIAL VISION

In this section, I would like to discuss what I believe is the main reason for the adhesion of transpersonal scholars to perennialism, a reason that, in my opinion, may also be behind both Maslow's early perennialism and the wide acceptance of Wilber's ideas in the transpersonal community. What I would like to suggest here is that *there is a relation of mutual influence between the experiential vision and the perennial philosophy.*[22] In other words, I believe that, against the background of certain Cartesian assumptions, the experiential vision decisively contributed to the long-standing acceptance of the perennial vision in the transpersonal community. And conversely, that the universalist premises of early transpersonal theory influenced and reinforced, in turn, an experiential understanding of transpersonal and spiritual phenomena. Let us take a closer view at each one of these relations.

On the one hand, I am suggesting that the experiential vision is one of the main determinants of the transpersonal commitment to the perennial philosophy. As we have seen, the humanistic and transpersonal turn to experience stems not only from the rightful endeavor of reclaiming human inner life as a valuable source of knowledge, but also from the attempt to legitimize transpersonal psychology as an empirical, and therefore scientific, discipline of knowledge. Therefore, we have seen too, transpersonal theorists generally attempt to justify spiritual knowledge claims appealing to an inner empiricism whose validity is essentially anchored in inner replicability and intersubjective agreement (see chapter 3). But what transpersonalists did not foresee is that the acceptance of these experiential and consensual premises would force them to make a premature commitment to the universalism of the perennial philosophy. That is, *once a consensual theory of truth for the validity of spiritual and transpersonal experiences was posited, a universalist vision of spirituality was made nearly imperative.* If there is not a perennial philosophy, transpersonalists may have feared, if there is not a unity in mysticism and a consensus about the world view that spiritual experiences convey, then transpersonal and spiritual knowledge claims would run the risk of being charged again with subjectivism, solipsism, or even seen as pathological. Of course, it needs to be added, considering the intellectual climate of the late 1960s, 1970s, and even 1980s, there were actually grounds for these worries. Both the modern marginalization of spirituality as subjective and epistemically sterile, and the view of valid knowledge as essentially objective and public, were still widely accepted during those years and made these concerns inevitable and justified.

The problem with these anxieties, of course, is that they only arise in the context of objectivist epistemologies. In other words, the accusation of subjectivism only troubles those who accept objectivist standards of knowledge. It only affects those who still believe that valid knowledge needs to be purely objective, that is, grounded in the structure of a pregiven reality that exists independently of the human psyche. What I am suggesting here is that behind worries of falling into subjectivism lurks necessarily a tacit commitment to a Cartesian epistemology and model of cognition. However, as we have seen, Cartesianism should be precisely one of the targets of transpersonal theory: To talk of objectivism in the context of transpersonal theory— and probably in any other discipline as well—is not only confusing but also inadequate, and ultimately undermines the transpersonal perspective itself, whose central claim is that human consciousness (so-called human subjectivity) can expand to include other elements of life and cosmos (the so-called objective universe).

On the other hand, I am also proposing that the universalist agenda of the early transpersonalists influenced in turn their commitment to the experiential vision. As we have seen, Maslow's perennialism rests on a sharp distinction between a core-religious experience (the peak-experience), which was universal and unmediated, and its interpretation, which was contextual and mediated.[23] Faced with the evident diversity of mystical conceptions and cosmologies, many transpersonalists adopted Maslow's defense of the unity of the human spirit in terms of an experiential mystical core, that is, a nonconceptual direct apprehension of reality which is free from cultural influences and doctrinal "dogmas."[24] In the context of the world spiritual traditions, that is, the universalist leitmotif of Maslow's approach to humanistic psychology naturally took the shape of an experiential perennialism.[25] In sum, the experiential and universalistic premises of humanistic psychology reinforced each

other and led transpersonal psychology to embrace and maintain a perennialist vision of spirituality for decades.

SUMMARY AND CONCLUSIONS

The humanistic origins of transpersonal theory, with the universalistic impetus of Maslow's work, along with the ecumenical spirit of the 1960s and
1970s, were fertile soil in which perennialist ideas naturally propagated in
transpersonal circles. As we have seen, faced with the plurality of spiritual
world views, on the one hand, and bewitched by objectivist spells, on the
other, transpersonalists defended the spiritual unity of humanity in the form
of an experiential or structuralist perennialism. If transpersonal and spiritual
claims were to be recognized as valid and scientific, transpersonalists believed,
they had to be shown to be universal, and this spiritual consensus could only
be found either in an artificially constructed core-religious experience (à la
Maslow) or in abstract and anonymous deep structures (à la Wilber). In other
words, *objectivist assumptions made the legitimization of transpersonal psychology
dependent upon the truth of the perennial philosophy.*

In this chapter, however, we have seen that the perennial vision suffers
from several basic tensions and shortcomings. These include an a priori
commitment to a nondual monistic metaphysics and an endorsement of
objectivism and essentialism in knowledge claims about ultimate reality. We
also noted that Wilber's structuralist account of the perennial philosophy is
subject to a number of problems and weaknesses, such as elevationism and
essentialism, lack of structuralist validity, "bad" hermeneutics, and arbitrariness in the ranking of traditions. Taken together, these claims and presuppositions not only predispose toward subtle forms of religious exclusivism and
intolerance, but also hinder spiritual inquiry and limit the range of valid spiritual choices through which we can creatively participate in the Mystery out
of which everything arises.

For these reasons, I suggest that the exclusive commitment of transpersonal theory to the perennial philosophy would be detrimental to its continued creative vitality. To put it somewhat dramatically, perennialism was a
comfortable home for transpersonal theory for some time, but this home has
become a prison, and many of its prisoners agoraphobic. It may be time for
transpersonal theory to become self-critical of its own assumptions, and
explore alternative visions to the perennial philosophy to approach the
nature of both human spirituality and interreligious relations.

Before concluding this chapter, I would like to point out that my intention has not been to refute the perennial philosophy. Rather, my main purpose has been to highlight the tacit commitment of transpersonal theory to the perennial philosophy, and suggest the potential limitations of this adherence by describing the fundamental assumptions and pitfalls of perennialism. It is my hope that the exposition and airing of the presuppositions of perennialism will help create an open space in which transpersonal theory need not subordinate alternative perspectives but can enter into genuine engagement and a fertile dialogue with them.

I need to stress here, however, that I personally believe not only that the ecumenical search for common ground is an important and worthy enterprise, but also that some perennialist claims are plausible and may prove to be valid. At least, I have the conviction that it is possible to identify certain elements common to most contemplative traditions (some form of attentional training, certain ethical guidelines, an intentional moving away from self-centeredness, a sense of the sacred, etc.).

Nevertheless, I also believe that to assume the essential unity of mysticism paradoxically can betray the truly essential message of the different spiritual traditions. Perhaps the longed-for spiritual unity of humankind can only be found in the multiplicity of its voices. If there is a perennial philosophy, this needs to be established on the basis of interreligious inquiry and dialogue, and not presumed as an unassailable axiom from which inquiry must depart and to which dialogue must lead. And if there is not a perennial philosophy, this is no reason to despair. As we will see in Part II of this book, once we give up the Cartesian assumptions of the experiential vision, alternatives to perennialism naturally emerge that allow us to look at the transpersonal project with refreshed eyes: eyes that discern that transpersonal theory does not need the perennial philosophy as its fundamental metaphysical framework; eyes that appreciate and honor the multiplicity of ways in which the sense of the sacred can be not only conceptualized, but also intentionally cultivated, embodied, and lived; eyes that recognize, in short, that the sacred need not be univocally universal to be sacred.

PART II

RECONSTRUCTION

Part II of this book introduces a participatory vision of human spirituality alternative to the perennialism and experientialism prevalent in transpersonal theory. Chapter 5 (The Participatory Nature of Spiritual Knowing) outlines the main epistemic features of this participatory turn and shows how they not only overcome the limitations of the experiential vision, but also situate transpersonal studies in greater alignment with the aims of the spiritual quest. Chapter 6 (An Ocean with Many Shores: The Challenge of Spiritual Pluralism) unpacks the metaphysics of the participatory vision and provides a pluralistic understanding of spiritual knowledge, spiritual liberation, and spiritual ultimates. Chapter 7 (After the Participatory Turn) explores some of the emancipatory implications of the participatory turn for interreligious relations, transpersonal developmental models, the problem of conflicting truth-claims in religion, the validity of spiritual truths, the problem of mediation in spiritual knowledge, and spiritual liberation. Chapter 8 (A More Relaxed Spiritual Universalism) presents the kind of spiritual universalism implicit in the participatory vision and offers some concluding reflections on the dialectic between universalism and pluralism, between the One and the Many, in the creative unfolding of Spirit.

5

THE PARTICIPATORY NATURE

OF SPIRITUAL KNOWING

Spiritual knowing is a participatory event: It can involve the creative participation of not only our minds, but also our hearts, bodies, souls, and most vital essence. Furthermore, spiritual energies are not confined to our inner world, but can also flow out of relationships, communities, and even places. In this chapter, I describe these basic features of spiritual knowing, and show how a participatory understanding naturally helps us avoid the dangers of spiritual narcissism and integrative failure as described in chapter 2. I also suggest that this participatory account is more consistent with the view of spiritual knowing embraced by most contemplative traditions.

AFTER THE DECONSTRUCTION carried out in Part I of this book, the more challenging task of reconstruction is called for. As I have suggested, the main aim of this task should be to develop a framework that is no longer limited by the objectivist and individualistic premises that dominate modern transpersonal studies. In Part II of this book, I want to propose that this reconstruction is possible, and that it needs to take the form of a participatory turn (i.e., a radical shift of emphasis from intrasubjective experiences to participatory events in our understanding of transpersonal and spiritual phenomena). In this chapter, then, I offer a very general sketch of the main epistemic features of the participatory vision, and in the following chapters I spell out some of its main metaphysical and spiritual implications.

THE PARTICIPATORY TURN

As we have seen, transpersonal phenomena dismantle the intentional structure inherent in the modern notion of experience. Both the Cartesian subject and the Cartesian object, as grammatical as well as experiential categories, are rendered implausible by the very nature of transpersonal phenomena. In the wake of the nonintentional nature of transpersonal phenomena, it becomes imperative to go beyond the modern notion of experience and reframe our understanding of transpersonal phenomena in a way that does not connote intentionality.

But to take this alternative path leaves us in an even more perplexing predicament. If transpersonal and spiritual phenomena are not intrasubjective experiences, what in the world are they? Briefly, I want to propose that transpersonal phenomena can be more adequately understood as *multilocal participatory events* (i.e., *emergences of transpersonal being that can occur not only in the locus of an individual, but also in a relationship, a community, a collective identity, or a place*). In other words, I am suggesting that what has been commonly called a transpersonal experience can be better conceived as the emergence of a transpersonal participatory event. The basic idea underlying the participatory turn, then, is not that an expansion of individual consciousness allows access to transpersonal contents, but rather that the emergence of a transpersonal event precipitates in the individual what has been called a transpersonal experience. Thus understood, the ontological dimension of transpersonal phenomena is primary and results in the experiential one. Transpersonal experiences do not lead to transpersonal knowledge, but rather transpersonal participatory events elicit in the individual what have been commonly called transpersonal experiences.[1]

It goes without saying that I am not denying the existence of an intrasubjective dimension in transpersonal phenomena. On the contrary, the emergence of a transpersonal event in the locus of an individual demands the participation of his or her consciousness. However, the participatory vision reframes this experiential dimension as the participation of an individual consciousness in a transpersonal event. What the participatory vision radically rejects is the anthropocentric, and ultimately egocentric, move to infer from this participation that transpersonal phenomena are essentially human inner experiences. As virtually all mystical traditions maintain, spiritual phenomena are not to be understood merely in phenomenological terms, but rather as stemming from the human participation in spheres of being and awareness that transcend the merely human. Listen, for example, to St. John of the Cross (1979) concerning the union of the human soul with God:

> When God grants this supernatural favor to the soul, so great a union is caused that all the things of both *God and the soul become one in participant transformation*, and the soul appears to be God more than a soul. Indeed, *it is God by participation*. Yet truly, its being (even though transformed) is naturally as distinct from God as it was before, just as the window, although illumined by the ray, has being distinct from the ray's. (pp. 117–118; italics added)

In other words, the participatory vision is reacting against intrasubjective reductionism, that is to say, the reduction of transpersonal and spiritual phenomena to the status of individual inner experiences.

Let us now have a closer look at this view of transpersonal phenomena as *multilocal participatory events*. The participatory vision conceives transpersonal phenomena as (1) *events,* in contrast to intrasubjective experiences; (2) *multilocal*, in that they can arise in different loci, such as an individual, a relationship, a community, a collective identity, or a place; and (3) *participatory*, in that they can invite the generative power and dynamism of all dimensions of human nature to interact with a spiritual power in the cocreation of spiritual worlds. In the remainder of this section, I attempt to clarify these three features, and, in a following section, I indicate how they help us to avert the limitations of the experiential vision.

TRANSPERSONAL PHENOMENA AS EVENTS

The participatory vision regards transpersonal phenomena as events, rather than as inner experiences.[2] In order to clarify the contrast between experiences and events, I would like to draw an analogy with the celebration of a party. A party is a participatory celebration of life and of the other. A party is not anyone's property because it cannot be possessed. A party "occurs" whenever a certain combination of elements comes together, and the most we can do to facilitate it is to optimize these conditions. We can, for example, get psychologically ready for celebration; dress in a more festive, elegant, or colorful manner; invite open, interesting, or like-minded people; arrange special and vivid decoration; cook succulent and nurturing food; or prepare games, rituals, or activities that promote self-expression, mutual participation, and openness to life energies. A party can also occur spontaneously, for example, out of the fortuitous encounter of several old friends in a café. An important point to notice is that both external and internal conditions seem to be important for participating in a party. As we know so well, if for some reason we feel detached or closed towards others or life energies, even the most festive environment will not be a party for us. Therefore, a party is neither objective nor subjective, but rather a participatory phenomenon. A party is not an intrasubjective experience, but an experiential event in which we can participate given the presence of certain external and internal conditions.

In drawing this analogy, I want to suggest that transpersonal phenomena are like a party in the sense that they are not individual inner experiences but participatory events; they are neither objective nor subjective; they cannot be possessed (they are not anyone's property); they can be optimized but never forced; and they can emerge spontaneously with the coming together of certain conditions.[3]

Let us look now at the implications of this distinction between experiences and events for our understanding of spiritual phenomena, for example, the visionary transfiguration of the world that occurs in nature mysticism. In nature mysticism, as well as during certain ritual uses of entheogens, the natural world can be drastically transformed and unfold with an exalted quality of depth, pregnant meaning, profound numinosity, luscious Life, and sacred Mystery. In the context of the participatory vision, *this transfiguration of the world is not seen as a mere change in our individual experience of a pregiven world, but as the emergence of an ontological event in reality in which our consciousness creatively participates.* In other words, it is not so much our experience of the world that changes, but rather our experience-and-the-world that undergo a mutually codetermined transformation.

The idea of transpersonal and spiritual phenomena as participatory events is consistent with Gadamer's (1990) notion of truth as an event of self-disclosure of Being. For Gadamer, truth should not be understood as correspondence with ahistorical facts or experiences, but as an ontological "happening" of Being in the locus of human historical existence. In Gadamer's words: "Being is self-presentation and . . . all understanding is an event" (p. 484). In his discussion of Gadamer's notion of truth, Carpenter (1995) points out that: "As an event, truth is something one experiences. But this experience (in the sense of the German *Erfahrung*) cannot be understood as simply 'subjective' experience (*Erlebnis*), since all experience is a part of the historical context in which it occurs" (p. 195).[4]

TRANSPERSONAL PHENOMENA AS MULTILOCAL

In contrast to the individualist focus of the experiential vision, the participatory vision recognizes that transpersonal phenomena are multilocal in that they can occur not only in an individual, but also in a relationship, a community, a collective identity, or a place.

To offer an adequate explanation of the multilocal nature of transpersonal events goes beyond the scope of this section, so I will merely indicate here that this notion finds extensive support in the world's spiritual literature. First, we are indebted to Martin Buber (1970) for having offered one of the most compelling expositions of a relational understanding of spirituality. In his shift from a mystical conception of spirituality—centered on individual inner experiences (*Erlebnis*)—to a dialogical one—geared to the intersubjective and the community (*Gemeinschaft*)—Buber (1970) proposes that the true place of spiritual realization is not the individual experience, but the community, the Between. In Buber's (1970) words: "Spirit is not in the I but between I and you, it is not like the blood that circulates you, but like the air in which you breathe" (p. 89). Or as Mendes-Flohr (1989) puts it summarizing Buber's views: "The realm of the Between, that which establishes 'authentic' *Gemeinschaft*, is the locus of God's realization" (p. 115). And this community (*Gemeinschaft*), said Buber, "is an event that arises out of the Center between men" (quoted in Mendes-Flohr, 1989, p. 117). It is important to stress than Buber is not talking in metaphoric terms. For Buber, the realm of the Between or the interhuman (*das Zwischenmenschliche*) has an extramental, independent ontological status, and it is precisely this realm, not the one of individual inner experience, that is the locus of genuine spiritual realization.[5]

Second, communal spiritual events have also been frequently reported in the religious literature. This is the case in the Christian tradition, for example, with the descent of the Holy Spirit on the apostles at Pentecost or their communion with God at the Eucharist. As Johnston (1995) points out, "all through The Acts of the Apostles we find the Spirit descending on the group, communicating gifts and filling all with his presence" (p. 214). Communal spiritual events are also well known in other spiritual systems, as illustrated by the first phase of the Sinai revelation of God to the people of Israel,[6] the dance of the Whirling Dervishes in the Melveli Sufi order, or the ayahuasca ceremonies in certain South American native traditions.

Third, transpersonal events can also occur in the locus of collective identities, such as the ones that can emerge from archetypal, phylogenetic, ancestral, racial, or cultural morphic fields. Integrating and creatively expanding the work of Grof (1985, 1988) and Sheldrake (1981, 1988), Bache (2000) argues that many of the transpersonal experiences that occur in psychedelic sessions need to be understood as involving not only individual human consciousness, but also larger fields of conscious identities that "include knowing, planning, and innovating" (p. 80). Talking about the participation in the homo sapiens species-mind, for example, he tells us:

> the experience is not one of becoming something other than what we are, but rather of reaching into deeper levels of what we already are. We do not take on the species-mind, but rather we open to that part of our being where we already are the species-mind. (p. 81)

Finally, there also exists a vast literature on sacred places, places identified by religious traditions as being particularly charged with spiritual power or presence (Eliade, 1959; Olsen, 1996; Swan, 1990, 1991). Every spiritual tradition has one or more sacred places whose special spiritual quality makes them privileged locations for ritualistic and religious practices such as, for instance, purification and healing, prayer and contemplation, vision quests and pilgrimages, or, more generally, spiritual renewal. Examples of these sacred places, by which even the modern self feels captivated, include Palenque, Mount Arafat, Delphi, Mecca, Mount Sinai, and Lourdes, among many others. Although clothed in experiential language, the following passage by Swan (1988) is revealing of the nature of sacred places: "If we find that many people, regardless of cultural heritage or prior awareness of the 'power' of a place, go to that place and have a transpersonal experience there, then perhaps we can begin to better understand why shamans revere the so-called places of power" (p. 22).

I conclude this section with the words of Joan Halifax (1998), who beautifully captures the essence of this expanded understanding of spirituality: "I hesitate calling myself spiritual," she tells us, "my sense is that the spiritual flows between beings, be they with humans or other beings" (p. 8).

TRANSPERSONAL PHENOMENA AS PARTICIPATORY

The most important feature of transpersonal events is that they are participatory. In this context, the term *participatory* has three different but equally important meanings. First, participatory alludes to the fact that, after the break with Cartesianism, transpersonal events—and the knowledge they usually convey—can no longer be objective, neutral, or merely cognitive. On the contrary, *transpersonal events engage human beings in a participatory, connected, and often passionate knowing that can involve not only the opening of the mind, but also of the body, the heart, and the soul.* Although transpersonal events may involve only certain dimensions of human nature, all dimensions can potentially come into play in the act of *participatory knowing,* from somatic transfiguration to the awakening of the heart, from erotic communion to visionary cocreation, and from contemplative knowing to moral insight, to mention only a few.

Second, participatory refers to the role that individual consciousness plays during transpersonal events. This relation is not one of appropriation, possession, or passive representation of knowledge, but of *communion* and *cocreative participation.* As we will see, this participatory character of transpersonal knowing has profound implications for spiritual epistemology and metaphysics.

Finally, participatory also refers to the fundamental ontological predicament of human beings in relation to spiritual energies and realities. Human beings are—whether they know it or not—always participating in the self-disclosure of Spirit by virtue of their very existence. This participatory predicament is not only the ontological foundation of the other forms of participation, but also the epistemic anchor of spiritual knowledge claims and the moral source of responsible action.

THE NATURE OF PARTICIPATORY KNOWING

It is fundamental to stress that whenever I talk in the following pages about participatory knowing, this should not be understood as if I were talking exclusively of a mental, intellectual, or cognitive activity. Far from that. As used in this work, *participatory knowing refers to a multidimensional access to reality that includes not only the intellectual knowing of the mind, but also the emotional and empathic knowing of the heart, the sensual and somatic knowing of the body, the visionary and intuitive knowing of the soul, as well as any other way of knowing available to human beings.*[7] As Chirban (1986) points out in his discussion of Eastern Orthodox Christianity, for example:

> The [spiritual] knowledge about which the Fathers speak is more than intellectual; it is moral, affective, experiential, ontological. . . . Intellectual knowledge alone is viewed as placing limitations upon the subject and object. So,

even a superior degree of knowledge (as conceptual and intellectual) remains partial without the moral, affective and experiential. True understanding comes from the dynamics of all these dimensions. (p. 294)

For St. Basil, he adds: "'knowing' God occurs by participation in the 'true life . . . returning to the original good.' In this participation God offers 'intimacy,' a result of our 'affective' and 'moral' knowledge of God" (p. 304).

In this chapter, I am going to outline the basic features of participatory knowing, and suggest how they can help us not only to overcome the limitations of the experiential vision, but also to reconnect transpersonal studies with spiritual goals. The practical ways in which these features impact transpersonal and spiritual studies will become clear in the following chapters, so I appeal here to the patience of the reader while reading the following, admittedly sketchy and somewhat abstract, exposition.

Briefly, transpersonal phenomena are participatory events that involve ways of knowing that are presential, enactive, and transformative. Let us look at each of these features one by one.

1. *Participatory knowing is presential:* Participatory knowing is knowing by presence or by identity. In other words, in a transpersonal event, knowing occurs by virtue of being. To be sure, it may be tempting to explain this knowing by saying that "one knows X by virtue of being X." However, this account is misleading because it suggests a knowing subject and a known object, the very epistemic categories that transpersonal events so drastically dismantle. Faced with the difficulties of adequately expressing presential knowing, many mystics devised a new mode of discourse—the via negativa or apophatic language—which allowed them to convey the nonintentional nature of their realizations through a displacement of the grammatical object of their locutions (Sells, 1994). At this point, I choose to depict presential knowing as knowing by virtue of being.

At any rate, what should be clear here is that participatory knowing is not geared to a Cartesian subject-object model of cognition. In contrast to traditional epistemologies, participatory knowledge is not knowledge of something by someone. Rather, participatory knowledge is lived as the emergence of an embodied presence pregnant with meaning that transforms both self and world. We could say, then, that *subject and object, knowing and being, epistemology and ontology, are brought together in the very act of participatory knowing.*

2. *Participatory knowing is enactive:* Following the groundbreaking work of Maturana and Varela (1987), and Varela, Thompson, and Rosch (1991), the participatory vision embraces an enactive paradigm of cognition.[8] Participatory knowing, then, is not a mental representation of pregiven, independent spiritual objects, but an enaction, the bringing forth of a world or domain of distinctions cocreated by the different elements involved in the participatory event. Some central elements of transpersonal and spiritual participatory events include individual intentions and dispositions; cultural, religious, and historical horizons; archetypal and subtle energies; and, as we will see, an indeterminate and dynamic spiritual power of inexhaustible creativity.

The enactive nature of participatory knowing is crucial for its emancipatory power.[9] Were the participatory vision to embrace a representational paradigm of cognition—according to which knowledge is the inner subjective representation of an independent objective reality—it would automatically relapse into the Cartesianism of the experiential vision and be burdened by many of its maladies. Contra Rorty (1979) and Habermas (1987a), however, not all epistemic discourse can be assimilated to foundationalist, objectivist, or representational frameworks. Participatory knowing, we will see in the next chapters, is not necessarily afflicted by the problems of Cartesian modes of consciousness.

3. *Participatory knowing is transformative:* Participatory knowing is transformative at least in the following two senses. First, the participation in a transpersonal event brings forth the transformation of self and world. And second, a transformation of self is usually necessary to be able to participate in transpersonal knowing, and this knowing, in turn, draws forth the self through its transformative process in order to make possible this participation.

The transformative quality of the human participation in transpersonal and spiritual phenomena has been observed by a number of modern consciousness researchers (e.g., Grof, 1985, 1988; Harman, 1994) and scholars of mysticism (e.g., Barnard, 1994, Staal, 1975). One needs to be willing to be personally transformed in order to access and fully understand most spiritual phenomena. The epistemological significance of such personal transformation cannot be emphasized enough, especially given that the positivist denial of such a requisite is clearly one of the main obstacles for the epistemic legitimization of transpersonal and spiritual claims in the modern West. As Evans (1993) points out, one of the main dogmas of skepticism concerning spiritual realities what he calls "impersonalism": "the dogmatic rejection of any truth claim that requires personal transformation to be adequately understood and appraised" (p. 101).

THE EMANCIPATORY VALUE OF THE PARTICIPATORY TURN

One the main advantages of this participatory account is that it radically undermines most of the shortcomings of the experiential vision, such as intrasubjective reductionism, subtle Cartesianism, spiritual narcissism, and integrative arrestment. Let us briefly look at how the participatory vision counteracts these limitations.

INTRASUBJECTIVE REDUCTIONISM

A multilocal conception of transpersonal phenomena is clearly inimical to the intrasubjective reductionism of the experiential vision. If transpersonal phenomena can occur not only in the individual, but also in relationships, communities, collective identities, and places, then their confinement to the realm of individual inner experience must be both inadequate and erroneous. As we have seen, modernity regarded spiritual phenomena as individual inner experiences without epistemic value. We have also seen how transpersonal theory, although reclaiming the epistemic status of spiritual phenomena, is still committed in several fundamental respects to the modern interpretation of spirituality as primarily private and individual. In affirming the multilocality of transpersonal events, the participatory vision gives the second, and perhaps final, step towards the emancipation of spirituality from this restrictive space. As our example of the visionary transfiguration of the world illustrates, in maintaining that transpersonal events are multilocal, the participatory vision frees Spirit from its inner and individualistic constraints, and extends its reach to the entire universe—from which, of course, it never actually departed.

SUBTLE CARTESIANISM

To view transpersonal phenomena as participatory events rather than as intrasubjective experiences eradicates subtle Cartesianism at its roots. As we have seen, events in which human beings participate are neither of something or by someone, nor can they be understood as objective or subjective. In addition, the presential and enactive nature of transpersonal knowing maintained by the participatory vision averts the structuration of transpersonal phenomena in terms of a subject knowing or having experiences of transpersonal objects. To regard transpersonal phenomena as nonintentional events in which human beings can participate, then, effectively shortcircuits transpersonal theory's commitment to a Cartesian model of cognition.

Spiritual Narcissism

To draw transpersonal and spiritual phenomena out of the realm of inner experience is to pull them out of the domain where the ego believes itself sovereign and relentlessly struggles to dominate. And in doing so, I believe, the participatory vision thwarts to a large extent the illegitimate egoic appropriation of spirituality that I have called spiritual narcissism. Furthermore, the understanding of transpersonal phenomena as events undermines these distorted forms of spiritual participation insofar as, in contrast to intrasubjective experiences, events are not things that the ego can have or take possession of. Since the most the ego can do is to participate in the event, the chances of egoic appropriation of spiritual energies are substantially diminished.

Integrative Arrestment

The integrative arrestment typical of the experiential vision is also undermined because, understood in terms of participatory knowing rather than of transient experiences, transpersonal events can be lived as realizations that, once learned, transform how we see ourselves and guide our actions in the world. As Amis (1995) puts it in regard to spiritual knowledge (logos, *gnosis*) in esoteric Christianity: "This special kind of knowledge has the power to create this special kind of discrimination. Having the right knowledge, we become able to make the right choice" (p. 76). A series of compelling and evocative examples of the transforming power of spiritual insights in our times can be found in Ring's (1998) recent study on the existential consequences of near-death experiences (NDEs).[10] What is more, as we will see in the next section, the participatory vision helps us reconnect the transpersonal enterprise with contemplative goals and values. In doing so, it offers a more adequate framework for understanding the nature of spirituality and for fostering the integration of transpersonal and spiritual events in everyday life.

In addition to these gains, the participatory vision releases transpersonal studies from the *dualism between experience and knowledge*, according to which transpersonal experiences lead to transpersonal knowledge. From this participatory viewpoint, this dualism is seen as not only unnecessary, but also misleading and problematic. It is unnecessary because what has been called a transpersonal experience is now better understood as the participation of an individual consciousness in a transpersonal event. It is misleading because it suggests the centrality of human individual experience in spiritual phenomena, overlooking both the multilocal nature of transpersonal events and the transhuman sources of spiritual creativity. And it is problematic because this dualism engenders the problems of epistemic mediation and construction, objectivism and subjectivism, and absolutism and relativism, intrinsic to any Cartesian-Kantian model of knowledge and cognition. In the next two chapters, I show in some detail how the participatory vision frees us from these epistemological myths and dissolves their pernicious implications.

To conclude this section, I would like to raise and respond to a possible objection to the emancipatory value of the participatory vision. It may be argued that, although the participatory vision can free us, in theory, from Cartesianism, it cannot fulfill its promises in practice because the subject-object duality cannot be solved through any type of formal model or discourse, but can only be transcended in the territory of human life. This seems to be, for example, Wilber's (1997b) view on this matter, who points out that the subject-object dualism can only be overcome in postformal stages of consciousness development. I totally agree with the spirit of this remark: The value of non-Cartesian frameworks is close to nothing if they merely become new "theories" for the Cartesian ego. However, I should add that different metaphors and conceptual frameworks can either perpetuate Cartesian consciousness or promote its transcendence. For the reasons espoused above, I firmly believe that the participatory vision is a powerful tool for fostering such a transformation.

PARTICIPATORY KNOWING AND THE SPIRITUAL QUEST

Having shown how the participatory vision prunes many of the adverse ramifications of the modern experiential understanding of transpersonal phenomena, I want to suggest now that it is also more harmonious with the spiritual goals of the contemplative traditions. This point is extremely important because, in my opinion, transpersonal studies should not be dissociated from the spiritual quest, but rather be in the service of the spiritual transformation of self, relationships, and world.

In brief, the participatory turn situates transpersonal studies in greater alignment with the spiritual quest because the aim of most contemplative traditions is not "to have experiences," but rather to realize and participate in special states of discernment. In this account, William James's (1902/1961) often quoted words are quite pertinent: "Although so similar to states of feeling, mystical states seem to those who experience them to be also states of knowledge. They are states of insight into depths of truth unplumbed by the discursive intellect. They are illuminations, revelations, full of significance and importance" (p. 300). Or as Bolle (1968) puts it in his minor classic book on the study of religion: "More than 'mere' experience, the mystic experience is knowledge" (p. 113).

These states of discernment are special in that they have an emancipatory nature: Spiritual knowledge is knowledge that liberates. To be sure, the nature of this liberation may differ substantially among traditions. I should make clear here that I am not advancing a universalist thesis about spiritual knowledge or liberation. As I see it, there may be different ways in which human beings cocreate their participation in the Mystery and move away from self-centered ways of being. What I am merely saying is that most contemplative traditions are primarily concerned with the emergence of certain participatory ontological-epistemic events associated with such terms as "liberation," "salvation" or "enlightenment."[11]

This should not come as a surprise. After all, most contemplative traditions—especially those spawned in India—state the spiritual problem of humankind in essentially epistemological terms: Existential and spiritual alienation are ultimately rooted in ignorance (*avidya*), in misconceptions about the nature of self and reality which lead to craving, attachment, self-centeredness, and other unwholesome dispositions. Therefore, the attainment of final liberation (*moksa, nirvana*, etc.) does not result from meditative experiences per se, but from wisdom (*prajña*), from the direct knowledge of "things as they really are" (e.g., Hopkins, 1971; Potter, 1991).[12] The ultimate goal of most contemplative traditions, then, is not realized by entering any type of altered state, ecstasy, or trance, but by the overcoming of delusion and ignorance. In the words of Sankara: "Since the root cause of this transmigratory existence is ignorance, its destruction is desired. Knowledge of *Brahman* therefore is entered on. Final beatitude results from this knowledge" (*Upadesasahasri*, I: 5; in Mayeda, 1992, p. 103). Or, as Nasr (1989) puts it in relation to the goal of virtually all spiritual traditions: "The sapiential perspective envisages the role of knowledge as the means of deliverance and freedom, of what the Hindu calls *moksa*. To know is to be delivered" (p. 309).[13]

The previous quotations may suggest a causal relationship between knowledge and liberation, a view of spiritual knowledge as leading to or resulting in liberation. However, according to most traditional accounts, it is inappropriate to talk in terms of causality between knowledge and liberation because, in the final analysis, there is no difference between them: Final liberation is not other than spiritual knowledge. Listen, again, to Sankara: "Liberation is not an effect—it is but the destruction of bondage (ignorance)" (*Brhadaranyaka Upanisad Sankara Bhasya*, 3.3.I; in Indich, 1980, p. 107). Or, as Hollenback (1996) writes in reference to *kaivalyam* (isolation), the ultimate goal of the Samkhya system and Patañjali's Yoga: "Isolation is not a mental state where the subject-object distinction has disappeared. Isolation is not a mental state because it is a condition of naked insight in which the soul [*purusa*] has utterly escaped bondage from prakrti and samsara" (p. 591).

I should stress here that this description of transpersonal and mystical events in terms of participatory knowing should not be understood as excluding the equally fundamental presence of affective qualities. On the contrary, as I suggested earlier, the participatory nature of transpersonal knowing not only entails an opening of the mind and the soul, but also of the body and the heart. In Christian mysticism, for example, knowledge of God, or the participation in the Divine Intellect, invariably involves a profound love towards God, the creation, and humanity (*agape, caritas*) (McGinn, 1996b). Similarly, in Mahayana Buddhism, the disclosure of wisdom (*prajña*) is inseparable from the development of compassion (*karuna*) (P. Williams, 1989). The same can be said of Sufism, where Ibn al-'Arabi's path of knowledge is beautifully balanced by Rumi's path of passionate love for the Divine (Chittick, 1983, 1989). These examples of the mutual interpenetration of love and knowledge in the spiritual journey could be multiplied endlessly.

An important point that follows from this analysis is that mystical ecstasies, trances, and absorptions are neither the final goal of the contemplative traditions nor should they be equated with final liberation.[14] Actually, most traditions warn that these mystical states are not to be sought for their own sake, but are usually a psychospiritual preparation to participate in special states of discernment. Although an adequate justification of this claim would require a thorough exploration of different mystical texts that would move us away from our present focus, it may be helpful to offer at least several examples extracted from different traditions.

The trance of cessation (*nirodhasamapatti*), culmination of the four formless *jhanas* in Theravada Buddhism (Buddhaghosa, 1976; Griffiths, 1986), the state of absorption without support (*asamprajñata samadhi*) of the Yoga Sutras of Patañjali (Patañjali, 1977), or the state of transcendence of all duality (*nirvikalpa samadhi*) in Sankara's Advaita Vedanta (Mayeda, 1992), are neither synonymous nor should be confused with the achievement of final liberation in each of these traditions. Although these states are often regarded as important steps, it would be a serious mistake to confound them with final liberation as envisaged by these traditions: *nirvana* in Theravada Buddhism, *kaivalyam* (isolation) in Samkhya-Yoga, or *moksa* in Sankara's Advaita Vedanta. And what is, according to these traditions, the nature of this final liberation? The nature of final liberation is essentially epistemic, that is, participation in spiritual states of insight. More precisely, *nirvana* is objectless discernment free from the mind constructing activities and defilements (lust, hatred, and delusion), that is, the double knowledge of the destruction of the fluxes (*asravaksayajñana*) and their absolute future nonarising (*anutpadajñana*) (C. Cox, 1992; Harvey, 1995); *kaivalyam* (isolation) is the penetrating insight into the eternal self (*purusa*) which is independent from any kind of mental or material phenomena (*prakrti*) (Patañjali, 1977); and, finally, *moksa* is knowledge of Brahman (*Brahmajñana*), or the direct recognition of the ultimate identity between one's innermost self (*Atman*) and the ultimate ground of the Universe (*Brahman*) (Mayeda, 1992). In other words, *nirvana*, *kaivalyam*, and *moksa* are not merely intrasubjective experiences, but participatory epistemic events, emergences of liberating knowing.

The case of Zen Buddhism deserves particular attention, especially since its widely claimed experiential emphasis impacted so decisively Western conceptions not only of Zen in particular but also of Eastern spirituality in general. Interestingly enough, historical analyses indicate that this experiential focus was not an original aspect of traditional Zen, but rather emerged at the turn of the twentieth century as a response to the modern Western critique of religion as dogmatic, irrational, and unscientific (Sharf, 1995a, 1995b). As Sharf (1995a) points out: "The Buddhist emphasis on 'inner experience' is in part a product of modern and often lay-oriented reform movements, most notably those associated with the *vipassana* revival in Southest Asia, and those associated with contemporary Zen movements in Japan" (p. 246). This experiential turn is evident, for example, in the Japanese Kyoto school, especially in the writings of Nishida Kitaro, D. T. Suzuki, and Nishitani Keiji. These modernized movements became in turn the main vehicles of transmission of Buddhism to the West. In particular, D. T. Suzuki's popular accounts of *satori* as a direct nondual experience, heart of all genuine spiritual traditions, substantially shaped not only the West's understanding of Zen Buddhism, but also its overall approach to Eastern religions (Faure, 1993). Nevertheless, this experiential emphasis is absent in traditional Zen teachings, treatises, or practices. In this account, the following passage by historian of religions Sharf (1995a) deserves to be quoted at some length:

> The irony of this situation is that the key Japanese terms for "experience"— *keiken* and *taiken*—are rarely attested in premodern Japanese texts. Their contemporary currency dates to the early Meiji, when they were adopted to render Western philosophical terms for which there was no ready Japanese equivalent. One searches in vain for premodern Chinese or Japanese equivalent to the phenomenological notion of experience. Nor is it legitimate to interpret such technical Zen terms as *satori* (literally, to understand), or *kensho* (to see one's original nature), as denoting some species of "unmediated experience" in the sense of Nishida's *junsui keiken*. (p. 249)[15]

But then, what is the original meaning of these terms for final liberation in Zen Buddhism? Sharf (1995a) offers us the answer:

> In traditional Chinese literature, such terms are used to denote *the full comprehension and appreciation of central Buddhist tenets such as emptiness, Buddha-nature, or dependent origination.* There are simply no a priori grounds for conceiving such *moments of insight* in phenomenological terms. Indeed, Chinese Buddhist commentators in general, and Ch'an exegetes in particular, tend to be antipathetic to any form of phenomenological reduction. (p. 249; italics added)

Before concluding this section, I should stress that I am not claiming that this account of liberation in terms of participatory knowing is paradigmatic for every mystic in every mystical tradition. Some mystics, like St. John of the Cross or St. Teresa for example, frequently expressed their insights in experiential language, and it therefore will not be difficult to find passages in the religious literature that seemingly contradict my thesis.[16] The mystical literature is so vast, rich, and diverse that one can probably find disconfirmation for any generalized statement about mysticism. What I do contend, in contrast, is that an understanding of spiritual liberation in terms of participatory knowing is more consistent with the dominant trends of most schools of Buddhism, Hinduism, Western esotericism, and also of many forms of Christian, Islamic, and Jewish mysticism, and probably shamanism as well.[17]

In any event, in the light of this prevalent identity of participatory knowing and liberation in most accounts, it is my belief that the participatory vision may help us not only to situate transpersonal studies in greater alignment with the spiritual quest but also to deepen our understanding of the nature of spirituality and the goals of the contemplative traditions.

SUMMARY AND CONCLUSIONS

My main intention in this chapter has been to introduce an account of spiritual knowing that is no longer limited by inner and individualistic premises. Transpersonal and spiritual phenomena, I have argued, are not individual inner experiences but participatory events (i.e., emergences of transpersonal being that can occur in the locus of a person, a relationship, a community, a collective identity, or a place). While affirming the existence of an individual consciousness that may participate in transpersonal events, the participatory vision challenges the anthropocentric and egocentric move of inferring from this participation that spiritual phenomena are fundamentally human inner experiences.

Basically, then, what I am proposing is a translation of the entire transpersonal project from a intrasubjective framework, geared to a subject–object model of cognition, into a participatory framework that is free from rusty Cartesian moorings. This basic move enables us to emancipate transpersonal theory from many of its current conceptual and practical constraints. Some of the main direct consequences that follow from this conceptual revision are: (1) a more integral understanding of spirituality free from intrasubjective reductionism, (2) the dismantling of Cartesianism, and, as we will see, the dissolution of many of the dilemmas inherent in a subject–object model of cognition, (3) the undermining of spiritual narcissism and integrative arrestment, and (4) the realignment of transpersonal studies with the spiritual quest.

But there is more. Once we free transpersonal theory from the Cartesian prejudices of the experiential vision and take seriously the participatory nature of spiritual knowing, alternatives to the perennialism that predates transpersonal studies naturally emerge that allow us to look at the transpersonal project with fresh eyes. This new transpersonal vision has profound implications not only for our understanding of interreligious relations, but also for the justification of spiritual claims and even our approach to spiritual liberation. The next two chapters explore some of the spiritual landscapes disclosed by this alternative vision.

6

AN OCEAN WITH MANY SHORES

THE CHALLENGE OF SPIRITUAL PLURALISM

Our assumptions about the nature of spiritual knowing guide our religious choices and judgments. In this chapter, I argue that the basic epistemological assumptions that ground the current understanding of spirituality contribute to the alienation characteristic of modern times and the impoverishment of our spiritual lives. A new epistemological soil for our "spiritual trees" is essential to bring forth a richer spiritual harvest. Here I start cultivating these new grounds and suggest that spirituality emerges from human cocreative participation in an always dynamic and indeterminate spiritual power. This understanding not only makes universal spiritual hierarchies appear misconceived, but also reestablishes our direct connection with the source of our being and expands the range of valid spiritual choices that we as individuals can make.

IN CHAPTER 4, we saw some of the fundamental problems of a perennialist account of spirituality. Assuming a pregiven ultimate reality, perennialism regards the variety of contemplative goals (*unio mystica, moksa, sunyata, theoria, nirvana, devekut, kaivalyam,* etc.) as different interpretations, dimensions, or levels of a single spiritual ultimate. Then, while ecumenically claiming to honor all those truths, perennialism consistently grades spiritual insights and traditions according to how closely they approach or represent this pregiven spiritual reality (e.g., nondual traditions over dual ones, monistic over theistic, impersonal over personal, etc.). We also noticed the mutually reinforcing relation between perennialism and an experiential account of spirituality, and suggested that, once we give up the Cartesian assumptions underlying both approaches, alternative visions naturally emerge that allow us to look at the spiritual life with more discerning eyes.

It is now time to start using these new eyes and see how far their gaze reaches: What kind of spiritual landscape do they reveal? What new understandings do they yield? How to envision in this new light our participation in spiritual knowledge? How do interreligious relations look under this glow? What about spiritual liberation? And so forth. To start approaching these fundamental questions, I want to offer in this chapter the general contours of a vision of spirituality alternative to the perennialism characteristic of transpersonal studies. In the next chapter, then, I explore some of the implications of this vision for transpersonal and spiritual studies.

Before proceeding, however, I should stress that although I believe that this vision is more sensitive to the spiritual evidence and better honors the diversity of ways in which the sense of the sacred can be embodied, by no means do I claim that it conveys the final Truth about the Mystery of being in which we creatively participate. In contrast, my main intention is to open avenues to rethink and live spirituality in a different, and I believe more fruitful, manner. Likewise, although I believe this vision is advantageous for both interreligious relations and individual spiritual growth, it should be obvious that its ultimate value is a practical challenge that needs to be appraised by others as they personally engage it and critically decide whether it fosters their spiritual understanding and blossoming. It is in this spirit of offering, invitation, inquiry, and perhaps skillful means that I advance the ideas of this chapter.

After these caveats, we can initiate our discussion with a brief review of some contextualist alternatives to perennialism already existent in the literature. Although it offers valuable insights, I argue that contextualism is also limited by highly questionable epistemological assumptions, and that a fresher view is needed that integrates the merits of perennialism and contextualism while eschewing their shortcomings. In the remainder of the chapter, I offer the basic contours of an alternative vision that, free from the Cartesian-Kantian moorings that restrain these approaches, discloses a radical plurality not only of spiritual paths, but also of spiritual liberations and spiritual ultimates.

CURRENT TRENDS IN THE MODERN STUDY OF MYSTICISM

Classic definitions of mysticism explain mystical knowledge in terms of an identification with, or direct experience of, the ultimate Ground of Being, which is variously described in capitalized terms such as God, the Transcendent, the Absolute, the Noumenal, Ultimate Reality, or, more simply, the Real (e.g., Carmody & Carmody, 1996; Hick, 1992; Huxley, 1945; Schuon, 1984a; Underhill, 1955).[1] These definitions are typically perennialist insofar as they assume the existence of a single, ready-made ultimate reality that is directly accessed, partially or totally, by mystics of all kinds and traditions. If mystical knowledge is direct and ultimate reality is One, so the reasoning goes, mystical experiences must either be phenomenologically identical, or, if different, correspond to different dimensions, perspectives, or levels of this singular spiritual ultimate. As Perovich (1985a), a contemporary perennialist, puts it: "The point [of the perennial philosophers] in insisting on the identity of mystical experiences was, after all, to bolster the claim that the most varied mystics have established contact with 'the one ultimate truth'" (p. 75).

The perennialist logic rests then on three fundamental premises: (1) There is a single referent for all mysticisms, (2) this referent corresponds to the ultimate nature of reality or the Divine, and (3) mystics can directly access this single ultimate reality. These three interrelated assumptions have been seriously challenged by a number of scholars of modern comparative mysticism, who share an emphasis on the importance of contextual determinants of mystical insights and experiences. Let us briefly look at some of the main features of this debate between perennialists and contextualists.

Ever since the publication of Steven Katz's (1978a) seminal collection, *Mysticism and Philosophical Analysis*, the contemporary conversation on mysticism has orbited around the issues of the universality versus plurality of mystical aims and experiences, the direct versus mediated nature of mystical knowledge, and the ontological status of the spiritual realities that mystics claim to access.[2] Although with different emphases, Katz and other contextualist[3] scholars claim that *mystical experiences are no different from other human experiences in that they are fully mediated, shaped, and constituted by the language, culture, doctrinal beliefs, and soteriological expectations of the traditions in which they occur* (I call this view the "strong thesis of mediation").[4] What contextual and conceptual factors influence, then, is not only the interpretation of mystical states (as most perennialists admit), but also their very phenomenological content: "The experience itself as well as the form in which it is reported is shaped by concepts which the mystic brings to, and which shape, his experience" (Katz, 1978b, p. 26). Therefore, for contextualists, there is not a variously interpreted universal mystical experience, but at least as many distinct types as contemplative traditions (see, e.g., Almond, 1982).[5] What is more, these types of mysticism do not necessarily correspond to different dimensions or levels of a single spiritual ultimate, but may be independent contemplative goals determined by particular practices, and whose meaning and soteriological power largely depend on their wider religious and metaphysical frameworks. Consequently, as Katz's (1978b) original essay concludes, "'God' can be 'God,' 'Brahman' can be 'Brahman' and *nirvana* can be *nirvana* without any reductionistic attempt to equate the concept of 'God' with that of 'Brahman', or 'Brahman' with *nirvana*" (p. 66). Or, as he forcibly put it some years later:

> Straightforwardly, what is argued is that, for example, the Hindu mystic does not have an experience of x which he describes in the, to him, familiar language and symbols of Hinduism, but rather he has a Hindu experience; his experience is not an unmediated experience of x but is itself the at least partially preformed anticipated Hindu experience of Brahman. Again, the Christian mystic does not experience some unidentified reality which he then conveniently labels 'God', but rather has the at least partially, prefigured Christian experiences of God, or Jesus, and so forth. Moreover, as one might anticipate, it is my contention, *based on what evidence there is,* that the Hindu experience of Brahman and the Christian experience of God are not the same. (Katz, 1983b, pp. 4–5)

Needless to say, such a direct threat to the widely cherished idea of a common spiritual ground for humankind did not go unnoticed or unchallenged. On the contrary, the writings of Katz and his collaborators set the stage for two decades of lively, and often heated, debate among a plethora of *more*-perennialist and *more*-contextualist oriented scholars.[6] Although I cannot offer here an exhaustive review of this debate, it may be helpful to give at least a brief résumé of its main features.

In the perennialist camp, four main lines of reasoning are usually developed. First, some perennialist authors argue for the existence of a cross-cultural pure consciousness experience that, due to its nonconceptual nature, must be both immediate and universal (Evans, 1989; Forman, 1990a, 1998a). Second, they defend the deconstructive nature of the mystical path, that is to say, a view of mystical practices such as meditation as processes of deautomatization (Deikman, 1966) or deconditioning of socially learned conceptual schemes and cognitive structures through which we apprehend ourselves and the world (Brown, 1986; Forman, 1989, 1990b, 1993; Rothberg, 1989, 1990). Third, perennialists refer to scriptural data that apparently contradict the contextualist thesis; for example, if all spiritual experiences are molded by doctrinal beliefs and expectations, the unexpected and sometimes heretical insights reported by many mystics (such as Meister Eckhart, Isaac Luria, or even the Buddha) should not occur (Forman, 1989, 1990b; Perovich, 1985a; Stoeber, 1992, 1994). Finally, they accuse contextualists of both working upon questionable epistemological assumptions (e.g., that all experience, including the mystical, is mediated), and being self-contradictory: If all knowledge is constructed, the contextualist thesis is also a construct without universal or absolute value, and if so, why should we prefer it? (Evans, 1989; Forman, 1989; Rothberg, 1989; Wilber, 1995).[7]

Contextualist authors, for their part, typically argue for their position along one or several of the following lines. First, they offer detailed textual and historical accounts that indicate the radical contextuality of mystical practices and aims, and the resulting phenomenological differences among mystical experiences (Fenton, 1995; Gimello, 1978, 1983; Hollenback, 1996; Katz, 1978b). The primary goal of these analyses is to show how mystical experiences and referents are progressively shaped and constituted through specific doctrinal commitments and practices (e.g., Klein, 1986). Second, they describe the mystical path as a reconstructive process aimed at the reconditioning of cognitive structures and conceptual schemes that allow mystics to apprehend self and world according to their doctrinal beliefs (Gimello, 1978; Katz, 1978b). Third, contextualists hold that there is an inescapable reciprocity between experience and interpretation, where "all experience becomes *interpreted* experience, while all interpretation is mediated by experience" (Dupré, 1996, pp. 3–4). No experience comes with its interpretation, and since the lenses to understand the meaning of spiritual experiences always derive from some external (and usually doctrinal) framework, mysticism is not in a privileged epistemological position (R. H. Jones, 1993; Moore, 1978; Proudfoot, 1985). Fourth, they challenge the existence of "pure consciousness experiences" and assert that, even if such contentless states exist, they may not be cognitive of any ultimate or divine reality (Bagger, 1991; R. H. Jones, 1993). Finally, some contextually oriented authors accuse the perennialist program of being essentialist, ideological, authoritarian, patriarchal, and overlooking the spirituality of women, indigenous people, and other marginal groups (Heron, 1998; Jantzen, 1994; Raphael, 1994; Wright, 1995).

This is not the place to assess the value of each one of these arguments. For our present purposes, I would rather like to suggest that both perennialism and contextualism are rooted in interrelated ontological and epistemological presuppositions whose exposure and criticism can break through the impasse that characterizes this modern debate.

BEYOND PERENNIALISM AND CONTEXTUALISM

In the previous pages, I have dealt with the problems of perennialism at length (chapter 4) while offering a much briefer account of those of contextualism— the postmodern adversary of perennialism. This is because perennialism, not contextualism, has been the foundational framework of transpersonal theory. Although these two approaches are often seen as opposed alternatives, I now want to argue that both perennialism and contextualism are actually shaped by a set of complementary epistemological presuppositions. Let us briefly look at the nature of these assumptions.

THE CARTESIAN ROOTS OF PERENNIALISM

We have already seen how perennialism subscribes to an objectivist model of knowledge and reality. Perennialists generally assume that there is a pregiven spiritual ultimate that can be objectively known by mystics of all traditions. A corollary of this assumption is the belief that this spiritual ultimate has certain pregiven features (e.g., nondual, monistic, impersonal, etc.) which are independent of human participation in it. Because consensus about such attributes is virtually absent among mystics (except perhaps, and vaguely enough, about its intrinsically benevolent nature), perennialists try to preserve the unity of mysticism by invoking perspectivist, hierarchical, and/or structuralist views.

A serious drawback shared by all these approaches, however, is that they import to spiritual realities the notorious Myth of the Given of empiricist science, and with it, most of its insurmountable problems.[8] The appeal to the given has been diversely articulated throughout the history of Western philosophy, for example, in terms of "sense-data," "objects of the world," or "immediate experiences."[9] In the context of our discussion, by the Myth of the Given I understand the following two interrelated theses: (1) The world has pregiven features independent of any cognitive activity (ontological thesis), and (2) human knowledge finds its justification by matching its claims with this pregiven world (epistemological thesis).

As is well known, both theses have been seriously undermined by contemporary developments in the human sciences and hermeneutics, anthropology and linguistics, the philosophy and sociology of science, feminist and indigenous epistemologies, and modern cognitive science, among other disciplines. From different perspectives, these approaches have made evident that once we take seriously the interpretive nature of human knowledge and the collapse of the representational paradigm of cognition, the very idea of a pregiven world becomes not only naive, but also misleading and unnecessary. But let us be clear here: None of these modern disciplines claims that there is not a world out there apart from human ideation. In contrast, what they strongly suggest is that the features of this world are not independent, objective, or fixed, but rather codetermined, malleable, and dynamic. In other words, the world does not have an intrinsic nature waiting to be discovered and represented by human cognition, but discloses itself in a variety of ways partially contingent on the dispositions, intentions, and modes of consciousness of the knower.

I cannot explain with any detail here why so many contemporary philosophers and scientists reject the idea of the given, so I will simply refer the reader to some key works in which this essentialist myth is mercilessly exposed and devastated, in all its forms—see Quine's (1953, 1990) critique of the "two dogmas of empiricism," Sellars's (1956, 1963) attack on "the idea of givenness," Kuhn's (1970a) challenge to the "neutral nature of observation," Goodman's (1978) "ways of world-making," Rorty's (1979) deconstruction of the metaphor of "mind as the mirror of nature," Davidson's (1984) refutation of an "uninterpreted reality," von Glasersfeld's (1984) "radical constructivism," Gadamer's (1990) notion of "truth-events," Varela, Thompson, and Rosch's (1991) enactive paradigm of cognition, and Tarnas's (1991) participatory epistemology, to mention only a few.

Although heavily criticized by philosophers for decades, the Myth of the Given is not easy to dispose altogether. Indeed, some contemporary thinkers hold a weaker version of the Myth that posits the existence of very rough and malleable but still intrinsic features in the sensoriomotor world.[10] Without the existence of such intrinsic features, it is usually argued, our conversations about the natural world would be rendered unintelligible, and our scientific discoveries and technological advances unexplainable (e.g., Searle, 1995). While a Jamesian pragmatist epistemology can probably explain these unexplainable facts without resorting to essentialist discourse, I believe that it is legitimate to talk conventionally about intrinsic features of the world in such a weaker sense. Although malleable and codetermined to a large extent, the sensoriomotor world does present itself to us in nonarbitrary ways.

I should add, however, that this weakness needs to be emphasized even more strongly when we move to mental and spiritual realities. What I am suggesting here is that *the creative element of human cognition plays an even more fundamental formative role in hermeneutic and spiritual knowing than in empirical domains.* In other words, as we move from the more gross to the more subtle, the gap between being and knowing, between the ontological and the epistemological, is increasingly abridged. Accordingly, it becomes less and less adequate to anchor the soundness of knowledge claims on any kind of intrinsic features, and more and more necessary to discern validity standards of a different kind. As we will see in this chapter, in spirituality this formative role takes the form of an intentional creative participation that accounts for and justifies a variety of independent and valid spiritual paths, spiritual liberations, and even spiritual ultimates.

Perennialists generally recognize the closing gap between ontology and epistemology in spiritual knowing. However, their claim that ultimate reality has universally pregiven features (e.g., nondual, impersonal, monistic) and that the perennial Truth conveys "things as they really are," reveals the residual objectivism of their approach. Herein lie the Cartesian roots of perennialism.[11]

THE NEO-KANTIAN ROOTS OF CONTEXTUALISM

Whereas perennialism leans back to Cartesianism, contextualism subscribes to Neo-Kantian epistemological assumptions about the nature of knowledge and reality.[12] As we have seen, contextualists convincingly argue that spiritual knowledge is mediated and molded by cultural factors, doctrinal commitments, and soteriological expectations. That mystics generally experience and report the knowledge cultivated by their traditions is obviously accurate, and these authors should be credited for having emphasized the radical plurality of spiritual claims.

From this valid insight, however, contextualism goes on to deny or bracket the ontological and metaphysical import of human participation in spiritual realities.[13] According to Cupitt (1998), for example, "The [postmodern] mysticism of secondarieness is mysticism *minus* metaphysics, mysticism *minus* any claim to special or privileged knowledge, and mysticism without any other world than this one" (p. 8). Although it would probably be unfair to charge all contextualist authors with psychologism, subjectivism, or reductionism,[14] it is safe to say, I believe, that they typically operate under the spell of what Popper (1970, 1994) calls the Myth of the Framework. In our present context, this Myth would suggest the idea that *mystics are prisoners of their conceptual frameworks and that spiritual knowledge is always constituted, shaped, or screened through them.* Listen to Gimello (1983): "Mystical experience is simply the psychosomatic enhancement of religious beliefs and values or of beliefs and values which are held 'religiously'" (p. 85). These religious concepts, beliefs, values, and expectations, he adds,

> are of the essence of mystical experience. They engender it. They inform its very identity. Were one to substract from mystical experience the beliefs which mystics hold to be therein confirmed and instantiated, all that would be left would mere hedonic tone, a pattern of psychosomatic or neural impulse signifying nothing. (p. 62)

Contrary to mystical claims, no direct knowledge of spiritual realities is therefore possible, and, for some contextualist authors, these may not even exist.

As we have seen, one way to challenge this myth is to show that mystics report insights that their doctrines and beliefs could not have prepared them to expect or allowed them to constitute. Although mysticism does tend to be conservative in its reaffirming of previous doctrinal beliefs (Katz, 1983b), perennialists are right in noting the emergence of novel and truly revolutionary mystical events that cannot be fully explained by ordinary constructive variables or acquired conceptual frameworks. We will return to this crucial issue in the next sections. Here it should suffice to say that this legitimate rejoinder reveals the shortcomings of the contextualist "strong thesis of mediation." However, there is still a more fatal stroke to be given to the Myth of the Framework, a stroke that, I believe, paves the way naturally for the emergence of the participatory vision.

As I see it, the crucial flaw of the contextualist logic is not the denial that mystics can transcend their conceptual frameworks, but *the very postulation of a dualism of conceptual framework and uninterpreted reality.*[15] This Dualism of Framework and Reality, however, is widely regarded as implausible, especially in the wake of Donald Davidson's (1984) celebrated essay "On the Very Idea of a Conceptual Scheme." Taking the translatability of languages as a paradigmatic case, Davidson argues that the idea of alternative conceptual frameworks necessarily presupposes a larger common ground that makes these frameworks truly alternative and whose existence renders the idea unintelligible: "Different points of view make sense, but only if there is a common co-ordinate system on which to plot them; yet the existence of a common system belies the claim of dramatic incomparability" (p. 184). According to Davidson, the dissolution of this third dogma of empiricism (after Quine) undermines not only the existence of conceptual frameworks (and its related self-defeating conceptual relativisms), but also the idea of an uninterpreted reality (the Myth of the Given).[16] In his own words: "In abandoning this search [for a common uninterpreted reality], we abandon the attempt to make sense of the metaphor of a single space within which each scheme has a position and provides a point of view" (p. 195).

But there is more. As Tarnas (1991) suggests, this epistemic dualism contributes in fundamental manners to the existential estrangement of the modern self. By placing the individual inexorably out of touch with the real world, the alienating Cartesian gap between subject and object is epistemologically affirmed and secured: "Thus the cosmological estrangement of modern consciousness initiated by Copernicus and the ontological estrangement initiated by Descartes were completed by the epistemological estrangement initiated by Kant: a threefold mutually enforced prison of modern alienation" (p. 419).[17] For our present purposes, Tarnas's analysis is particularly helpful because, in contrast to other critiques, it brings to the foreground the pernicious implications of this dualism for the human participation in spiritual knowledge:

> The Cartesian-Kantian paradigm both expresses and ratifies a state of consciousness in which experience of the unitive numinous depths of reality has been systematically extinguished, leaving the world disenchanted and the human ego isolated. Such a world view is, as it were, a kind of metaphysical and epistemological box. (p. 431)

Once we give up the Dualism of Framework and Reality, however, we can, with Davidson (1984), "re-establish unmediated touch with the familiar objects whose antics make our sentences true or false" (p. 198). It is crucial to realize at this point that since the overcoming of this dualism implies not only dropping ideas about conceptual frameworks, but also "the concept of an uninterpreted reality" (Davidson, 1984, p. 198), these objects can no longer be taken to mean the pregiven objects of positivism, empiricism, or naïve realism. On the contrary, giving up this dualism calls us *to move beyond objectivism and subjectivism towards the recognition of the simultaneously interpretive and immediate nature of human knowledge.* And this movement can only be fully honored and consistently performed, I believe, by embracing a participatory vision of knowledge and reality. In a participatory epistemology, Tarnas (1991) tells us,

> the interpretive and constructive character of human cognition is fully acknowledged, but the intimate, interpenetrating and all-permeating relationship of nature to the human being and human mind allows the Kantian consequence of epistemological alienation to be entirely overcome. (p. 435)[18]

Put simply, to transcend the dualistic side of Kant is to redeem our participatory, connected, and direct relationship with reality and the source of our being.

To look at this shift in the context of the participatory turn illustrates the nature of its emancipatory power. The flight to inner experience in religious studies was in large part aimed to protect religion from the Enlightenment critique of metaphysics, especially at the hands of Descartes and Kant (Proudfoot, 1985).[19] It is natural, therefore, that to liberate spirituality from the Cartesian-Kantian "epistemological box," to use Tarnas's words, entails not only a movement away from an overemphasis on inner experience, but also *the recovery of the metaphysical import of spiritual knowledge.*

To conclude this section, I would like to point out that both perennialism and contextualism are parasitic of the experiential vision of spiritual phenomena. On the one hand, as we have seen, the appeal to an uninterpreted mystical experience is pivotal for the perennialist defense of the universality of human spirituality (e.g., Evans, 1989; Forman, 1990a, 1998a; Shear, 1994). On the other hand, contextualist analyses primarily focus on how mystical experiences are mediated, shaped, constructed, and reported. Although some contextualists assure us that we should not mistake their approach with psychologism or subjectivism, the fact is that these authors typically remain silent about the ontological and metaphysical implications of mystical events. To be sure, a generous reading may see in this attitude a healthy agnosticism, but I believe that we are in a position to see it now as a metaphysical bias contingent on Neo-Kantian prejudices that can and should be abandoned.[20]

In sum, both perennialism and contextualism heavily depend on the Dualism of Framework and Reality. Perennialist approaches tend to emphasize one pole of the dualism, holding onto the idea of an uninterpreted reality and falling prey to the problems inherent in the Myth of the Given. Contextualist approaches tend to emphasize the other pole, getting trapped in conceptual maps and falling under the spell of the Myth of the Framework.[21] As we have seen, however, this splitting of reality into two halves is not only epistemologically suspect but also existentially and spiritually alienating. The agenda, then, is clear: We need a model that integrates the merits of perennialism and contextualism into a vision of spirituality free from Cartesian-Kantian dualisms and myths. The remainder of this chapter attempts to offer such a vision.

AN OCEAN WITH MANY SHORES

Having shown the limitations of both perennialism and contextualism, the task remains of how to better understand the nature of spiritual knowledge and the diversity of spiritual claims. In the rest of this chapter, I introduce a participatory vision that combines the merits of these perspectives with modern epistemological insights so as to achieve a more satisfactory account of spirituality.

Let us begin our story by departing from a classic perennialist account. As we have seen, perennialism postulates a single spiritual ultimate which can be directly known through a transconceptual, and presumably ineffable, metaphysical intuition. This insight, so the account goes, provides us with a direct access to "things as they really are," that is, the ultimate nature of reality and our innermost identity. Central to this view is the idea that once we lift the manifold veils of cultural distortions, doctrinal beliefs, egoic projections, the sense of separate existence, and so forth, the doors of perception are unlocked and the true nature of self and reality is revealed to us in a flashing, liberating insight. From a classic perennialist perspective, every spiritual tradition leads, in practice, to this identical, single vision. Or to use one of the most popular perennialist metaphors, spiritual traditions are like rivers leading to the same ocean.

In chapter 4, we saw the implausibility of this metaphor in its ordinary usage (i.e., to refer to a cross-cultural spiritual ultimate). Here, however, I would like to suggest that, although distorted, there is a hidden truth abiding in this metaphor. I propose that most traditions do lead to the same ocean, but not the one portrayed on the perennialist canvas. The ocean shared by most traditions does not correspond to a single spiritual referent or to "things as they really are," but, perhaps more humbly, to *the overcoming of self-centeredness*, and thus a liberation from corresponding limiting perspectives and understandings.

With perennialism, then, I believe that most genuine spiritual paths involve a gradual transformation from narrow self-centeredness towards a fuller participation in the Mystery of existence.[22] To be sure, this self-centeredness can be variously overcome (e.g., through the compassion-raising insight into the interpenetration of all phenomena in Mahayana Buddhism, the knowledge of Brahman in Advaita Vedanta, the continuous feeling of God's loving presence in Christianity, the cleaving to God in Judaism, or the commitment to visionary service and healing in many forms of shamanism), to name only a few possibilities. In all cases, however, we invariably witness a liberation from self-imposed suffering, an opening of the heart, and a commitment to a compassionate and selfless life.[23] It is in this spirit, I believe, that the Dalai Lama (1988) thinks of a common element in religion:

> If we view the world's religions from the widest possible viewpoint, and examine their ultimate goal, we find that all of the major world religions . . . are directed to the achievement of permanent human happiness. They are all directed toward that goal. . . . To this end, the different world's religions teach different doctrines which help transform the person. In this regard, all religions are the same, there is no conflict. (p. 12)

For the sake of brevity, and mindful of the limitations of this metaphor, since most traditions identify the liberation from self-centeredness as pivotal for this transformation, I will call this common element the Ocean of Emancipation.[24]

Furthermore, I concur with perennialism in holding that the entry into the Ocean of Emancipation may be accompanied, or followed by, a transconceptual disclosure of reality. Due to the radical interpenetration between cognizing self and cognized world, once the self-concept is deconstructed, the world may reveal itself to us in ways that transcend conceptualization.

Nevertheless, and here is where we radically depart from perennialism, I maintain that there is *a multiplicity of transconceptual disclosures of reality*. Resolutely committed to the Myth of the Given, perennialists erroneously assume that this transconceptual disclosure of reality must be necessarily One. In other words, perennialists generally believe that plurality emerges from concepts and interpretations, and that the cessation of conceptual proliferation must then result in a single apprehension of "things as they really are."[25]

This equation of transconceptuality with a single insight as the goal of all contemplative traditions is both unwarranted and misconceived, for at least the following three reasons. Firstly, diversity does not merely derive from the superimposition of concepts upon a seamless reality. Reality in itself is plural. Diversity exists not only at a conceptual level, but also at non-conceptual and transconceptual ones. To mention a few examples of non-conceptual diversity from our everyday life may be helpful here. The intense flavors of mustard, cheese, and chocolate are not unlike because we conceive them differently, but due to their own codetermined presentational qualities. And the same can be said about the manifold colors, forms, sounds, textures, and scents that make our lives so rich and interesting. As experimental psychology showed more than half a century ago, for example, people can distinguish colors without having the conceptual terms that would supposedly allow such judgments. To equate nonconceptuality with oneness, then, is like suggesting that all these qualities are identical and only become different when they are conceptualized. Secondly, absence of conceptual content is not equivalent to phenomenological identity. As William James points out, in his *Principles of Psychology*, "there are innumerable consciousnesses of emptiness, no one of which taken in itself has a name, but all different from each other. The ordinary way is to assume that they are all emptinesses of consciousness, and so the same state. But the feeling of an absence is *toto coelo* other than an absence of a feeling: it is an intense feeling" (quoted in Barnard, 1997, p. 137). And the same can be said about the so-called ineffable states: Ineffability does not warrant phenomenological or ontological identity (Fenton, 1995). Finally, I should add here, a transconceptual disclosure of reality may not necessarily be the goal of many spiritual traditions or the zenith of human spirituality. Although space does not allow me to document this claim here adequately, I would like to suggest that the entry into the Ocean of Emancipation and the access to transconceptual cognition are not always the end, but in some cases the starting point of genuine spiritual inquiry. From the truths of the Ocean of Emancipation and transconceptual cognition, then, perennialism draws the erroneous conclusion that this transconceptual unfolding of reality must necessarily be one and the same for all traditions.[26]

But to enter the Ocean of Emancipation does not inevitably tie us to a particular disclosure of reality, even if this is transconceptual. In contrast, what the mystical evidence suggests is that there are a variety of possible spiritual insights and ultimates (Tao, Brahman, *sunyata*, God, *kaivalyam*, etc.) whose transconceptual qualities, although sometimes overlapping, are irreducible and often incompatible (personal versus impersonal, impermanent versus eternal, dual versus nondual, etc.). The typical perennialist move to account for this conflicting evidence is to assume that these qualities correspond to different interpretations, perspectives, dimensions, or levels of a single ultimate reality. As we have seen, however, this move is both unfounded and problematic. A more cogent way to explain the diversity of spiritual claims is—and this is where contextualist analyses are helpful—to hold that *the various traditions lead to the enactment of different spiritual ultimates and/or transconceptual disclosures of reality.* Although these spiritual ultimates may apparently share some qualities (e.g., nonduality in *sunyata* and *Brahmajñana*), they constitute independent religious aims whose conflation may prove to be a serious mistake. In terms of our metaphor, we could say, then, that *the Ocean of Emancipation has many shores.*[27]

The idea of different spiritual "shores" receives support from one of the few rigorous cross-cultural comparative studies of meditative paths. After his detailed analysis of Patañjali's *Yogasutras*, Buddhaghosa's *Visudhimagga*, and the Tibetan *Mahamudra*, Brown (1986) points out that:

> The conclusions set forth here are nearly the opposite of that of the stereotyped notion of the perennial philosophy according to which many spiritual paths are said to lead to the same end. According to the careful comparison of the traditions we have to conclude the following: there is only one path, but it has several outcomes. There are several kinds of enlightenment, although all free awareness from psychological structure and alleviate suffering. (pp. 266–267)

Whereas Brown, Wilber, and other transpersonalists have rightly identified certain parallels across contemplative paths, contextualists have correctly emphasized that the enaction of different spiritual insights and ultimates requires specific mystical teachings, trainings, and practices. Or put in traditional terms, particular "rafts" are needed to arrive at particular spiritual "shores": If you want to reach the shore of *nirvana*, you need the raft of the Buddhist *dharma*, not the one provided by Christian praxis. And if you want to realize knowledge of Brahman (*Brahmajñana*), you need to follow the Advaitin path of Vedic study and meditation, and not the practice of Tantric Buddhism, devotional Sufi dance, or psychedelic shamanism. And so forth. In this account, the Dalai Lama (1988) is straightforward:

> Liberation in which "a mind that understands the sphere of reality annihilates all defilements in the sphere of reality" is a state that only Buddhists can accomplish. This kind of *moksa* or nirvana is only explained in the Buddhist scriptures, and is achieved only through Buddhist practice. (p. 23)

What is more, different liberated awarenesses and spiritual ultimates can be encountered not only among different religious traditions, but also within a single tradition itself. Listen once again to the Dalai Lama (1988):

> *Questioner:* So, if one is a follower of Vedanta, and one reaches the state of *satcitananda*, would this not be considered ultimate liberation?

> *His Holiness:* Again, it depends upon how you interpret the words, "ultimate liberation." The mokṣa which is described in the Buddhist religion is achieved only through the practice of emptiness. And this kind of nirvana or liberation, as I have defined it above, cannot be achieved even by Svatantrika Madhyamikas, by Cittamatras, Sautrantikas or Vaibhasikas. The follower of these schools, *though Buddhists,* do not understand the actual doctrine of emptiness. Because they cannot realize emptiness, or reality, they cannot accomplish the kind of liberation I defined previously. (pp. 23–24)

What the Dalai Lama is suggesting here is that the various spiritual traditions and schools cultivate and achieve different contemplative goals. He is adamant in stressing that adherents to other religions, and even to other Buddhist schools, cannot attain the type of spiritual liberation cultivated by his own. There are alternative understandings and awarenesses of emptiness even among the various Buddhist schools: From the Theravadin *pugdala-sunyata* (emptiness of the person; existence of the aggregates) to the Mahayana *dharma-sunyata* (emptiness of the person and the aggregates) and the Madhyamika *sunyata-sunyata* (emptiness of emptiness). And from Dogen's Buddha-Nature = Impermanence to Nagarjuna's *sunyata* = *pratitya-samutpada* or to Yogachara's, Dzogchen's, and Hua-Yen's more essentialist understandings in terms of Pure Mind, Luminous Presence, or Buddhahood (*Tathagatagarbha*).[28] To lump together these different awarenesses into one single spiritual liberation or referent reachable by all traditions may be profoundly distorting. Each spiritual shore is independent and needs to be reached by its appropriate raft.

I should stress that my defense of many viable spiritual paths and goals does not preclude the possibility of equivalent or common elements among them. In other words, although the different mystical traditions enact and disclose different spiritual universes, two or more traditions may share certain elements in their paths and/or goals (e.g., belief in a personal Creator, attention training, ethical guidelines, etc.). In this context, Vroom's (1989) proposal of a "multicentered view of religion" that conceives traditions as displaying a variety of independent but potentially overlapping focal points should be seriously considered:

> The overlapping of the various religions would then no longer occur in the one focus—belief in a Creator. There would be many overlaps. The similarities all relate to such dimensions of religion as ethical injunctions, ways of experiencing community, interpretation of basic experiences, and the content of belief. (p. 383)[29]

As I see it, this model not only makes the entire search for a common core simplistic and misconceived, but also avoids the pitfall of strict incommensurability of spiritual traditions, thus paving the way for different forms of comparative scholarship.[30]

To recapitulate, the common ocean to which most spiritual traditions lead is not a pregiven spiritual ultimate, but the Ocean of Emancipation, a radical shift in perspective that involves the deconstruction of the Cartesian ego, the eradication of self-imposed suffering, and the rise of selfless perception, cognition, and action. The entry into the Ocean of Emancipation, however, is not necessarily the zenith of spiritual development, but may rather be the starting point of genuine spiritual inquiry. Furthermore, although this access may be ushered in by the emergence of transconceptual cognition, there are a variety of transconceptual disclosures of reality, some for which the spiritual traditions are vehicles, and others whose enaction may presently require a more creative participation. In other words, the Ocean of Emancipation has many spiritual shores, some of which are enacted by the world spiritual traditions, and others of which, as the last section of this chapter stresses, may not have emerged as yet.

A PARTICIPATORY ACCOUNT OF
GROF'S CONSCIOUSNESS RESEARCH

Before proceeding further, I should mention here an important exception to this generally contextual enaction of spiritual shores. Modern consciousness research has revealed that traditional spiritual shores can become available in special states of consciousness, such as those facilitated by entheogens, breathwork, and other technologies of consciousness.[31] As the groundbreaking research of Stanislav Grof (1985, 1988, 1998) indicates, human beings can enact and understand spiritual insights and cosmologies belonging to specific religious worlds even without previous exposure to them. In Grof's (1988) words:

In nonordinary states of consciousness, visions of various universal symbols can play a significant role in experiences of individuals who previously had no interest in mysticism or were strongly opposed to anything esoteric. These visions tend to convey instant intuitive understanding of the various levels of meaning of these symbols.

As a result of experiences of this kind, subjects can develop accurate understanding of various complex esoteric teachings. In some instances, persons unfamiliar with the Kabbalah had experiences described in the Zohar and Sepher Yetzirah and obtained surprising insights into Kabbalistic symbols. Others were able to describe the meaning and function of intricate mandalas used in the Tibetan Vajrayana and other tantric systems. (p. 139)

As I see it, Grof's data not only reveals the limitations of the contextualist program in the study of spirituality, but also can be regarded as the empirical refutation of its strong thesis of mediation. For contextualists, let us remember here, all spiritual knowledge and experience is always mediated by doctrinal beliefs, intentional practices, and soteriological expectations. As contextualist scholar Moore (1978) puts it, for example, "the lack of doctrinal presuppositions might prevent the mystic not only from understanding and describing his mystical states but even from experiencing the fullness of these states in the first place" (p. 112). Whether or not Grof's subjects experience the fullness of mystical states and attain a complete understanding of traditional spiritual meanings is an open question. But even if this were not the case, the evidence provided by Grof's case studies is sufficient, I believe, to consider the contextualist strong thesis of mediation empirically refuted. Grof's subjects report experiences that should not occur if the strong thesis of mediation is correct.

In the context of the participatory vision, Grof's experiential data show that, once a particular spiritual shore has been enacted, it becomes potentially accessible—to some degree and in special circumstances—to the entire human species.[32] But then Grof's experiential data do not need to be interpreted as supporting a perspectivist account of the perennial philosophy.[33] The various spiritual ultimates accessed during special states of consciousness, rather than being understood as different ways to experience the same Absolute Consciousness—which implicitly establishes a hierarchical ranking of spiritual traditions with monistic and nondual ones like Advaita Vedanta at the top—can be seen as independently valid enactions of a dynamic and indeterminate spiritual power. As should be obvious, any hierarchical arrangement of spiritual insights or traditions necessarily presupposes the existence of a pregiven spiritual ultimate relative to which such judgements can be made. Whenever we drop the Myth of the Given in spiritual hermeneutics, however, the very idea of ranking traditions according to a paradigmatic standpoint becomes not only suspect but also misleading and superfluous.[34]

BREAKING THE CARTESIAN-KANTIAN
SPELL IN SPIRITUAL STUDIES

Although the metaphor of an ocean with many shores is helpful to illustrate the partial truths of perennialism and contextualism, it should be obvious that it is ultimately inadequate to convey the participatory and enactive nature of spiritual knowing advanced here. As with all geographical metaphors, one can easily get the mistaken impression that these shores are pregiven, some-how waiting out there to be reached or discovered. This view, of course, would automatically catapult us back to a modified perspectival perennialism beset by the problems of the Myth of the Given.

The participatory vision should not then be confused with the view that mystics of the various kinds and traditions simply access different dimensions or perspectives of a ready-made single ultimate reality. This view is obviously under the spell of the Myth of the Given and merely admits that this pre-given spiritual referent can be approached from different vantage points. In contrast, the view I am advancing here is that *no pregiven ultimate reality exists, and that different spiritual ultimates can be enacted through intentional or sponta-neous creative participation in an indeterminate spiritual power or Mystery.*[35]

To be sure, as Grof's research shows, once enacted, spiritual shores become more easily accessible and, in a way, "given" to some extent for indi-vidual consciousness to participate in. Once we enter the Ocean of Emanci-pation, transpersonal forms which have been enacted so far are more readily available and tend more naturally to emerge (from mudras to visionary land-scapes, from liberating insights to ecstatic types of consciousness, etc.). But the fact that enacted shores become more available does not mean that they are predetermined, limited in number, or that no new shores can be enacted through intentional and creative participation. Like trails cleared in a dense forest, spiritual pathways traveled by others can be more easily crossed, but this does not mean that we cannot open new trails and encounter new won-ders (and new pitfalls) in the always inexhaustible Mystery of being.

It is with this vision in mind, I believe, that Heron (1998) rightfully cri-tiques certain authoritarian tendencies of many spiritual traditions. Once we accept that new shores can be enacted, traditional spiritual goals and paths, although a rich source of inspiration, guidance, and wisdom, can no longer be regarded as prescriptive or paradigmatic for all individual spiritual development (Heron, 1998). Each individual is faced with a complex set of spiritual dispositions, options, and choices for which traditional paths may, or may not, be the adequate answer. Furthermore, it is quite probable that there are a number of genuine spiritual potentials whose emergence and expression may not be encouraged or cultivated in traditional spiritual practices. This seems to be the case, for example, of the spiritual transformation of human dimensions that have been historically overlooked or marginalized in traditional settings, such as primary instincts, sexuality, interpersonal intimacy, conscious parenting, emotional intelligence, creative imagination, or spiritual potentials perhaps specific to race, gender, and sexual orientation. Seen in this light, the increasing spiritual eclecticism observable today in Euroamerica, although not without serious hazards and potential abuses, may be seen as the vanguard of an emergent awareness striving to include these other dimensions into a more integral understanding of spirituality.

It is fundamental to distinguish clearly our position not only from perspectival perennialism but also from spiritual relativism and anarchy. The threat of spiritual anarchy is short-circuited by the fact that there are certain transcendental constraints upon the nature of spiritually enacted realities. In other words, there is a spiritual power or Mystery out of which everything arises which, although indeterminate, does impose restrictions on human visionary participation.

As Varela, Thompson, and Rosch (1991) suggest in relation to evolution, the key move "is to switch from a prescriptive logic to a proscriptive one, that is, from the idea that what is not allowed is forbidden to the idea that what is not forbidden is allowed" (p. 195). In our context, we could say that although there are restrictions that invalidate certain enactions, within these parameters an indefinite number of them may be feasible.

A central task for philosophy of religion and the interreligious dialogue, then, is the identification of these parameters or restrictive conditions for the enaction of valid spiritual realities. If I ventured to speculate, I would suggest that the nature of these parameters may have to do not so much with the specific contents of visionary worlds (although certain restrictions may apply), but with the moral values emerging from them, for example, the saintly virtues in Christianity, the perfections (*paramitas*) in Buddhism, and so forth. In this regard, it is noteworthy that, although there are important areas of tension, religions have usually been able to find more common ground in their ethical prescriptions than in doctrinal or metaphysical issues.[36] In any event, the regulative role of such parameters not only frees us from falling into spiritual anarchy, but also, as we will see in the next chapter, paves the way for making qualitative distinctions among spiritual insights and traditions.

Admittedly, to postulate that human intentionality and creativity may influence or even affect the nature of the Divine—understood here as the source of being—may sound somewhat heretical, arrogant, or even inflated. This is a valid concern, but I should add that it stems from a conventional view of the Divine as an isolated and independent entity disconnected from human agency, and that it becomes superfluous in the context of a participatory cosmology: Whenever we understand the relationship between the divine and the human as reciprocal and interconnected, we can, humbly but resolutely, reclaim our creative spiritual role in the divine self-disclosure (cf. Heron, 1998).

The idea of a reciprocal relationship between the human and the divine finds precedents in the world mystical literature. Perhaps its most compelling articulation can be found in the writings of ancient Jewish and Kabbalistic theurgical mystics.[37] For the theurgic mystic, human religious practices have a profound impact not only in the outer manifestation of the divine, but also in its very inner dynamics and structure. Through the performance of the commandments (*mizvot*), the cleaving to God (*devekut*), and other mystical techniques, the theurgic mystic conditions Divine activities such as the restoration of the sphere of the *sefirots*, the unification and augmentation of God's powers, and even the transformation of God's own indwelling (Idel, 1988). As Idel puts it, the theurgic mystic "becomes a cooperator not only in the maintenance of the universe but also in the maintenance or even formation of some aspects of the Deity" (p. 181).

Furthermore, as both Dupré (1996) and McGinn (1996c) observe, this understanding is not absent in Christian mysticism. In the so-called affective mystics (Richard of Saint Victor, Teresa of Avila, Jan van Ruusbroec, etc.), for example, we find the idea that the love for God substantially affects divine self-expression and can even transform God himself. In his discussion of Ruusbroec's mysticism, Dupré (1996) points out:

> In this blissful union the soul comes to share the dynamics of God's inner life, a life not only of rest and darkness but also of creative activity and light. . . . The contemplative accompanies God's own move from hiddenness to manifestation within the identity of God's own life. (p. 17)

And he adds:

> By its dynamic quality the mystical experience surpasses the mere awareness
> of an already present, ontological union. The process of loving devotion *real-*
> *izes* what existed only as potential in the initial stage, thus creating a *new*
> ontological reality. (p. 20)

Although space does not allow me to document this claim here, I believe
that the idea of a spiritual cocreation—"one that many have assumed but few
have dared to express" (Dupré, 1996, p. 22)—is also present in devotional
Sufism, as well as in many Indian traditions such as Shaivism and Buddhism.
In any event, my intention here is not to suggest the universality of this
notion (which clearly is not the case), but merely to show that it has been
maintained by a variety of mystics from different times and traditions.

The Cartesian reduction of spiritual knowledge to an awareness of a
pregiven divinity has also been challenged by a number of contemporary
authors.[38] For example, Heron (1998) recently advanced a participatory theology that posits a dynamic divine becoming which evolves, at least in part,
through human creative participation: "For the theology of action, humans
are co-creators on the crest of divine becoming" (p. 252). In alignment with
our view, Heron (1998) conceives the spiritual path as aimed not at the
encounter with a pregiven divinity, but at the cocreated expression of an
indeterminate and unpredictable divine unfolding. In his own words:

> Based on the notion of our inclusion within innovative divine becoming. . . .
> I believe that we may co-create our path in dynamic relation with a set of
> options emerging from the spiritual life within. (p. 53)

As we have seen, Wilber (1995, 1998a) has also emancipated, to some
extent, his integral theory from the tyranny of spiritual pregivens through
the incorporation of certain elements of the enactive paradigm. For Wilber
(1995), spiritual worldspaces are "not simply given and then merely represented via a correspondency" (p. 541), but codetermined by the interaction
of individual, social, internal, and external factors. Against the idea of spiritual pregivens, he writes:

> [a given spiritual] referent exists *only* in a *worldspace* that is itself *only* disclosed
> in the process of development, and the *signified* exists only in the *interior per-*
> *ception* of those who have developed to that worldspace. . . . The words
> *Buddha-nature* and *Atman* and *Spirit* and *Dharmakaya* are signifiers whose *refer-*
> *ents* exist only in the transpersonal or *spiritual worldspace,* and they therefore

require, for their understanding, a *developmental signified*, and appropriately developed interior or Left-Hand dimension. (1995, p. 272)

Let us remember, however, that Wilber assimilates the enactive paradigm into a vision that upholds a universal sequence of still pregiven deep spiritual structures. In this regard, Wilber (1995) tells us, "Enaction of the presently given worldspace is not just based on *past* structural coupling. Rather, based also on the emergent pressure of the future [the next pregiven deep structure], the present world is enacted" (p. 714). As Heron (1998) comments, however,

> the idea of deep invariance and surface innovation takes away much more than it gives. For it undermines human creativity with an account of its inescapable superficiality. If we already know today the underlying deep structure of future innovation, in what possible sense can it be authentically innovative? Nor does the idea say much for divine originality, if it has nothing new in store for us at the level of deep structures. (p. 81)

Notice here that the acceptance of direction or telos in spiritual evolution does not require either any predetermined pathway or prefixed goal. In other words, teleological thinking does not require a monolithic final causality.

Finally, after his devastating assault on the Cartesian-Kantian paradigm, Tarnas (1991) also urges the need for a participatory epistemology in which human beings are regarded as an essential vehicle for the creative self-unfolding of reality. Speaking in the context of philosophy of science concerning the spiritual dimensions of nature, Tarnas states:

> The essential reality of nature is not separate, self-contained, and complete in itself, so that the human mind can examine it "objectively" and register it from without. Rather, nature's unfolding truth emerges only with the active participation of the human mind. Nature's reality is not merely phenomenal, nor is it independent and objective; rather, it is something that comes into being through the very act of human cognition. . . . Both major forms of epistemological dualism—the conventional precritical and the post-Kantian critical conceptions of human knowledge—are here countered and synthesized. On the one hand, the human mind does not just produce concepts that "correspond" to an external reality. Yet on the other hand, neither does it simply "impose" its own order on the world. Rather, the world's truth realizes itself within and through the human mind. (p. 434)

SUMMARY AND CONCLUSIONS

We began this chapter exploring the merits and shortcomings of perennialist and contextualist accounts of spiritual knowledge. Perennialism rightly emphasizes the existence of common or analogous elements among spiritual traditions, the ontological status of spiritual realities, and their formative role in human spiritual knowledge. And contextualism rightfully draws our attention to the radically contextual nature of spiritual knowledge, the interrelationship of spiritual paths and goals, and the ensuing diversity of spiritual aims and liberations.

Both approaches, however, are burdened by a host of Cartesian-Kantian prejudices that not only reduce their explanatory power, but also force spiritual possibilities into very limiting molds. More specifically, perennialism and contextualism are both contingent on the Dualism of Framework and Reality (i.e., a vision of human knowledge as mediated through conceptual frameworks which can neither directly access nor fully convey a supposedly uninterpreted reality). This basic dualism naturally engenders two interdependent epistemological myths: The Myth of the Given (there is a single pregiven reality out there independent of any cognitive activity), and the Myth of the Framework (we are epistemic prisoners trapped in our conceptual frameworks). Although representatives of these approaches tend to subscribe to both myths to some degree, perennialists seem particularly bewitched by the Myth of the Given, while contextualists tend to be especially constrained by the Myth of the Framework. These epistemological myths, we have seen here, not only create all sorts of pseudo-problems about the nature of spiritual knowing, but also contribute in fundamental ways to human alienation by severing our direct connection with the source of our being.

As a natural remedy for this situation, I have integrated the partial truths of perennialism and contextualism with modern and postmodern epistemological insights into a participatory vision of spirituality. This vision radically overcomes the Dualism of Framework and Reality and enables us to free spirituality from its associated myths. Taking a typical perennialist metaphor as starting point, I suggested that most spiritual traditions lead to the same ocean. However, this ocean is not a single ultimate reality, but a radical overcoming of limiting self-centeredness which can be accompanied by a variety of transconceptual disclosures of reality. This Ocean of Emancipation, as I called it, has different shores that correspond to independent spiritual ultimates to which the various religious traditions are geared. The various spiritual ultimates, rather than being understood as different levels, dimensions, or interpretations of a pregiven Ground of Being, can be seen as independently valid enactions of a dynamic and indeterminate spiritual power. Although there are certain constraints on their nature, these constraints are not absolutely establishable in advance, and the number of feasible enactions of spiritual worlds and ultimates may be, within these boundaries, virtually limitless. As an ancient Islamic proverb says, "God never reveals himself twice in the same form."

Once we *fully* overcome the Dualism of Framework and Reality, then, spiritual paths can no longer be seen either as purely human constructions (Myth of the Framework) or as concurrently aimed at a single, predetermined ultimate reality (Myth of the Given). Once we *fully* exorcise the Cartesian-Kantian spell in spiritual studies and give up our dependence on essentialist metaphysics, in contrast, the various spiritual traditions can be better seen as vehicles for the participatory enaction of different spiritual ultimates and transconceptual worlds. In Panikkar's (1984) words: "The different religious traditions become expressions of the creativity of being striking ever new adventures into the real" (p. 97). In a participatory cosmos, human intentional participation creatively channels and modulates the self-disclosing of Spirit through the bringing forth of visionary worlds and spiritual realities. Spiritual inquiry then becomes a journey beyond any pregiven goal, an endless exploration and disclosure of the inexhaustible possibilities of an always dynamic and indeterminate Mystery. Krishnamurti notwithstanding, spiritual truth is perhaps not a pathless land, but a goalless path.

AFTER THE PARTICIPATORY TURN

Changing our root assumptions about the nature of spiritual knowing has implications for our understanding of many perennial spiritual problems and concerns. In this chapter, I briefly explore how the participatory vision offers new perspectives for our approach to interreligious relations, spiritual developmental models, traditional meditative maps, spiritual epistemology, and the very idea of spiritual liberation.

A FULL DISCUSSION of the manifold implications of the participatory turn for transpersonal and spiritual studies lies beyond the scope of this work. However, this book would be incomplete without mentioning at least a few of them in relation to the following six basic subjects: (1) the ranking of spiritual traditions, (2) transpersonal developmental models, (3) the problem of conflicting truth-claims in religion, (4) the validity of spiritual truths, (5) the problem of mediation in spiritual knowledge, and (6) the very idea of spiritual liberation.

ON RANKING SPIRITUAL TRADITIONS

The participatory turn has important ramifications for our understanding of interreligious relations. Here I revisit the idea of ranking spiritual traditions, and later on I address the associated problem of conflicting truth-claims in religion.

As we have seen, spiritual gradations stem from the postulation of an ultimate referent from which the relative, partial, or lower value of religious systems and insights is assigned. In terms of our metaphor of an ocean with many shores, we could say that, after reaching a previously laid down spiritual shore or enacting a new one, mystics have typically regarded other shores as incomplete, inferior, or simply false. As we suggested in chapter 4, however, there is no agreement whatsoever among mystics about either the nature of this spiritual ultimate or this hierarchy of spiritual insights. This lack of consensus, of course, is not only one of the most puzzling riddles in philosophy of religion, but also an overriding source of debate in contemporary interreligious dialogue. What is even more important, the idea of a universal spiritual ultimate for which traditions compete has profoundly affected how people from different creeds engage one another, and, even today, engenders all types of religious conflicts, quarrels, and even holy wars. Before suggesting a tentative solution to such a conundrum, and in order to grasp its complexity and pervasiveness, I first offer a few cross-cultural examples of spiritual gradations.

Hierarchical gradations of spiritual traditions have been developed in all major religious traditions. As is well known, Christianity often regarded previous pagan religions as incomplete steps towards the final Christian revelation. Likewise, in Islam, the teachings of Jesus and the ancient prophets of Israel are recognized as relatively valid but imperfect versions of the final Truth revealed in the Koran.

The profusion of alternative spiritual gradations in Hinduism is also well known. For example, while Sankara subordinates the belief in a personal, independent God (*Saguna Brahman*) to the nondual monism of Advaita Vedanta,[1] Ramanuja regards the monistic state of becoming Brahman as a stage "on the way to union with [a personal] God" (Zaehner, 1960/1994, p. 63) and claimed that the entire system of Advaita Vedanta was resting on wrong assumptions (Thibaut, 1904). But there is more: Udayana, from the Nyaya school, arranged the rest of Hindu systems into a sequence of distorted stages of understanding of the final truth embodied in his "ultimate Vedanta," which holds the ultimate reality of the "Lord" (*isvara*) (Halbfass, 1991). And "Vijñanabhioksu, the leading representative of the revival of classical Samkhya and Yoga in the sixteenth century, states that other systems are contained in the Yoga of Patañjali and Vyasa just as rivers are preserved and absorbed by the ocean" (Halbfass, 1988a, p. 415). As any scholar of Hinduism can easily realize, these examples could be endlessly multiplied.[2]

In the Buddhist tradition we also find a number of conflicting hierarchies of spiritual insights and schools. As Buswell and Gimello (1992) point out,

> Buddhist schools often sought to associate particular stages along the marga
> [the path], usually lower ones, with various of their sectarian rivals, while
> holding the higher stages to correspond to their own doctrinal positions. . . .
> The purpose of such rankings was not purely interpretive; it often had an
> implicit polemic thrust. (p. 20)

We have already seen, in the words of the Dalai Lama, how Tibetan Buddhism considers the Theravadin and Yogacarin views of emptiness as preliminary and incomplete. It is important to stress that, for Tibetan Buddhists,
their understanding of emptiness is not merely different but more refined,
accurate, and soteriologically effective.[3] Needless to say, this is not an opinion
shared by representatives of other Buddhist schools, which consider their
doctrines complete in their own right, and sufficient to elicit the total awakening described by the Buddha. To mention only one other of the many
alternative Buddhist hierarchies, Kukai, the founder of the Japanese Shingon,
offered a very exhaustive ranking of Confucian, Taoist, and Buddhist systems
culminating in his own school (see, e.g., Kasulis, 1988). In Kukai's "ten
abodes for the mind" (jujushin), Buswell and Gimello (1992) explain,

> the fourth abiding mind corresponds to the Hinayanists, who recognize the
> truth of no-self . . . whereas the sixth relates to the Yogacarins, who generate
> universal compassion for all. Kukai's path then progresses through stages cor-
> responding to the Sanron (Madhyamika), Tendai (T'ien-t'ai), and Kegon
> (Hua-yen) systems, culminating in his own Shingon Esoteric school. (p. 20)

Only in the tenth stage, corresponding to the Shingon school, Kukai considers the Buddhist practitioner fully liberated.

Interestingly enough, contemporary discussions of spiritual gradations
strikingly mirror some of these ancient debates. For example, whereas Wilber
tries to persuade us (à la Sankara) of the more encompassing nature of nonduality when contrasted to dual and theistic traditions, Stoeber's (1994)
theo-monistic model establishes (à la Ramanuja) a mystical hierarchy where
nondual, impersonal, and monistic experiences are subordinated to dual,
personal, and theistic ones.[4] Since we have already seen some of Wilber's
standards and arrangements, let us listen here to Stoeber (1994):

> It is possible in a theistic teleological framework to account for monistic
> experiences in terms of the nature of theistic experiences, treating these as
> necessary and authentic experiences in the mystic theology. But the reverse
> does not hold true in a monistic framework. In a monistic framework theistic
> experiences are not regarded as necessary to the monistic ideal. (pp. 17–18)

What at first sight is more perplexing about these rankings is that their advocates, apparently operating with analogous criteria (such as encompassing capacity), reach radically opposite conclusions about the relationship between nondual and theistic spirituality. When examined more closely, however, this should not be too surprising. The criteria proposed are often vague enough that they can be interpreted to favor one's preferred tradition upon the rest. Take, for example, Wilber's guideline that "a higher level has extra capacities than previous ones." Obviously, what counts as "extra capacities" can be, and actually is, differently judged by the various authors and traditions according to their doctrinal commitments (e.g., nonduality versus the personal and relational qualities of the Divine).

After the participatory turn, however, these interreligious rankings can be recognized as parasitic upon the Cartesian-Kantian assumptions we have gradually uncovered and questioned. Hierarchical arrangements of spiritual insights, that is, heavily depend on the assumption of a universal and pregiven spiritual ultimate relative to which such judgments can be made. To put it another way, these interreligious judgments make sense only if we first presuppose one or another version of the Myth of the Given, and/or the existence of a single noumenal reality behind the multifarious spiritual experiences and doctrines. Whenever we drop these assumptions, however, the very idea of ranking traditions according to a paradigmatic standpoint becomes both fallacious and superfluous. Do not misunderstand me. I am not suggesting that spiritual insights and traditions are incommensurable, but merely that it may be seriously misguided to compare them according to any pre-established spiritual hierarchy. In a moment, I will suggest some directions where these comparative grounds can be sought, but let us first examine the elaboration of transpersonal developmental models in light of our discussion about hierarchical gradations.

TRANSPERSONAL DEVELOPMENTAL MODELS

Briefly, I would like to offer here some words of caution about distilling transpersonal developmental models from traditional meditative cartographies. Traditional meditative maps have been generally regarded by transpersonal psychologists as phenomenological descriptions of spiritual experiences occurring during meditation. What is more, some transpersonal authors have drawn universalist conclusions—both descriptive and prescriptive—about cross-cultural stages of human spiritual development out of the comparative analysis of Eastern meditative maps (e.g., Brown, 1986; Wilber, 1995, 1996b).[5]

However, it is fundamental to remember, and this is something invariably overlooked by transpersonal authors, that *most traditional meditative maps were derived from didactic gradations of spiritual insights, and may therefore not have so much to do with firsthand meditative experiences as with apologetics and scholasticism.*

In his rigorous analysis of Buddhist modernism, for example, Sharf (1995a) indicates how misguided it may be to interpret works such as Buddhagosa's *Visuddhimagga* as based on phenomenological descriptions of meditative experience—as it is frequently understood in transpersonal works (e.g., Brown, 1986; Goleman, 1977; Walsh, 1984, 1990, 1993b; Wilber, 1996b). In this influential work, Buddhaghosa explicitly states that his account of the Buddhist path relies on the study of scripture, and nowhere does he suggest that it is founded on his or others' meditative experiences (Sharf, 1995a). The same can be said of other popular meditative treatises such as Asanga's *Bodhisattvabhumi* ("Stages of the Boddhisattva's Path"), Tsong kha pa's *Lam rim chen mo* ("Great Book of the Stages of the Path"), or Kamalasila's *Bhavanakrama* ("Course of Practice"):

> Rarely if ever do the authors of these compendiums claim to base their expositions on their own experience. On the contrary, the authority of exegetes such as Kamalasila, Buddhaghosa, and Chih-I lay not in their access to exalted spiritual states but in their mastery of, and rigorous adherence to, sacred scripture. (Sharf, 1998, p. 99)[6]

This eminently scriptural foundation of meditation manuals should not come as a surprise. After all, before the Hindu renaissance (i.e., Rammohan Roy, Radhakrishna, etc.) and the modernization of Buddhism (i.e., the *vipassana* revival of South Asia, the Kyoto school of Kitaro Nishida, the Westernized Buddhism of D. T. Suzuki, etc.), spiritual experiences were not considered the goal of practice, and their epistemological status was also usually judged as ambiguous and deceptive (Faure, 1991, 1993; Halbfass, 1988b; Sharf, 1998). For example, two of the most celebrated Buddhist epistemologists, Dharmakirti and Candrakirti, strongly reject the validation or legitimization of spiritual knowledge on the grounds of meditative experiences (see Halbfass, 1988b, p. 393; Hayes, 1997).

In general, then, traditional descriptions of stages of the path should be understood not so much as descriptions of meditative states, but as *prescriptions for spiritual development according to doctrinal commitments and scriptural canons.* What is more, in some cases they may not even have played this pre-scriptive role either, but merely had a scholastic intention. As Buddhologists Buswell and Gimello (1992) warn us,

> Although the design of an intellectually consistent and logically indefeasible marga, in which all stages of the path serve a necessary function, may have been an interesting scholastic device, it may also have little if anything to do with actual meditative practice. In the mind of the Buddhist scholastics who created these elaborate schemes, personal spiritual experience need not always have been at issue. While this is no doubt a pejorative conclusion—and one that the scholastic traditions themselves would probably have rejected—the evidence demands that we make it.
>
> Indeed, the elaborate and meticulous construction of hierarchies of religious understanding may derive from a breakdown in religious praxis. Such failure might well have forced the creation of conceptual systems as an attempt to explain religious transitions that seemed problematic because they were no longer being achieved. It may be, then, that in some cases hierarchically arranged and progressive margas were not intended as guides to actual experience. (pp. 19–20)

Stressing this scholastic (versus practical) nature of stage maps of the Buddhist path, Pandith Vajragnana (1997) states: "It is not absolutely necessary to pass all the stages; Buddha never explained things in this way. The later teachers systematized things in the form of stages. A meditator does not try to pass these stages one by one in sequence" (p. 184).

In any event, what should be clear is that the development of traditional meditative maps generally occurred in the context of scholastic exegesis or apologetic hierarchical gradations. The prescriptive character of traditional meditative cartographies obviously presents a serious challenge to common transpersonal interpretations. *If meditative guides were not so much based on phenomenological reports, but were written as injunctions to enact particular spiritual doctrines, and if these doctrines are, as even perennialists admit, different and often incompatible, then the abstraction of a universal spiritual path out of them may be seriously flawed.*

From our viewpoint, however, the eminently prescriptive nature of traditional meditative maps is no longer cause for difficulty or despair. On the contrary, once we let go of universalist agendas in spiritual hermeneutics, the value of these maps can be fully understood and honored. Specifically, these maps can now be regarded as highly sophisticated *enactive codes* of particular spiritual shores. In other words, each meditative guide contains a set of injunctions, practices, rituals, symbols, and parameters that function as the ignition key and regulative system for the enaction and embodiment of particular spiritual liberations, spiritual ultimates, and/or transconceptual disclosures of reality. In this light, the scholastic and apologetic nature of these cartographies stops being a potential shortcoming. Although the actual effectiveness of these enactive codes is an open question (Buswell & Gimello, 1992), their creative potential to bring forth a plurality of spiritual insights and realities can now be fully appreciated and celebrated.

THE PROBLEM OF CONFLICTING TRUTH CLAIMS IN RELIGION

Closely related to the ranking of traditions is the so-called problem of conflicting truth-claims in religion. Roughly, this problem refers to the incompatible ultimate claims religious traditions make about the nature of reality, spirituality, and human identity (see, e.g., Christian, 1972; Griffiths, 1991; Hick, 1974, 1983). Since all religions have been imagined to aim at the same spiritual end, the diversity of religious accounts of ultimate reality is not only perplexing, but also conflicting and problematic.

Although with different nuances, the attempts to explain such divergences have typically taken one of the three following routes: dogmatic exclusivism ("my religion is the only true one, the rest must be false"), hierarchical inclusivism ("my religion is the most accurate or complete, the rest must be lower or partial"), and ecumenical pluralism ("there may be real differences between our religions, but all must ultimately lead to the same end").[7] Alternatively, to put it in terms of the models outlined above, contextualism invokes conceptual frameworks, and perennialism appeals to hierarchical gradations of traditions and/or to esotericist, perspectivist, or structuralist explanations. All these stances, we can now see, are still animated by the Cartesian-Kantian dualisms and myths we exposed and challenged in the last chapter.

After the participatory turn, however, a more satisfactory response to this conundrum naturally emerges. In short, my thesis is that once we give up Cartesian-Kantian assumptions about a pregiven or noumenal spiritual reality common to all traditions, the so-called problem of conflicting truth-claims becomes, for the most part, a pseudoproblem.[8] In other words, the diversity of spiritual claims is a problem only when we have previously presupposed that they are referring to a single, ready-made spiritual reality.[9] However, if rather than resulting from the access and visionary representation of a pregiven reality, spiritual knowledge is enacted, then spiritual truths need no longer be conceived as "conflicting." Divergent truth-claims are conflicting only if they intend to represent a single referent of determined features. As Heim (1995) suggests in relation to the various spiritual fulfillments: "Nirvana and communion with God are contradictory only if we assume that one or the other must be the sole fate for all human beings" (p. 149). But if we see such a spiritual referent as malleable, indeterminate, and open to a multiplicity of disclosures contingent on human creative endeavors, then the reasons for conflict vanish like a mirage. In this light, the threatening snake we saw in the dark basement can now be recognized as a peaceful and connecting rope.

In short, by giving up our dependence on Cartesian-Kantian premises in spiritual hermeneutics, religious traditions are released from their predicament of metaphysical competition and a more constructive and fertile interreligious space is naturally engendered. To break the Cartesian-Kantian spell in spiritual studies, that is, leads to affirming the uniqueness and legitimacy of each tradition in its own right, and only from this platform, I believe, can a genuine interreligious dialogue be successfully launched. Once traditions stop thinking of themselves as superior or closer to *the* Truth, peoples from diverse belief systems can encounter each other in the spirit of open dialogue, collaborative inquiry, and mutual transformation.[10]

The diversity of spiritual truths and cosmologies, then, rather than being a source of conflict or even cause for considerate tolerance, can now be reason for wonder and celebration. Wonder in the wake of the inexhaustible creative power of the self-unfolding of being. And celebration in the wake of the recognition of both our participatory role in such unfolding, and the emerging possibilities for mutual respect, enrichment, and cross-fertilization out of the encounter of traditions. "This plurality of consensual beliefs," Irwin (1996) tells us,

> need not lead to the error that one must choose among alternatives or be lost, must accept the validity of a particular visionary world or suffer the consequences of indecision or despair. *There is a creative power in the plurality of visionary worlds*, a convergence of forms and ideas of immeasurable depth. (p. 34; italics added)

Conceived as diverse but not conflicting visions, traditions can stop their quarrels about which one embodies the final Truth, philosophers of religion can let go of the tensions created by the irreconcilable religious ultimate claims, and perhaps people from different creeds can encounter one another in the spirit of mutual respect, enrichment, and transformation.

Two points need to be stressed at this point of our discussion. First, in my view, spiritual pluralism does not exist only at a doctrinal level, but at a metaphysical one. Plurality is not merely an exoteric diversion, but fundamentally engrained in the innermost core of each tradition. As Panikkar (1984) forcefully puts it: "Pluralism penetrates into the very heart of the ultimate reality" (p. 110).[11] And second, there is not a necessary, intrinsic, or a priori hierarchical relationship among the various spiritual universes. There is no final, privileged, or more encompassing spiritual viewpoint. There is neither a "view from nowhere" (Nagel, 1986), nor a "view from everywhere" (H. Smith, 1989). No human being can claim access to a God's eye that can judge from above which tradition contains more parcels of a single Truth, not because this Truth is noumenally inaccessible, but because it is intrinsically indeterminate, malleable, and plural.

Needless to say, this double recognition does not snare us in spiritual anarchy or relativist cul-de-sacs. The malleable and indeterminate nature of reality does not mean that anything goes in spiritual matters. True, as William James (1975) points out, "the world stands really malleable, waiting to receive its final touches at our hands" (p. 123).[12] But a participatory vision is not an idealist one. Although reality does not have a fixed essence, it presents us with identifiable qualities, tendencies, and restrictions. And these conditions, though allowing for a rich variety of possible enactions, not only preclude the arbitrariness of the spiritual universes, but also impose limitations on the human creative participation and expression of spiritual truths. In spiritual matters, as in anything else, anything does *not* go and everything matters.

THE VALIDITY OF SPIRITUAL TRUTHS

As for the thorny issue of the validity of spiritual insights, I should say that the criteria stemming from a participatory account of spiritual knowing can no longer be simply dependent on the picture of reality disclosed (although, again, certain restrictions may apply), but on the kind of transformation of self, community, and world facilitated by their enaction and expression. That is, once we fully accept the creative link between human beings and the real in spiritual knowing, judgments about how accurately spiritual claims correspond to or represent ultimate reality become nearly meaningless. The goal of contemplative systems is not so much to describe, represent, mirror, and know, but to prescribe, enact, embody, and transform. Or to put it in terms of the Buddhist notion of skillful means (*upaya*): "The chief measure of a teaching's truth or value is its efficacy unto religious ends, rather than any correspondence with facts" (Buswell & Gimello, 1992, p. 4). In other words, *the validity of spiritual knowledge does not rest in its accurate matching with any pre-given content, but in the quality of selfless awareness disclosed and expressed in perception, thinking, feeling, and action.*

It cannot be stressed strongly enough that to reject a pregiven spiritual ultimate referent does not prevent us from making qualitative distinctions in spiritual matters. To be sure, like beautiful porcelains made out of amorphous clay, traditions can not be qualitatively ranked according to their accuracy in representing any original template. However, this does not mean that we cannot discriminate between more evocative, skillful, or sophisticated artifacts. Grounds to decide the comparative and relative value of different spiritual truths can be sought, for example, not in a prearranged hierarchy of spiritual insights or by matching spiritual claims against a ready-made spiritual reality, but by assessing their emancipatory power for self and world, both intra- and interreligiously. By the *emancipatory power* of spiritual truths I mean their *capability to free individuals, communities, and cultures from gross and subtle forms of narcissism, egocentrism, and self-centeredness.* In very general terms, then, and to start exploring these potential qualitative distinctions, I believe that we can rightfully ask some of the following questions: How much does the cultivation and embodiment of these truths result in a movement away from self-centeredness? How much do they lead to the emergence of selfless awareness and/or action in the world? How much do they promote the growth and maturation of love and wisdom? To what degree do they deliver the promised fruits? How effective are they in leading their followers to harmony, balance, truthfulness, and justice within themselves, their communities, and towards the world at large? And so forth.

Apart from their emancipatory power, there is another orientation relevant to the making of qualitative distinctions among spiritual insights. Essentially, I see the project of constructing frameworks to portray a supposedly pregiven reality the hallmark of false knowing, that is, the pretension of a proud mind to represent a ready-made reality without the collaboration of other levels of the person (instinct, body, heart, etc.), which, I believe, are crucial for the construction of genuine knowledge. In contrast, I propose that an enaction of reality is more valid when it is not only a mental-spiritual matter, but a multidimensional process that involves all levels of the person. Although space does not allow me to elaborate this point here, I believe that we are in direct contact with an always dynamic and indeterminate Mystery through our most vital energy. When the various levels of the person are cleared out from interferences (e,g., energetic blockages, bodily embedded shame, splits in the heart, pride of the mind, and struggles at all levels), this energy naturally flows and gestates within us, undergoing a process of transformation through our bodies and hearts, ultimately illuminating the mind with a knowing that is both grounded in and coherent with the Mystery. Because of the dynamic nature of the Mystery, as well as our historically and culturally situated condition, this knowing is never final, but always in constant evolution.

This being said, qualitative distinctions can be made among the various enactions by not only judging their emancipatory power, but also discriminating how grounded in or coherent with the Mystery they are. For example, it is likely that, due to a number of historical and cultural variables, most past and present spiritual visions are to some extent the product of dissociated ways of knowing—ways of knowing that emerge predominantly from the mental access to subtle dimensions of transcendent consciousness, but that are ungrounded and disconnected from vital and immanent spiritual sources. This type of spiritual knowledge, although certainly containing important and genuine insights, is both prey to numerous distortions and, at best, a partial understanding that claims to portray the totality. As I experience it, our lived engagement with both transcendent and immanent spiritual energies not only renders a priori hierarchical spiritual gradations obsolete, but also provides an orientation to critique more or less dissociated constructions.

Therefore, a sharp distinction needs to be drawn between "knowledge that is matched with a pregiven reality" and "knowing that is grounded in, aligned to, or coherent with the Mystery." As I see it, the former expression inevitably catapults us into objectivist and representational epistemologies in which there can exist, at least in theory, one single most accurate representation. The latter expressions, in contrast, as well as my understanding of truth as attunement to the unfolding of being, emancipate us from these limitations and open us up to a potential multiplicity of visions that can be firmly grounded in, and equally coherent with, the Mystery. This is why there may be a variety of valid ontologies which nonetheless can be equally harmonious with the Mystery and, in the realm of human affairs, manifest through a similar ethics of love, compassion, and commitment to the blooming of life in all its constructive manifestations (human and nonhuman).

Two important qualifications need to be made about these suggested guidelines. The first relates to the fact that, as the Dalai Lama (1988, 1996) stresses, some spiritual paths and liberations may be more adequate for different psychological and cultural dispositions, but this does not make them universally superior or inferior. The well-known four yogas of Hinduism (reflection, devotion, action, and experimentation) come quickly to mind in this regard, as well as other spiritual typologies that can be found in both Hinduism and other traditions (see, e.g., Beena, 1990; H. Smith, 1994). The second refers to the complex difficulties inherent in any proposal of cross-cultural criteria for religious truth (see, e.g., Vroom, 1989; Dean, 1995; Stenger, 1995). It should be obvious, for example, that my emphasis on the overcoming of narcissism and self-centeredness, although I believe it central to most spiritual traditions, may not be shared by all. A related problem is the fact that values such as wisdom, justice, freedom, harmony or truthfulness may be more representative of certain traditions than others, and some probably reflect a Western bias. To complicate these matters even more, what constitutes wisdom, freedom, or harmony may be diversely understood in various traditions.

These and other difficulties make it imperative to stress the very tentative and conjectural status of any cross-cultural criteria for spiritual truth. But there is more. I do not think that any resolution about cross-cultural spiritual criteria can be legitimately attained by scholars, religious leaders, or even mystics on a priori grounds. What I am suggesting is that the search for criteria for cross-cultural religious truth is not a logical, rational, or even spiritual problem to be solved by isolated individuals or traditions, but a *practical task* to be accomplished in the fire of interreligious dialogue and in actual practices and their fruits. In other words, the difficulties in finding such criteria are due to the fact that they may well not exist as yet, but are waiting to emerge in dialogical space and in the fruits of actual practices, not in the individual minds of scholars or even living mystics.[13]

But then, where does all this leave us? Once again, Irwin (1996) offers a discerning perception of the situation:

If we reject the absolute claims of any one system and reject the abstract construction of a "transcendent unity" embedded in a Western dialectical ontology, then we are left with an open, permissive horizon of transpersonal encounters. This relativizes the epistemological claims of any exclusive system, mystical, rational or artistic and shifts the emphasis toward more symbolically constructed transpersonal paradigms. (p. 180)

In a similar vein, after his critique of universalist and absolutist visions of religion, Panikkar (1988) concludes:

The alternative is neither anarchy nor irrationalism. . . . The alternative is a dynamic notion of freedom, of Being, and the radical relativity of everything with everything, so that all our explanations are not only for the time being, because ours is a being in time, but also because no Absolute can encompass the complexity of the Real, which is radically free. (p. 145)

THE PROBLEM OF MEDIATION IN SPIRITUAL KNOWLEDGE

An exhaustive treatment of mediation in spiritual knowledge would require at least an entire chapter, so I will merely suggest here how its supposedly pernicious implications are dissolved by the participatory turn. *Mediation* is generally understood, after Kant, as the process or processes by which human beings access, filter, organize, and know the world through a series of constructions and dispositions, such as deep structures, cultural understandings, world views, paradigms, epistemes, conceptual frameworks, languages, cognitive schemes, and a number of neurophysiological mechanisms. These processes, we are told, not only operate at conscious and unconscious levels of awareness, but also limit and shape in fundamental ways what we can possibly know about ourselves and the world. Central to the notion of mediation is that it is only through these constructions and mechanisms that human beings can make intelligible the raw input of an otherwise inscrutable reality.[14]

One of the most radical and controversial claims of mysticism is that, contrary to the modern thesis of mediation, mystical awareness allows human beings to transcend all mediating lenses and directly realize their essential identity, ultimate reality, or the divine. As we have seen, mystical claims to immediacy were one of the main targets of the contextualist program in the study of mysticism. According to Katz (1978b), let us remember,

there are *no* pure (i.e., unmediated) experiences. Neither mystical experience nor more ordinary forms of experience give any indication, or any grounds for believing, that they are unmediated. That is to say, all experience is processed through, organized by, and makes itself available to us in extremely complex epistemological ways. The notion of unmediated experience seems, if not self-contradictory, at best empty. (p. 26)

In response, some perennialist scholars have suggested that these mediating factors, rather than causing, contaminating, or constituting mystical experiences, are the catalyst or context in which truly universal and direct insights emerge (Forman, 1990b; Perovich, 1985a; Wilber, 1995). In his critique of Katz, for example, Wilber (1995) tells us that "I find myself in *immediate* experience of *mediated* worlds" (p. 601). Although not a perennialist, Heron (1998) also offers an understanding of mystical knowledge in terms of mediated-immediacy:

> My experience is subjective and mediated because I shape it within my context, including my intersubjective social context and my participation in nature and cosmos—the field of interbeing. It is objective and immediate because through it I meet and touch what there is, given Being. (p. 15)

These are, I believe, valid rejoinders to the contextualist challenge, and here I would like to expand this response with a further argument against the thesis of mediation not only in mystical but also in human knowledge in general.[15]

The first step to take is to recognize that the notion of mediation presupposes the Dualism of Framework and Reality we deconstructed in last chapter. On the one hand, we have an unfathomable pregiven reality or "thing-in-itself," and, on the other, a variety of mediating mechanisms through which such reality becomes phenomenally accessible to us. In the Cartesian-Kantian paradigm, then, mediation becomes both inescapable and alienating. It is inescapable because a bridge needs to be built between subject and object, as well as between phenomenal and noumenal realities. And it is alienating because, as Tarnas (1991) convincingly argues, these dualisms ineluctably place us out of touch from a reality that is the very source of our being.

But if, as I have argued, the Dualism of Framework and Reality is implausible, and if the belief in a pregiven reality is perhaps no more than mere fiction, then the very idea of mediation cannot be but misleading and dispensable. The so-called problem of mediation, I am suggesting here, is nothing but another Kantian myth engendered by the illusory Dualism of Framework and Reality.

In a participatory epistemology free from these Cartesian-Kantian molds, the so-called mediating principles (languages, symbols, etc.) are no longer imprisoning, contaminating, or alienating barriers that prevent us from a direct, intimate contact with the world. On the contrary, once we accept that there is not a pregiven reality to be mediated, these factors are revealed as the vehicles through which reality or being self-manifests in the locus of the human. Like Gadamer's (1990) revision of the nature of historical prejudices, that is, *mediation is transformed from being an obstacle into the very means that enable us to directly participate in the self-disclosure of the world.* Tarnas (1991) gets to the heart of the matter:

> All human knowledge of the world is in some sense determined by subjective principles [mediating factors]; but instead of considering these principles as belonging ultimately to the separate human subject, and therefore not grounded in the world independently of human cognition, this participatory conception held that these subjective principles are in fact an expression of the world's own being, and that the human mind is ultimately the organ of the world's own process of self-revelation. (pp. 433–434)

It is in this vein, I believe, that Panikkar (1996) argues that the problem of mediation arises from the split between ontology and epistemology in modern philosophy. Although maintaining the onetime need of this split for the achievement of self-reflective awareness, Panikkar points out that it needs to and can be healed through "a more mature philosophy, which being aware of the distinction (epistemology/ontology, subject/object) does not break it in two pieces" (p. 232). Once this integration is attained, Panikkar (1996) continues,

> There is no need of epistemological mediation because ontologically everything is ultimate mediation, or rather *communion*. Everything is, because it mediates. Everything is in relation because everything is relation. (p. 235)

In other words, *a participatory epistemology transforms the "problem of mediation" into intimate communion with the cosmos.* The quality of intimacy emerging from this shift suggests, I believe, that our most basic participation in reality needs to be understood, not so much in terms of a hermeneutics of discovery (of pregiven meanings and objects) or a hermeneutics of suspicion (of distorting and contaminating factors), but of a *hermeneutics of the heart* (of love, trust, and communion with reality).

The rationale for such an hermeneutics of the heart is evocatively illustrated by the following thought experiment provided by Tarnas (1998):

> Imagine you are the universe, a deep, beautiful, ensouled universe, and you are being courted by a suitor. Would you open your deepest secrets to the suitor—that is, to the methodology, the epistemology—who would approach

you as though you were unconscious, utterly lacking in intelligence or purpose, and inferior in being to him; who related to you as though you were ultimately there for his exploitation, development, and self-enhancement; and his
motivation for knowing you is driven essentially by a desire for prediction and
control for his own self-betterment? Or would you open your deepest secrets
to that suitor—that epistemology, that methodology—who viewed you as
being at least as intelligent and powerful and full of mystery as he is, and who
sought to know you by uniting with you to create something new? (p. 59)

The moral of this thought experiment, of course, is that for its deeper secrets
to be revealed, the world needs less suspicion and domination, and more love
and cosmic trust. We need to cultivate, as Panikkar (1988) puts it, a "cosmic
confidence in reality" whose ultimate ground "lies in the almost universal
conviction that reality is ordered—in other words, is good, beautiful, and
true. It is a divine Reality" (p. 144). When we look deeply into the nature of
such trust, Panikkar (1996) adds, we realize that this

> cosmic confidence is not trust in the world, confidence in the cosmos. It is
> the confidence of the cosmos itself, of which we form a part inasmuch as we
> simply are.... The confidence itself is a cosmic fact of which we are more or
> less aware, and which we presuppose all the time. (p. 281)

To reiterate, the universe needs less obsession and paranoia and more
love. Only by our becoming its sincere and unconditional lovers is the cosmos likely to reciprocate and offer us its intimate secrets and precious pearls.
And, which are these precious pearls? To be sure, they are as infinite as the
universe itself. Nevertheless, I would like to venture here, the most valuable
gifts we can receive are probably answers to what Needleman (1982) calls
the Great Questions of Life, namely, Who am I? Why are we here? What's
the meaning of life? Is there life after death? What can we know? Is there a
God? How should we live? And so forth. As Needleman stresses, the
response to these questions cannot be given to us in propositional or objectivist fashion, but gracefully offered as states of being in which these mysteries turn into Mysteries, ceasing to be the cause of sorrow and anxiety, and
becoming the source of boundless wonder, joy, and celebration.

SPIRITUAL LIBERATION

The thesis of a plurality of spiritual ultimates also has important implications
for our understanding of spiritual liberation. Traditionally, spiritual liberation
is said to involve two interrelated dimensions:

1. Soteriological-phenomenological, or the attainment of human fulfill-
ment, salvation, redemption, enlightenment, or happiness.

2. Epistemological-ontological, or the knowledge of "things as they really
are," ultimate reality, or the Divine.[16]

Interestingly, according to most traditions, there is a relation of mutual causality and even final identity between these two defining dimensions of spiritual
emancipation: To know is to be liberated, and if you are free, you know.

It has been my contention that, although most traditions concur in that
liberation implies an overcoming of limiting self-centeredness and associated
restricted perspectives, this can be cultivated, embodied, and expressed in a
variety of independent ways. Likewise, I also advanced the even more radical
thesis that this spiritual plurality is not only soteriological or phenomenological, but also epistemological, ontological, and metaphysical. Put simply, there is
a multiplicity of spiritual liberations and spiritual ultimates. The tasks remain,
however, to address the tension between our account and the traditional claim
that liberation is equivalent to knowing "things as they really are," as well as to
explore the implications of our viewpoint for spiritual blossoming.

To begin with, I should admit straight off that this tension is a real one,
and that the participatory vision will probably not be acceptable to those
who firmly believe in the exclusive or privileged truth of their religions.
While respecting the many thoughtful and sensitive individuals who maintain exclusivist or inclusivist stances, I see these pretensions as problematic
assumptions that not only cannot be consistently maintained in our pluralistic contemporary world, but also frequently lead to a deadlock in the interfaith dialogue.

The practice of authentic dialogue requires not only the willingness and
ability to actively listen to and understand others, but also the openness to be
challenged and transformed by their viewpoints. As we have seen, the basic
problem with absolutist stances in this regard is that once one believes to be
in possession of the Truth about "things as they really are," dialogue with
people maintaining conflicting viewpoints cannot but become an uninteresting and sterile monologue. At worst, the conflicting viewpoints are
regarded as less evolved, incoherent, or simply false. At best, the challenges
presented are assimilated within the all-encompassing absolutist framework.
In both cases, absolutists appear not to be able to listen to what other people
are saying, because all new or conflicting information is screened, processed,

or assimilated in terms of his or her own framework. Therefore, a genuine or symmetrical encounter with the other in which opposing viewpoints are regarded as real options is rendered unlikely (Ferrer, 1998a).

The many arguments showing the untenability of religious absolutism are well known and need not be repeated here (see, e.g., Byrne, 1995; Panikkar, 1984; Wiggins, 1996). To the standard ones, I would like to add two. The first is that the very idea of a unique and privileged access to the one spiritual Truth heavily depends on the Cartesian–Kantian assumptions whose dubious nature I hope to have convincingly suggested in the last chapter (the Myth of the Given, the Dualism of Framework and Reality, etc.). The second is that it may be argued that religious absolutism is inconsistent with the nature of spiritual liberation as maintained by those religious traditions themselves. Most traditions equate spiritual liberation with boundless freedom. But if we rigidly maintain the exclusive Truth of our tradition, are we not binding ourselves to a particular, limited disclosure of reality? And if we tie our very being to a singular, even if transconceptual, disclosure of reality, then, we can rightfully wonder, how truly boundless is our spiritual freedom? Is this freedom truly boundless or rather a subtle form of spiritual bondage? And if so, is this the promised spiritual freedom we are truly longing for?

As I see it, the apparent tension between the participatory vision and the mystical claims of metaphysical ultimacy can be relaxed by simultaneously holding that (1) all traditions are potentially correct in maintaining that they lead to a direct insight into "things as they *really* are," and (2) this "really" does not refer to a Cartesian pregiven reality. Despite our deep-seated dispositions to equate Cartesian objectivity with reality, it is fundamental to realize that to reject the Myth of the Given is not to say good-bye to reality, but to pave the way for encountering it in all its complexity, dynamism, and mystery. From this perspective, the expression "things as they really are" is misguided only if understood in the context of objectivist and essentialist epistemologies, but not if conceived in terms of participatory enactions of reality free from egocentric distortions. After all, let us remember here, what most mystical traditions offer are not so much descriptions of a pregiven ultimate reality to be confirmed or falsified by experiential evidence, but prescriptions of ways of "being-*and*-the-world" to be intentionally cultivated and lived. The descriptive claims of the contemplative traditions primarily apply to the deluded or alienated ordinary human predicament, as well as to the various visions of self and world disclosed throughout the unfolding of each soteriological path. But since there are many possible enactions of truer and more liberated self and world, it may be more accurate to talk about them not so much in terms of "things as they really are," but of "things as they really can be" or even "things as they really should be." While the expression "things as they really can be" would remain more neutral, the expression "things as they really should be" would stress the all-important ethical dimension of the contemplative endeavor, for example, in terms of moral criticism of egocentric understandings of reality and associated ways of life.

Whatever expression we choose to use (and all of them are valid having made the appropriate qualifications), it should be clear that when we say that this "really" refers to an understanding of reality free from the distorting lenses of narcissism and self-centeredness, we are not limiting contemplative claims to their phenomenological dimension. On the contrary, a participatory epistemology can fully explain, in a way that no Cartesian paradigm can, why most traditions consider these two dimensions of liberation (phenomenological and ontological) radically intertwined. *If reality is not merely discovered but enacted through cocreative participation, and if what we bring to our inquiries affects in important ways the disclosure of reality, then the fundamental interrelationship, and even identity, between phenomenology and ontology, between knowledge and liberation, in the spiritual search stops being a conundrum and becomes a natural necessity.* And if this is the case, there is no conflict whatsoever for the participatory vision to simultaneously maintain that there exist a plurality of spiritual ultimates and that all of them may disclose "things as they really are."

But, what about ecumenical pluralism? It is important to note that traditional religious pluralism emerged within the modern Cartesian-Kantian world view. Ecumenical pluralism understands religious traditions as leading to different interpretations, dimensions, or phenomenal awarenesses of an ineffable single spiritual ultimate. Tolerance among traditions is then attained, but at the cost of inadvertently invalidating some of the most fundamental mystical claims, such as the direct nature of mystical knowledge or that spiritual liberation leads to "things as they really are." In his excellent study of reference and realism in mysticism, Byrne (1995) reaches a similar conclusion:

> If pluralism is true, then rich, living, doctrinally loaded accounts of the nature of transcendental reality and of salvation are both necessary and inevitably flawed. They are necessary for the moulding of the practical and experiential complexes by means of which humankind can genuinely relate to the sacred.

They are inevitably flawed, for from the nature of the case they cannot claim strict truth with any certainty. (p. 201)

Recapitulating our discussion so far, neither religious absolutism (exclusivist or inclusivist) nor ecumenical pluralism can truly honor both the plurality of spiritual ultimate claims and the fact that they may all be disclosing "things as they really are." Only a participatory vision of the sort espoused here can consistently explain, and epistemologically anchor, spiritual pluralism while simultaneously preserving the ontological claims of mysticism.

Finally, after this participatory emancipation of spirituality out of its modern experiential confinement, spiritual liberation can no longer be conceived as a merely individual or private affair. Once our understanding of the nature of spirituality is expanded to include our relationships and the world, the locus of spiritual realization needs to be accordingly expanded too. Liberation is not an intrasubjective experience, nor is it a merely personal event. This move towards a more relational approach to liberation is in perfect alignment, I believe, with emergent spiritual trends such as feminist spirituality, deep ecology, liberation theology, socially engaged spirituality, as well as with the possibility of collective transformation via participation in morphic fields of collective identities (Bache, 2000). Related to this is the fact that, if total, liberation needs to transform all the dimensions of our being, not only perceptual and cognitive, but also emotional, sexual, interpersonal, somatic, imaginal, intuitive, and so forth (Rothberg, 1996a, 1996b, 1999; Wilber, 1997a).

Furthermore, I would argue that this expanded vision of spiritual liberation is implicit in the very idea of transpersonal identity. If our transpersonal identity encompasses other beings and even the entire cosmos, can we then be fully liberated when our relationships with others are deeply problematic? Can we be fully liberated when people around us suffer? Can we be fully liberated when our world is moving towards ecological collapse? In the light of this awareness, of course, a commitment to the liberation of all beings becomes an existential imperative.

SUMMARY AND CONCLUSIONS

In this chapter, I have explored some of the implications of the participatory turn for transpersonal and spiritual studies. This analysis revealed that the participatory vision casts light and suggests new directions in at least the following six areas: the ranking of spiritual traditions, transpersonal developmental models, the problem of conflicting truth claims in religion, the validity of spiritual truths, the problem of mediation in spiritual knowledge, and the nature of spiritual liberation. Rather than repeating here these numerous implications, I would like to conclude this chapter by addressing an interesting paradox that threatens to corrode my presentation.

Briefly, the paradox I am referring to results from the fact that my account of the indeterminate nature of ultimate reality may be seen to be, legitimately I believe, more in alignment with some spiritual traditions than others. It can be said, for example, that to suggest that the Mystery of Being has no pregiven essence is more consistent with certain Buddhist understandings of emptiness (*sunyata*) than with traditional accounts of the Christian God or the Advaitin Brahman.[17] As is well known, emptiness (*sunyata*) was depicted by Nagarjuna and other Buddhist thinkers as the lack of intrinsic nature of reality (*svabhava*), which leads to the avoidance of all reifying views and a radical openness to reality. But then, the participatory vision can be accused of severely undermining some of its own fundamental intentions. To wit, if the participatory vision subtly favors some traditions over others, is it not then implicitly establishing the kind of hierarchical gradation whose death it triumphantly announces? Or even worse, if the participatory vision holds that central to spiritual liberation is the emancipation from any particular disclosure of ultimate reality, is it not situating itself above all traditions? In any case, is not the participatory vision then sabotaging the very spiritual pluralism that it advocates? Is not the participatory vision then blatantly self-defeating or self-contradictory?

Of course, since there is no neutral spiritual ground, paradoxes like this inevitably emerge from any cross-cultural account of spirituality. The task remains, however, to see if this paradox is truly pernicious or self-contradictory. To begin with, I would like to stress that *the denial of pregiven attributes is not equivalent to constructing a positive theory about the divine, which could then be hierarchically posited as superior to other views.* Interestingly, a parallel point has been repeatedly stressed by apophatic mystics from all traditions, East and West. Because of the frequent misunderstandings about mystical apophasis, the following passage by Sells (1994) deserves to be quoted at some length:

> Much discussion of mystical union and comparative mysticism has been based upon substantialist language of whatness and quiddity. Do adherents of differing traditions "worship the same God," "believe the same thing," or

"experience the same thing"—i.e., is *what* someone from tradition X experiences or believes the same or different from that experienced or believed by someone from tradition Y.

The nonsubstantialist understanding of the transcendent common to apophatic mystics does not fit the premises of such questions. In the words of Plotinus, there is no thus or not-thus. In the words of Eriugena, the transcendent is nothing, i.e., no-thing, beyond all entity and quiddity. The apophatic language of disontology, in continually moving toward a removal of the "what" (a removal that is never achieved, always in progress), suggests a different mode of comparison, one less likely to reduce the particularities of differing traditions to a "what," to a homogenous set of doctrines, propositions, or descriptions of experience. (pp. 11–12)

In this spirit, I suggest that the claims of the participatory vision do not fit with certain premises common to most modern philosophies. Consistent with the pluralistic impulse that animates the participatory vision, for example, my claims are not advanced in any absolutist or universalist fashion. Actually, one of my main goals has been precisely to question absolutist, universalist, and objectivist assumptions about the existence of pregiven spiritual ultimates and standards. To interpret this denial as a self-refuting positive theory is both fallacious and question-begging. In other words, *the possible self-contradictory nature of the participatory vision only emerges when it is judged by standards appropriate only in an absolutist domain of discourse.* The participatory vision would be inconsistent only if it is supposed to make objectivist or universalist knowledge claims.

Another way to dismantle these charges is to stress, again in harmony with our thesis, the eminently performative and prescriptive (versus descriptive) nature of the present theorizing. In both cases, once we drop objectivist assumptions, the threatening paradox vanishes and the possible self-contradiction becomes self-exemplification.[18]

While we cannot consistently maintain the universal or absolute superiority of this account over others, we can highlight its advantageous value and prefer it on those grounds. In this sense, we could say, for example, that the participatory vision: (1) is more generous in terms of recognizing the infinite creativity of spirit than other meta-perspectives, contributing therefore to the actual generativity of spiritual unfolding (e.g., allowing, impelling, and catalyzing Spirit's creative urges through human embodied participation), (2) better honors the diversity of spiritual traditions, insights, and ultimates than other approaches, affirming, supporting, and legitimizing the largest number of spiritual perspectives and traditions on their own terms, (3) provides a more fertile ground for a constructive and egalitarian interreligious dialogue, as well as for greater respect and harmony among people holding different religious beliefs, (4) dissolves many epistemological dualisms, myths, riddles, and alienating consequences of other models of spiritual knowing, and (5) has emancipatory consequences for our individual participation in the self-disclosure of reality, for example, in terms of expanding the range of viable creative options to cultivate, embody, and express the sacred. At any rate, this is where I am walking in order to dialogue with others about spiritual matters.

8

A MORE RELAXED
SPIRITUAL UNIVERSALISM

Against the modern anxiety that tells us that if we cannot find universal truths we are doomed to fall into a self-contradictory vulgar relativism, I argue that the participatory vision paves a middle way between the extremes of absolutism and relativism. Although thus far I have stressed the plurality of spiritual worlds and truths, here I argue that the participatory vision also brings forth a more relaxed and fertile spiritual universalism that passionately embraces the variety of ways in which we can cultivate and embody the sacred in the world. Rather than being hierarchical in nature, however, the dialectic between universalism and pluralism, between the One and the Many, may well be one of the deepest dynamics of the self-unfolding of Spirit.

IN PART I OF THE BOOK (Deconstruction), I have examined three fundamental tenets or assumptions of most transpersonal scholarship so far: (1) *experientialism*, an understanding of transpersonal and spiritual phenomena in terms of individual inner experiences, (2) *inner empiricism*, an empiricist account of transpersonal inquiry and epistemic justification, and (3) *perennialism*, an essentially universalist view of spiritual knowledge, spiritual liberation, and spiritual ultimates. The main goal of Part I of this book has been to show that these proposals, although once valuable and necessary, are today beset by a host of serious problems that ultimately corrode the aims of the transpersonal orientation from within. Let me recapitulate here the nature of these shortcomings.

First, experientalism can be conceptually charged with intrasubjective reductionism (i.e., the reduction of spiritual and transpersonal phenomena to the status of individual private experiences), and subtle Cartesianism (i.e., an inadequate understanding of spiritual and transpersonal phenomena according to a subject–object model of knowledge and cognition). Pragmatically, we have also seen how experientialism tends to foster spiritual narcissism (i.e., the misuse of spiritual energies to bolster narcissistic or self-centered ways of being), and integrative arrestment (i.e., the hindrance of the natural integrative process that translates transpersonal and spiritual realizations into everyday life towards the spiritual transformation of self, relationships, and world). Second, inner empiricism typically results in an empiricist colonization of spirituality that not only burdens spiritual inquiry with objectivist anxieties and pseudo-problems, but also has detrimental consequences for the sorely needed contemporary legitimization of spirituality. Third, the transpersonal adhesion to perennialism is a premature commitment that has been uncritically taken for granted, even when the perennial philosophy is not well supported by modern scholarship in comparative mysticism and builds important obstacles for transpersonal hermeneutics, interreligious dialogue, and spiritual inquiry.

In Part II of the book (Reconstruction), I have suggested that these limitations can be overcome through a *participatory turn* in transpersonal and spiritual studies. The crux of this participatory turn is a radical shift from intrasubjective experiences to participatory events in our understanding and engagement of transpersonal and spiritual phenomena. In a nutshell, the participatory turn conceives transpersonal and spiritual phenomena, not as individual inner experiences, but as participatory events that can occur in different loci, such as an individual, a relationship, a community, a larger collective identity or a place. The intrasubjective dimension of these phenomena, then, can now be better understood as the participation of individual consciousness in these events, and not as its fundamental essence or basic nature. In contrast, the emergence of a transpersonal event can potentially engage the creative participation of all dimensions of human nature, from somatic transfiguration to the awakening of the heart, from erotic communion to visionary cocreation, and from contemplative knowing to moral insight. In this book, I have used the term *participatory knowing* to refer to this creative and multidimensional human access to reality.

This revision entails a number of important emancipatory implications for transpersonal and spiritual studies. I will mention here a few of the most significant. To begin with, the emphasis on participatory knowing liberates transpersonal studies from their tacit commitment to a Cartesian epistemology and situates them in greater alignment with the goals of the spiritual quest, which has traditionally aimed at the attainment, not of special experiences or altered states, but of liberating discernment and practical wisdom. In addition, this move releases transpersonal studies from its restraining empiricist moorings and paves the way for the articulation of an *emancipatory epistemology* that anchors the validity of spiritual knowledge, not on its matching pregiven spiritual realities, but on its liberating power for self and world (i.e., its capability to move individuals, communities, and cultures away from egocentric understandings of reality and associated forms of life). Finally, the participatory turn overcomes the essentialism and reductionism of the perennial philosophy by conceiving of a plurality of potentially overlapping but independently valid spiritual liberations and ultimates, which are enacted through human creative participation in an always dynamic and indeterminate spiritual power. This move automatically facilitates a more dialogical interreligious space, renders a priori hierarchical spiritual gradations misconceived, and emancipates individual spiritual choices from external religious authority.

The main fruit of this revision is the emergence of a *participatory vision of human spirituality*: a vision that embraces both parallels and differences among religious traditions without falling into the faulty essentialisms of the perennial philosophy; a vision that accepts the formative role of contextual factors in human spirituality while simultaneously stressing and fostering the inexhaustible creative power of Spirit; a vision that redeems the ontological and metaphysical status of spiritual knowledge without reifying any pregiven spiritual ultimate; a vision that emphasizes the centrality of liberation in assessing the validity of spiritual knowledge claims without falling into spiritual relativism or moral anarchy; a vision, in sum, that reestablishes our intimate connection with the source of our being and opens the range of valid spiritual choices through which we can creatively participate in the Mystery out of which everything arises.

By way of concluding this book, I would like to offer some final reflections on (1) the relationship between the experiential and the participatory visions; (2) the participatory turn in the context of a movement beyond absolutism and relativism in spiritual studies; and (3) the dialectic of universalism and pluralism in Spirit's unfolding.

THE RELATIONSHIP BETWEEN THE EXPERIENTIAL AND PARTICIPATORY VISIONS

To avoid any possible misunderstanding of my position, I would like to offer here some concluding remarks on the relationship between the experiential and participatory visions. Although the problems of the experiential vision are legion, the participatory turn does not demand its total abandonment, but rather its limitation to certain dimensions or stages of transpersonal inquiry. In other words, my critique of the experiential vision should not be taken as arguing for its repudiation and replacement. Rather, what is argued here is the need to move beyond a purely individual and intrasubjective experiential account of transpersonal and spiritual phenomena towards an understanding grounded on participatory knowing and practical wisdom. Let me try to clarify here what I mean exactly by limiting the experiential vision to certain dimensions or stages of transpersonal inquiry.

On the one hand, I believe that experiential discourse can be legitimately used to refer to the individual inner dimension of spiritual and transpersonal phenomena. From our previous discussions, it should be obvious that the participatory vision does not deny or eradicate, of course, the inner and individual aspects of spirituality. Rather, the participatory vision simply reconceives this intrasubjective dimension in terms of the participation of an individual consciousness in transpersonal or spiritual events. The important point to realize, then, is that the experiential, although important, is only an aspect of spiritual events, and this recognition prevents the pitfall I have called *experiential reductionism*. As most traditions tell us, spiritual events cannot be reduced to human experiences, because they flow from dimensions of existence in which human beings can participate but that transcend the merely human.[1] With this in mind, it is safe to use, I believe, experiential talk to refer to the individual inner dimension of transpersonal and spiritual phenomena.

On the other hand, it may be possible to regard the relationship between the experiential and participatory visions in a sequential manner.[2] As transpersonal theorists Wade (1996), Washburn (1995), and Wilber (1996b) point out, Cartesian consciousness may be the necessary starting point of spiritual inquiry (in the modern West, I would qualify). From this viewpoint, the descriptive value of the experiential vision—geared to a Cartesian model of cognition—may be limited to the first stages of the spiritual path, in which the spiritual seeker undergoes temporary openings which are typically interpreted in Cartesian terms as transient experiences, being more prone to fall into spiritual narcissism and integrative arrestment. As the spiritual seeker deepens his or her understanding of these insights, as well as begins to embody and live them in the world, the limits of this experiential account become gradually evident and the participatory vision may start looking like a more adequate framework to understand transpersonal and spiritual phenomena. At this juncture, for example, individuals may tend to feel that spirituality is not so much about having special private experiences, but about cultivating emancipatory understandings that transform not only their inner being, but also their relationships and the world. What I am suggesting here, then, is that the adequacy and validity of the experiential and participatory visions may be relative to different—though not necessarily mandatory—stages of spiritual development.[3] In any case, seen as valid to refer to certain dimensions or stages of transpersonal inquiry, the experiential vision is not abandoned, but simply qualified and situated by what I believe is a more fruitful understanding of human spirituality.[4]

But, do I believe that the participatory vision is not only a more fruitful but a final understanding of transpersonal and spiritual phenomena? I can only answer this question with a firm no. As I mentioned earlier, by no means do I claim that the participatory vision discloses the final truth about the nature of Spirit. Neither the indeterminate nature of Spirit nor the dynamic quality of spiritual unfolding can be fully captured by any conceptual framework. As the history of ideas shows, claims of ultimacy have been invariably proven to be both naïve and deceptive. What is more, claims about final truths are hostile to the nature of being and knowing espoused by the participatory vision. If, rather than pregiven or objective, being and knowing are enacted, dynamic, and participatory, then it should be obvious that claims about final, immutable, or universal truths are both misleading and distorting.

There is no doubt, then, that the participatory vision will be refined, modified, and eventually deconstructed and situated in due time. Were the participatory vision to be embraced at some point by transpersonal scholars, for example, it will surely be only a question of time before its limitations emerge (especially if it is reified or taken too seriously!). Whenever this occurs, I would be more than ready to join its critics, ask for its abandonment, and celebrate its assimilation or replacement by more adequate understandings. The thesis of this book is not that the participatory vision is true in an absolute or objective way, but rather that it is both more consistent with the goals of world spiritual traditions,[5] and a more fruitful way to think and live spiritual and transpersonal phenomena today. It is only in this qualified sense, I believe, that we could say that the participatory vision reveals more truth (understood here as attunement to the unfolding of being) than the experiential one without falling into the extremes of rigid absolutism or vulgar relativism. The next section elaborates on some aspects of this movement beyond absolutism and relativism in spiritual studies.

BEYOND ABSOLUTISM AND RELATIVISM IN SPIRITUAL STUDIES

The participatory turn can be seen as an attempt to pave a middle way between the Scylla of an authoritarian absolutism and the Charybdis of a self-contradictory and morally pernicious relativism. I believe that this move is pivotal not only for spiritual studies, but also for contemporary philosophy and science, and this book would be incomplete without some final reflections about the complex difficulties involved in its undertaking.

Let me begin by admitting that going beyond absolutism and relativism is not an easy task. It calls us to transcend many strongly engrained habits of our thinking and to participate in the mystery and paradox that pervade our universe. It calls us to overcome deeply rooted fears and to humbly encounter uncertainty and complexity. It calls us to simultaneously admit, against absolutism, that there is not a single True story, and against relativism, that some stories are better than others—and that some may be plainly distorting and problematic. Admittedly, to dwell on the razor's edge of such a middle way can be perplexing and distressing, especially in the context of a cultural matrix still bewitched by the hubris of absolutist metaphysics, and constrained by the assumptions of the Cartesian-Kantian legacy. As we have seen, however, many of the disconcerting paradoxes involved in going beyond absolutism and relativism may be more apparent than real. More precisely, they only emerge when these attempts are considered within an absolutist universe of discourse, and dissolve when approached from alternative paradigms of understanding, such as the participatory one introduced here.[6]

Here I would like to add that even in the case that some of the self-referential or paradoxical nature of nonabsolutist approaches would still remain in these alternative paradigms of understanding, this does not necessarily mean that they should be dismissed as self-contradictory.[7] To be sure, to turn paradoxes into self-contradictory statements is tempting, but I would argue that the transpersonal eye may see in this more a retreat into Cartesian habits of thinking, rather than, for example, a movement towards transconceptual and contemplative modes of cognition. From a transpersonal perspective, that is, the movement beyond absolutism and relativism can be seen not as self-contradictory, but as paradoxical. As paradoxical, the issues it raises cannot be completely solved in the arena of formal (bivalent) logic or by newer, improved, or more encompassing paradigms.[8] Although paradoxes cannot be conceptually solved, they can be transcended in the realm of human action and experience. In my opinion, for example, many of the paradoxes raised by nonabsolutist approaches disappear when one realizes that, rather than philosophical positions to be logically defended in an absolutist domain of discourse, they are attitudes towards life and other human beings characterized by both an openness to understand and be enriched by what is different, and a surrendering to the Mystery that can never be fully apprehended by the mind. As attitudes towards life rather than as philosophical positions, these approaches can be criticized, but not refuted. And here is where the potential transformative power of paradox truly emerges: Paradoxes are doorways to transpersonal ways of being because, by ineluctably (and often humorously) showing the limits of rational-logical thinking, they invite us to expand our consciousness and enter the space of transrational modes of being and cognition.

A MORE RELAXED SPIRITUAL UNIVERSALISM

In this book, I have introduced a participatory spiritual pluralism as a more adequate metaphysical framework than the perennialism typical of most transpersonal works. If I have argued so forcefully for spiritual pluralism it is because (1) a naïve or rigid universalism has been generally taken for granted in transpersonal studies, (2) I believe that pluralism should be the starting point of interfaith inquiry and dialogue, (3) pluralism is more consistent with my own participatory understanding of spiritual states of discernment, and (4) conceiving a plurality of spiritual liberations and ultimates not only is more generous in recognizing, but also can foster, the infinite creativity of Spirit. Although for these and other reasons my work emphasizes the metaphysical plurality of spiritual worlds, I should stress here that I do not believe that either pluralism or universalism per se are spiritually superior or more evolved. And it is now time to make explicit the kind of spiritual universalism implicit in the participatory vision.

There is a way, I believe, in which we can legitimately talk about a shared spiritual power, one reality, one world, or one truth. On the one hand, the discussion about whether there is one world or a multiplicity of different worlds can be seen as ultimately a semantic one, and metaphysically a pseudo-problem. On the other hand, a shared spiritual ground needs to be presupposed to make interreligious inquiry and dialogue possible and intelligible. After all, traditions do understand each other and frequently developed and transformed themselves through rich and varied interreligious interactions. The strict incommensurability of traditions needs to be rejected on logical, pragmatic, and historical grounds. Thus, it may be possible to talk about a common spiritual dynamism underlying the plurality of religious insights and ultimates. But let us be clear here, this spiritual universalism does not say that the Tao is God, that emptiness (*sunyata*) is structurally equivalent to Brahman, and similar, quite empty I believe, equations. And neither does it suggest the equally problematic possibility that these spiritual ultimates are different cuts, layers, or snapshots of the same pie. As I see it, the *indeterminate nature of Spirit* cannot be adequately depicted through any positive attribute, such as nondual, dual, impersonal, personal, and so forth. This is why, I believe, so many Western and Eastern mystics chose the so-called *via negativa* or apophatic language to talk about the Divine, and why such nonexperiential language was regarded by most traditions as closer to the Divine than any positive statement of its qualities.[9]

The spiritual universalism of the participatory vision, then, does not establish any a priori hierarchy of positive attributes of the divine: Nondual insights are not necessarily higher than dual, nor are dual higher than nondual. Personal enactions are not necessarily higher than impersonal, nor impersonal higher than personal. And so forth. Since the Mystery is intrinsically indeterminate, spiritual qualitative distinctions cannot be made by matching our insights and conceptualizations with any pregiven features. In contrast, I suggest that qualitative distinctions among spiritual enactions can be made by not only evaluating their emancipatory power for self, relationships, and world, but also discriminating how grounded in or coherent with the Mystery they are. Moreover, because of their unique psychospiritual and archetypal dispositions, individuals and cultures may emancipate themselves better through different enactions of the spiritual power, and this not only paves the way for a more constructive and enriching interreligious dialogue, but also opens up the creative range of valid spiritual choices potentially available to us as individuals. In sum, *this vision brings forth a more relaxed and permissive spiritual universalism that passionately embraces (rather than reduces, conflates, or subordinates) the variety of ways in which the sacred can be cultivated and embodied, without falling into spiritual anarchy or vulgar relativism.*

The relationship between pluralism and universalism cannot be characterized consistently in a hierarchical fashion, and even less in terms of spiritual evolution.[10] While there are lower and higher forms of both universalism and pluralism (more or less emancipatory, grounded in the Mystery, sophisticated, encompassing, explanatory, etc.), my sense is that *the dialectic between universalism and pluralism, between the One and the Many, displays what may well be the deepest dynamics of the self-disclosing of Spirit.* From the rigid universalism of rational consciousness to the pluralistic relativism of some postmodern approaches, from perennialist universalisms to the emerging spiritual pluralism of the interfaith dialogue, Spirit seems to swing from one to the other pole, from the One to the Many and from the Many to the One, endlessly striving to more fully manifest, embody, and embrace love and wisdom in all its forms. Newer and more embracing universalist and pluralistic visions will continue to emerge, but the everlasting dialectical movement between the One and the Many in the self-disclosing of Spirit makes any abstract or absolute hierarchical arrangement between them misleading. If I am right about the generative power of the dialectical relationship between the One and the Many, then to get stuck in or freeze either of the two poles as the Truth cannot but hinder the natural unfolding of Spirit's creative urges. This is why, although originally offered in a different context, the following remark by Habermas (1992) seems pertinent here: "The metaphysical priority of unity above plurality and the contextualist priority of pluralism above unity are secret accomplices" (pp. 116–117).

To conclude, I would like to emphasize that it is only after traveling through the tremendously rich, complex, and multifaceted spiritual waters that we can, I believe, afford to immerse ourselves in the profound ocean of this more open, fertile, and relaxed universalism; a universalism that calls to be realized, not so much in isolated individual inner experiences, grandiose visions, or metaphysical intuitions, but through intimate dialogue and communion with other beings and the world.

NOTES

CHAPTER 1
TRANSPERSONAL THEORY: NOW AND THEN

1. The term *transpersonal* was first suggested by Stanislav Grof in a conversation with Abraham Maslow to refer to the emergent field of transpersonal psychology. See Sutich (1976) for an historical account of the choice of the term transpersonal, and Vich (1988) for a review of some of its earlier uses in the works of William James, C. G. Jung, and Dane Rudhyar.

2. For lucid summaries of the influence of some of these thinkers upon transpersonal theory, see Battista (1996), Epstein (1996), Scotton (1996), Taylor (1996), and Yensen and Dryer (1996), all of which can be found in the excellent *Textbook of Transpersonal Psychiatry and Psychology* (Scotton, Chinen, & Battista, 1996). On Jung and transpersonal psychology, see also Levy (1983).

3. On some of these Western philosophical roots of transpersonal theory, see R. McDermott (1993), Hannah (1993a, 1993b), Wilber (1995), and Judy (1996).

4. For a concise history of the *vipassana shanga*, see Rawlinson (1997). A more critical account of this movement can be found in Sharf (1995a).

5. In this work I refer to transpersonal, spiritual, and mystical phenomena somewhat interchangeably. Although the meaning of these terms sometimes overlaps, it is important not to lump them together. To be sure, since there is no consensus among scholars about how to define any of these three phenomena (e.g., Brainard, 1996; Dupré, 1987; Evans, 1993; Helminiak, 1996; Lajoie & Shapiro, 1992; Rothberg, 1996b; Shapiro, 1994; Wilber, 1997a; Zinnbauer et al., 1997), the relationships among them largely depend on the semantic distinctions with which one chooses to work. Rather than trying to offer a priori simple definitions of such complex phenomena as spirituality or mysticism—which today is both naïve and preposterous—I will simply say here that, in my opinion, their relationship is more one of family-resemblance than of identity, equivalence, or inclusion. For example, while certain phenomena can be regarded as both transpersonal and mystical (e.g., certain states of nonduality) all transpersonal phenomena are not mystical (e.g., a self-identification with botanical processes that may occur during a psychedelic session) nor are all mystical phenomena transpersonal (e.g., certain visions or locutions not involving an expansion of individual consciousness). This family resemblancelike relation operates, I believe, not only between transpersonal and mystical phenomena, but also between mystical and spiritual phenomena, and between spiritual and transpersonal phenomena.

6. The reason I am stressing the diversity of transpersonal expressions is because I believe that there are a variety of transpersonal modes of being that cannot be reduced to any singular way of life. Although all transpersonal in their overcoming of limiting self-centeredness, the ways in which this transformation can occur and be manifested in our intimate relationships, communal life, social structures, etc. can be, I believe, drastically different.

7. Whether we can say that the world is intrinsically transpersonal or not largely depends on how we understand the term *world*. In the context of the participatory vision presented in this book, the nature of the world, rather than being intrinsic, is considered relational. In other words, the variety of ways in which the world unfolds is contingent upon how it is engaged, enacted, and lived. It is in this qualified sense that we can say, I believe, that the aim of transpersonal theory is to bring forth a transpersonal world (i.e., to provide human beings with both conceptual understandings and practical injunctions to enact and live the world transpersonally).

8. Compare Tarnas's (1991) description of one of the foundations of the modern world view:

> Conceptions involving a transcendent reality were increasingly regarded as beyond the competence of human knowledge; as useful palliatives for man's emotional nature; as aesthetically satisfying imaginative creations; as potentially valuable heuristic assumptions; as necessary bulwarks for morality or social cohesion; as political-economic propaganda; as psychologically motivated projections; as life-impoverishing illusions; as superstitious, irrelevant, or meaningless. (p. 286)

9. I want to thank Larry Spiro who, in a series of stimulating dialogues, confirmed my then growing awareness of the many problems of an experiential account of transpersonal and spiritual phenomena.

10. For two presentations of this epistemic approach to transpersonal and spiritual phenomena, see Ferrer (1999b, 2000a).

11. Crucial for this turn was a conversation with Richard Tarnas, who kindly challenged the arbitrary dichotomy between experience and knowledge of the epistemic approach and suggested a number of thoughtful directions towards a more adequate articulation of the shift I was trying to convey.

12. In the second part of this book, I call this multidimensional human access to reality "participatory knowing."

CHAPTER TWO

THE EXPERIENTIAL VISION OF HUMAN SPIRITUALITY

1. In this book, I use the term *experiential* to refer to the individual inner or intrasubjective character of the modern understanding of human experience. Notice, however, that the notion of experience can be used as the bearer of wider semantic contents that can be non-Cartesian and even transhuman (for example, in the philosophies of James, Whitehead, or Nishida). These expanded meanings free the notion of experience from its modern intrasubjective constraints and are therefore in harmony with the participatory vision of spirituality introduced in this book.

2. Walsh and Vaughan's (1993) definition of transpersonal experiences is probably the most widely used in the literature. In my opinion, this wide reception lies in the conceptual ambiguity inherent in their definition. In contrast to other transpersonal definitions in which the access to external sources of knowledge is explicitly maintained (e.g., Grof, 1972, 1988), Walsh and Vaughan's (1993) definition leaves unclear if the expansion of the sense of self with which they characterize transpersonal experiences provides extrapsychic information about nonbiographical aspects of humanity, life, and cosmos or, by contrast, is solely an intrapsychic phenomenon. In other words, in talking about the sense of identity or self, it is not clear if these authors are presupposing the extrapsychic epistemic value of transpersonal experiences (realist interpretation), or if they are rather confining it to the realm of the human psyche (phenomenological interpretation). Parenthetically, notice

how the fundamental epistemological issue of transpersonal theory (i.e., the nature of transpersonal knowledge) naturally emerges in the very attempt to define transpersonal experiences.

Rather than a shortcoming, however, I suggest that this conceptual ambiguity should be regarded as a virtue, especially if the definition is taken in a nominal sense—as a statement about the meaning of the expression "transpersonal experience" in the transpersonal community of discourse—rather than in a real sense—as a statement claiming to reflect the nature of transpersonal phenomena. As Brainard (1996) maintains in relation to mysticism, a certain degree of vagueness in definitions of phenomena that are not well known may have great heuristic value. This is certainly the case, I believe, with Walsh and Vaughan's (1993) transpersonal definition. Because both realist and phenomenological readings of transpersonal phenomena can be found in the transpersonal literature, the heuristic value of this definition should be obvious: It is a definition of transpersonal experiences with which most transpersonal authors would agree. And this heuristic value stems precisely from the ambiguity of the definition, not in spite of the same.

3. Listen, for example, to Nietzsche (1984), voicing the spirit of the Enlightenment in relation to "the value of religion for knowledge": "*Never, neither indirectly nor directly, neither as a dogma nor as an allegory, has religion yet held any truth*" (p. 79).

4. For a general critical analysis of the uses of the notion of experience in modern religious studies, see Sharf (1998).

5. This humanistic emphasis on experiences did not emerge in a vacuum. For an interesting collection of essays suggesting the deep-seated nature of experientialism in the American cultural and philosophical tradition, see J. J. McDermott (1976).

6. In Maslow's views about the nature of peak-experiences, then, we find not only the seeds of the experiential vision, but also the genesis of the common adhesion of transpersonal theory to a perennialist vision of spirituality: "The very beginning, the intrinsic core, the essence, the universal nucleus of every known high religion . . . has been the private, lonely, personal illumination, revelation, or ecstasy of some acutely sensitive prophet or seer" (1970, p. 19). The relationship between transpersonal theory and the perennial philosophy is critically addressed in chapter 4. Here, I am merely pointing out that the roots of this association can be traced to the very birthplace of the transpersonal orientation, that is, Maslow's seminal works. Maslow's most clear perennialist manifesto can be found in chapter 3 of his *Religions, Values, and Peak-Experiences* (1970), adequately entitled "The 'Core-Religious,' or 'Transcendent,' Experience." Two earlier evaluations of the relationship between transpersonal theory and the perennial philosophy can be found in Ferrer (1999a, 2000c).

7. Despite Jung's interest in Eastern thinking (Taoism, Yoga, Buddhism), he consistently maintained that Westerners need to create their own yoga, largely based on the Christian tradition, and avoid adopting or imitating Eastern spiritual practices. As modern commentators point out, Jung's readings of Eastern doctrines were also heavily shaped by his own psychological theories and Neo-Kantian epistemological assumptions. On Jung and the East, see Clarke (1994), Coward (1985a), and Meckel and Moore (1992).

8. I should add here that, shortly before his death, Maslow raised many questions about the experiential and individualistic emphasis of his earlier works. For example, in the preface to the paperback edition of *Religions, Values, and Peak-Experiences* (1970)—posthumously published with slight modifications as "Comments on 'Religions, Values, and Peak-Experiences'" (1971)—Maslow regards this book as "too imbalanced toward the individualistic" (p. xiii), and stresses the need to connect experientialism with social reform. In this important essay, he repeatedly warns us against the traps of seeking peak-experiences per se, and falling into an experiential narcissism that would

exalt "the peak experience . . . as the best or even *only* path to knowledge, and thereby all the tests and verifications of the *validity* of the illumination may be tossed aside" (1970, p. ix). Maslow's concerns about the potential hazards of an overemphasis on inner experience were perhaps most evident in his severe critique of the early experientialism of the Esalen Institute under the charges of anti-intellectualism and self-absorption (see E. Hoffman, 1988, pp. 328–329). Though Maslow's overall vision of spirituality was basically inner and individualistic, then, we can observe in his late thinking an increasing critical awareness of the pitfalls of the experiential vision.

9. The present critique focuses exclusively on the experiential assumptions of the modern understanding of transpersonal phenomena. However, I should mention here that to define the transpersonal as "beyond ego"—or "beyond self," or "beyond the personal," and so forth—is not entirely without problems. As several authors have already argued (Epstein, 1988; Wilber, 1995, pp. 226–231), to equate transpersonality with beyond ego without clarifying what is meant by ego, or which egoic components are transcended in transpersonal phenomena, can be deeply confusing. One of the main sources of this confusion is that since the transpersonal is *per definitionem* relative to the personal (or the transegoic to the egoic, etc.), the way the personal is understood and lived determines what can be regarded as transpersonal. Any definition of transpersonality as "beyond the personal" (or "beyond ego," "beyond self," etc.) needs to be preceded by an elucidation of what it is meant by personal, ego, or self.

In this account, an additional complication to the ones pointed out by Epstein (1988) and Wilber (1995) is that the self or the personal may be diversely understood and lived in different cultures and traditions (e.g., Marsella, Devos, & Hsu, 1985; Roland, 1988; Shweder, 1991). In an attempt to offer a more culturally sensitive definition, transpersonal anthropologist Laughlin (1994) defines transpersonal experiences as *"those experiences that bring the cognized-self into question"* (p. 7). Thus defined, then, what constitutes a transpersonal experience may vary across cultures. However, the problem is not completely solved. Again, a clear understanding of what is meant by *cognized-self* not only as a theoretical construct but also as it is lived across different cultures, would still have to precede these definitions of transpersonal experiences.

Even bracketing for a moment the well-documented cross-cultural diversity in self-identity, a second complication arises from the dynamics of psychospiritual development. On the one hand, imagine two individuals, the first whose self is prevalently identified with the body-mind, and the second whose self-identity has incorporated in a stable manner certain elements that transcend but include the body-mind complex (e.g., witness-consciousness). In such a case, the presence of witness-consciousness may be lived as a transpersonal phenomenon by the first individual, but not by the second, insofar as it is already part of his or her ordinary mode of being-in-the-world. On the other hand, a parallel argument can be made in the case of the same individual at two different stages of his or her spiritual development: What at a certain time is experienced as a transpersonal phenomenon would cease to be lived as such whenever that aspect of being is incorporated into everyday consciousness.

In sum, defined this way, *what constitutes a transpersonal experience may vary not only among different cultures (cross-culturally), but also between different individuals in a single culture (interpersonally), and even between different stages of development of a single individual (intrapersonally)*. It should be obvious, then, that to define transpersonal phenomena as experiences "beyond the sense of personal identity," "beyond self," or even "beyond the cognized-self" entails such a degree of conceptual nebulousness that renders this type of definition inadequate. What is needed, I believe, is not to embark oneself on the arduous (and probably futile) task of elucidating the multifarious meanings the transpersonal can take in all possible situations, but a radically different way to think about transpersonal phenomena.

10. In a later work, however, Habermas (1992) seems to have qualified his earlier claim that all religious meanings have been conclusively overcome by the modern rational world view. Even after the modern deflation of metaphysics, he tells us,

> ordinary life, now fully profane, by no means is immune to the shattering and subversive intrusion of extraordinary events. Viewed from without, religion, which has largely been deprived of its world view functions, is still indispensable in ordinary life for normalizing intercourse with the extraordinary. . . . Philosophy, even in its postmetaphysical form, will be able neither to replace nor to repress religion as long as religious language is the bearer of a semantic content that is inspiring and even indispensable, for its content eludes (for the time being?) the explanatory force of philosophical language and continues to resist translation into reasoning discourses. (p. 51)

For a lucid essay arguing for the potential validity of contemplative knowledge claims in the context of Habermas's theory of communicative action, see Rothberg (1986a).

11. Habermas (1984): "On the one hand, a decentered [differentiated] understanding of the world opens up the possibility of dealing with the world of facts in a cognitively objectified [*versachlicht*] manner and with the world of interpersonal relations in a legally and morally objectified manner; on the other hand, it offers the possibility of a subjectivism freed from imperatives of objectification in dealing with individualized needs, desires, and feelings [*Bedürfnisnatur*] (p. 216).

12. At first sight, Wilber (1995) seems to place a very heavy weight for the undertaking of this integrative task on the individual, that is, on the emergence of vision-logic cognition. However, Wilber stresses that individual cognitive competencies always develop intersubjectively and against the background of adequate metaphorical models, so the emergence of vision-logic should probably be seen as both an individual and a social phenomenon.

13. By Cartesian Anxiety, Bernstein (1985) means "the anxiety that unless we can specify a firm foundation for our knowledge claims, unless we can appeal to clear determinate ahistorical criteria for deciding what is true and false, correct and incorrect, then the only alternative is to fall into the abyss of a self-refuting relativism where 'anything goes'" (p. 309). As I argue elsewhere (Ferrer, 1998a), this anxiety is alive and well in contemporary transpersonal scholarship, especially in Wilber's recent works (1995, 1996a).

14. Note that Hollenback (1996) is not proposing any type of solipsistic or projective psychologism in which mystics merely "create" their spiritual universes by exerting the faculty of their empowered imagination. On the contrary, Hollenback believes that the empowered imagination can actually transcend the mystic's belief systems and become a source of novel revelations and creative spiritual insights. Hollenback's (1996) work is important not only for having articulated a spiritual cognitive mechanism (*enthymesis*) able to account for the constructive elements of mystical knowing, but also for having introduced paranormal evidence and indigenous spirituality in the contemporary discussion on mysticism. For another exception to the typical neglect of indigenous spirituality in mystical studies, see Carmody and Carmody (1996).

15. Note that in addition to objects for consciousness, we can also have intersubjective relations not only in the extrapsychic, but also in the intrapsychic space. In her *The Intersubjectivity of the Mystic,* for example, Frohlich (1993) proposes, following Lonergan, to understand some forms of mysticism in terms of "mystical intersubjectivity," that is to say, as the mediation of the transcendent ground of consciousness (i.e., God) within the immediate ground of human consciousness. In her own words: "Mystical experience . . . is not an experience of God as an 'object,' not of oneself as a

sheer 'subject,' but of a state of 'mystical intersubjectivity.' It is a non-objectifiable presence of the divine at the level of one's own presence" (p. 140).

From a different standpoint, Washburn (1994a, 1994b, 1995) explains transpersonal development as an essentially intersubjective process (in terms of the relationships between the ego and the Dynamic Ground) taking place in intrapsychic space. Therefore, both the I-It (subject-object) and the I-Thou (intersubjective) distinctions can be made in both extrapsychic and intrapsychic spaces.

16. Levin (1988b) rightly argues that the pronouncement of objectivist claims betrays the transpersonal orientation because it assumes the very Cartesian epistemology from which it struggles to be free. The solution, for Levin, is that transpersonal claims should be articulated in a strictly phenomenological language (i.e., as statements referring exclusively to human experience). I believe that Levin is correct in his condemnation of objectivist language in transpersonal studies, and his paper is particularly helpful in showing how transpersonal phenomena render the structural opposition between subject and object suspect. However, as the present work should make obvious, to prescribe phenomenology as a remedy for transpersonal studies is to prescribe the illness for the cure.

17. This may be, I believe, related to Wilber's critique of Grof's approach to the study of transpersonal experiences. According to Wilber (1995), Grof's works "simply *describe* the monological subject having monological experiences: the Cartesian subject has an experience, sees an archetypal image, experiences volcanic pleasure/pain, identifies with plants, has an out-of-body experience, relives birth, or perhaps dissolves altogether" (p. 745, n. 17). For Wilber's understanding of the term "monological," see chapter 3, note 9 (this volume).

18. As I argue in chapter 7, this Cartesian account of spiritual phenomena is at the root of the riddles of epistemic mediation and construction that predate the modern study of mysticism (see, e.g., Forman, 1990a, 1998a; Gill, 1984, 1989; R. H. Jones, 1993; Katz, 1978a, 1983a; Perovich, 1985b; Rothberg, 1989, 1990; Short, 1996). Having implicitly posited a subject-object model of cognition, that is, Kantian questions naturally arise about both the mediation between subject and object, and the construction of the objects of knowledge by the structures of subjectivity. As we will see, however, the abandonment of these experiential prejudices naturally results in the dissolution of these insidious conundrums.

19. An early critique of the narcissistic pitfalls of spiritual experientialism can be found in Bregman (1982). Like Bregman, other critical theorists such as Adorno, Jacoby, and Lasch tend to lump together pathological forms of narcissism and authentic processes of self-transformation. For these thinkers, most forms of interiorization are seen as both a narcissistic withdrawal from social and political responsibility, and a concession to the dominant capitalist system. See Gendlin (1987) for a clarification of this confusion.

20. In this context, however, it seems important to distinguish between pathological or unnecessary narcissism and the normal narcissism that inevitably accompanies the aspirant throughout the spiritual path, and is said to be completely eradicated only in final realization (Almaas, 1996; Epstein, 1986; Wilber, 1986).

21. In his in-depth study of narcissism and spirituality, for example, Almaas (1996) depicts narcissism as "a direct consequence of the lack or disturbance of self-realization" (p. 10).

22. Another author who connects Cartesianism and narcissism is Levin (1987): "Narcissistic pathology takes over in metaphysics with the triumph of Cartesian subjectivism. This subjectivism is very deceptive, very difficult to grasp—much like the narcissistic personality, in fact. Descartes's subjectivism is in reality a retreat into weakness and self-delusion, which manages to appear as a triumph of strength, self-mastery, and rational control" (p. 507).

23. This is illustrated, for example, by the consideration of *lectio/meditatio* (meditative reading and repetition of texts) as giving fruit to *oratio* (prayer) and *contemplatio* (contemplation) in Christian monastic mysticism (McGinn, 1996a), or the need for *sravana* (listening) and *manana* (reflection) of *sruti* (revealed scripture) before *nididhyasana* (meditation) in Sankara's Advaita Vedanta (Rambachan, 1991). One of the most compelling articulations of the need for an adequate conceptual understanding as a prerequisite for enacting direct spiritual knowledge can be found in Klein's (1986) excellent study of the Gelukba order of Tibetan Buddhism.

24. Actually, as I suggest in the concluding chapter, an intrasubjective account of spirituality may be in many cases both the starting point and the foundation of more integral and emancipated spiritual understandings.

CHAPTER THREE
THE EMPIRICIST COLONIZATION OF SPIRITUALITY

1. On the question of the public observation of states of consciousness, see Globus's (1993) two letters submitted to the journal *Science* in response to Tart's (1972) suggestion to study altered states of consciousness following the tenets of empirical science. See below for a summary of Tart's original proposal.

2. I should add here that Braud and Anderson (1998) conclude their work urging for a pluralistic epistemology that implies a pluralistic ontology. Obviously, to embrace epistemological pluralism would naturally emancipate transpersonal studies from the exclusivity of empiricist approaches.

3. For two lucid discussions of Jung's philosophical and epistemological assumptions, see Clarke (1992) and Nagy (1991).

4. On Jung and mysticism, see Coward (1985b), Dourley (1998), and Jaffé (1989).

5. Note here that religious empiricism is a long-standing tradition in Western religious studies. Probably catalyzed by William James's recommendation of an association of religion and empiricism, this tradition reached its height with the so-called Chicago School of empirical theology (see, e.g., Meland, 1969). See also Gelpi (1994) for a review of the turn to experience in contemporary Western theology.

6. For a lucid feminist critique of this position, see Davaney (1987).

7. For an examination of this charge, see Ferrer (1998a), and chapter 8, note 10 (this volume).

8. Note, however, that Kuhn (1970b) was one of the most effective critics of Popper's falsifiability criterion for scientific knowledge, and this suggests that Wilber's account of science (as well as of Kuhn) may be somewhat artificial and distorting.

9. Wilber (1998a) defines the term *monological* as follows: "*Monological* comes from 'monologue,' which means a single person talking by him- or herself. Most empirical science is monological, because you can investigate, say, a rock without ever having to talk with it" (p. 36). As I see it, Wilber's characterization of empirical science as monological reveals the residual objectivism of his integral vision. In contrast, the participatory epistemology advanced in the present work embraces the more dialogical approach pioneered by the feminist revision of science. According to Keller (1983), for example, Barbara McClintock's scientific approach entails listening to "hear what the material has to say to you . . . [to] let it come to you" (p. 198). On the feminist revision of science, see Keller (1985), Keller and Longino (1996), Shepherd (1993), and Schiebinger (1999).

10. This is also the case in classic Buddhist theories of knowledge. For Dharmakirti, perhaps the most celebrated Buddhist epistemologist, only "the experience of the person whose interpretation of

his experience is consistent with the basic doctrines of Buddhism validates exactly those doctrines" (Hayes, 1997, p. 117). Naturally, for Hayes, this epistemic justification is ultimately "a disappointing return to dogmatism" (p. 117). In Part II of this book, however, we will see that once we free our understanding of spiritual inquiry from Cartesianism, the apparent dogmatism of most religious epistemologies can be seen in a more sympathetic light.

11. Compare Hoffman's (1982) parable of the *bhikkhu*.

12. For classic discussions on the falsifiability of religious claims, see Barnhart (1977), Blackstone (1963), Flew and MacIntyre (1955), Kellenberger (1969), and McKinnon (1970). For other critiques of Wilber's account of spiritual inquiry, see Helminiak (1998) and Heron (1996b, 1998).

13. Note that this move is not original to the transpersonal movement. An analogous turn can be found, for example, in Schleiermacher's early account of religion as immediate experience. As Proudfoot (1985) observes,

> the turn to religious experience was motivated in large part by an interest in freeing religious doctrine and practice from dependence on metaphysical beliefs and ecclesiastical institutions and grounding it in human experience. This was the explicit aim of Scheleiermacher's *On Religion*, the most influential statement and defense of the autonomy of religious experience." (p. xii)

14. Although used to refer to the nascent field of comparative religion, the term "science of religion" can be traced to the writings of Max Müller, in particular to his highly influential *Introduction to the Science of Religion* (1893).

CHAPTER FOUR
TROUBLE IN PARADISE:
THE PERENNIAL PHILOSOPHY REVISITED

1. Earlier versions of several portions of this chapter appeared in Ferrer (1999a, 2000c). Also, some sections were presented in a panel on "Multiculturalism and Transpersonal Psychology" at the Institute of Transpersonal Psychology, Palo Alto, February, 1998, and at the Grof Transpersonal Conference, Esalen Institute, Big Sur, March, 2000.

2. See also Faivre's (1994) historical account of the perennial philosophy in the context of Western esotericism.

3. Other influential figures who contributed to the popularity of perennialist ideas in the following decades include Joseph Campbell, Thomas Merton, D. T. Suzuki, and Alan Watts.

4. For several discussions contrasting the perennial philosophy and the philosophical discourse of postmodernity—more specifically with Gadamer's hermeneutics, postmodern process theology, and Rorty's neopragmatism—see, respectively, Dean (1984), Griffin and Smith (1989), and Isenberg and Thursby (1985). For two perennialist responses to Dean's critical essay, see Nasr (1985) and Olson (1985).

5. Compare Almond's (1982) five models of the relationship between mystical experience and its interpretation.

6. For an interesting critique of the typological approach in the comparative study of mysticism, see Price (1987).

7. For a sympathetic analysis of involutionary and evolutionary versions of the perennial philosophy, see Isenberg and Thursby (1984–86).

8. In several works, Wilber (1990a, 1995, 1997a) also suggests the possibility of validating perennialist claims on the basis of the experiential content of mystical experiences. As we will see, however, this claim is not only highly questionable but also parasitic of the experiential vision. The reader interested in exploring this issue can consult the works by Grof (1998), Wilber (1990a) and Shear (1994) for different arguments suggesting that the principles of the perennial philosophy can find epistemic support in mystical experiences. For the contrary view, that is, that mystical experiences offer no evidential value for a perennialist metaphysic, see Angel (1994), Fenton (1995), Griffiths (1991), Jones (1983), and H. Smith (1987).

9. The Neo-Hindu flavor of transpersonal perennialism should not be surprising, especially given that two of its main sources were the Westernized Vedanta of Huxley's (1945) seminal work, *The Perennial Philosophy*, and the Hindu-oriented primordial tradition of Huston Smith's (1976) *Forgotten Truth*.

10. Some transpersonal theorists suffer from analogous anxieties. See, for example, my "Beyond Absolutism and Relativism in Transpersonal Evolutionary Theory" (Ferrer, 1998a) for an analysis of some of the problems stemming from these Cartesian worries in the context of Wilber's recent work.

11. Apart from abundant textual and historical data, substantial disagreements among mystics are also evident in the contemporary interreligious monastic dialogue. In the recent Gethsemani encounter among Buddhist and Christian monastics, for example, important differences in their spiritual beliefs (on ultimate reality, on God, on grace, on intuition, etc.) were widely acknowledged as a source of mutual enrichment (Mitchell & Wiseman, 1997).

12. Interestingly enough, in spite of his great reliance on Piaget, Wilber's structuralist account of spiritual diversity is much closer to Chomsky's universal grammar and Lévi-Strauss's structural anthropology than to Piaget's genetic constructivism. Although resisting the structuralist label, Chomsky was the first author who explicitly postulated a two-level structuralist approach (i.e., a theory that posits the existence of surface versus deep structures in the universal organization of language). To be more precise, Chomsky's theory of language distinguishes between surface structures (syntactically interpretable, what we hear), deep structures (semantically interpretable, what we understand), and basic structures (innate mental dispositions that generate the deep structures of language) (Caws, 1997). As is well known, Chomsky openly aligned himself with the Cartesian-Kantian tradition in maintaining that the basic structures of the mind are innate, pregiven, and independent of experience. For a retrospective account of the debates around Chomsky's deep structures in linguistic theory, see Huck and Goldsmith (1995).

In a way, we could say that Wilber has done with Chomsky what Lévi-Strauss did with de Saussure: to extend the structuralist logic beyond the boundaries of linguistics to include the full spectrum of human sciences. Wilber clearly follows Chomsky in both postulating a two-level structuralist model, and regarding the deep structures as pregiven and independent of existential and historical contingencies. In contrast to Chomsky, however, Wilber seems to systematically conflate deep and basic structures, although it is not clear if and how this may affect the integrity of his model. Perhaps a connected problem is that, in Wilber's theory, parallels among surface structures (e.g., the nonduality of Atman–Brahman and the nonduality of *sunyata*) are invariably taken to manifest a common underlying deep structure (the nondual level). However, what Chomsky's transformational grammar shows is precisely the contrary: Syntactically similar surface structures (e.g., "John is eager to please" and "John is easy to please") can be associated with different semantic deep structures, that is, have different underlying meanings; and syntactically different surface structures (e.g., "John ate the orange" and "The orange was eaten by John") can be sustained by the same semantic deep structure, that is, have an identical meaning.

As for Piaget's genetic structuralism, it is important to note that the notion of structure invoked by Wilber is not the Piagetian one. Piaget's structuralism is animated by a radical epistemological constructivism that leaves little room for Wilber's transcendental, pregiven, and permanent deep structures. Actually, Piaget struggled to find a middle way between an absolute predetermined sequence of innate, permanent structures (à la Lévi-Strauss or Chomsky) and a merely contingent emergence of structures (à la Foucault's epistemes). For Piaget (1968), this middle way exists and can be paved by the epistemological notions of self-construction and self-regulation—notions that, by the way, prefigured in important ways Varela, Thompson, and Rosch's enactive paradigm. In this regard, Piaget tells us: "We conclude that there is room for an alternative that falls between absolute preformation of logical structures on the one hand, and their free or contingent invention on the other. Construction, in being constantly regulated by equilibration requirements . . . finally yields a necessity that is a non-temporal, because reversible, law" (p. 67). In the same vein, he asks, "is it not quite plausible to think of the nature that underlies physical reality as constantly in process of construction rather than as a heap of finished structures?" (p. 68). Furthermore, critiquing the innatist model that Chomsky and Wilber embrace, Piaget (1968) writes: "We must admit that we do not really understand why the mind is more truly honored when turned into a collection of permanent schemata [Wilber's deep structures] than when it is viewed as the as yet unfinished product of continual self-construction" (p. 114). And he adds: "Man [sic] can transform himself and the world by transforming the world and can structure himself by constructing structures; and these structures are his own, for they are not eternally predestined either from within or from without" (p. 119). Finally, indicating what is ultimately at stake in the discussion of this issue, Piaget (1968) concludes that: "The basic epistemological alternatives are predestination or some sort of constructivism" (p. 141). Perhaps the most simple way to describe the fundamental difference between Piaget and Wilber would be to say that Piaget chose constructivism and Wilber predestination.

13. There are different versions of the Great Chain of Being. Although Wilber has posited as many as seventeen levels, he generally refers to ten: sensoriomotor, phantasmic-emotional, representational, rule/role, reflexive-formal, vision-logic, psychic, subtle, causal, nondual (1997a). Sometimes, he also uses a more simplified version involving only five levels: matter, body, mind, soul, and spirit (1993b).

14. Note that Wilber claims that this model is not an a priori construction, but an a posteriori reconstruction based on the study of those individuals who have already realized these potentials (Sankara, Christ, the Buddha, etc.): "The involutionary theories . . . are all attempts to take into account that the depths of the higher structural potentials are already present but not seen" (1995, p. 634). What Wilber is suggesting, then, is that involutionary models inductively emerged to explain the existence of higher deep structures. What I am claiming here, by contrast, is that the postulation of predetermined and universal deep structures stems from a previous commitment to such an involutionary scheme. On the one hand, considering the variety of spiritual goals described in the world religious literature, it is hard to understand how Wilber's arrangement of these deep structures could actually emerge from an impartial structural analysis of mystical texts and biographies. On the other hand, it should be noted that Wilber's prestructuralist writings were already perennialist (see, e.g., 1975, 1977). For example, in his early work on a perennial psychology, he writes, "whether Reality is called Brahman, God, Tao, Dharmakaya, Void, or whatever is of no great concern, for all alike point to that state of non-dual Mind wherein the universe is not split into seer and seen" (1977, p. 79). This strongly suggests that Wilber's structuralist analyses were guided by a perennialist agenda and a prior commitment to nondual spiritual traditions, of which he is a practitioner (Wilber, 1999a), and which perennial philosophers have generally regarded as the most accurate articulation of the perennial Truth.

15. However, as perennialist scholar of religion Borg (1991) points out: "to identify the great chain of being and the primordial tradition too closely conflicts with the claim that the primordial tradition is nearly universal; the implication that all pre-modern cultures are forms of Neoplatonism seems rightfully suspect" (p. 35).

16. For several introductions to the structuralist movement, see Boyne (1996), Caws (1997), Gardner (1981), and Lane (1970). See also Piaget (1968) for a summary of his genetic structuralism, and Harland (1987) and Frank (1989) for two good overviews of the shift from structuralism to poststructuralism or neostructuralism.

17. More specifically, besides Paul Ricoeur, the structuralist influence in religious studies is apparent in the works of authors such as Anthony Thiselton, Daniel Patte, John Dominic Crossan, and Georges Dumézil (Caws, 1997; Stiver, 1996). As for Chomsky's two-level structuralism, although already implicit in Jung's views of noumenal (universal) and phenomenal (culturally specific) archetypes, and in Eliade's comparative studies of myth, it reached an explicit formulation in the hands of Dick Anthony and Thomas Robbins (see, e.g., Anthony, 1982; Anthony & Robbins, 1975). A relatively recent defense of structuralism as an adequate method for the study of religion can be found in Penner (1989). For several interesting applications of the two-level structuralist approach to the study of new religious movements, see Anthony and Ecker (1987), Cox (1981), and Wilber (1987). For a concise review and critique of structuralism in religious studies, see Stiver (1996).

18. After reading an earlier version of the following critique, Wilber (1999d) qualified his views about the nature of deep structures in important ways. Incorporating some of the following critical points and presenting them as his current views, he tells us, for example, that "I would eventually come to believe that most of the deep features [structures] of holons were not given ahistorically, but rather were laid down in the process of evolution and development itself" (p. 6). Still later, he adds, "once laid down as evolutionary memory, they tend to become fixed habits (or a priori structures) in their domains, acting as teleonomic omega points for all future members of the class" (p. 6). In any event, while reading the following critique, the reader should bear in mind that although I believe it is valid regarding Wilber's theorizing so far, judging from his recent moves, it may of course not adequately represent Wilber's future views about these matters. Indeed, I believe that a full incorporation of this critique into his integral model would situate Wilber's views in closer alignment with the participatory vision presented in this book.

19. See Kelly (1998a, 1998b) for a compelling critique of Wilber's adoption of the Great Chain of Being as an adequate root metaphor for transpersonal development and evolution. Interestingly, in response to Kelly's criticisms, Wilber (1996d) admits that "my suggestion to open up the Great Chain of Being by seeing it, not as a monolithic pole but rather as numerous different streams traversing various waves, substantially alters the root metaphor (possibly fatally)" (p. 400).

20. Wilber devotes considerable efforts to explain the dynamics of the movement of surface structures (which he calls "translation") and the movement of deep structures (which he calls "transformation"), but fails to specify the rules governing the relation between a specific deep structure and its surface structures (which he calls "transcription") (see 1984, pp. 45–54; 1996b, pp. 46–52). More recently, Wilber (1995) mentions that Chomsky and Piaget offered transcription rules that explain how "the potentials of the deep structure are unfolded in actual surface structures" (p. 531, note 45). However, he has not yet offered the transcription rules that sustain his own model.

21. For an interesting hermeneutic dialogue involving the Advaitin nonduality and the Christian doctrine of the Trinity, see von Brück (1991).

22. There may be, however, an even a deeper cultural reason for this adhesion. As Tarnas suggests, the transpersonal loyalty to Neo-Hindu forms of perennial philosophy may have been in part a reaction to a Western religious matrix dominated by dogmatic forms of Christianity: "Historically, the abstract universalism of the European Enlightenment project had already served this rebellion against dogmatic Christianity. When this modern Western commitment is combined with (a usually decontextualized) Eastern mysticism, we see the basic contours of transpersonal perennialism" (personal communication, April 19, 2001).

23. As Dupré (1996) points out, however, the perennialist distinction between mystical experience and interpretation is misconceived:

> Underlying this position is a rather simplistic assumption—possibly derived from eighteenth-century empiricist theories—that experience consists of an immediate mental content and is not the function that mediates the mind with reality. If one accepts the latter position, as we do, all experience becomes *interpreted* experience, while all interpretation is mediated by experience. This implies that the religious tradition within which the mystical experience tales place is itself informed and shaped by experience. Nor does the presence of common features "override" the difference: the differences remain, and they remain essential. (pp. 3–4)

24. I should probably say here some words about the most recent systematic attempt to ground a perennialist account of spirituality in experience. I am referring to Forman's search for pure consciousness events (PCEs) across the traditions (e.g., Forman, 1990a, 1993, 1998a). According to Forman (1993) a PCE is a type of mystical experience "during which the subject remains conscious (wakeful, alert—not sleeping or unconscious) yet devoid of all mental content" (p. 708). To illustrate the nature of these events, Forman (1993) reports his own experience of pure consciousness during a neo-Advaitin meditation retreat:

> I had been meditating alone in my room all morning when someone knocked on my door. I heard the knock perfectly clearly, and upon hearing it I knew that, although there was no "waking up" before hearing the knock, for some indeterminate length of time prior to the knocking I had not been aware of anything in particular. I had been awake but with no content for my consciousness. *Had no one knocked I doubt that I would ever have become aware that I had not been thinking or perceiving. The experience was so unremarkable, as it felt like, in retrospect, just regular me though utterly without content, that I simply would have begun at some point to recommence thinking and probably would never have taken note that I had been conscious yet devoid of mental content.* (p. 708, italics added)

What these PCEs reveal, Forman (1998b) believes, is the "innate human capacity" to be conscious of consciousness itself, of awareness per se. More specifically, Forman (1998b) suggests that the PCEs of mysticism are the expression of psychophysiological structures of the human mind which are independent of tradition, culture, and era. Furthermore, Forman (1990a, 1998a) and his associates claim to have found evidence for the occurrence of these PCEs in religious traditions such as Samkhya-Yoga, and certain Buddhist, Jewish, Sufi, and Christian schools and mystics. And on these grounds, Forman (1998b) hypothesizes the existence of a Perennial Psychology:

> What mysticism and the above arguments reveal is a *psychologia perennis*, a Perennial Psychology. . . . The claim of the Perennial Psychology is not that there exists a commonality of philosophical claims but rather that in the human psyche there are certain deep and consistent psychological structures. (p. 28)

Interestingly, Forman neglects to mention Wilber's (1975) proposal of this very term more than twenty years ago to refer to a very similar approach.

As I see it, there is much in Forman's research program that is both salutary and significant. Apart from showing some of the limitations of Katz's (1978a, 1983a) contextualist approach to mysticism, Forman's shift from experience to event to refer to mystical phenomena, and his depiction of knowledge by identity as the epistemic mode of mysticism, are important moves in harmony with the participatory vision presented in Part II of this book. However, Forman also falls into several pitfalls that need at least a brief consideration.

First, we have seen that Forman (1993) describes his PCE as an unnoticeable and unremarkable phenomenon experienced by "just the regular me though utterly without content" (p. 708). If this report is supposed to be paradigmatic for a PCE (as Forman presents it), however, I have serious doubts that he and the mystics are talking about the same animal. Mystical awareness is not an "unremarkable," wakeful but objectless consciousness experienced by "the regular me" which can pass unnoticed or be easily forgotten. On the contrary, mystical PCEs are pregnant with deep meaning, blissful and ecstatic feelings, and usually involve a drastic transformation of individual consciousness whose occurrence is hardly unnoticed or forgotten. Forman's description of mystical PCEs in terms of contentless awareness completely ignores not only the affective qualities and heightened depth and presence characteristic of mystical PCEs, but also the profound existential and/or cosmological meaning that they intrinsically carry. This leads me to believe that Forman's unremarkable PCEs, although surely fascinating psychophysiological phenomena, are not the PCEs of mysticism.

Second, a related and highly questionable claim made by Forman (1998b) is that mystical notions as diverse as the Buddhist *sunyata*, the Hindu Atman, or the Christian "highest power in the soul" are just different ways of speaking about consciousness itself: "It makes sense to think that mystics could be talking in a variety of languages—applying different beliefs and background claims—about the same phenomenon and experience. . . . Mysticism and awareness per se are, in important respects, nonpluralistic" (p. 33). Nonetheless, to depict these distinct nondual states as referring to "consciousness itself" is a distorting oversimplification of what the traditions actually say about these phenomena. To be sure, Forman's description may conceivably suit the nondual goals of traditions like Samkhya-Yoga or Advaita Vedanta, but it certainly does not conform to the prevalent trends in Buddhist, Christian, or Jewish spirituality. Contra Forman (1998b), for example, sunyata is not "awareness per se . . . devoid of the subject/object distinction and of any content of specifiable shape" (p. 33), but the direct insight into the codependent arising of phenomena, insight which is at the root of the emergence of both Buddhist wisdom (*prajña*) and compassion (*karuna*). Likewise, what most Christian mystics report is not an inconspicuous experience of their own contentless consciousness, but a sublime and awesome participation in or union with God's divine Being. Finally, from the perspective of the wisdom traditions, Forman's program can also be charged with anthropocentrism and reductionism in its insistence that the PCEs are a reflection of the "psychophysiological structures of the human mind." By contrast, virtually all spiritual traditions maintain that mystical events do not result merely from human psychophysiology, but from the participation in spheres of being and knowledge that transcend the merely human. In my opinion, what all this suggests is that in order to find deep commonalities among the different traditions, Forman had to bracket all metaphysics and develop a reductionistic and anthropocentric account of mysticism as the awareness of the psychophysiological structures of the human mind. As we have seen, this reductionistic approach naturally leads to important distortions of the traditions and severely undermines Forman's otherwise valuable cross-cultural research.

25. Notice here that this is not necessarily the case with Wilber's neo-perennialism. If I understand Wilber correctly, he is defending universality on a structural, and not on an experiential,

level. Therefore, it would be possible, and perhaps inevitable, that mystics from different traditions would have different experiences, at least of the psychic, subtle, and causal levels. The only level where Wilber seems to claim universality on not only structural but experiential terms is the non-dual level, where this distinction, as well as any other, would dissolve into the direct apprehension of Reality as it really is. In the next chapters, however, we will see how misleading this claim can be.

CHAPTER FIVE
THE PARTICIPATORY NATURE OF SPIRITUAL KNOWING

1. In order to highlight the contrasts between the participatory and the experiential visions, I am talking here of transpersonal events as they occur in the locus of the individual. However, it should be kept in mind that one of the fundamental features of the participatory vision is that transpersonal events are multilocal, that is, they can occur not only in an individual, but also in a relationship, a community, a collective identity, or a place.

2. Although to my knowledge the term "event" has never been applied in a participatory manner to transpersonal or spiritual phenomena, it may be necessary to mention two uses of this term in the modern literature on mysticism. First, Forman (1990a, 1993) proposes the locution "pure consciousness event" to talk about a type of mystical experience "during which the subject remains conscious (wakeful, alert—not sleeping or unconscious) yet devoid of all mental content" (1993, p. 708). For Forman, pure consciousness events are nonintentional experiences devoid of mental content that can be found in virtually all mystical traditions. Second, Sells (1994) suggests that we talk about mysticism not as experiences but as "meaning events." According to Sells, a mystical meaning event is the semantic reenactment of mystical experiences, that is, the meaning of the mystic's linguistic expressions. In his own words: "In contrast to the realization as an instance of mystical union which entails a complete psychological, epistemological, and ontological transformation, the meaning event is a semantic occurrence" (p. 9). As I see it, Sells's intention is primarily methodological. What he is suggesting is to bracket issues about what mystics encounter, experience, or know, and focus on the study of mystical modes of discourse, such as the apophatic one. A similar suggestion has been recently made by Idel (1996) in his plea to focus on mystical expressions, rather than on mystical experiences.

Although neither Forman nor Sells talks about participatory events, it is noteworthy that, facing the nonintentionality of some mystical states, these authors chose to refer to them as events. The fundamental difference between my approach and these proposals is that while Forman uses the term *event* to refer to an experiential state that is epistemically void, and Sells uses it to talk about the semantic meaning of mystical utterances, I use it to refer to the participatory nature of transpersonal and most mystical phenomena.

3. Much of the early transpersonal research focused on the elucidation of the factors that facilitate the occurrence of a transpersonal event. Although these are important and valuable efforts, I believe that there will always exist a certain degree of indeterminacy in this matter. That is, I do not think that we will ever arrive at an exhaustive list of operational conditions whose presence would definitively warrant the emergence of a given transpersonal or spiritual event. This indeterminacy is illustrated in the traditional literature by the analogy between the attainment of enlightenment and the growth of a tree. When growing a tree, we can facilitate certain conditions for its healthy development (e.g., good soil, adequate watering and nutrients, a place that receives light, and so on), but there will always be elements that escape human control (e.g., the weather, plagues, the genetic quality of the seed, etc.). The indeterminacy of spiritual events is explained by the various

traditions in several ways (e.g., in terms of accumulated karma from past lives in many Hindu and Buddhist schools, in terms of Divine grace in Christianity, etc.). In any event, all this suggests, I believe, that an element of indeterminacy regarding spiritual realizations is somehow embedded in the human condition.

4. For two lucid discussions about the often overlooked Gadamerian notion of "truth event," see Carpenter (1994) and DiCenso (1990). Interestingly, Carpenter's (1994) essay traces the roots of Gadamer's notion of "truth event" to the Neoplatonic doctrine of emanation. In another work, Carpenter (1995) applies this idea as a hermeneutic tool to compare the nature of spiritual revelation in Bhartrhari and Bonaventure. In total harmony with the conception of spiritual knowledge here espoused, Carpenter (1995) concludes with the following words:

> I would like to suggest that the striking similarities in Bhartrhari's and Bonaventure's descriptions of the actual reception of revelation, through which the individual moves from a naïve experience of the world as given, as objective, *in se*, as *vikara*, to the disclosure of the world as relational, as expressio, as anukara, point to an experience of truth in this sense. (p. 198)

And he adds:

> In the actual *event* of revelation, there is no self-same 'object' 'out there' that remains beyond our purely subjective powers of knowing. Rather, *revelation as an event can perhaps best be understood as the disclosure of a reality that is itself dynamic and relational.* (p. 199, italics added)

5. On relational spiritual approaches, see also Achterberg and Rothberg's (1998) reflections on relationship as spiritual practice, Hershock's (1996) account of Ch'an enlightenment in terms of interpersonal intimacy, and Wade's (1998, 2000) original research on sexuality and spiritual knowing.

6. Before the well-known second phase of the Sinai revelation, in which Moses became a mediator and received detailed spiritual teachings at the top of the Mountain of God, the book of Exodus relates a first phase in which God himself came down and revealed the Ten Commandments to the people of Israel in a communal fashion. As Holdrege (1996) points out in her rigorous study, *Veda and Torah*, "the Zohar thus represents the theophany at Mount Sinai as a collective experience, in which the mysteries contained in the Ten Words were apprehended by the people of Israel as a whole" (p. 323). Interestingly, Holdrege (1996) describes the Vedic and Sinai revelations as paradigmatic spiritual "events" to be reenacted by the Hindu and Jewish communities respectively (pp. 334–339).

7. For different perspectives on empathic knowing, see Hart (1999), Jaggar (1990), Jordan (1997), and Orange (1995); on somatic knowing, see Bollas (1987), Grosz (1993), and Jaggar and Bordo (1990); on imaginal-inspirational knowing, see Hart (2000); on intuitive knowing, see Shepherd (1993) and Vaughan (1979); and on spiritual/contemplative knowing, see Hart, Nelson, and Puhakka (2000), H. Smith (1993), and Wilber (1990a).

8. For a summary and further refinement of the enactive paradigm, see Thompson (1996). For a lucid review of Varela, Thompson, and Rosch's (1991) groundbreaking work, *The Embodied Mind*, see Puhakka (1993).

9. As we have seen, Wilber (1995, 1996a) incorporates some of the central insights of the enactive paradigm in his integral theory of evolution, such as the rejection of the representational paradigm, the emancipation from the constraints of a pregiven reality, and the notion of "enacted worldspaces" (i.e., intersubjectively shared worlds of referents that are disclosed in the process of the mutually codetermined evolution of consciousness and the world). Wilber should be credited for

having extended the scope of the enactive paradigm from the sensoriomotor world to mental and spiritual realms. However, the truly emancipatory potential of this expansion gets truncated by his subordination of the enactive paradigm to a universal sequence of pregiven evolutionary deep structures. According to Wilber (1995), let us remember here, although the different "worldspaces" are not pregiven but enacted, their unfolding follows a predetermined evolutionary pathway that reverses a prior involutionary process. With this move, Wilber betrays the raison d'être of the enactive paradigm, which was not only devised to provide a middle way between absolutism and nihilism, but also developed in the context of a view of evolution by natural drift that is inimical to any determined evolutionary path. In contrast, I maintain that the idea of pregivens needs to be rejected not only in the surface manifestations of spiritual power, but also in its innermost nature and creative dynamism (deep structures, in Wilber's terms).

10. The evolution of Ring's (1985, 1998) thinking nicely illustrates the shift of emphasis from experiences and altered states to the transforming participatory knowing advocated in the present work.

11. I am not suggesting, then, an identical or structurally equivalent goal for all contemplative traditions. As we have seen, the adhesion of transpersonal theory to a perennialist metaphysics may not only have been premature, but also have problematic consequences for transpersonal hermeneutics, interreligious dialogue, and spiritual inquiry. In contrast to the essentialist reductionism of the perennial philosophy, in the next chapter I explain how the participatory vision celebrates the diversity of mystical claims by embracing a stance of spiritual pluralism. For different articulations of a more pluralistic vision of spirituality and mysticism, see the works by Dean (1995), Griffiths (1991), Heim (1995), Irwin (1996), Katz (1978a, 1983a), and Vroom (1989).

12. As we have seen in chapter 3, however, some Western-influenced scholars have reinterpreted Eastern contemplative teachings in an empirical fashion (i.e., as experientially originated and verifiable) with the apologetic intention of making them more harmonious with scientific views of valid knowledge.

13. Compare Jones (1993): "The purpose of the mystical paths to enlightenment is to depict and illustrate the way to overcome the nescience blocking the enlightening knowledge (as defined by the particular mystic's tradition)" (p. 4).

14. This mistake is related to the spiritual disorder that Wilber (1986) calls "pseudo-nirvana" (i.e., "the mistaking of subtle or archetypal forms, illuminations, raptures, ecstasies, insights, or absorptions for final liberation") (p. 123).

15. Note that these statements may not hold true for other Buddhist schools. As Gyatso (1999) shows, for example, Tibetan Buddhism does refer to meditative states through several lexemes (e.g., *myong-ba* and *nyams*) which seem to be synonymous of the English term experience. Although Gyatso personally regards spiritual insights as "varieties of enlightened experiences" (p. 120), she tells us that, in Tibetan Buddhism, "when distinction between subject and object dissolves entirely, however, it is usually not labelled with any of the terms for experience discussed thus far but rather is cast as an enlightened realization, often termed *rtogs*" (pp. 119–120). And she adds: "*Nyams* [experience] in particular is, in fact, frequently contrasted with *rtogs* [realization], especially in the Mahamudra literature, where meditative experiences are sometimes said to precede, but in themselves to be bereft of realization" (p. 120).

16. Note, however, that although both St. John of the Cross and St. Teresa talked about spiritual experiences, they did not consider them constitutive of the truly mystical. As Turner (1995) explains, whereas "John's 'dark nights' are the metaphors not *of* experience, but of a dialectical *cri-*

tique of experientialist tendencies" (p. 227), Teresa valued her raptures and visions mainly as signposts for the Mansions and not as the essence of genuine contemplation. Although their mysticisms differ in important ways, Turner (1995) continues, both John and Teresa thought of the mystical as ultimately beyond experience.

17. The examples selected here derive exclusively from Eastern sources because these are the traditions that the proponents of the experiential vision usually rely on. Notice, however, that a parallel case can be made in the case of most Western traditions. For example, a classic account of Christian mysticism in terms of mystical knowing can be found in Maritain's (1932/1959) magnum opus, *The Degrees of Knowledge*, in which a hierarchy of forms and modes of knowledge (*sensible, praeter-real, transsensible*) leading to the ultimate goal of knowledge of God is presented. Likewise, in his highly acclaimed work, *The Foundations of Mysticism*, McGinn (1994) has recently criticized the modern tendency to describe mysticism in terms of inner experiences or altered states, and found "the term 'presence' (of God) a more central and more useful category for grasping the unifying note in the varieties of Christian mysticism" (p. xvii). According to McGinn (1996b), even for the so-called "affective mystics" like Bernard of Clairvaux or John of the Cross, love of God included some form of intuitive knowing (*intelligentia amoris*). Likewise, the Islamic tradition has always emphasized sacred knowledge as both the core and goal of its mysticism and soteriology (Chittick, 1989). Experiences of self-annihilation (*fana'*) are not the salvific end in the Sufi path; the goal, in contrast, is to know God (*ma'rifa*), to be a perfect human being by being with God (Chittick, 1989). According to the Islamic mystic and philosopher Ha'iri Yazdi (1992), for example, "mysticism is a form of presence-knowledge . . . a form of human noetic consciousness in the sense that mystical moods and experiences are assertive and profoundly informative. Mysticism is characterized throughout by an orderly awareness of the world of reality. It puts something before us as the truth of this world" (p. 113). Finally, the attainment of metaphysical knowledge has also been the primary goal of the diverse traditions often amalgamated under the term "Western esotericism" such as Hermeticism, Gnosticism, Theosophy, and so forth (Faivre, 1994; Faivre & Needleman, 1995). For a traditionalist account of the centrality of knowledge in most contemplative traditions, East and West, see Nasr (1989).

CHAPTER SIX
AN OCEAN WITH MANY SHORES:
THE CHALLENGE OF SPIRITUAL PLURALISM

1. The difficulties in offering a precise and inclusive definition of mysticism have been repeatedly noticed by modern researchers and scholars (e.g., Dupré, 1987; Forman, 1990b; Haas, 1997; Lukoff & Lu, 1988). The term *mysticism* stems from the Greek *musteion* and *mistikos*, which mean "to close," and more specifically, "to close the eyes and/or the mouth" (Armstrong, 1993; Bouyer, 1980). Etymological analyses, however, are not too helpful in defining mysticism because, although many mystical practices do entail silence and inwardness, others involve outward activities such as singing, dancing, or visionary engagement of the environment—as Stace's (1960) classical division of mysticism into introvertive and extrovertive nicely conveys. For an excellent recent attempt at clarifying the meaning of this elusive notion, see Brainard (1996).

2. To quote only a few of the most relevant works see, for various articulations and defenses of perennialism, Byrne (1984), Evans (1989), Forman (1989, 1990a, 1993, 1998a), Hick (1992), King (1988), Perovich (1985a, 1985b), J. R. Price, III (1985), Rothberg (1989), Shear (1994), H. Smith (1987), Stoeber (1992, 1994), and Wainwright (1981). For critiques of perennialism and proposals of more contextualists approaches, see Almond (1982), Bagger (1991), Cupitt (1998), Dean (1984),

Fenton (1995), Gill (1984, 1989), Griffiths (1991), Heron (1998), Hollenback (1996), Idel and McGinn (1996), Jones (1993), Katz (1978a, 1983a, 1985, 1988, 1992a), McGinn (1994), Proudfoot (1985), and Raphael (1994). See also Short (1996) for a somewhat misleading attempt to reconcile both perspectives.

3. Contextualist approaches are commonly called "constructivist" by their critics (e.g., Forman, 1990a, 1998a; Rothberg, 1989). If I use the term *contextualist* here, it is because it is the one preferred by many of these authors. For example, Katz (1992b) tells us: "I have been, of late, referred to as a 'constructivist,' but given the meaning attached to this designation by my critics, I reject this term, preferring to describe my approach as 'contextualist'" (p. 34).

4. The "strong thesis of mediation" asserts that all mystical experiences are always necessarily mediated (i.e., that the phenomenology of mysticism can be fully explained by resorting to constructive variables such as the concepts, doctrines, and expectations that mystics bring to their experiences). In contrast, what we may call the "weak thesis of mediation" asserts that most mystical experiences are heavily mediated by contextual variables, but that mystical phenomenology is the product of a complex interaction between constructive variables, the intentional creative participation of the mystic, and an indeterminate spiritual power of inexhaustible creativity. Later on, I suggest that whereas Stanislav Grof's consciousness research renders the strong thesis of mediation highly implausible, the participatory vision of human spirituality presented here embraces the weak thesis of mediation.

5. Note that contextualist approaches to mysticism did not originate with the work of Katz and collaborators. As early as 1909, Rufus Jones, in his *Studies in Mystical Religion*, states that:

> There are no "pure experiences", no experiences which come wholly from *beyond* the person who has them . . . Mystical experiences will be, perforce, saturated with the dominant ideas of the group to which the mystic belongs, and they will reflect the expectations of that group and period. (quoted in Almond, 1982, p. 163)

Likewise, the eminent scholar of Jewish mysticism Gershom Scholem (1946) points out that:

> There is no such thing as mysticism in the abstract, that is to say, a phenomenon or experience which has no particular relation to other religious phenomena. There is no mysticism as such, there is only the mysticism of a particular religious system, Christian, Islamic, Jewish mysticism and so on. (pp. 5–6)

6. I am stressing here "more" perennialist and "more" contextualist because, as the dialogue between these camps evolved, their differences have gradually become more of emphasis than of radical disagreement. For example, most perennialist authors would readily recognize today, although against a universalist background, some degree of contextuality in mysticism and a reciprocity between mystical experience and interpretation.

7. As I argue elsewhere (Ferrer, 1998a), the charge of self-contradiction cannot be consistently maintained against many contextualist and pluralist approaches. The charge of self-contradiction or self-refutation is the classic argument against relativism used by virtually all absolutist philosophers even since Plato's quarrels with the Sophists (e.g., see Burnyeat, 1990). In its general form, the argument runs as follows: Relativism (or constructivism, contextualism, pluralism, etc.) is self-refuting because it cannot be stated consistently without becoming some form of absolutism (or objectivism, universalism, etc.). That is, to say that all views are relative (or constructed, contextual, etc.) renders the relativist thesis either relative itself or claiming to be an exception to its own logic. If the relativist thesis does not have absolute and universal value, the absolutist philosopher

argues, then there is no reason to consider it more valid than any other view. Conversely, if the relativist thesis is claimed to have absolute value, it either contradicts itself or falls into what Mandelbaum (1982) called the "self-excepting fallacy."

To be sure, a vulgar relativism maintaining that everything is the same as everything else, and that no distinctions can be therefore made between what is good or bad, right or wrong, true or false is both blatantly self-contradictory and morally repulsive. However, many alternatives to absolutism, such as certain types of pluralism, perspectivism, pragmatism, and moderated forms of relativism and constructivism, are not necessarily inconsistent. What all these approaches have in common is not to be self-refuting, but to challenge absolutist, universalist, and objectivist beliefs in the existence of transcultural and transhistorical standards of rationality, truth, and morality. As Adorno (1979) warns, to interpret this denial as a self-refuting positive theory is both fallacious and question-begging.

In short, what I am suggesting here is that *the self-refuting nature of most nonabsolutist approaches only emerges when they are either believed to have absolutist purposes or judged by standards (notions of absolute truth, rationality, etc.) only appropriate in an absolutist domain of discourse.* In other words, these approaches are self-refuting only when they are supposed to have an absolutist agenda, that is, to make absolutist claims.

The persuasiveness of the argument for the self-refuting nature of nonabsolutist approaches, then, rests on the acceptance of an absolutist domain of discourse. However, human discourse can have different purposes apart from arguing for the absolute truth or falsehood of knowledge claims, viewpoints, or paradigms. For example, when Meiland (1980) examines the claim that "if relativism is *only* relatively true, then we have no reason for taking it seriously," he points out that this statement presumes that only that which is purely absolute or objective is worth expressing. By bringing evidence contra universals and absolutes, relativists may be attempting to rationally persuade the nonrelativist of the relativity of all conceptual frameworks, including the relativist one. This appears to be, for example, the path taken by Goodman (1978), who emphasizes the local (vs. universal) validity of relativist knowledge claims. Stated in this way, then, the relativist thesis, far from being self-refuting, is rather self-exemplifying (B. H. Smith, 1993). Furthermore, I should add, they may be appealing to the reasonableness, appropriateness, and even "truthness" of the relativist thesis without operating in the domain of a bivalent theory of truth—according to which a statement is either true or false (not true), instead of having different degrees of "truthness" (Negoita, 1985). Finally, as Rothberg (1994) points out, arguments for self-contradiction such as Habermas's performative paradox (to question discourse is self-refuting because it assumes discourse) are only legitimate if one presumes the impossibility of going beyond the structures of communicative rationality—and this assumption is precisely what most spiritual traditions challenge! In all these cases, relativism is not self-refuting and is worth expressing. Needless to say, analogous arguments can be made, *mutatis mutandis*, in defense of many other nonabsolutist approaches such as certain forms of pluralism (Matilal, 1991; Panikkar, 1996; Rescher, 1993), contextualism (Lynch, 1998), perspectivism (MacIntyre, 1988), or moderated relativism (Hales, 1997; MacIntyre, 1987, 1988; Margolis, 1986, 1989; Tianji, 1991).

To recapitulate, although vulgar relativism is clearly self-contradictory, the validity of this charge against many nonabsolutist approaches assumes an absolutist domain of discourse. However, both the existence of absolutist standards (of reason, truth, and value), and the exclusive or privileged legitimacy of an absolutist domain of discourse, is precisely what is denied or put into question by these approaches. But then, the argument for self-refutation against relativism is only well-founded if relativism, the view that it is trying to discredit, is mistaken (that is, if there really exist absolute standards of reason, knowledge, and value). Once it is revealed that the hidden premises of the self-refutation charge against non-absolutist approaches presuppose its conclusion, this reasoning becomes what logicians call a syllogistic fallacy. This is probably why a nonabsolutist philosopher such as Fuchs (1992) can tranquilly point out that "The methodological horror of relativism and its paradoxes scares and occupies only those who still search for safe epistemic foundations" (p. 30).

8. The term "Myth of the Given" was coined by Sellars (1956) in his seminal lectures on empiricism and philosophy of mind under the title "The Myth of the Given: Three Lectures on Empiricism and the Philosophy of Mind," published later as "Empiricism and the Philosophy of Mind." Earlier critiques of the essentialist ideas denounced by Sellars can be found in the philosophical pragmatism of Charles Sanders Peirce, the absolute idealism of F. H. Bradley, and the philosophical behaviorism of Gilbert Ryle (e.g., see Ross, 1970). For some enlightening discussions on Sellars's assault on the Myth of the Given, see Gutting (1977), Robinson (1975), and Rottschaefer (1978).

9. For a classic critical survey of theories of the given, see Ross (1970). See also Wild (1940) for an early critique of the idea of the given in empiricist philosophy.

10. For two contemporary accounts of the Myth of the Given, for example, see Searle (1995) and Nagel (1997). For a critical review of Nagel's work, see Williams (1998).

11. An apparent exception to the perennialist adhesion to the Myth of the Given can be found in Wilber's recent works (1995, 1996a, 1998a). In contrast to most perennialists, Wilber is well aware of the problems with the Myth of the Given, and maintains instead a qualified *correspondence theory of truth* which, while admitting the interpretive nature of knowledge, preserves an objective component that anchors these interpretations. Both his Four Quadrant Model, and especially his notion of worldspaces ("enacted domains of distinctions") clearly indicate that Wilber is trying to free the spiritual life from the many tyrannies dictated by this Myth. In spite of these valuable efforts, I believe that the Myth of the Given is still lurking in Wilber's integral theory. It breathes with ease, for example, in both his defense of a pregiven sequence of deep structures (linked to Neo-Hindu involutionary ideas), and his insistence on pregiven features of ultimate reality (strikingly following a monistic metaphysics: Oneness, nonduality, etc.). This subtle but unequivocal retention of objectivist prejudices effectively subverts the profound emancipatory potential of his integral model. To mention only one example, it leads to a universal (and ultimately doctrinal) gradation of spiritual insights and traditions that may unnecessarily constrain not only human spiritual evolution, but also the creative range of valid spiritual choices (cf. Heron, 1998, pp. 80–82).

12. Note that perennialist accounts can also be neo-Kantian. According to Hick (1992), for example, the different spiritual ultimates "represent different phenomenal awarenesses of the same noumenal reality" (p. 15). For a critique of Hick's Neo-Kantianism, see Eddy (1994), and for an excellent analysis of the "hyper-Kantianism" of Katz and other contextualists, see Forgie (1985). Another Kantian-like defense of perennialism was recently articulated by Ingram (1997).

13. Two important exceptions are Stoeber's (1994) experiential constructivism and Hollenback's (1996) theory of mystical empowerment (*enthymesis*). While endorsing the mediated and contextual nature of mystical experiences, these authors maintain that spiritual realities can have a creative impact on the content of mystical knowledge, which explains the emergence of novel spiritual insights and mystical heresies. As I see it, these works are harmonious with the participatory vision developed in this chapter.

14. Responding to these charges, Katz (1988) states: "My view—and it's important that it be understood—is that while such transcendental realities or Reality may well exist, it (or He, She or It) can only be known by us in the way such metaphysical realia became available to us given the sort of beings we are" (p. 754). Although Katz's position leaves open the existence of spiritual reali-

ties, it is animated by a Neo-Kantian, and ultimately dualistic, agnosticism regarding their ontological nature. In other words, metaphysical or noumenal realities may exist, but we can only access our
situated phenomenal awareness of them.

15. The Dualism of Framework and Reality pervades contemporary religious studies. Apart
from the writings of contextualist scholars of mysticism and the above mentioned works by Hick, see
Lindbeck (1984) for a very influential defense of religions as interpretative schemes. Lindbeck's work
is particularly helpful in making obvious the limitations of the two main modern approaches to religion, the "experiential expressive" (perennialist) and his favored "cultural-linguistic" (contextualist).

See also Runzo (1986) for a thoughtful but ultimately misguided theological defense of religions as conceptual schemes. Although containing valuable insights, Runzo's work nicely illustrates,
I believe, how the adherence to conceptual frameworks inevitably places a noumenal spiritual reality out of reach from human consciousness, which then becomes trapped in a merely phenomenal
world. Furthermore, since all religious truth-claims are relative to conceptual frameworks, skepticism can only be avoided by resorting to an exhausted absolute commitment to faith.

Note also how much the influential work of J. Z. Smith (1978) subtly perpetuates this dualism. In his celebrated essay, "Map is Not Territory," after rightly critiquing the idea of a pregiven territory (the Myth of the Given), Smith concludes: "'Map is not territory'—but maps are all we
possess" (p. 309). In the same vein, for Baudrillard (1994): "The territory no longer precedes the
map, nor does it survive it. It is nevertheless the map that precedes the territory—*precession of simulacra*—that engenders the territory" (p. 1). For these postmodern authors, that is, all we can have
access to are our constructions, or, as Nelson Goodman (1978) puts it, our versions of reality and
never reality itself. This postmodern move, however, far from dissolving or transcending the Dualism
of Framework and Reality (or map and territory), reinforces it by fatally obliterating one of its poles
(reality) and then desperately elevating the other (frameworks, maps, or versions of reality). "The
world well lost," as Rorty's (1972) famous essay celebrated.

For an analysis of the uses and abuses of the idea of conceptual frameworks in religious studies, see Godlove (1984, 1997). Following Davidson, Godlove proposes that once the dualism of
scheme and content is deconstructed, we need to give up the idea of religions as conceptual frameworks. Interestingly, Godlove (1997) argues that Kant himself may be free from such pernicious
dualism insofar as his categories are transcendental and therefore "could provide our judgments
with the possibility of empirical truth" (p. 37).

16. For two lucid critiques of some aspects of Davidson's essay, see Rescher (1980) and Quine
(1981). Although rejecting the Myth of the Given, both authors question that linguistic translatability is an adequate ground to refute the existence of alternative conceptual schemes. Rescher (1980),
for example, suggests that the test to judge the presence of alternative conceptual schemes is not
translatability but interpretability. Rescher's essay is especially helpful in showing how any plausible
retention of the idea of a conceptual scheme needs to let go of both its original Kantian moorings
and the notion of a pregiven world. Free from these specters, Rescher continues, potentially different conceptual schemes are no longer seen as alternative or competing a priori interpretations of a
ready-made world, but simply diverse a posteriori creative innovations stemming from our empirical inquiries and ontological commitments (in our terms, alternative conceptual schemes become
different enactions of the world).

17. The relationship between epistemological and existential alienation has also been noted
by Carr (1992) in her excellent work on modern nihilism:

> Existential nihilism . . . is in fact secondary; it is derived from alethiological, episte-
> mological, or ethical nihilism. It is because we believe there is no truth that we con-

clude that the world is pointless; it is because we think that knowledge is mere illusion that we describe life as meaningless; it is because we see no moral fabric in the universe that we see our existence as without value. (p. 20)

18. Since Tarnas's (1991) account not only shows the tragic existential implications of the Cartesian-Kantian world view, but also the need to overcome it through a shift towards a participatory epistemology, we will return to his work in the next chapter.

19. This move was apparent, for example, in the writings of American Transcendentalists such as Emerson, Parker, or Brownson. As Gelpi (2000) puts it, "The first Transcendentalists . . . all wanted to get beyond, to transcend, if you will, the limitations of Enlightenment religion. They sought to rescue religious experience from the skeptical consequences of Enlightenment nominalism by developing an account of religious intuition" (p. vii). For example, Gelpi tells us, "Parker defended the subjective intuition of the objective truth of Enlightenment religion" (p. vii).

20. These Neo-Kantian prejudices are also present in transpersonal works. For example, talking about the ontological status of spiritual power, Washburn (1995) points out that "we simply cannot know . . . whether the power of the Ground, in addition to being an intrapsychic phenomenon, is also an extrapsychic (metaphysical, cosmic) noumenon" (p. 130). And he adds, although "Spirit may have its ultimate origin in a metaphysical source lying completely beyond the soul, . . . the ego can have no experience, and therefore no knowledge, of the power of the ground as it may (or may not) exist beyond these boundaries" (pp. 130–131).

21. Although I believe that both the Myth of the Given and the Myth of the Framework are the natural progeny of the more fundamental Dualism of Framework and Reality, this dualism is also frequently derived from the commitment to the idea of an uninterpreted reality (the Myth of the Given). This is the case, for example, with Hick (1992) who, assuming that the Real is One and faced with the diversity of mystical revelations, is forced to postulate an inaccessible noumenal reality behind such multiplicity. Of course, the price for Kantian spectacles is always high: Apart from reintroducing the classic Kantian dualism to account for this perplexing tension, Hick is forced to reject mystical claims about the immediate nature of spiritual knowledge. As we will see, the participatory vision can harmoniously house both the irreducible diversity of spiritual revelations and their direct or immediate nature.

22. Compare Evans (1993): "Spirituality consists primarily of a basic transformative process in which we uncover and let go of our narcissism so as to surrender into the Mystery out of which everything continually arises" (p. 4). In the same vein, Hick (1992) understands spiritual liberation as "the transformation of human existence from self-centeredness to Reality-centeredness" (p. 14). Similarly, M. J. Augustine (1986) argues that, although holding different spiritual Ultimates, both Buddhism and Christianity share a common anthropology aimed at transforming egocentric perception and action into selfless ones. And finally, Ingram (1997) suggests that the "different conceptions of salvation or final liberation share a generic commonality: all, in their own historically and culturally specific way, are concerned with the transformation of human existence from self-centeredness to a new and mutually creative relationship with the relatively inaccessible Sacred" (p. 185).

23. This movement away from limiting self-centeredness can also be expressed, among and within traditions, through different existential stances (e.g., monasticism, asceticism, contemplation, devotional service, selfless action in the world, etc.) For a survey of some of these expressions in the major religious traditions, see Kieckhefer and Bond's (1988) interesting study of sainthood in world religions. Of related interest is Parrinder's (1982) excellent comparative study of the idea of avatar

(incarnation of the divine in human form) across religious traditions, which, by the way, explicitly refutes Huxley's (1945) claims about its universality.

24. This overcoming of limiting self-centeredness should not be confused with the erroneous belief that liberation involves a total transcendence or annihilation of the egoic system or individual personality. As transpersonal theorists have taken pains to stress, what is overcome in the spiritual path is not our personal identity, but our exclusive and restrictive self-identification with the construct of a separate self (see, e.g., Epstein, 1988; Wilber, 1997a).

25. Let us admit straight off that this belief is also held by many contemplative traditions, especially those spawned in India. In the next chapter, I address the apparent tension between the participatory vision and the essentialist claims of these traditions.

26. This faulty reasoning undermines much of Forman's (1990a, 1998a) case for a universal pure consciousness event on the grounds of its nonconceptuality. Although ultimately retreating to a stance of perspectival perennialism, Loy (1988) provides an excellent presentation of a variety of transconceptual forms of nonduality.

27. The idea of different spiritual salvations has recently received a compelling articulation in the hands of Heim (1995). Heim's work is helpful in revealing the contradictions of other so-called pluralistic approaches (like Hick's or W. C. Smith's) which nonetheless defend an equivalent end point for all traditions. A true religious pluralism, Heim claims, needs to acknowledge the existence of alternative religious aims, and to put religions on a single scale will not do it: There are "many true religions . . . and each the only way" (p. 219). Although suggesting several possibilities, Heim remains agnostic about the metaphysical vision behind his "more pluralistic hypothesis" (see, e.g., p. 146), and ultimately slips back, inconsistently I believe, to the Myth of the Given: "Among the various religions," he tells us, "one or several or none may provide the best approximate representation of the character of that cosmos, explaining and ordering these various human possibilities within it" (p. 215). This relapse is also evident when, after comparing the different religious ends to different cities, he says that "I regard these cities as sites within a single world, whose global mapping has a determinate character" (p. 220). In these statements, it becomes obvious that Heim's more pluralistic hypothesis is only pluralistic at a phenomenological or soteriological level (admitting different human spiritual fulfillments), but not at an ontological or metaphysical one (at the level of spiritual knowledge and reality).

28. For several discussions of different Buddhist views about the nature of ultimate reality, see Cook (1989), Hopkins (1988), and Küng (1989). For a good introduction to some of the controversies among Buddhist schools regarding the substantiality of ultimate reality, see Chinchore (1995).

29. For a more detailed exploration of the merits of a multicentered account of interreligious relations, see Hoffman (1993). This multicentered account is consistent with a view of religion and mysticism as "family resemblance" concepts (e.g., Dupré, 1987; Hick, 1992; O'Leary, 1996; Smart, 1973). According to this view, although there is not an essence in mysticism, each mystical tradition is similar in important respects to some others in the family, but not in all respects to any, or in any respect to all. For some problems in defining religion in family resemblances terms, however, see Fitzgerald (1996).

30. Roughly, these comparisons may potentially lead to the identification of at least four different types of equivalencies: (1) *cognitive*: common beliefs, doctrines, or ethical guidelines (e.g., belief in reincarnation, or the Golden Rule); (2) *functional*: spiritual doctrines, notions, or practices that, while having different meanings, play an analogous role in two or more religious traditions

(e.g., *qi/prana* and soul as mediators between body and spirit [Lipman, 1995]—this would be analogous to what Panikkar (1996) calls "homeomorphic equivalents"); (3) *homoversal*: human invariants or universal truths for the human species (e.g., in relation to waking, dream, and dreamless sleep states of consciousness—the term "homoversal" was coined in a different context by Rosemont, 1988); and (4) *ontological*: overlapping elements in different participatory enactions of ultimate reality (e.g., union with a personal God in Judaism, Christianity, and Islam) (Idel & McGinn, 1996).

31. Of course, the all-important distinction between state and trait is pertinent here. Although the transient access to spiritual shores can be breathtaking, inspiring, and deeply transforming, very rarely if ever is it a substitute for sailing in the adequate raft, especially regarding the permanent integration of these understandings in everyday life. As is well known in modern consciousness research, many spiritual insights, apparently fully penetrated during nonordinary states, are frequently forgotten, partially or totally, after these events. Although there may be some exceptions (see, e.g., Ring [1985, 1998] for an exposition of the spiritual aftereffects from near-death experiences), it is safe to say, I believe, that in general only a continued intentional spiritual commitment can facilitate the stabilization of these insights in everyday life.

32. An intriguing question raised by these phenomena is why this transpersonal access to cross-cultural spiritual symbolism had not been reported before in the world religious literature or pictorial history, even in those traditions that ritually used entheogens, breathing, or other technologies of consciousness modification, such as many shamanic cultures, and certain schools of Sufism, Tantra, and Hinduism (Grof, 1988; Jesse, 1996; Metzner, 1999). In other words, if transpersonal consciousness allows human beings to access cross-cultural religious symbolism, why do we not find, for example, Buddhist or Christian motifs in indigenous pictorial art? Or reports of Kabbalistic symbols and experiences in the Tantric or Sufi literature? Many of these traditions were very prone to describe—either pictorially or literally—their spiritual visions in great detail, and had their members encountered the powerful symbolic motifs that Grof's subjects report, it would be reasonable to expect finding at least some records of them, and to my knowledge we have found none.

In the wake of this striking situation, the modern mind may be tempted to explain away the phenomena reported by Grof in terms of cryptoamnesia (i.e., the subjects had forgotten their previous exposure to those symbols and the special state of consciousness simply brings these memories to consciousness). In my opinion, however, this explanation needs to be ruled out because Grof's subjects not only can see the form of these religious and mythological symbols, but also gain detailed insight into their deeper esoteric meaning. Furthermore, although the cryptoamnesia hypothesis may explain some of the cases reported by Grof (e.g., the self-identification of some Japanese people with the figure of Christ in the Cross), it would be very difficult to explain in these terms many of the cases Grof reports, in which an individual accesses detailed knowledge of mythological and religious motifs of barely known cultures like the Malekulans in New Guinea (Grof, 1998, pp. 19–21). In these cases, the possibility of previous intellectual exposure to such detailed information of a barely known culture is remote enough, I believe, to rule out the cryptoamnesia hypothesis as a plausible general explanation of these phenomena.

In my opinion, Grof suggests a more plausible explanation: The contemporary transpersonal access to cross-cultural symbolism may reflect the emergence of a novel evolutionary potential of the human psyche, associated with the capability of accessing deeper, cross-cultural layers of the collective unconscious. As I see it, the emergence of this potential, which may mirror in the unconscious the greater interconnectedness of human consciousness in our global times (e.g., through media, television, and especially cyberspace), may have been facilitated by a combination of the following interrelated factors: (1) the lack, after the decline of Christianity, of an unequivocal religious matrix in the modern West that would provide a definite symbolic container for spiritual experiences; (2) the fact that the ritual space for psychedelic and breathwork sessions is not usually structured according to any specific traditional religious symbolism or soteriological aim (as it was generally the case with the ritual use of entheogens in traditional settings); (3) the "seeking" impetus of the modern spiritual quest in Euro-America, arguably especially strong in individuals who feel drawn to experiment with psychedelics or breathwork (e.g., see Roof's [1993, 1999] characterization of modern American spirituality as a "quest culture" composed by a "generation of seekers"); and (4) the importation of modern Western understandings of open inquiry to spiritual matters. As I see it, the combination of these factors may have paved the way for a more open-ended search for, and receptivity to, sacred forms and spiritual meanings, and fostered the emergence of spiritual awarenesses cultivated by different religious traditions.

33. Note that I am not saying that the perennial philosophy cannot find support in Grof's data, or that Grof's research disconfirms a perennialist metaphysics. As Grof's (1998) recent book, *The Cosmic Game*, clearly shows, the psychedelic evidence can be interpreted in ways that are consistent with perennialism. What I am simply suggesting is that Grof's empirical findings are also consistent with a more pluralist participatory vision of human spirituality that is free from the limitations of perennialist thinking.

34. This more pluralist account of Grof's findings is consistent with the recent synthesis of the psychedelic evidence carried out by Merkur (1998). After indicating that most interpretations of the psychedelic evidence so far have been biased in favor of the idea of a universal mysticism, Merkur emphasizes that the empirical data have always pointed to a rich diversity of psychedelic spiritual states. More concretely, Merkur distinguishes twenty-four types of psychedelic unitive states, and suggests that some of them may be more representative of certain religious traditions than others. What characterizes the psychedelic state, he tells us, is that it "provides access to all" (p. 155). Furthermore, although some of these states can be arranged in terms of increasing complexity, Merkur points out that "their development is not unilinear but instead branches outward like a tree of directories and subdirectores on a computer" (p. 98). Note, however, that Merkur's psychoanalytic account of psychedelic experiences is both reductionistic and severely constrained by the Myth of the Framework. For Merkur, all psychedelic experiences are pseudohallucinations explicable in terms of intense intrapsychic fantasizing. In his own words: "psychedelic unions are all experiences of imagination" (p. 156).

35. Although with Christian overtones, the indeterminate nature of ultimate reality has been recently suggested by Bracken (1995) and Neville (1991).

36. A promising starting point can be found in *A Global Ethic: The Declaration of the Parliament of the World's Religions* (Küng & Kuschel, 1993). For a plea for the need of interfaith dialogue in the search for a global ethic, see Küng (1991), and for two lucid papers pointing out some of the pitfalls and difficulties involved in the establishment of a global ethic, see King (1995) and Knitter (1995).

37. According to Idel (1988), in Jewish mysticism, "the term *theurgy*, or *theurgical* . . . refer(s) to operations intended to influence the Divinity, mostly in its own inner state or operations, but sometimes also in its relationship to man" (p. 157). Kabbalistic theurgy should be distinguished from the different meanings of this term in Christian and Neoplatonic mysticism, as, for example, in the writings of Dionysius the Areopagite. For accounts of theurgical practices in these traditions, see Dodds (1951) and Norris (1987). Interestingly, Idel (1988) explains how the theurgical aspect of the Kabbalah was lost and transformed into gnosis by Christianity (pp. 260–264), which suggests a shift from a more reciprocal and participatory relationship with a dynamic divinity to a

more unilateral and passive knowledge or vision of an immutable and pregiven God. As I see it, this is a shift from an open Divinity to a closed one—a transformation of a Divine Thou into a Divine It or an immutable He.

38. For other accounts of participatory cosmologies, see Barfield (1957), Berman (1981), Heron and Reason (1997), Kremer (1992a, 1992b, 1994, 1997), Reason (1994), and Skolimowski (1994). Note, however, that some of these accounts (like Barfield's) subscribe to a Kantian metaphysics and, accordingly, restrict the creative power of human participation to phenomenal awarenesses of an unknowable (noumenal) reality.

CHAPTER SEVEN
AFTER THE PARTICIPATORY TURN

1. Although Advaita Vedanta generally considers theism (*Saguna Brahman*) as an inferior level of understanding, it should be stressed that Sankara did not offer a hierarchical gradation of spiritual systems. In contrast to the more inclusivistic projects of Kumarila, Bhartrhari, and most Neo-Hinduist thinkers, Sankara simply rejects as false, in his *Brahamasutrabhasya* for example, most other systems and philosophies, such as Samkhya, Yoga, and Buddhism. Because these systems are not based on the Vedic revelation, Sankara argues, they are unable to convey any truth whatsoever about the nature of ultimate reality. In this account, see Halbfass's (1991) excellent essay, "Vedic Orthodoxy and the Plurality of Religious Traditions," in his *Tradition and Reflection*, 51–85.

2. For a critical analysis of spiritual gradations in Neo-Hinduism, see Halbfass's (1988c) "'Inclusivism and 'Tolerance' in the Encounter Between India and the West," in his *India and Europe*, 403–418.

3. Some transpersonal theorists like Wilber endorse this view of a continuum of spiritual progress across the three Buddhist vehicles (e.g., Wilber, 1998a, p. 168). Nevertheless, given the multifarious historical, cultural, and experiential contingencies in the development of these Buddhist schools, insights, and understandings, this suggestion seems unwarranted. Again, I am not saying that there cannot be deeper understandings or higher truths in spiritual matters. But to put the three Buddhist vehicles—which, by the way, are well and alive today—on a continuum of spiritual progress not only confuses appearing later in time with being more refined, but also strikes me as an apologetic move spurred by the endorsement of one tradition over others.

4. There are many precedents to this position in Western religious studies. To quote only two distinguished examples, Buber (1961) regards the I-Thou relationship with God as spiritually higher than the monistic experience of nonduality, and Zaehner (1957) argues that the monistic ideal is transcended in theistic mysticism. According to Zaehner (1957), Sankara's monistic liberation (*moksa*) is a primitive stage of the process of deification. More recently, the preeminence of theism over Wilber's nondual mysticism has also been argued by Helminiak (1996, 1998). For Zaehner's critique of Huxley's Vedantic perennial philosophy, see Newell (1981).

5. In two important essays, Rothberg (1996a, 1999) recently questioned the adequacy of stage models to account for spiritual development.

6. Compare Lopez (1992) on the Buddhist path: "The scholastic delineations of the path read not as records of personal experience but as the pronouncements of theorists and technicians, who do not speak from the end of a path that they themselves have reached" (p. 148).

7. For a concise overview of these three typical models of interreligious relations (exclusivism, inclusivism, and pluralism) in the context of Christian attitudes towards other religions, see

D'Costa (1986). See also Hick and Knitter (1987) for a representative defense of ecumenical pluralism and critique of exclusivism and inclusivism, and D'Costa (1990) for various critiques of ecumenical pluralism and suggestions of more pluralistic attitudes towards interreligious relations.
Critiques of ecumenical pluralism can also be found in Heim (1995), Panikkar (1984, 1988, 1996),
and Vroom (1989). For two good critical surveys of some varieties of religious pluralism, see Knitter
(1985) and Yandell (1993b).

Although there is today a plethora of pluralistic approaches to religion (phenomenalist, ethical, ontological, etc.), the main factor distinguishing between ecumenical pluralism and the new
pluralist models is that whereas the former retains a common goal for all traditions, the latter insist
on the irreducible diversity of religious aims. In this context, the participatory vision not only
embraces this new radical pluralism, but also attempts to articulate some of its epistemological and
metaphysical foundations.

8. I should stress here that my discussion about the "problem of conflicting truth claims" is
limited to religious ultimate claims, that is, about the nature of reality, spiritual ultimates, and so
forth. It should be obvious that religions make other types of truth claims (empirical, transempiri-
cal, historical, mythical, etc.) which, I readily admit, may be not only in real conflict with each other,
but also be potentially true or false (supernatural events, reincarnation theories, stories of creation,
eschatologies, etc.). The elucidation of the nature and evaluation of these claims involves complex
philosophical questions which cannot be addressed here. For valuable discussions about the assessment of cross-cultural religious truth claims, see Dean (1995), Griffiths and Lewis (1983), Hick
(1981), and Vroom (1989).

9. Some authors suggest the possibility of maintaining a plurality of noumenal realities to
which the different traditions are geared (e.g., Heim, 1995, p. 146). This hypothesis, however, unnecessarily perpetuates, and even multiplies, dubious and alienating Kantian dualisms. For a classic critique of the Kantian "thing in itself," see Schrader (1967).

10. The idea of mutual transformation as the answer to the interreligious question was originally proposed by Streng (1993). In harmony with our approach, Streng qualifies that "mutual
transformation . . . is not just individual or inner change; rather, this phrase suggests that there is no
self-contained 'inner' as opposed to a separate 'outer,' no 'individual' separate from a physical and
social context" (p. 122). See also Ingram and Streng (1986) for a collection of essays on the Buddhist-
Christian dialogue written in this spirit.

From a Whiteheadian perspective, Cobb (1982, 1990, 1996) has been gradually developing an
approach to interreligious relations that eschews the problems of contextualist and perennialist
views by paving a middle way that celebrates the uniqueness of each tradition while urging their
openness to positive transformation out of the encounter with others, a stance that he describes as
"mutual openness leading to mutual transformation" (1996, p. 55)

11. Throughout his prolific academic career, Panikkar (1984, 1988, 1996) has done probably
more than anyone else to pursue the metaphysical and ontological implications of spiritual pluralism. For an excellent Festschrift on Panikkar's work, see Prabhu (1996).

12. This participatory and pluralistic account of spiritual knowing, as well as our emphasis on
transformation in the assessment of spiritual claims, is consistent, I believe, with William James's
pragmatist epistemology and pluralist metaphysics. Although not without tensions and ambiguities,
James's work generally rejects the view of a pregiven reality and, contrary to widespread belief,
insists on the irreducible diversity of mystical claims. In his late and often ignored essay, "A
Pluralistic Mystic," James stresses that "I feel now as if my own pluralism were not without the kind

of support which mystical corroboration may confer. Monism can no longer claim to be the only beneficiary of whatever right mysticism may possess to lend *prestige*" (in Barnard, 1997, p. 31). And he adds: "The monistic notion of oneness, a centred wholeness, ultimate purpose, or climateric result of the world, has wholly given way. Thought evolves no longer a centred whole, a One, but rather a numberless many" (in Barnard, 1997, p. 31). Barnard's (1997) work is the most complete account to date of William James's views on mysticism.

13. Interreligious dialogues are celebrated by scholars, religious leaders, or contemplatives, but very rarely do we witness encounters including representatives from all three groups (for an exception, see, e.g., Coward & Pennelhum, 1976). I would like to urge here the need for interreligious dialogues involving not only these groups, but also the voices of women and other marginalized ethnic and social groups. Only this kind of multidimensional interreligious dialogue—a dialogue that actively encourages the participation of reason and faith, intellect and mystical awareness, the masculine and the feminine, and so forth—may have some chance to arrive at comprehensive cross-cultural criteria for spiritual truth. As Sugunasiri (1996) convincingly argues, interfaith dialogue needs to pave the way for a spiritual interaction that not only involves verbal exchange, but also body intimation and the inclusion of other aspects of human nature into the exchange.

14. For some classic presentations of the inevitability of mediation in human knowledge, see Lewis (1929) and H. H. Price (1932)

15. For other valuable discussions of mediation in mystical knowledge, see Bernhardt (1990), Frohlich (1993), Gill (1984, 1989), Perovich (1985b), J. R. Price, III (1998), and Rothberg (1990).

16. For a concise survey of this claim to Reality in the major religious traditions, see Hick's (1992), especially the chapter on "Religion and Reality." For a more comprehensive analysis of different truth claims in world religions, see Vroom (1989).

17. The harmony between the participatory vision and Madhyamaka Buddhism should not be surprising, especially considering that the enactive paradigm of cognition was developed in conjunction with Buddhist notions of emptiness (see Varela, Thompson, & Rosch, 1991). However, it is my contention that the participatory vision of human spirituality is also consistent with the thinking of most apophatic mystics across traditions, Jewish theurgical mysticism, Kashmir Śaivism, as well as with Christian understandings of the Logos as an always open and dynamic creative spiritual power.

18. For more extended discussions of the futility of the charge of self-refutation against many pluralistic approaches, see chapter 6, note 7 (this volume), and Ferrer (1998a).

CHAPTER EIGHT
A MORE RELAXED SPIRITUAL UNIVERSALISM

1. Some readers of this work suggest that this shift may have some parallels with Hillman's (1983, 1992) archetypal revision of Jungian psychology. Whereas Jung talked about the archetypes mainly in Neo-Kantian and phenomenological terms (i.e., from the perspective of human experience), Hillman shifted this anthropocentric focus and founded a psychology geared to the perspective of the archetypes themselves. Hillman's writings mercilessly dethrone the human ego from its traditional hegemonic position in the psyche, and posit a polytheistic psychic space primarily ruled by archetypal forces. In a similar vein, some commentators note, the participatory vision may be seen not only as a shift of emphasis from intrasubjective experience to participatory knowing, but also as a shift from the perspective of a participating subjectivity to one geared to the larger spiritual

dimension in which humans participate but that transcends the merely human. A similar shift can be found, I believe, in Bache's (2000) important revision of Grof's transpersonal theory. According to Bache, "We must conceptualize everything that happens in psychedelic therapy from the perspective of both the individual subject *and the larger life form we are*" (p. 298).

2. I am indebted to Steve Dinan (personal communication, May 5, 1999) for this suggestion.

3. Note that I am using the term *stages* in a broad sense to refer to different moments of spiritual insight and by no means am I suggesting my endorsement of rigid stage models of spiritual development. As I argue in chapter 7, most traditional stage models of spiritual development are not derived from meditative practice but from doctrinally oriented scholastic endeavors. On the adequacy of stage models to account for spiritual growth, see Rothberg (1996a, 1999), Wilber (1997a, 1999b), and Mitchell and Wiseman (1997).

4. Perhaps a related question is whether it is too early for the participatory vision. Some colleagues, for example, although persuaded by the emancipatory value of the participatory turn, consider that it may be too early for its adoption. In their eyes, human inner experience is still awaiting legitimization not only in psychology, but also in philosophy and science, and the acceptance of its epistemological value may be a prerequisite to move forward. Only then, these friendly critics believe, will it make full sense to embrace the participatory turn here proposed. To embrace it beforehand, they add, may be counterproductive, like a premature baby with birth defects.

Although I do not share these concerns, I believe that these critics raise valid and important points. The epistemological value of inner experience needs still to be legitimized in contemporary social, academic, and religious milieus. And the task of humanistic, existential, and transpersonal psychology is unfinished in this regard. This is why I deeply sympathize with the attempts of many contemporary thinkers to ground spiritual studies on William James's radical empiricism or other expanded forms of empiricism. Apart from challenging intrasubjective reductionism, an appeal of these proposals is that they build bridges between spirituality and science, thereby giving a scientific outlook to spiritual studies and making room for the revaluation of their experiential knowledge claims. There can be no doubt that this move has positively influenced the reconsideration of the epistemic value of spirituality, especially in popular and mainstream circles. When examined closely, however, the bridges between empiricist science and spirituality are not as solid as they seem and, as we have seen, this fragility ultimately forces spirituality into limiting scientific molds and has self-defeating consequences for its legitimization. My hope is that this work may serve as a warning of the potential pitfalls and limitations of most empiricist accounts of spirituality.

Furthermore, in my judgment, the participatory vision fosters the legitimization of human inner experience as a source of valid knowledge. If spiritual experiences are regarded as the fruit of human participation in a dynamic spiritual power that is ontologically real, then their epistemic value can be firmly anchored and affirmed. To be sure, self-deception is always possible, and each knowledge claim needs to be independently evaluated according to a variety of standards (context, internal and external coherence, transforming power, etc.). In this connection, I firmly believe that the emancipatory epistemology advanced in the present work provides more adequate guidelines than empiricism for the evaluation of spiritual knowledge claims. Once we give up Cartesian assumptions about spiritual realities, the validity of spiritual claims cannot be consistently anchored in their matching pregiven spiritual referents. The validity of spiritual knowing can be more adequately established, I have proposed, by assessing its emancipatory power for self, relationships, and world.

5. Some readers of my work, particularly those affiliated with traditional religions, note that an analogous deconstruction and reconstruction of the transpersonal project can be carried out from the perspective of certain contemplative traditions (such as Neoplatonism, Sufism, Kabbalah, Tibetan

Buddhism, or Advaita Vedanta). And some even conclude that what the participatory vision really shows is the need to close the transpersonal project altogether and rechannel the modern spiritual search through traditional religions. In other words, these individuals read my work as suggesting that transpersonal theory is in bankruptcy and should therefore be abandoned.

I agree in part with their first observation, but I strongly object to their conclusion. As we have seen, both the participatory vision and most spiritual traditions emphasize participatory knowing over intrasubjective experience in the spiritual quest. Therefore, an analogous revision of transpersonal theory can probably be launched from a traditional perspective. However, the participatory vision differs in fundamental ways from the majority of traditional accounts. Most traditions, for example, typically upheld their cosmologies and revelations in an absolutist, universalist, and exclusivist fashion. Religious traditions developed prior to the emergence of interfaith dialogue in cultural and political conditions conducive to the pronouncement of exclusivist claims. The participatory vision, in contrast, rejects the exclusivity of any tradition and maintains instead an *open spiritual pluralism grounded in the postulation of a dynamic and indeterminate spiritual power that can be variously enacted and expressed in the world.*

The solution to our present spiritual predicament, then, cannot be a mere return to traditionalism (as many representatives of the traditions are acutely aware today). To be sure, both transpersonal theory and modern spiritual movements can learn tremendously from the wisdom traditions. In the wake of the secularization of the modern West, religious traditions have been precious containers for the cultivation of the sacred, and it is natural that the modern spiritual quest looks to them for guidance and inspiration. However, this does not mean that our goal is merely the recovery of the traditional sense of the sacred. In spite of the profound wisdom of traditional teachings and practices, we cannot ignore that most religious traditions are still beset not only by intolerant exclusivist and absolutist tendencies, but also by patriarchy, authoritarianism, dogmatism, conservatism, transcendentalism, body-denial, sexual repression, and hierarchical institutions. As I see it, then, one of the goals of the transpersonal project is to carry out a *critical reconnection with the sacred that will lead to novel, more integral, and more emancipatory spiritual understandings and practices.* Transpersonal theory, that is, although working in close alliance with the traditions towards the resacralization of the world, has to engage them in the spirit of open-ended inquiry, critical dialogue, and mutual transformation. From this encounter, it can be reasonably expected, not only will many traditional forms be challenged, as will transpersonal theory itself, but also new spiritualities more sensitive to contemporary needs and concerns will emerge.

6. See chapter 6, note 7 (this volume), and Ferrer (1998a).

7. The reader interested in the issues raised by the self-referentiality of the different varieties of relativism can consult the anthologies by Bernstein (1983), Harré and Krausz (1996), Hollis and Lukes (1982), Krausz (1989), Krausz and Meiland (1982), Margolis (1986), Siegel (1987), and Wilson (1970). For several works explicitly challenging the self-refuting nature of relativism, see Hales (1997), Krausz (1997), Meiland (1980), and B. H. Smith (1988, 1993). And for a variety of arguments showing the non-self-refuting nature of pluralism, see Berlin (1991), Hoy, (1994), Matilal (1991), Panikkar (1996), and Rescher (1993); of contextualism, see Lynch (1998); of perspectivism, see MacIntyre (1988); and of moderated forms of relativism, see MacIntyre (1987), Margolis (1986, 1989), and Tianji (1991).

8. This may be related, I believe, to the well-known difficulties in articulating a conclusive philosophical refutation of relativism. For example, listen to Gadamer (1990):

That the thesis of skepticism or relativism refutes itself to the extent that it claims to be true is an irrefutable argument. But what does it achieve? The reflective argument that proves successful here rebounds against the arguer, for it renders the truth value of reflection suspect. It is not the reality of skepticism or of truth-dissolving relativism but the truth claim of all formal argument that is affected. Thus the formalism of such relative argument is of specious philosophical legitimacy. In fact it tells us nothing. (p. 344)

On Gadamer and relativism, see the collection of essays edited by Schmidt (1995). Also, on the refutation of relativism, MacIntyre (1987) writes:

> For relativism, like skepticism, is one of these doctrines that have by now been refuted a number of times too often. Nothing is perhaps a surer sign that a doctrine embodies some not-to-be-neglected truth that in the course of the history of philosophy it should have been refuted again and again. Genuinely refutable doctrines only need to be refuted once. (p. 385)

9. For two recent discussions of the problems of using the term *experience* in apophatic mysticism, see Carlson (1999) and Turner (1995). For Carlson (1999), "the mystical moment can in fact *not* be articulated in terms of categories of what we commonly know and express as experience" (p. 256–257) because "at the very heart of mystical experience there can lie a certain 'nonexperience,' a certain 'impossibility' of experience for the subject of experience" (p. 262).

Similarly, for Turner (1995), mystical apophasis is concerned not with an "experience of absence" but with an "absence of experience" (p. 264). Turner's work is especially helpful in showing the problems of the modern "experientialist" account of mysticism in referring to the message of most Christian medieval mystics. Turner argues that what characterizes most medieval mystics (from Eckhart to the author of *The Cloud of Unknowing* and even to St. John of the Cross) is precisely both a forceful rejection of the mystical experience as the means to and location of the union with God, and a severe critique of such distorting experientialisation of the mystical path. In contrast to the search for the mystical through the cultivation of special inner experiences, the medieval mind thought of the mystical as "an exoteric dynamic *within* the ordinary, as being the negative dialectic *of* the ordinary" (p. 268). "Experientalism," Turner concludes, "is, in short, the 'positivism' of Christian spirituality. It abhors the experiential vacuum of the apophatic, rushing in to fill it with the plenum of the psychologistic" (p. 259).

10. Recently, Ken Wilber (1999c, 2000) characterized a number of cultural and spiritual visions that emphasize pluralism and dialogue as emerging from a lower level of spiritual understanding and evolution, which he calls, following the work of Clare Graves and Don Beck, the green meme. According to Wilber, the following are some of the features of the "green meme" world view: "Permeable self, relational self, group intermeshing. Emphasis on dialogue, relationships. . . . Strongly egalitarian, anti-hierarchy, pluralistic values, social construction of reality, diversity, multiculturalism, relativistic value systems; this worldview is often called pluralistic relativism" (1999c, p. 113). Typical green meme approaches, for Wilber, include humanistic psychology, liberation theology, cooperative inquiry, the World Council of Churches, Greenpeace, animal rights, ecofeminism, diversity movements, ecopsychology, Martin Buber's I-Thou spirituality, among others. In his typical evolutionary and hierarchical fashion, Wilber situates the green meme between the rational-scientific world view and the universal integralism that characterizes his own approach.

The green meme, Wilber tells us, has both merits and shortcomings. Merits include that it transcends the "rigid universalisms of formal rationality" and attempts to incorporate formerly marginalized peoples and ideas. Its two main shortcomings are that it falls into a pluralistic relativism that is both self-contradictory and morally pernicious, and that it champions forms of dialogue that, while hiding superiority claims, are often not more than a fruitless sharing of views and feelings that lacks discriminative power concerning which decisions and courses of actions are better to take. In what follows I would like to briefly (1) discuss the coherency of the category of "green meme"; and (2) offer some final reflections on the claim that pluralism is necessarily relativistic.

Before proceeding, I should say here that I believe that Wilber is correct in highlighting the potential shadow of certain pluralistic stances and dialogical practices: Yes, some pluralistic approaches can fall into relativistic contradictions, and dialogue can degenerate exactly in the ways Wilber describes. However, it is one thing to point out the potential shadow of these approaches, but quite another to present this shadow as their essence and then, on these shaky grounds, lump them all together as spiritually less evolved. This move is not only distorting but also fallacious because pluralism can be maintained and dialogue can be practiced in ways that avoid these shortcomings and embody genuine spiritual awarenesses.

Interestingly, Wilber (2000) attributes the apparent lack of dialogue between himself and a number of leading transpersonal thinkers (see Rothberg and Kelly, 1998) to their operating mainly through the green meme. He tells us that "many philosophical debates are not really a matter of the better objective argument, but of the subjective level of those debating. . . . This is why 'cross-level' debates are rarely resolved, and all parties usually feel unheard and unappreciated" (2000, p. 13). Then he quotes in approval the opinion of Don Beck about his recent debate with contemporary transpersonal authors: "This book is partly a series of typical green-meme attacks on second-tier [i.e., spiritually more evolved integral universalism]. There is much ideology, little evidence" (2000, p. 43).

Let us first have a look at the cogency of the green meme as a semantic category. As I see it, one of the main problems with Wilber's depiction of the green meme is that it fails to discriminate between linguistic form (how X is expressed) and depth of awareness (the quality of awareness from which X is expressed). What I am suggesting here is that the language of dialogue, pluralism, intimacy, and relationship can be expressive of very different levels of consciousness, and Wilber's account tends to systematically lump them all together under the superficial and relativistic artificial category of the green meme.

This, I believe, is profoundly distorting: Dogen's account of enlightenment as "intimacy with all beings," for example, is not emerging from a relativistic awareness or a lower level of spiritual understanding, but from a liberated state in which we are continuously awakened by our intimate connection with reality and each of its wondrous dwellers. Actually, what many of the approaches Wilber lumps together under the green meme rubric have in common is not to be necessarily relativistic or to belong to a lower level of spiritual evolution, but rather to stress *relational forms of spirituality*: Buber's I-Thou, like Tich Nath Hanh's (1995) "inter-being," emphasizes the realm of the Between and the community as the locus of spiritual realization; many ecopychological and ecofeminist approaches cultivate spiritual understandings that emerge out of our relationship with vegetal, animal, and planetary awarenesses; liberation theology and some diversity movements are forms of socially engaged spirituality that, far from being relativistic, offer rigorous critical analysis of society (of capitalism, of discrimination, of marginalization, of social injustice, of the polarization of rich and poor, etc.) and attempt to respond to these challenges in spiritually informed ways.

Wilber's tendency towards negative sweeping generalizations, for example, about ecopsychological and ecofeminist approaches, has been already noted by environmental philosophers such as M. Zimmerman (1998):

> Wilber sometimes either discounts the best work of deep ecology theory, or else confuses such theory with foolish pronouncements made by environmental activists who manifest regressive tendencies. . . . Regarding ecofeminism, Wilber reveals the

same disconcerting tendency to toss distinct positions onto the same undifferentiated heap. (p. 202)

I am not saying that all the approaches Wilber lists under the green meme rubric are necessarily spiritually oriented or that none of them ever falls into relativistic dilemmas. What I am saying is that *Wilber's green meme is a mixed bag that conflates relational and socially engaged spiritual approaches into a pluralistic relativism to which many of them are actually hostile.* All this suggests, in my opinion, that, despite having recently made room in his integral theory for relational and socially engaged forms of spirituality, Wilber's seems to be still biased in favor of a spirituality primarily based on individualistic practice and tends to prejudge intersubjective spiritual approaches as spiritually less evolved.

Second, in the same vein, Wilber conflates all pluralistic approaches into an artificial pluralistic relativism that is both self-contradictory and morally pernicious. He tells us, for example, that:

> If "pluralism" is really true, then we must invite the Nazis and the KKK to the multicultural banquet, since no stance is supposed to be better or worse than another, and so all must be treated in an egalitarian fashion, at which point the self-contradictions of undiluted pluralism come screaming to the fore. (1999c, p. 118)

And identifying pluralistic approaches with vulgar relativism, he states:

> What is true for you is not necessarily true for me; what is right is simply what individuals or cultures happen to agree on at any given moment; there are no universal claims for knowledge or truth; each person is free to find his or her own values, which are not binding for anybody else. "You do your thing, I do mine," is a popular summary of this stance. (1999c, p. 117)

As we have seen in this book, however, many forms of pluralism, contextualism, and even moderate forms of relativism can be maintained without falling into the performative contradictions and moral anarchy of vulgar relativism. What is more, as the participatory vision shows, pluralism may have ontological, metaphysical, and even spiritual foundations and its adoption can have deeply emancipatory implications for spiritual growth and understanding.

About Wilber's claim that pluralism leads to moral anarchy, I should say that *it cannot be repeated too often that the absence of absolute or universal standards does not mean that there are no standards at all, or that any value judgment is arbitrary.* Clearly, what is lurking behind Wilber's presentation is what Bernstein (1985) calls the Cartesian Anxiety, i.e., the belief that the rejection of absolute or universal standards ineluctably leads to both vulgar relativism and moral anarchy. But nonabsolutist philosophers are well aware of the dangers of falling into what B. H. Smith (1988) calls the Egalitarian Fallacy, that is, to assert "that, unless one judgment can be said or shown to be [objectively, absolutely, universally] more 'valid' than another, then all judgments must be 'equal' or 'equally valid'" (p. 98). In the same manner, modern cultural anthropologists warn us against this faulty reasoning. According to Robbins (1993), for example, the flight from ethnocentrism should not lead anthropologists into the "relativistic fallacy," the morally intolerable "idea that it is impossible to make moral judgments about the beliefs and behaviors of others" (p. 9). The examples of modern thinkers who, while adopting pluralist or contextualist positions, avoid falling into vulgar relativism could be multiplied endlessly. Actually, I do not know of any serious contemporary philosopher who holds the view that any belief or practice should be regarded as good as any other, so I fail to discern who are the real targets of Wilber's critique of the view that "no stance is supposed to be better or worse than another, and so all must be treated in an egalitarian fashion" (p. 113).

A related problem with Wilber's presentation is that it completely ignores the possibility of historically embedded spiritual values. For example, judgments about what is better or worse can be legitimately made either on pragmatic/contextual grounds such as local adequacy, applicability, emancipatory power, and so forth, or resolved in a situation of "concourse" where we not only rationally consider abstract moral postulates, but also openly listen to the voice of our bodies, our emotions, and our souls (Kremer, 1992b, 1994). And contrary to cultural solipsisms, Bernstein (1991) points out that, although each tradition has its own standards of rationality and morality, cross-cultural qualitative judgments are possible because we can examine both how a tradition fulfills its own standards, and how successful it is in meeting the challenges of rival traditions. Therefore, "The rational superiority of a tradition can be vindicated without (falsely) presupposing that there are universally neutral, ahistorical standards of rationality. There is not 'rationality as such'" (p. 91). A similar point has been made by Hoy (1994) in his critique of Habermas' universalism: "To criticize one community or set of social practices, we do not need to imagine some ideal standpoint that is independent of any contingent concrete standpoint. More substantively, we may judge that community, not from outside our own standpoint (since there is no such outside), but from the standpoint of other communities, or other self-understandings, that we know to be, or to have been, viable" (p. 203).

In other words, the rejection of universal standards does not necessarily snare us in either the absurd endorsement of all forms of life (like the Nazis or the KKK) or the ethnocentric hubris and provinciality of thinking that our standards are to be preferred to all others. All of us are already participating in diverse planetary communities, and this participation allows us to criticize not only others' standards, but also our own. By stepping outside our own particular community and looking at our context from other contexts, we can practice self-criticism and open ourselves to learn and be transformed by other perspectives. In this way, ethnocentrism is avoided while conserving grounds for cross-cultural criticism. The assumption that without absolute or universal standards, rational criticism of others and ourselves is not possible is another Enlightenment myth that must be laid to rest.

I have already argued both in this book (chapter 6, note 7) and elsewhere (Ferrer, 1998a) that conflating pluralism and vulgar relativism is fallacious, so rather that repeating these arguments here, I would like say that my sense is that both Wilber and I are attempting to offer visions that honor the delicate balance between universalism and pluralism, between the One and the Many. Wilber's retention of determinate features of a common spiritual ultimate for all traditions (e.g., the One, nonduality), insistence on a universal evolutionary sequence of pregiven deep spiritual structures, and consistent ranking as evolutionarily inferior of spiritual visions that refuse to fit in his scheme seem to me too nostalgic of exhausted universalisms. Conversely, it is probable that my emphasis on spiritual pluralism, rejection of these deep common features, and nonhierarchical a priori understanding of interreligious relations, may make me look too relativist in his eyes. But the important, practical point, I believe, is that we both stress the need for and possibility of making qualitative distinctions in spiritual matters. While Wilber uses a hierarchical gradation of spiritual insights and traditions essentially based on the notion of holistic capacity (which strikes me as too dependent on Neovedantic and Neoplatonic metaphysics), I argue that these distinctions cannot be made on a priori grounds, that they should be essentially based upon the emancipatory power of spiritual practices and insights, and that they ultimately constitute a *practical task* to be accomplished in the fire of the living interreligious dialogue and spiritual inquiry.

REFERENCES

Abhishiktananda, Swami. (1974). *Saccinananda: A Christian approach to Advaitic experience.* New Delhi, India: I.S.P.C.K.

Achterberg, J., & Rothberg, D. (1998). Relationship as spiritual practice. In D. Rothberg & S. Kelly (Eds.), *Ken Wilber in dialogue: Conversations with leading transpersonal thinkers* (pp. 261–274). Wheaton, IL: Quest.

Adorno, T. (1979). *Negative dialectics.* (E. B. Ashton, Trans.). New York: Seabury Press.

Ahumada, J. (1997). Disclosures and refutations: Clinical psychoanalysis as a logic of enquiry. *International Journal of Psychoanalysis, 78*(6), 1105–1118.

Almaas, A. H. (1996). *The point of existence: Transformations of narcissism in self-realization.* Berkeley, CA: Diamond Books.

Almond, P. C. (1982). *Mystical experience and religious doctrine: An investigation of the study of mysticism in world religions.* New York: Mouton.

Alston, W. P. (1991). *Perceiving God: The epistemology of religious experience.* Ithaca, NY: Cornell University Press.

Amis, R. (1995). *A different Christianity: Early Christian esotericism and modern thought.* Albany, NY: State University of New York Press.

Angel, L. (1994). *Enlightenment East and West.* Albany: State University of New York Press.

Anthony, D. (1982). A phenomenological structuralist approach to the scientific study of religion. *ReVision, 5*(1), 50–66.

Anthony, D., & Ecker, B. (1987). The Anthony typology: A framework for assessing spiritual and consciousness groups. In D. Anthony, B. Ecker, & K. Wilber (Eds.), *Spiritual choices: The problem of recognizing authentic paths to inner transformation* (pp. 35–105). New York: Paragon House.

Anthony, D., & Robbins, T. (1975). From symbolic realism to structuralism: Review essay on the work of Robert Bellah. *Journal for the Scientific Study of Religion, 14,* 403–413.

Armstrong, K. (1993). *A history of God: The 4000-year quest of Judaism, Christianity and Islam.* New York: Alfred A. Knopf.

Augustine, M. J. (1986). The sociology of knowledge and Buddhist-Christian forms of faith, practice, and knowledge. In P. O. Ingram & F. J. Streng (Eds.), *Buddhist-Christian dialogue: Mutual renewal and transformation* (pp. 35–51). Honolulu: University of Hawaii Press.

Bache, C. M. (2000). *Dark night, early dawn: Steps to a deep ecology of mind.* Albany: State University of New York Press.

Bagger, M. (1991). Ecumenicalism and perennialism revisited. *Religious Studies, 27*, 399–411.

Bamford, G. (1996). Popper and his commentators on the discovery of neptune: A close shave for the Law of Gravitation. *Studies in History and Philosophy of Science, 27*(2), 207–232.

Barfield, O. (1957). *Saving the appearances: An study in idolatry.* London: Faber and Faber.

Barnard, G. W. (1994). Transformations and transformers: Spirituality and the academic study of mysticism. *Journal of Consciousness Studies, 1*(2), 256–260.

Barnard, G. W. (1997). *Exploring unseen worlds: William James and the philosophy of mysticism.* Albany: State University of New York Press.

Barnhart, J. E. (1977). *The study of religion and its meaning: New explorations in light of Karl Popper and Emile Durkheim.* New York: Mouton.

Barnhart, M. (1994). Sunyata, textualism, and incommensurability. *Philosophy East and West, 44*, 647–658.

Barrett, S. R. (1997). *Anthropology: A student's guide to theory and method.* Toronto: University of Toronto Press.

Baruss, I. (1996). *Authentic knowing: The convergence of science and spiritual aspiration.* West Lafayette, IN: Purdue University Press.

Battista, J. R. (1996). Abraham Maslow and Roberto Assagioli: Pioneers of transpersonal psychology. In B. W. Scotton, A. B. Chinen, & J. R. Battista (Eds.), *Textbook of Transpersonal Psychiatry and Psychology* (pp. 52–61). New York: Basic Books.

Baudrillard, J. (1994). *Simulacra and simulation.* (S. F. Glaser, Trans.) Ann Arbor, MI: University of Michigan Press.

Bechtel, W. (1988). *Philosophy of science: An overview for cognitive science.* Hillsdale, NJ: Erlbaum.

Beena, C. (1990). *Personality typologies: A comparison of Western and ancient Indian approaches.* New Delhi, India: Commonwealth.

Berlin, I. (1991). *The crooked timber of humanism.* New York: Alfred A. Knopf.

Berman, M. (1981). *The reenchantment of the world.* Ithaca, NY: Cornell University Press.

Bernhardt, S. (1990). Are pure consciousness events unmediated? In R. K. C. Forman (Ed.), *The problem of pure consciousness: Mysticism and philosophy* (pp. 220–236). New York: Oxford University Press.

Bernstein, R. J. (1985). *Beyond objectivism and relativism: Science, hermeneutics and praxis.* Philadelphia: University of Pennsylvania Press.

Bernstein, R. J. (1991). Incommensurability and otherness revisited. In E. Deutsch (Ed.), *Culture and modernity: East-West philosophical perspectives* (pp. 85–103). Honolulu: University of Hawaii Press.

Blackstone, W. (1963). *The problem of religious knowledge.* Englewood Cliffs, NJ: Prentice-Hall.

Bollas, C. (1987). *The shadow of the object: Psychoanalysis and the unthought known.* London: Free Association Books.

Bolle, K. W. (1968). *The freedom of man in myth.* Nashville, TN: Vanderbilt University Press.

Bordo, S. (1987). *The flight to objectivity.* Albany: State University of New York Press.

Borella, J. (1995). René Guénon and the traditionalist school. In A. Faivre & J. Needleman (Eds.), *Modern Esoteric Spirituality: Vol. 21. World spirituality: An encyclopedic history of the religious quest* (pp. 330–358). New York: Crossroad.

Borg, M. (1991). Root images and the way we see: The primordial tradition and the biblical tradition. In A. Sharma (Ed.), *Fragments of infinity: Essays in religion and philosophy* (pp. 31–45). Bridport, Dorset, UK: Prism Press.

Boucouvalas, M. (1980). Transpersonal psychology: A working outline of the field. *Journal of Transpersonal Psychology, 12*(1), 37–46.

Boucouvalas, M. (1999). Following the movement: From transpersonal psychology to a multi-disciplinary transpersonal orientation. *Journal of Transpersonal Psychology, 31*(1), 27–39.

Bouyer, L. (1980). Mysticism. An essay of the history of the word. In R. Woods (Ed.), *Understanding Mysticism* (pp. 42–55). Garden City, NY: Doubleday.

Boyne, R. (1996). Structuralism. In B. S. Turner (Ed.), *The Blackwell companion to social theory.* Malden, MA: Blackwell.

Bracken, J. A. (1995). *The divine matrix: Creativity as link between East and West.* Maryknoll, NY: Orbis.

Bragdon, E. (1990). *The call for spiritual emergency: From personal crisis to personal transformation.* San Francisco: Harper & Row.

Brainard, F. S. (1996). Defining "Mystical Experience." *Journal of the American Academy of Religion, 64*(2), 359–393.

Braud, W., & Anderson, R. (1998). *Transpersonal research methods for the social sciences.* Thousand Oaks, CA: Sage.

Bregman, L. (1982). *The rediscovery of inner experience.* Chicago: Nelson-Hall.

Brown, D. P. (1986). The stages of meditation in cross-cultural perspective. In K. Wilber, J. Engler, & D. Brown (Eds.), *Transformations of consciousness: Conventional and contemplative perspectives on development* (pp. 219–284). Boston: Shambhala.

Buber, M. (1961). *Between man and man.* London: Collins.

Buber, M. (1970). *I and thou.* (W. Kaufmann, Trans.). New York: Scribner.

Buddhaghosa, Bhadantacariya. (1976). *The path of purification (Visuddhimagga):* 2 vol. (Bhikkhu Nyanamoli, Trans.). Berkeley: Shambhala.

Bullock, A. (1985). *The humanistic tradition in the West.* London, Great Britain: Thames & Hudson.

Burnyeat, M. F. (1990). Protagoras and self-refutation in Plato's *Theaetetus.* In S. Everson (Ed.), *Companions to ancient thought 1. Epistemology* (pp. 39–59). New York: Cambridge University Press.

Buswell, R. E., & Gimello, R. M. (1992). Introduction. In R. E. Buswell & R. M. Gimello (Eds.), *Paths to liberation: The marga and its transformations in Buddhist thought* (pp. 1–36). Honolulu: University of Hawaii Press.

Byrne, P. (1984). Mysticism, identity and realism: A debate reviewed. *International Journal for Philosophy of Religion, 16,* 237–243.

Byrne, P. (1995). *Prolegomena to religious pluralism: Reference and realism in religion*. New York: St. Martin's Press.

Caldwell, B. J. (1984). Some problems with falsificationism in economics. *Philosophy of the Social Sciences, 14*(4), 489–495.

Caplan, M. (1999). *Halfway up the mountain: The error of premature claims to enlightenment*. Prescott, AZ: Hohm Press.

Capra, F. (1982). *The turning point*. New York: Simon & Schuster.

Carlson, T. A. (1999). *Indiscretion: Finitude and the naming of God*. Chicago: University of Chicago Press.

Carmody, D. L., & Carmody, J. T. (1996). *Mysticism: Holiness East and West*. New York: Oxford University Press.

Carpenter, D. (1994). Emanation, incarnation, and the truth-event in Gadamer's *Truth and Method*. In B. R. Wachterhauser (Ed.), *Hermeneutics and truth* (pp. 98–122). Evanston, IL: Northwestern University Press.

Carpenter, D. (1995). *Revelation, history, and the dialogue of religions: A study of Bhartrhari and Bonaventure*. Maryknoll, NY: Orbis Books.

Carr, K. L. (1992). *The banalization of nihilism: Twentieth-century responses to meaninglessness*. Albany: State University of New York Press.

Caws, P. (1973). Structuralism. In P. P. Wiener (Ed.), *Dictionary of the history of ideas: Vol. IV* (pp. 322–330). New York: Scribner.

Caws, P. (1997). *Structuralism: A philosophy for the human sciences*. (2nd ed.). Atlantic Highlands, NJ: Humanities Press.

Chalmers, A. (1990). *Science and its fabrication*. Buckingham, UK: Open University Press.

Chaudhuri, H. (1977). *The evolution of integral consciousness*. Wheaton, IL: Quest.

Chinchore, M. R. (1995). *Anatta/Anatmata: An analysis of the Buddhist anti-substantialist crusade*. New Delhi, India: Sri Satguru Publications.

Chirban, J. T. (1986). Developmental stages in Eastern Orthodox Christianity. In K. Wilber, J. Engler, & D. Brown (Eds.), *Transformations of consciousness: Conventional and contemplative perspectives on development* (pp. 285–314). Boston: Shambhala.

Chittick, W. C. (1983). *The Sufi path of love: The spiritual teaching of Rumi*. Albany: State University of New York Press.

Chittick, W. C. (1989). *The Sufi path of knowledge: Ibn al'-Arabis metaphysics of imagination*. Albany: State University of New York Press.

Chomsky, N. (1965). *Aspects of the theory of syntax*. Cambridge: MIT Press.

Chomsky, N. (1968). *Language and mind*. New York: Harcourt Brace Jovanovich.

Christian, W. A. (1972). *Oppositions of religious doctrines: A study in the logic of dialogue among religions*. New York: Herder & Herder.

Cioffi, F. (1985). Psychoanalysis, pseudo-science and testability. In G. Currie & A. Musgrave (Eds.), *Popper and the Human Sciences* (pp. 13–44). Boston: Martinus Nijhoff.

Clarke, J. J. (1992). *In search of Jung: Historical and philosophical enquiries*. New York: Routledge.

Clarke, J. J. (1994). *Jung and Eastern thought. A dialogue with the Orient*. New York: Routledge.

Clarke, J. J. (1997). *Oriental enlightenment: The encounter between Asian and Western thought.* New York: Routledge.

Cobb, J. B., Jr. (1982). *Beyond dialogue: Toward a mutual understanding. transformation of Christianity and Buddhism.* Philadelphia: Fortress Press.

Cobb, J. B., Jr. (1990). Beyond "pluralism." In G. D'Costa (Ed.), *Christian uniqueness reconsidered: The myth of a pluralistic theology of religions* (pp. 81–95). Maryknoll, NY: Orbis Press.

Cobb, J. B., Jr. (1996). Metaphysical pluralism. In J. Prabhu (Ed.), *The intercultural challenge of Raimon Panikkar* (pp. 46–57). Maryknoll, NY: Orbis Books.

Collins, J. (1962). The problem of a perennial philosophy. In *Three paths in philosophy* (pp. 255–279). Chicago: Henry Regnery.

Comans, M. (1998). Swami Abhisiktananda (Henri Le Saux, O.S.B.) and Advaita: The account of a spiritual journey. In G. A. Oddie (Ed.), *Religious traditions in South Asia: Interaction and change* (pp. 107–124). Surrey, Great Britain: Curzon Press.

Cook, F. H. (1989). Just this: Buddhist ultimate reality. *Buddhist-Christian Studies, 9,* 127–142.

Corless, R. J. (1993). The coming of the dialogian: A transpersonal approach to interreligious dialogue. *Dialogue and Alliance, 7*(2), 3–17.

Cortright, B. (1997). *Psychotherapy and spirit: Theory and practice in transpersonal psychotherapy.* Albany: State University of New York Press.

Coward, H. (1985a). *Jung and Eastern thought.* Albany: State University of New York Press.

Coward, H. (1985b). Mysticism in the psychology of Jung and the Yoga of Patañjali. In *Jung and Eastern thought* (pp. 124–144). Albany: State University of New York Press.

Coward, H., & Pennnelhum, T. (Eds.). (1976). *Mystics and scholars: The Calgary Conference on Mysticism 1976.* Waterloo, ON, Canada: Wilfred Laurier University Press.

Cox, C. (1992). Attainment through abandonment: The Sarvastivadin path of removing defilements. In R. E. Buswell, Jr. & R. M. Gimello (Eds.), *Paths to liberation: The Marga and its transformations in Buddhist thought: Vol. 7. Studies in East Asian Buddhism* (pp. 63–105). Honolulu: University of Hawaii Press.

Cox, H. (1981). Deep structures in the study of new religions. In J. Needleman & G. Baker (Eds.), *Understanding the new religions* (pp. 122–130). New York: Seabury Press.

Cupitt, D. (1998). *Mysticism after modernity.* Malden, MA: Blackwell.

Curd, M., & Cover, J. A. (1998). *Philosophy of science: The central issues.* New York: W. W. Norton.

Cutsinger, J. S. (1997). *Advice to the serious seeker: Meditations on the teaching of Frithjof Schuon.* Albany: State University of New York Press.

Dalai Lama, H. H. (1988). *The Bodhgaya interviews.* (Ed. by J. I. Cabezón). Ithaca, NY: Snow Lion.

Dalai Lama, H. H. (1996). *The good heart: A Buddhist perspective on the teachings of Jesus.* Boston: Wisdom Publications.

Daly, M. (1984). *Pure lust*. Boston: Beacon Press.

Damasio, A. (1995). *Descartes' error: Emotion, reason and the human brain*. New York: Putnam.

Davaney, S. G. (1987). The limits of the appeal to women's experience. In C. W. Atkinson, C. H. Buchanan, & M. R. Miles (Eds.), *Shaping new vision: Gender and values in American culture*. (pp. 31–49). Harvard Women's Studies in Religion Series. Ann Arbor, MI: UMI Research Press.

Davidson, D. (1984). *Inquiries into truth and interpretation*. New York: Oxford University Press.

Davidson, L. (1994). Philosophical foundations of humanistic psychology. In F. Wertz (Ed.), *The humanistic movement: Recovering the person in psychology* (pp. 24–44). Lake Worth, FL: Gardner Press.

D'Costa, G. (1986). *Theology and religious pluralism: The challenge of other religions*. New York: Basil Blackwell.

D'Costa, G. (Ed.). (1990). *Christian uniqueness reconsidered: The myth of a pluralistic theology of religions*. Maryknoll, NY: Orbis Books.

Dean, T. (1984). Primordial tradition or postmodern hermeneutics? A review essay of A. M. Olson & L. S. Rouner (Eds.), *Transcendence and the sacred* and S. H. Nasr, *Knowledge and the sacred, The Gifford Lectures 1981*. *Philosophy East and West, 34*(2), 211–226.

Dean, T. (Ed.). (1995). *Religious pluralism and truth: Essays on cross-cultural philosophy of religion*. Albany: State University of New York Press.

Deikman, A. (1966). Deautomatization and the mystic experience. *Psychiatry, 29,* 324–338.

Derrida, J. (1978). *Writing and difference*. (Alan Bass, Trans.). Chicago: University of Chicago Press.

Deutsch, E. (Ed.). (1991). *Culture and modernity: East-West philosophical perspectives*. Honolulu: University of Hawaii Press.

DiCenso, J. (1990). *Hermeneutics and the disclosure of truth: A study in the work of Heidegger, Gadamer, and Ricoeur*. Charlottesville: University Press of Virginia.

Dodds, E. R. (1951). Theurgy and its relationship to neoplatonism. In *The Greeks and the Irrational* (pp. 283–311). Berkeley: University of California Press.

Doore, G. (1990). Epilogue: What should we believe? In G. Doore (Ed.), *What survives?: Contemporary explorations of life after death* (pp. 273–279). Los Angeles: J. P. Tarcher.

Dourley, J. (1998). The innate capacity. Jung and the mystical imperative. In R. K. C. Forman (Ed.), *The innate capacity: Mysticism, psychology, and philosophy* (pp. 123–136). New York: Oxford University Press.

Duhem, P. (1953). *The aim and structure of physical theory*. Princeton: Princeton University Press.

Dupré, L. (1987). Mysticism. In M. Eliade (Ed.), *The Encyclopedia of Religion, Vol. 10* (pp. 245–261). New York: Macmillan.

Dupré, L. (1996). Unio Mystica: The state and the experience. In M. Idel & B. McGinn (Eds.), *Mystical union in Judaism, Christianity, and Islam: An ecumenical dialogue* (pp. 3–23). New York: Continuum.

Eddy, P. R. (1994). Religious pluralism and the divine: Another look at John Hick's Neo-Kantian proposal. *Religious Studies, 30*(4), 467–478.

Eliade, M. (1959). *The sacred and the profane.* New York: Harcourt Brace Jovanovich.

Epstein, M. (1986). Meditative transformations of narcissism. *Journal of Transpersonal Psychology, 18*(2), 131–158.

Epstein, M. (1988). The deconstruction of the self: Ego and "egolessness" in Buddhist insight meditation. *Journal of Transpersonal Psychology, 20*(1), 61–69.

Epstein, M. (1996). Freud's influence on transpersonal psychology. In B. W. Scotton, A. B. Chinen, & J. R. Battista (Eds.), *Textbook of transpersonal psychiatry and psychology* (pp. 29–38). New York: Basic Books.

Evans, D. (1989). Can philosophers limit what mystics can do? A critique of Steven Katz. *Religious Studies, 25*, 53–60.

Evans, D. (1993). *Spirituality and human nature.* Albany: State University of New York Press.

Faivre, A. (1994). *Access to Western esoterism.* Albany: State University of New York Press.

Faivre, A., & Needleman, J. (Eds.). (1995). *Modern esoteric spirituality: Vol. 21. World spirituality: An encyclopedic history of the religious quest.* New York: Crossroad.

Faure, B. (1991). *The rhetoric of immediacy: A cultural critique of Chan/Zen Buddhism.* Princeton: Princeton University Press.

Faure, B. (1993). *Chan insights and oversights: An epistemological critique of the Chan tradition.* Princeton: Princeton University Press.

Fay, B. (1996). *Contemporary philosophy of social science.* Cambridge: Blackwell.

Fenton, J. Y. (1995). Mystical experience as a bridge for cross-cultural philosophy of religion: A critique. In T. Dean (Ed.), *Religious pluralism and truth: Essays on cross-cultural philosophy of religion* (pp. 189–204). Albany: State University of New York Press.

Ferrer, J. N. (1998a). Beyond absolutism and relativism in transpersonal evolutionary theory. *World Futures: The Journal of General Evolution, 52*, 229–280.

Ferrer, J. N. (1998b). Speak now or forever hold your peace. An essay review of Ken Wilber's *The marriage of sense and soul: Integrating science and religion. Journal of Transpersonal Psychology, 30*(1), 53–67.

Ferrer, J. N. (1999a). Teoría transpersonal y filosofía perenne: Una evaluación crítica. [Transpersonal theory and the perennial philosophy: A critical evaluation]. In M. Almendro (Ed.), *La conciencia transpersonal* (pp. 72–92). Barcelona, Spain: Kairos.

Ferrer, J. N. (1999b). Una revisión de la teoría transpersonal. *Boletín de la Sociedad Española de Psicología y Psicoterapia Transpersonal, 3*, 24–30.

Ferrer, J. N. (2000a). El paradigma epistémico de la transpersonalidad. In F. Rodriguez Bornaetxea (Ed.), *Psicología transpersonal: Teoría y práctica.* Barcelona, Spain: La Liebre de Marzo.

Ferrer, J. N. (2000b). Transpersonal knowledge: A participatory approach to transpersonal phenomena. In T. Hart, P. Nelson, & K. Puhakka (Eds.), *Transpersonal knowing: Exploring the horizon of consciousness* (pp. 213–252). Albany: State University of New York Press.

Ferrer, J. N. (2000c). The perennial philosophy revisited. *Journal of Transpersonal Psychology, 32*(1), 7–30.

Feyerabend, P. (1975). *Against method*. London: Verso.

Feyerabend, P. (1995). *Killing time: The autobiography of Paul Feyerabend*. Chicago: Chicago University Press.

Fitzgerald, T. (1996). Religion, philosophy and family resemblances. *Religion, 26*, 215–236.

Flew, A. G. N., & MacIntyre A. (Eds.). (1955). *New essays in philosophical theology*. London: SCM Press.

Fontana, D. (1997). Authority in Buddhism and in Western scientific psychology. In J. Pickering (Ed.), *The authority of experience: Essays on Buddhism and psychology* (pp. 31–47). Surrey, Great Britain: Curzon Press.

Forgie, J. W. (1985). Hyper-Kantianism in recent discussions of mystical experience. *Religious Studies, 21*(2), 205–218.

Forman, R. K. C. (1989). Paramartha and modern constructivists on mysticism: Epistemological monomorphism versus duomorphism. *Philosophy East and West, 39*(4), 391–418.

Forman, R. K. C. (Ed.). (1990a). *The problem of pure consciousness: Mysticism and philosophy*. New York: Oxford University Press.

Forman, R. K. C. (1990b). Introduction: Mysticism, constructivism, and forgetting. In R. K. C. Forman (Ed.), *The problem of pure consciousness: Mysticism and philosophy* (pp. 3–49). New York: Oxford University Press.

Forman, R. K. C. (1993). Mystical knowledge. Knowledge by identity. *Journal of the American Academy of Religion, 61*(4), 705–738.

Forman, R. K. C. (Ed.). (1998a). *The innate capacity: Mysticism, psychology, and philosophy*. New York: Oxford University Press.

Forman, R. K. C. (1998b). Introduction: Mystical consciousness, the innate capacity, and the perennial psychology. In R. K. C. Forman (Ed.), *The innate capacity: Mysticism, psychology, and philosophy* (pp. 3–41). New York: Oxford University Press.

Fort, A. O. (1996). Review of A. Sharma, *The philosophy of religion and Advaita Vedanta: A comparative study in religion and reason. The Journal of Religion, 76*(4), 664–665.

Foucault, M. (1970). *The order of things: An archeology of the human sciences*. New York: Random House.

Frakenberry, N. (1987). *Religion and radical empiricism*. Albany: State University of New York Press.

Frank, M. (1989). *What is neostructuralism?* (S. Wilke & R. Gray, Trans.). Minneapolis: University of Minnesota Press.

Frohlich, M. (1993). *The intersubjectivity of the mystic: A study of Teresa of Avila's Interior Castle*. Atlanta, GA: Scholars Press.

Fuchs, S. (1992). *The professional quest for truth: A social theory of science and knowledge*. Albany: State University of New York Press.

Funk, J. (1994). Unanimity and disagreement among transpersonal psychologists. In M. E. Miller & S. R. Cook-Greuter (Eds.), *Transcendence and mature thought in adult-*

hood: The further reaches of adult development (pp. 3–36). Lanham, MD: Rowman & Littlefield.

Gadamer, H-G. (1990). *Truth and method* (2nd rev. ed.). (J. Weinsheimer & D. G. Marshall, Trans.). New York: Crossroad.

Gardner, H. (1981). *The quest for the mind: Piaget, Lévi-Strauss, and the structuralist movement* (2nd ed.). Chicago: University of Chicago Press.

Garfield, J. (1994). Dependent arising and the emptiness of emptiness. Why did Nagarjuna start with causation? *Philosophy East and West, 44,* 219–250.

Gatens-Robinson, E. (1993). Why falsificationism is the wrong paradigm for evolutionary epistemology: An analysis of Hull's Selection Theory. *Philosophy of Science, 60*(4), 535–557.

Gelpi, D. L. (1994). *The turn to experience in contemporary theology.* New York: Paulist Press.

Gelpi, D. L. (2000). *Varieties of transcendental experience: A study in constructive postmodernism.* Collegeville, MN: Liturgical Press.

Gendlin, E. T. (1987). A philosophical critique of the concept of narcissism: The significance of the awareness movement. In D. M. Levin (Ed.), *Pathologies of the modern self: Postmodern studies on narcissism, schizophrenia, and depression* (pp. 251–304). New York: New York University Press.

Gill, J. H. (1984). Mysticism and mediation. *Faith and Philosophy,* Jan (1), 111–121.

Gill, J. H. (1989). *Mediated transcendence: A postmodern reflection.* Macon, GA: Mercer University Press.

Gimello, R. M. (1978). Mysticism and meditation. In S. T. Katz (Ed.), *Mysticism and philosophical analysis* (pp. 170–199). New York: Oxford University Press.

Gimello, R. M. (1983). Mysticism in its contexts. In S. T. Katz (Ed.), *Mysticism and religious traditions* (pp. 61–88). New York: Oxford University Press.

Globus, G. (1993). Different views from different states. In R. N. Walsh & F. Vaughan, F. (Eds.), *Paths beyond ego: The transpersonal vision* (pp. 182–183). Los Angeles: J. P. Tarcher.

Godlove, T. (1984). In what sense are religions conceptual frameworks? *Journal of the American Academy of Religion, 52*(2), 289–305.

Godlove, T. (1997). *Religion, interpretation, and diversity of belief: The framework model from Kant to Durkheim to Davidson.* Macon, GA: Mercer University Press.

Goleman, D. (1977). *The varieties of meditative experience.* New York: E. P. Dutton.

Goodman, N. (1978). *Ways of worldmaking.* Indianapolis, IN: Hackett.

Griffin, D. R., & Smith, H. (1989). *Primordial truth and postmodern theology.* Albany: State University of New York Press.

Griffiths, P. J. (1986). *On being mindless: Buddhist meditation and the mind-body problem.* La Salle, IL: Open Court.

Griffiths, P. J. (1991). *An apology for apologetics: A study in the logic of interreligious dialogue.* Maryknoll, NY: Orbis Books.

Griffiths, P. & Lewis, D. (1983). On grading religions, seeking truth, and being nice to people—A reply to Professor Hick. *Religious Studies, 19*(1), 75–80.

Grinshpon, Y. (1997). Experience and observation in traditional and modern Patañjala Yoga. In E. Franco & K. Preisendanz (Eds.), *Beyond orientalism: The work of Wilhelm*

Halbfass and its impact on cross-cultural studies (pp. 557–566). Amsterdam-Atlanta, GA: Rodopi.

Grof, C., & Grof, S. (1990). *The stormy search for the self.* Los Angeles: J. P. Tarcher.

Grof, S. (1972). Varieties of transpersonal experiences: Observations from LSD psychotherapy. *Journal of Transpersonal Psychology, 4*(1), 45–80.

Grof, S. (1985). *Beyond the brain: Birth, death, and transcendence in psychotherapy.* Albany: State University of New York Press..

Grof, S. (1988). *The adventure of self-discovery: Dimensions of consciousness and new perspectives in psychotherapy and inner exploration.* Albany: State University of New York Press.

Grof, S. (1998). *The cosmic game: Explorations of the frontiers of human consciousness.* Albany: State University of New York Press.

Grof, S. (2000). *A psychology of the future: Lessons from modern consciousness research.* Albany: State University of New York Press.

Grof, S., & Bennet, H. Z. (1993). *The holotropic mind: The three levels of human consciousness and how they shape our lives.* New York: HarperCollins.

Grof, S., & Grof, C. (Eds.). (1989). *Spiritual emergency: When personal transformation becomes a crisis.* Los Angeles: J. P. Tarcher.

Grosz, E. (1993). Bodies and knowledges: Feminism and the crisis of reason. In L. Alcoff & E. Potter (Eds.), *Feminist epistemologies* (pp. 187–215). New York: Routledge.

Gutting, G. (1977). Philosophy of science. In C. F. Delaney, M. J. Loux, G. Gutting, & W. D. Solomon (Eds.), *The synoptic vision: Essays on the philosophy of Wilfrid Sellars* (pp. 73–104). Notre Dame, IN: University of Notre Dame Press.

Gyatso, J. (1999). Healings burns with fire: The facilitation of experience in Tibetan Buddhism. *Journal of the American Academy of Religion, 67*(1), 113–147.

Haas, A. M. (1997). What is mysticism? In B. Bäumer (Ed.), *Mysticism in Shaivism and Christianity* (pp. 1–36). New Delhi, India: D. K. Printworld.

Habermas, J. (1971). *Knowledge and human interests.* (J. J. Shapiro, Trans.). Boston: Beacon Press.

Habermas, J. (1984). *The theory of communicative action: Vol. 1. Reason and the rationalization of society.* (T. McCarthy, Trans.). Boston: Beacon Press.

Habermas, J. (1987a). *The philosophical discourse of modernity: Twelve lectures.* (F. Lawrence, Trans.). Cambridge: MIT Press.

Habermas, J. (1987b). *The theory of communicative action: Vol. II. Lifeworld and system: A critique of functionalist reason.* (T. McCarthy, Trans.). Boston: Beacon Press.

Habermas, J. (1988). *On the logic of the social sciences.* (S. W. Nicholsen & J. A. Stark, Trans.). Cambridge: MIT Press.

Habermas, J. (1992). *Postmetaphysical thinking: Philosophical essays.* (W. M. Hohengarten, Trans.). Cambridge: MIT Press.

Ha'iri Yazdi, M. (1992). *The principles of epistemology in Islamic philosophy: Knowledge by presence.* Albany: State University of New York Press.

Halbfass, W. (1988a). *India and Europe: An essay in understanding.* Albany: State University of New York Press.

Halbfass, W. (1988b). The concept of experience in the encounter between India and the West. In *India and Europe: An essay in understanding* (pp. 378–402). Albany: State University of New York Press.

Halbvass, W. (1988c). Inclusivism and "tolerance" in the encounter between India and the West. In *India and Europe: An essay in understanding* (pp. 403–418). Albany: State University of New York Press.

Halbfass, W. (1991). *Tradition and reflection: Explorations in Indian thought.* Albany: State University of New York Press.

Hales, S. D. (1997). A consistent relativism. *Mind, 106,* 33–52.

Halifax, J. (1998). *A Buddhist life in America: Simplicity in the complex.* New York: Paulist Press.

Hanegraaff, W. J. (1998). *New age religion and Western culture. Esotericism in the mirror of secular thought.* Albany: State University of New York Press.

Hanh, T. N. (1995). *The heart of understanding: Commentaries on the Prajñaparamita heart sutra.* Berkeley, CA: Parallax Press.

Hannah, F. J. (1993a). The transpersonal consequences of Hussrel's phenomenological method. *Humanistic Psychologist, 21,* 41–57.

Hannah, F. J. (1993b). Rigorous intuition: Consciousness, being, and the phenomenological method. *Journal of Transpersonal Psychology, 25*(2), 181–197.

Harland, R. (1987). *Superstructuralism: The philosophy of structuralism and post-Structuralism.* New York: Routledge.

Harman, W. (1988). The transpersonal challenge to the scientific paradigm: The need for a restructuring of science. *ReVision, 11*(2), 13–21.

Harman, W. (1994). The scientific exploration of consciousness: Towards an adequate epistemology. *Journal of Consciousness Studies, 1*(1), 140–148.

Harré, R., & Krausz, M. (1996). *Varieties of relativism.* Cambridge, MA: Blackwell.

Hart, T. (1999). The refinement of empathy. *Journal of Humanistic Psychology, 39*(4), 111–125.

Hart, T. (2000). Inspiration as transpersonal knowing. In T. Hart, P. Nelson, & K. Puhakka (Eds.), *Transpersonal knowing: Exploring the horizon of consciousness* (pp. 31–53). Albany: State University of New York Press.

Hart, T., Nelson, P., & Puhakka, K. (Eds.). (2000). *Transpersonal knowing: Exploring the horizon of consciousness.* Albany: State University of New York Press.

Harvey, P. (1995). *The selfless mind: Personality, consciousness and nirvana in early Buddhism.* Richmond, Surrey, UK: Curzon Press.

Hausman, D. M. (1985). Is falsificationism unpractised or unpractisable? *Philosophy of the Social Sciences,* 15(3), 313–319.

Hayes, R. P. (1994). Nagarjuna's appeal. *Journal of Indian Philosophy, 22,* 299–378.

Hayes, R. P. (1997). Whose experience validates what for Dharmakirti? In P. Bilimoria & J. N. Mohanty (Eds.), *Relativism, suffering and beyond: Essays in memory of Bimal K. Matilal* (pp. 105–118). New Delhi, India: Oxford University Press.

Hayward, J. H. (1987). *Shifting worlds, changing minds: Where the sciences and Buddhism meet.* Boston: Shambhala.

Heim, S. M. (1995). *Salvations: Truth and difference in religion.* Maryknoll, NY: Orbis Books.

Helminiak, D. A. (1996). *The human core of spirituality.* Albany: State University of New York Press.

Helminiak, D. A. (1998). *Religion and the human sciences.* Albany: State University of New York Press.

Heron, J. (1996a). *Co-operative inquiry: Research into the human condition.* Thousand Oaks, CA: Sage.

Heron, J. (1996b). Spiritual inquiry: A critique of Wilber. *Collaborative Inquiry, 18,* 2–10.

Heron, J. (1997). A way out for Wilberians. Unpublished manuscript.

Heron, J. (1998). *Sacred science: Person-centred inquiry into the spiritual and the subtle.* Ross-on-Wye, Herefordshire, UK: PCCS Books.

Heron, J. & Reason, P. (1997). A participatory inquiry paradigm. *Qualitative Inquiry, 3*(3), 274–294.

Hershock, P. D. (1996). *Liberating intimacy: Enlightenment and social virtuosity in Ch'an Buddhism.* Albany: State University of New York Press.

Hick, J. (Ed.). (1974). *Truth and dialogue on world religions: Conflicting truth claims.* Philadelphia: Westminster Press.

Hick, J. (1981). On grading religions. *Religious Studies, 17*(4), 451–467.

Hick, J. (1983). On conflicting religious truth-claims. *Religious Studies, 19*(4), 485–491.

Hick, J. (1992). *An interpretation of religion: Human responses to the transcendent.* New Haven: Yale University Press.

Hick, J., & Knitter, P. F. (Eds.). (1987). *The myth of Christian uniqueness.* Maryknoll, NY: Orbis Books.

Hillman, J. (1983). *Archetypal psychology: A brief account.* Dallas, TX: Spring Publications.

Hillman, J. (1992). *Revisioning psychology.* New York: HarperPerennial.

Hoffman, E. (1988). *The right to be human: A biography of Abraham Maslow.* Los Angeles: Jeremy P. Tarcher.

Hoffman, F. J. (1982). The Buddhist empiricist thesis. *Religious Studies, 18*(2), 151–158.

Hoffman, F. J. (1993). The concept of focal point in models for inter-religious understanding. In J. Kellenberger (Ed.), *Inter-religious models and criteria* (pp. 166–184). New York: St. Martin's Press.

Holdrege, B. A. (1996). *Veda and Torah: Transcending the textuality of scripture.* Albany: State University of New York Press.

Hollenback, J. B. (1996). *Mysticism: Experience, response, and empowerment.* University Park: Pennsylvania State University Press.

Hollis, M. (1994). *The philosophy of social science.* New York: Cambridge University Press.

Hollis, M. & Lukes, S. (Eds.). (1982). *Rationality and relativism.* Cambridge: MIT Press.

Hopkins, T. J. (1971). *The Hindu religious tradition.* New York: Harper & Row.

Hopkins, J. (1988). Ultimate reality in Tibetan Buddhism. *Buddhist-Christian Studies, 8,* 111–129.

Hoy, D. C. (1994). The contingency of universality: Critical theory as genealogical hermeneutics. In D. C. Hoy & T. McCarthy (Eds.), *Critical theory* (pp. 172–213). Cambridge, MA: Blackwell.

Huck, G. J., & Goldsmith, J. A. (1995). *Ideology and linguistic theory: Noam Chomsky and the deep structure debates.* New York: Routledge.

Hunt, H. T. (1984). A cognitive psychology of mystical and altered state experience. *Perceptual and Motor Skills, 58,* 467–513.

Hunt, H. T. (1985). Cognition and states of consciousness: The necessity of the empirical study of ordinary and non-ordinary consciousness for contemporary cognitive psychology. *Perceptual and Motor Skills, 60,* 239–282.

Hunt, H. T. (1995a). Some developmental issues in transpersonal experiences. *Journal of Mind and Behavior, 16*(2), 115–134.

Hunt, H. T. (1995b). *On the nature of consciousness: Cognitive, phenomenological, and transpersonal perspectives.* New Haven: Yale University Press.

Hunt, H. T., Gervais, A., Shearing-Johns, S., & Travis, F. (1992). Transpersonal experiences in childhood: An exploratory empirical study of selected adult groups. *Perceptual and Motor Skills, 75,* 1135–1153.

Huntington, C. W. with G. N. Wangchen (1989). *The emptiness of emptiness: An introduction to early Indian Mādhyamika.* Honolulu: University of Hawaii Press.

Hutchins, R. (1987). Ten simple ways to explain transpersonal psychology. PDTP Newsletter of the Proposed Division of Transpersonal Psychology in the American Psychological Association, 9–12.

Huxley, A. (1945). *The perennial philosophy.* New York: Harper & Row.

Idel, M. (1988). *Kabbalah: New perspectives.* New Haven: Yale University Press.

Idel, M. (1996). Universalization and Integration: Two conceptions of mystical union in Jewish mysticism. In M. Idel & B. McGinn (Eds.), *Mystical union in Judaism, Christianity, and Islam: An ecumenical dialogue* (pp. 27–57). New York: Continuum.

Idel, M., & McGinn, B. (Eds.). (1996). *Mystical union in Judaism, Christianity, and Islam: An ecumenical dialogue.* New York: Continuum.

Ihde, D. (1986). *Experimental phenomenology.* Albany: State University of New York Press.

Indich, W. M. (1980). *Consciousness in Advaita Vedanta.* Columbia, MO: South Asia Books.

Ingram, P. O. (1997). *Wrestling with the ox: A theology of religious experience.* New York: Continuum.

Ingram, P. O., & Streng, F. J. (Eds.). (1986). *Buddhist-Christian dialogue: Mutual renewal and transformation.* Honolulu: University of Hawaii Press.

Irwin, L. (1996). *Visionary worlds: The making and unmaking of reality.* Albany: State University of New York Press.

Isenberg, S. R., & Thursby, G. R. (1984–86). Esoteric anthropology: "Devolutionary" and "evolutionary" orientations in perennial philosophy. *Religious Traditions, 7–9,* 177–226.

Isenberg, S. R., & Thursby, G. R. (1985). A perennial philosophy perspective on Richard Rorty's Neo-Pragmatism. *International Journal for Philosophy of Religion, 17,* 41–65.

Jacoby, R. (1975/1997). *Social amnesia: A critique of contemporary psychology.* New Brunswick, NJ: Transaction Publishers.

Jaffé, A. (1989). *Was C. G. Jung a mystic? And other essays.* Einsiedeln, Switzerland: Diamon Verlag.

Jaggar, A. M. (1990). Love and knowledge. Emotions in feminist epistemology. In A. M. Jaggar & S. R. Bordo (Eds.), *Gender/body/knowledge: Feminist reconstructions of being and knowing* (pp. 145–171). New Brunswick: Rutgers University Press.

Jaggar, M. & Bordo, S. R. (Eds.) (1990). *Gender/body/knowledge: Feminist reconstructions of being and knowing.* New Brunswick: Rutgers University Press.

James, W. (1902/1961). *The varieties of religious experience.* New York: Collier Books, Macmillan.

James, W. (1975). *Pragmatism.* Cambridge: Harvard University Press.

Jantzen, G. M. (1994). Feminists, philosophers, and mystics. *Hypatia, 9*(4), 186–206.

Jayatilleke, K. N. (1963). *Early Buddhist theory of knowledge.* London: Allen and Unwin.

Jesse, R. (1996). Entheogens: A brief history of their spiritual use. *Tricycle: The Buddhist Review, 6*(1), 60–64.

Johnston, W. (1995). *Mystical theology: The science of love.* Maryknoll, NY: Orbis Books.

Jones, R. (1909). *Studies in mystical religion.* New York: Macmillan.

Jones, R. H. (1983). Experience and conceptualization in mystical knowledge. *Zygon: A Journal of Religion and Science, 18,* 139–165.

Jones, R. H. (1993). *Mysticism examined: Philosophical inquires into mysticism.* Albany: State University of New York Press.

Jordan, J. V. (1997). Clarity in connection: Empathic knowing, desire, and sexuality. In J. V. Jordan (Ed.), *Women's growth in diversity* (pp. 50–73). New York: Guilford Press.

Judy, D. H. (1996). Transpersonal psychology: Roots in Christian mysticism. In B. W. Scotton, A. B. Chinen, & J. R. Battista, J.R. (Eds.), *Textbook of transpersonal psychiatry and psychology* (pp. 134–144). New York: Basic Books.

Jung, C. G. (1935). *The Tavistock Lectures. Collected Works,* Vol. XVIII. (R. F. C. Hull, Trans.). Bollingen Series XX. Princeton: Princeton University Press.

Jung, C. G. (1968). *Aion: Researches into the phenomenology of the self.* Princeton: Princeton University Press.

Jung, C. G. (1992). Psychological commentary on The Tibetan Book of the Dead. In D. J. Meckel & R. L. Moore (Eds.), *Self and liberation: The Jung/Buddhism dialogue* (pp. 48–80). New York: Paulist Press.

Kalasunriya, A. D. P. (1981). On the notion of verification in Buddhism and in logical positivism. In N. Katz (Ed), *Buddhism and Western philosophy* (pp. 287–305). New Delhi, India: Stirling.

Kalansuriya, A. D. P. (1987). *A philosophical analysis of Buddhist notions.* New Delhi, India: Sri Satguru Publications.

Kalupahana, D. J. (1975). *Causality: The central philosophy in Buddhism.* Honolulu: University of Hawaii Press.

Kalupahana, D. J. (1986). *Nagarjuna: The philosophy of the middle way.* Albany: State University of New York Press.

Kasulis, T. P. (1988). Truth words: The basis of Kukai's theory of interpretation. In D. S. Lopez Jr. (Ed.), *Buddhist hermeneutics* (pp. 257–272). Honolulu: University of Hawaii Press.

Katz, S. T. (Ed.). (1978a). *Mysticism and philosophical analysis.* New York: Oxford University Press.

Katz, S. T. (1978b). Language, epistemology, and mysticism. In S. T. Katz (Ed.), *Mysticism and philosophical analysis* (pp. 22–74). New York: Oxford University Press.

Katz, S. T. (Ed.). (1983a). *Mysticism and religious traditions.* New York: Oxford University Press.

Katz, S. T. (1983b). The "conservative" character of mysticism. In S. T. Katz (Ed.), *Mysticism and religious traditions* (pp. 3–60). New York: Oxford University Press.

Katz, S. T. (1985). Recent work on mysticism. *History of Religions, 25,* 76–86.

Katz, S. T. (1988). On mysticism. *Journal of the American Academy of Religion, 56*(4), 751–757.

Katz, S. T. (Ed.). (1992a). *Mysticism and language.* New York: Oxford University Press.

Katz, S. T. (1992b). Mystical speech and mystical meaning. In S. T. Katz (Ed.), *Mysticism and language* (pp. 3–41). New York: Oxford University Press.

Kellenberger, K. (1969). The falsification challenge. *Religious Studies, 5*(1), 69–76.

Keller, E. F. (1983). *A feeling for the organism: The life and work of Barbara McClintock.* San Francisco: Freeman.

Keller, E. F. (1985). *Reflections on gender and science.* New Haven: Yale University Press.

Keller, E. F. & H. E. Longino (Eds.). (1996). *Feminism and science.* New York: Oxford University Press.

Kelly, S. (1998a). Revisioning the mandala of consciousness: A critical appraisal of Wilber's holarchical paradigm. In D. Rothberg & S. Kelly, S. (Eds.), *Ken Wilber in dialogue: Conversations with leading transpersonal thinkers* (pp. 119–130). Wheaton, IL: Quest.

Kelly, S. (1998b). Breaks in the chain. In D. Rothberg & S. Kelly, S. (Eds.), *Ken Wilber in dialogue: Conversations with leading transpersonal thinkers* (pp. 379–381). Wheaton, IL: Quest Books.

Kieckhefer, R., & Bond, G. D. (Eds.). (1988). *Sainthood: Its manifestation in world religions.* Berkeley: University of California Press.

King, S. B. (1988). Two epistemological models for the interpretation of mysticism. *Journal of the American Academy of Religion, 56*(2), 257–279.

King, S. B. (1995). It's a long way to a global ethic: A response to Leonard Swidler. *Buddhist-Christian Studies, 15,* 213–219.

Kitcher, P. (1982). *Abusing science: The case against creationism.* Cambridge: MIT Press.

Kitcher, P. (1984). *The nature of mathematical knowledge.* New York: Oxford University Press.

Klee, R. (1997). *Introduction to the philosophy of science.* New York: Oxford University Press.

Klein, A. (1986). *Knowledge and liberation: Tibetan Buddhist epistemology in support of transformative religious experience.* Ithaca, NY: Snow Lion Publications.

Klein, A. C. (1987). Finding a self: Buddhist and feminist perspectives. In C. W. Atkinson, C. H. Buchanan, & M. R. Miles (Eds.), *Shaping new vision: Gender and values in American culture* (pp. 191–218). Harvard Women's Studies in Religion Series. Ann Arbor, MI: UMI Research Press.

Knitter, P. F. (1985). *No other name?: A critical survey of Christian attitudes toward the world religions.* Maryknoll, NY: Orbis Books.

Knitter, P. F. (1995). Pitfalls and promises for a global ethics. *Buddhist-Christian Studies 15,* 221–229.

Krausz, M. (Ed.). (1989). *Relativism: Interpretation and confrontation.* Notre Dame, IN: University of Notre Dame Press.

Krausz, M. (1997). Relativism and beyond: A tribute to Bimal Matilal. In P. Bilimoria & J. M. Mohanty (Eds.), *Relativism, suffering and beyond. Essays in memory of Bimal K. Matilal* (pp. 93–104). New Delhi, India: Oxford University Press.

Krausz, M., & Meiland, J. W. (Eds.). (1982). *Relativism: Cognitive and moral.* Notre Dame, IN: University of Notre Dame Press.

Kremer, J. (1992a). The dark night of the scholar. *ReVision, 14*(4), 169–78.

Kremer, J. (1992b). Whither dark night of the scholar? *ReVision, 15*(1), 4–12.

Kremer, J. (1994). *Looking for Dame Yggdrasil.* Red Bluff, CA: Falkenblug Press.

Kremer, J. (1997). Are there indigenous epistemologies? Unpublished manuscript.

Kuhn, T. (1970a). *The structure of scientific revolutions* (2nd ed.). Chicago: University of Chicago Press.

Kuhn, T. (1970b). Logic of discovery or psychology of research. In I. Lakatos & A. Musgrave (Ed.), *Criticism and the growth of knowledge* (pp. 1–23). New York: Cambridge University Press.

Küng, H. (1989). Response to Francis Cook: Is it just this? Different paradigms of ultimate reality in Buddhism. *Buddhist-Christian Studies, 9,* 143–152.

Küng, H. (1991). *Global responsibility: In search for a new world ethic.* New York: Crossroad.

Küng, H., & Kuschel, K-J. (Eds.). (1993). *A global ethic: The declaration of the Parliament of the World Religions.* New York: Continuum.

Lajoie, D. H., & Shapiro, S. Y. (1992). Definitions of transpersonal psychology: The first twenty-three years. *Journal of Transpersonal Psychology, 24*(1), 79–98.

Lakatos, I. (1970). Falsification and the methodology of scientific research programmes. In I. Lakatos & A. Musgrave (Eds.), *Criticism and the growth of knowledge* (pp. 91–196). New York: Cambridge University Press.

Lakoff, G. (1987). *Women, fire, and dangerous things: What categories reveal about the mind.* Chicago: University of Chicago Press.

Lakoff, G., & Johnson, M. (1980). *Metaphors we live by.* Chicago: University of Chicago Press.

Lane, M. (Ed.). (1970). *Introduction to structuralism.* New York: Basic Books.

Lasch, C. (1978). *The culture of narcissism: American life in an age of diminishing expectations.* New York: W. W. Norton.

Laudan, L. (1996). *Beyond positivism and relativism: Theory, method, and evidence.* Boulder, CO: WestviewPress.

Laughlin, C. (1994). Transpersonal anthropology, then and now. *Transpersonal Review, 1*(1), 7–10.

Laughlin, C., & McManus, J. (1995). The relevance of the radical empiricism of William James to the anthropology of consciousness. *Anthropology of Consciousness, 6*(3), 34–46.

Laughlin, C., McManus, J., & D'Aquili, E. (1990). *Brain, symbol and experience.* Boston: Shambhala.

Lawson, A. E. (1993). On why falsifiability does not exist in theory testing: A reply to Smith and Siegel. *Journal of Research in Science Teaching, 30*(6), 603–606.

Leach, E. (1987). Structuralism. In M. Eliade (Ed.), *The encyclopedia of religion: Vol. 14* (pp. 54–64). New York: Macmillan.

Leder, D. (1990). *The absent body.* Chicago: University of Chicago Press.

Levin, D. M. (1987). Clinical stories: A modern self in the fury of being. In D. M. Levin (Ed.), *Pathologies of the modern self: Postmodern studies on narcissism, schizophrenia, and depression* (pp. 479–537). New York: New York University Press.

Levin, D. M. (1988a). *The opening of vision: Nihilism and the postmodern situation.* New York: Routledge.

Levin, D. M. (1988b). Transpersonal phenomenology: The corporeal scheme. *Humanistic Psychologist, 18*(2), 282–313.

Levy, J. (1983). Transpersonal psychology and Jungian psychology. *Journal of Humanistic Psychology, 23*(2), 45–51.

Lewis, C. I. (1929). *Mind and the world order.* New York: Scribner.

Lindbeck, G. A. (1984). *The nature of doctrine: Religion and theology in a postliberal age.* Philadelphia: Westminster Press.

Lipman, K. (1995). Between body and spirit: Eastern energetics and Western soulfulness. Unpublished manuscript.

Loemker, L. E. (1973). Perennial philosophy. In P. P. Wiener (Ed.), *Dictionary of the history of ideas: Vol. III* (pp. 457–463). New York: Scribner.

Lopez, D. S. (1992). Paths terminable and interminable. In R. E. Buswell & R. M. Gimello (Eds.), *Paths to liberation: The Marga and its transformations in Buddhist thought* (pp. 147–192). Honolulu: University of Hawaii Press.

Loy, D. (1988). *Nonduality. A study in comparative philosophy.* Atlantic Highlands, NJ: Humanities Press.

Lukoff, D., & Lu, F. G. (1988). Transpersonal psychology research review. Topic: Mystical experience. *Journal of Transpersonal Psychology, 20*(2), 161–184.

Lynch, M. P. (1998). *Truth in context: An essay on pluralism and objectivity.* Cambridge: MIT Press.

MacIntyre, A. (1987). Relativism, power, and philosophy. In K. Baynes, J. Bohman, & T. McCarthy (Eds.), *After philosophy: End or transformation?* (pp. 383–411). Cambridge: MIT Press.

MacIntyre, A. (1988). *Whose justice? Whose rationality?* Notre Dame, IN: University of Notre Dame Press.

Macy, J., & Rothberg, D. (1994). Asking to awaken. *ReVision, 17*(2), 25–33.

Mandelbaum, M. (1982). Subjective, objective, and conceptual relativisms. In M. Krausz & J. W. Meiland (Eds.), *Relativism: Cognitive and moral* (pp. 34–61). Notre Dame, IN: University of Notre Dame Press.

Margolis, J. (1986). *Pragmatism without foundations: Reconciling realism and relativism.* New York: Basil Blackwell.

Margolis, J. (1989). The truth about relativism. In M. Krausz (Ed.), *Relativism: Interpretation and confrontation* (pp. 232–255). Notre Dame, IN: University of Notre Dame Press.

Maritain, J. (1932/1959). *The degrees of knowledge* (4th ed.). (G. B. Phelan, Trans.). New York: Scribner.

Marsella, A. J., Devos, G., & Hsu, F. L. K. (Eds.). (1985). *Culture and self: Asian and Western perspectives.* New York: Tavistock Publications.

Marsh, J. L. (1988). *Post-Cartesian meditations: An essay in dialectical phenomenology.* New York: Fordham University Press.

Maslow, A. H. (1968). *Towards a psychology of being* (2nd ed.). New York: Van Nostrand.

Maslow, A. H. (1969). *The psychology of science: A reconnaissance.* Chicago: Henry Regnery, Gateway Edition.

Maslow, A. H. (1970). *Religions, values, and peak experiences.* New York: Viking Press.

Maslow, A. H. (1971). Comments on "Religions, Values, and Peak Experiences." In *The farther reaches of human nature.* New York: Viking Press.

Matilal, B. (1991). Pluralism, relativism, and interaction between cultures. In E. Deutsch (Ed.), *Culture and modernity: East-West philosophical perspectives* (pp. 141–160). Honolulu: University of Hawaii Press.

Maturana, H., & Varela, F. J. (1987). *The tree of knowledge: The biological roots of human understanding.* Boston: New Science Library.

Mayeda, S. (Ed.). (1992). *A thousand teachings: The* Upadesasahasri *of Sankara.* (S. Mayeda, Trans.). Albany: State University of New York Press.

McDermott, J. J. (1976). *The culture of experience: Philosophical essays in the American grain.* New York: New York University Press.

McDermott, R. (1993). Transpersonal worldviews: Historical and philosophical reflections. In R. Walsh & F. Vaughan (Eds.), *Paths beyond ego: The transpersonal vision* (pp. 206–213). Los Angeles: J. P. Tarcher.

McGinn, B. (1994). *The foundations of mysticism: Vol. I. The presence of God: A history of Western Christian mysticism.* New York: Crossroad.

McGinn, B. (1996a). *The growth of mysticism: Vol. II. The Presence of God: A history of Western Christian mysticism.* New York: Crossroad.

McGinn, B. (1996b). Love, knowledge and *Unio Mystica* in the Western Christian tradition. In M. Idel & B. McGinn (Eds.), *Mystical union in Judaism, Christianity, and Islam: An ecumenical ddialogue* (pp. 59–86). New York: Continuum.

McGinn, B. (1996c). Comments. In M. Idel & B. McGinn (Eds.), *Mystical union in Judaism, Christianity, and Islam: An ecumenical dialogue* (pp. 185–193). New York: Continuum.

McKinnon, A. (1970). *Falsification and belief.* Reseda, CA: Ridgeview.

Meckel, D. J., & Moore, R. L. (Eds.). (1992). *Self and liberation. The Jung/Buddhist dialogue.* New York: Paulist Press.

Meiland, J. W. (1980). On the paradox of cognitive relativism. *Metaphilosophy, 11,* 115–126.

Meland, B. E. (Ed.). (1969). *The future of empirical theology.* Chicago: University of Chicago Press.

Mendes-Flohr, P. (1989). *From mysticism to dialogue: Martin Buber's transformation of German social thought.* Detroit: Wayne State University Press.

Merkur, D. (1998). *The ecstatic imagination: Psychedelic experiences and the psychoanalysis of self-actualization.* Albany: State University of New York Press.

Miller, M. E. & Cook-Greuter, S. R. (1994). *Transcendence and mature thought in adulthood: The further reaches of adult development.* Lanham, MD: Rowman & Littelfield.

Min, A. K. (1997). Dialectical pluralism and solidarity of others: Towards a new paradigm. *Journal of the American Academy of Religion, 65*(3), 587–604.

Mishra, K. (1993). *Kashmir Śaivism: The central philosophy of Tantrism.* Portland, OR: Rudra Press.

Mitchell, D. W., & Wiseman, J. (Eds.). (1997). *The Getshemani encounter: A dialogue on the spiritual life by Buddhist and Christian monastics.* New York: Continuum.

Moore, P. (1978). Mystical experience, mystical doctrine, mystical technique. In S. T. Katz (Ed.), *Mysticism and philosophical analysis* (pp. 101–131). New York: Oxford University Press.

Müller, M. (1893). *Introduction to the science of religion.* London: Longmans Green.

Murphy, M. (1993). *The future of the body: Explorations into the further evolution of human nature.* New York: J.P. Tarcher/Perigee.

Murti, T. R. V. (1955). *The central philosophy of Buddhism.* London: Allen and Unwin.

Nagel, T. (1986). *The view from nowhere.* New York: Oxford University Press.

Nagel, T. (1997). *The last word.* New York: Oxford University Press.

Nagy, M. (1991). *Philosophical issues in the psychology of C. G. Jung.* Albany: State University of New York Press.

Nasr, S. H. (1985). Response to Thomas Dean's review of *Knowledge and the sacred. Philosophy East and West, 35*(1), 87–90.

Nasr, S. H. (1989). *Knowledge and the sacred.* Albany: State University of New York Press.

Nasr, S. H. (1993). *The need for a sacred science.* Albany: State University of New York Press.

Nasr, S. H. (1996). *Religion and the order of nature.* New York: Oxford University Press.

Needleman, J. (1982). *The heart of philosophy.* New York: Alfred A. Knopf.

Negoita, C. V. (1985). *Experts systems and fuzzy logic.* Menlo Park, CA: Benjamin/Cummings.

Nelson, J. E. (1994). *Healing the split: Integrating spirit in our understanding of the mentally ill.* Albany: State University of New York Press.

Nelson, P. L. (1990). The technology of the praeternatural: An empirically based model of transpersonal experiences. *Journal of Transpersonal Psychology, 22*(1), 35–50.

Nelson, P. L. (1998). Consciousness as reflexive shadow: An operational psychophenomenological model. *Imagination, Cognition and Personality, 17*(3), 215–228.

Neville, R. C. (1991). *Behind the masks of God: An essay toward comparative theology.* Albany: State University of New York Press.

Newell, W. L. (1981). *Struggle and submission: R. Z. Zaehner on mysticisms.* Washington: University Press of America.

Nietzsche, F. (1984). *Human, all too human: A book for free spirits.* (M. Faber, with S. Lehmann, Trans.). Lincoln: University of Nebraska Press.

Noll, R. (1994). *The Jung cult: Origins of a charismatic movement.* Princeton: Princeton University Press.

Norris, R. A. (1987). Theurgy. In M. Eliade (Ed.), *The encyclopedia of religion: Vol. 14* (pp. 481–483). New York: Macmillan.

Nuernberger, P. (1994). The structure of mind and its resources. In M. E. Miller & S. R. Cook-Greuter (Eds.), *Transcendence and mature thought in adulthood: The further reaches of adult development* (pp. 89–115). Lanham, MD: Rowman & Littlefield.

Nyanaponika Thera. (1973). *The heart of Buddhist meditation.* New York: Weiser.

O'Donovan-Anderson, M. (Ed.). (1996). *The incorporated self: Interdisciplinary perspectives of embodiment.* Lanham, MD: Rowman & Littelfield.

O'Hear, A. (1980). *Karl Popper.* London: Routledge & Kegan Paul.

O'Leary, J. S. (1996). *Religious pluralism and Christian truth.* Edinburgh, UK: Edinburgh University Press.

Olds, L. E. (1992). *Metaphors of interrelatedness: Toward a systems theory of psychology.* Albany: State University of New York Press.

Olsen, W. S. (1996). *The sacred place: Witnessing the holy in the physical world.* Salt Lake City: University of Utah Press.

Olson, A. M. (1985). On primordialism versus post-modernism: A response to Thomas Dean. *Philosophy East and West, 35*(1), 91–95.

Orange, D. M. (1995). *Emotional understanding: Studies in psychoanalytic epistemology.* New York: Guilford Press.

Otto, R. (1932). *Mysticism East and West: A comparative analysis of the nature of mysticism.* New York: Macmillan.

Outhwaite, W. (1996). The philosophy of social science. In B. S. Turner (Ed.), *The Blackwell companion to social theory* (pp. 83–106). Malden, MA: Blackwell.

Pandith Vajragnana (1997). Stages. In D. W. Mitchell & J. Wiseman (Eds.), *The Getshemani encounter: A dialogue on the spiritual life by Buddhist and Christian Monastics* (p. 184). New York: Continuum.

Panikkar, R. (1984). Religious pluralism: The metaphysical challenge. In L. S. Rouner (Ed.), *Religious pluralism* (pp. 97–115). Notre Dame, IN: University of Notre Dame Press.

Panikkar, R. (1988). The invisible harmony: A universal theory of religion or a cosmic confidence in reality. In L. Swidler (Ed.), *Toward a universal theology of religion* (pp. 118–153). Maryknoll, NY: Orbis Books.

Panikkar, R. (1996). A self-critical dialogue. In J. Prabhu (Ed.), *The intercultural challenge of Raimon Panikkar* (pp. 227–291). Maryknoll, NY: Orbis Books.

Paranjpe, A. C. (1984). *Theoretical psychology: The meeting of East and West.* New York: Plenum Press.

Paranjpe, A. C. (1988). A personality theory according to Vedanta. In A. C. Paranjpe, D. Y. F. Ho, & R. W. Rieber (Eds.), *Asian contributions to psychology* (pp. 185–213). New York: Praeger.

Parrinder, G. (1982). *Avatar and incarnation: A comparison of Indian and Christian beliefs.* New York: Oxford University Press.

Patañjali. (1977). *The Yoga-system of Patañjali*. (J. Haughton, Trans.). New Delhi, India: Motilal Banarsidass.

Penner, H. H. (1989). *Impasse and resolution: A Critique of the study of religion*. New York: Peter Lang.

Perovich, A. N., Jr. (1985a). Mysticism and the philosophy of science. *Journal of Religion, 65*, 63–82.

Perovich, A. N. Jr. (1985b). Mysticism or mediation: A response to Gill. *Faith and Philosophy*, April(2), 179–188.

Phillips, S. H. (1986). *Auorbindo's philosophy of Brahman*. New York: E. J. Brill.

Piaget, J. (1968). *Structuralism*. New York: Harper & Row.

Pinch, T. (1985). Theory testing in science—The case of solar neutrinos: Do crucial experiments test theories or theorists? *Philosophy of the Social Sciences, 15*(2), 167–187.

Polkinghorne, D. (1983). *Methodology for the human sciences: Systems of inquiry*. Albany: State University of New York Press.

Popper, K. (1959). *The logic of scientific discovery*. London: Hutchinson.

Popper, K. (1970). Normal science and its dangers. In I. Lakatos & A. Musgrave (Ed.), *Criticism and the growth of knowledge* (pp. 51–58). New York: Cambridge University Press.

Popper, K. (1994). The myth of the framework. In M. A. Notturno (Ed.), *The myth of the framework: In defense of science and rationality* (pp. 33–64). New York: Routledge.

Potter, K. H. (1991). *Presuppositions of India's philosophies*. New Delhi, India: Motilal Banarsidass.

Prabhu, J. (Ed.). (1996). *The intercultural challenge of Raimon Panikkar*. Maryknoll, NY: Orbis Books.

Price, H. H. (1932). *Perception*. London: Methuen.

Price, J. R., III. (1985). The objectivity of mystical truth claims. *The Thomist, 49*(1), 81–98.

Price, J. R., III. (1987). Typologies and the cross-cultural analysis of mysticism: A critique. In T. P. Fallon & P. B. Riley (Eds.), *Religion and culture: Essays in honor of Bernard Lonergan* (pp. 181–190). Albany: State University of New York Press.

Price, J. R., III. (1998). Mysticism, mediation, and consciousness. The innate capacity in John Ruusbroec. In R. K. C. Forman (Ed.), *The innate capacity: Mysticism, psychology, and philosophy* (pp. 111–120). New York: Oxford University Press.

Proudfoot, W. (1985). *Religious experience*. Berkeley, CA: University of California Press.

Puhakka, K. (1993). The reclaiming of knowledge by human experience [Review of *The embodied mind: Cognitive science and human experience*]. *Humanistic Psychologist, 21*(2), 235–246.

Puhakka, K. (2000). An invitation to authentic knowing. In T. Hart, P. L. Nelson, & K. Puhakka (Eds.), *Transpersonal knowing: Exploring the horizon of consciousness* (pp. 11–30). Albany: State University of New York Press.

Putnam, H. (1979). *Reason, truth and history*. Cambridge, NY: Cambridge University Press.

Quine, W. V. (1953). *From a logical point of view.* New York: Harper & Row.

Quine, W. V. (1981). On the very idea of a third dogma. In *Theories and things* (pp. 38–42). Cambridge: Belknap Press of Harvard University Press.

Quine, W. V. (1990). *In pursuit of truth.* Cambridge: Harvard University Press.

Quinn, W. W. (1997). *The only tradition.* Albany: State University of New York Press.

Rabinow, P. & Sullivan, W. M. (Eds.). (1987). *Interpretive social science: A second look.* Berkeley: University of California Press.

Radhakrishnan, S. (1923/1971). *Indian philosophy.* (2 Vol.). New York: Humanities Press.

Radhakrishnan, S. (1929/1957). *An idealist view of life* (5th ed.). London: Allen and Unwin.

Rambachan, A. (1991). *Accomplishing the accomplished: The Vedas as a source of valid knowledge in Sankara.* Honolulu: University of Hawaii Press.

Rambachan, A. (1994). *The limits of scripture.* Honolulu: University of Hawaii Press.

Raphael, M. (1994). Feminism, constructivism and numinous experience. *Religious Studies, 30,* 511–526.

Rawlinson, A. (1997). *Vippasana shanga.* In *The book of enlightened masters: Western teachers in Eastern traditions* (pp. 586–596). Chicago and La Salle, IL: Open Court.

Reason, P. (Ed). (1994). *Participation in human inquiry.* Thousand Oaks, CA: Sage.

Rescher, N. (1980). Conceptual schemes. In P. A. French, T. E. Uehling, Jr., & H. Wettstein (Eds.), *Midwest studies in philosophy: Vol. V. Studies in epistemology* (pp. 323–345). Minneapolis: University of Minnesota Press.

Rescher, N. (1993). *Pluralism: Against the demand for consensus.* New York: Oxford University Press.

Richards, G. (1978). *Sunyata*: Objective referent or *via negativa? Religious Studies, 14,* 251–260.

Ring, K. (1985). *Heading towards omega: In search of the meaning of the near-death experience.* New York: Quill.

Ring, K. (1998). *Lessons from the light: What we can learn from the near-death experience.* New York: Insight Books.

Robbins, R. H. (1993). *Cultural anthropology: A problem-based approach.* Itaca, IL: F. E. Peacock.

Roberts, B. (1984). *The experience of no-self.* Boston: Shambhala.

Robinson, W. S. (1975). The legend of the given. In H-N. Castañeda (Ed.), *Action, knowledge and reality: Critical studies in honor of Wilfred Sellars* (pp. 83–108). Indianapolis: Bobbs–Merrill.

Roland, A. (1988). *In search of self in India and Japan: Toward a cross-cultural psychology.* Princeton: Princeton University Press.

Roof, W. C. (1993). *A generation of seekers: The spiritual lives of the baby boom generation.* San Francisco: HarperSanFrancisco.

Roof, W. C. (1999). *Spiritual marketplace: Baby boomers and the remaking of American religion.* Princeton: Princeton University Press.

Rorty, R. (1972). The world well lost. *Journal of Philosophy, 69*(19), 649–665.

Rorty, R. (1979). *Philosophy and the mirror of nature.* Princeton: Princeton University Press.

Rosemont, H., Jr. (1988). Against relativism. In G. J. Larson & E. Deutsch (Eds.), *Interpreting across boundaries: New essays in comparative philosophy* (pp. 36–70). Princeton: Princeton University Press.

Ross, J. J. (1970). *The appeal to the given: A study in epistemology.* London: Allen and Unwin.

Rothberg, D. (1986a). Rationality and religion in Habermas' recent work: Some remarks on the relation between critical theory and the phenomenology of religion. *Philosophy and Social Criticism, 11,* 221–245.

Rothberg, D. (1986b). Philosophical foundations of transpersonal psychology: An introduction to some basic issues. *Journal of Transpersonal Psychology, 18*(1), 1–34.

Rothberg, D. (1989). Understanding mysticism: Transpersonal theory and the limits of contemporary epistemological frameworks. *ReVision, 12*(2), 5–21.

Rothberg, D. (1990). Contemporary epistemology and the study of mysticism. In R. K. C. Forman (Ed.), *The problem of pure consciousness: Mysticism and philosophy* (pp. 163–210). New York: Oxford University Press.

Rothberg, D. (1993). The crisis of modernity and the emergence of socially engaged spirituality. *ReVision, 15*(3), 105–114.

Rothberg, D. (1994). Spiritual inquiry. *ReVision, 17*(2), 2–12.

Rothberg, D. (1996a). How straight is the spiritual path? Conversations with Buddhist teachers Joseph Goldstein, Jack Kornfield, and Michelle McDonald-Smith. *ReVision, 19*(1), 25–40.

Rothberg, D. (1996b). Toward an integral spirituality. *ReVision, 19*(2), 41–42.

Rothberg, D. (1999). Transpersonal issues at the millennium. *Journal of Transpersonal Psychology, 31*(1), 41–67.

Rothberg, D. & Kelly, S. (Eds.). (1998). *Ken Wilber in dialogue. Conversations with leading transpersonal thinkers.* Wheaton, IL: Quest.

Rottschaefer, W. A. (1978). Ordinary knowledge and scientific realism. In J. C. Pitt (Ed.), *The philosophy of Wilfrid Sellars: Queries and questions* (pp. 135–161). Boston: D. Reidel.

Rowan, J. (1993). *The transpersonal: Psychotherapy and counseling.* New York: Routledge.

Runzo, J. (1986). *Reason, relativism and God.* New York: St. Martin Press.

Ruse, M. (1988). *Philosophy of biology today.* Albany: State University of New York Press.

Sanders, P. T., & Ho, M. W. (1982). Is Neo-Darwinism falsifiable—and does it matter? *Nature and Systems, 4,* 179–196.

Schiebinger, L. (1999). *Has feminism changed science?* Cambridge: Harvard University Press.

Schmidt, L. K. (Ed.) (1995). *The specter of relativism: Truth, dialogue, and phronesis in philosophical hermeneutics.* Evanston, IL: Northwestern University Press.

Schmitt, C. B. (1966). Perennial philosophy: From Agostino Steuco to Leibniz. *Journal of the History of Ideas, 27,* 505–532.

Scholem, G. (1946). *Major trends in Jewish mysticism.* New York: Schocken Books.

Schrader, G. (1967). The thing in itself in Kantian philosophy. In R. D. Wolff (Ed.), *Kant: A collection of critical essays* (pp. 172–188). Garden City, NY: Anchor Books.

Schuon, F. (1981). *Esoterism as principle and as way.* Pates Manor, Bedfont, Middlesex, UK: Perennial Books.

Schuon, F. (1984a). *The transcendent unity of religions.* Wheaton, IL: Quest.

Schuon, F. (1984b). *Logic and transcendence.* London: Perennial Books.

Schuon, F. (1997). *The eye of the heart: Metaphysics, cosmology, spiritual life.* Bloomington, IN: World Wisdom Books.

Scotton, B. W. (1996). The contribution of C. G. Jung to transpersonal psychiatry. In B. W. Scotton, A. B. Chinen, & J. R. Battista, (Eds.), *Textbook of transpersonal psychiatry and psychology* (pp. 39–51). New York: Basic Books.

Scotton, B. W., Chinen, A. B., & Battista, J. R. (Eds.). (1996). *Textbook of transpersonal psychiatry and psychology.* New York: Basic Books.

Searle, J. R. (1995). *The construction of social reality.* New York: Free Press.

Sellars, W. (1956). Empiricism and the philosophy of mind. In H. Feigl & M. Scriven (Eds.), *Minnesota studies in the philosophy of science: Vol. 1. The Foundations of the science and the concepts of psychology and psychoanalysis* (pp. 253–329). Minneapolis: University of Minnesota Press.

Sellars, W. (1963). *Science, perception and reality.* London: Routledge & Kegan Paul.

Sells, M. A. (1994). *Mystical languages of unsaying.* Chicago: University of Chicago Press.

Shanon, B. (1993). *The representational and the presentational.* Hemel Hempstead, UK: Harvester Wheatsheaf.

Shapiro, S. I. (1994). Religion, spirituality, and transpersonal psychology. *International Journal of Transpersonal Studies, 13*(1), 33–41.

Sharf, R. H. (1995a). Buddhist modernism and the rhetoric of meditative experience. *Numen 42*(3), 228–283.

Sharf, R. H. (1995b). Sambokyodan. Zen and the way of the new religions. *Japanese Journal of Religious Studies, 22*(3–4), 417–458.

Sharf, R. H. (1998). Experience. In M. C. Taylor (Ed.), *Critical terms for religious studies* (pp. 94–116). Chicago: University of Chicago Press.

Sharma, A. (1993). *The experiential dimension of Advaita Vedanta.* New Delhi, India: Motilal Banarsidass.

Sharma, A. (1995). *The philosophy of religion and Advaita Vedanta: A comparative study in religion and reason.* University Park: Pennsylvania State University Press.

Shear, J. (1994). On mystical experiences as support for the perennial philosophy. *Journal of the American Academy of Religion, 62,* 319–342.

Sheldrake, R. (1981). *A new science of life.* Los Angeles: J. P. Tarcher.

Sheldrake, R. (1988). *The presence of the past.* New York: Vintage.

Shepherd, L. J. (1993). *Lifting the veil: The feminine face of science.* Boston: Shambhala.

Short, L. (1996). Mysticism, mediation, and the non-linguistic. *Journal of the American Academy of Religion, 63*(4), 659–675.

Shweder, R. A. (1991). *Thinking through cultures: Expeditions in cultural psychology.* Cambridge: Harvard University Press.

Siegel, H. (1987). *Relativism refuted: A critique of contemporary epistemological relativism.* Dordrecht, Netherlands: Reidel.

Skolimowski, H. (1994). *The participatory mind: A new theory of knowledge and of the universe.* New York: Arkana, Penguin Books.

Smart, N. (1964/1992). *Doctrine and argument in Indian philosophy* (2nd rev. ed.). New York: E. J. Brill.

Smart, N. (1973). *The science of religion and the sociology of knowledge.* Princeton: Princeton University Press.

Smart, N. (1980). Interpretation and mystical experience. In R. Woods (Ed.), *Understanding mysticism* (pp. 78–91). Garden City, NY: Doubleday.

Smith, A. P. (1984). Mutiny on *The Beagle. ReVision,* 7(1), 19–34.

Smith, B. H. (1988). *Contingencies of value: Alternative perspectives for critical theory.* Cambridge: Harvard University Press.

Smith, B. H. (1993). Unloading the self-refutation charge. *Common Knowledge, 2,* 81–95.

Smith, H. (1976). *Forgotten truth: The primordial tradition.* New York: Harper & Row.

Smith, H. (1987). Is there a perennial philosophy? *Journal of the American Academy of Religion, 55,* 553–566.

Smith, H. (1989). *Beyond the postmodern mind* (2nd ed., rev.). Wheaton, IL: Theosophical Publishing House.

Smith, H. (1993). Educating the intellect: On opening the eye of the heart. In B. Darling-Smith (Ed.), *Can virtue be taught?* (pp. 17–31). Notre Dame, IN: University of Notre Dame Press.

Smith, H. (1994). Spiritual personality types: The sacred spectrum. In S. H. Nasr & K. O'Brien (Eds.), *In quest of the sacred: The modern world in the light of tradition* (pp. 45–57). Oakton, VA: Foundation for Traditional Studies.

Smith, J. E. (1968). *Experience and God.* London: Oxford University Press.

Smith, J. Z. (1978). *Map is not territory: Studies in the history of religions.* Leiden: Brill.

Sorell, T. (1991). *Scientism.* New York: Routledge.

St. John of the Cross (1979). The ascent to Mount Carmel. In K. Kavanaugh & O. Rodriguez, (Trans.), *The collected works of St. John of the Cross* (pp. 65–292). Washington, DC: Institute of Carmelite Studies. (Original Work Published 1585)

Staal, F. (1975). *Exploring mysticism.* Berkeley: University of California Press.

Stace, W. T. (1960). *Mysticism and philosophy.* Los Angeles: J. P. Tarcher.

Stamos, D. N. (1996). Popper, falsifiability, and evolutionary biology. *Biology and Philosophy, 11*(2), 161–191.

Stenger, M. A. (1995). Religious pluralism and cross-cultural criteria of religious truth. In T. Dean (Ed.), *Religious pluralism and truth: Essays on cross-cultural philosophy of religion* (pp. 87–107). Albany: State University of New York Press.

Stiver, D. R. (1996). *The philosophy of religious language: Sign, symbol and story.* Cambridge, MA: Blackwell.

Stoddart, W. (1994). Introduction. Meaning behind the absurd. In S. H. Nasr & K. O'Brien (Eds.), *In Quest of the sacred: The modern world in the light of tradition* (pp. 7–12). Oakton, VA: Foundation for Traditional Studies.

Stoeber, M. (1992). Constructivist epistemologies of mysticism: A revision and critique. *Religious Studies, 28,* 107–116.

Stoeber, M. (1994). *Theo-monistic mysticism: A Hindu-Christian comparison*. New York: St. Martin's Press.

Streng, F. J. (1967). *Emptiness: A study in religious meaning*. Nashville, TN: Abingdon Press.

Streng, F. J. (1993). Mutual transformation: An answer to a religious question. *Buddhist-Christian Studies, 13,* 121–126.

Sugunasiri, S. H. J. (1996). *Spiritual interaction*, not *interfaith dialogue*: A Buddhistic contribution. *Buddhist-Christian Studies, 16,* 143–165.

Sutich, A. J. (1969). Some considerations regarding transpersonal psychology. *Journal of Transpersonal Psychology, 1*(1), 11–20.

Sutich, A. J. (1976). The emergence of the transpersonal orientation. *Journal of Transpersonal Psychology, 8*(1), 5–19.

Swan, J. (1988). Sacred places in nature and transpersonal experiences. *ReVision, 10*(3), 21–26.

Swan, J. A. (1990). *Sacred places*. Santa Fe, NM: Bear.

Swan, J. A. (1991). *The power of place: Sacred ground in natural and human environments*. Wheaton, IL: Quest.

Swinburne, R. G. (1964). Falsifiability of scientific theories. *Mind, 73*(291), 434–436.

Tarnas, R. (1991). *The passion of the Western mind: Understanding the ideas that have shaped our world view*. New York: Ballantine Books.

Tarnas, R. (1998). The great initiation. *Noetic Sciences Review, 47,* 24–31, 57–59.

Tart, C. T. (1971). Scientific foundations for the study of altered states of consciousness. *Journal of Transpersonal Psychology, 3*(2), 93–124.

Tart, C. T. (1972). States of consciousness and state specific sciences. *Science, 176,* 1203–1210.

Tart, C. T. (1977). Science, states of consciousness, and spiritual experiences. The need for state-specific sciences. In C. T. Tart (Ed.), *Transpersonal Psychologies* (pp. 9–58). New York: Harper & Row.

Tart, C. T. (1983). *States of consciousness*. El Cerrito, CA: Psychological Processes.

Taylor, E. (1996). William James and transpersonal psychiatry. In B. W. Scotton, A. B. Chinen, & J. R. Battista (Eds.), *Textbook of transpersonal psychiatry and psychology* (pp. 21–28). New York: Basic Books.

Thibaut, G. (1904). *The Vedanta Sutras with the commentary of Ramanuja: Vol. 48. Sacred Books of the East*. Oxford: Clarendon Press.

Thompson, E. (1996). The mindful body: Embodiment and cognitive science. In M. O'Donovan-Anderson (Ed.), *The incorporated self: Interdisciplinary perspectives of embodiment* (pp. 127–144). Lanham, MD: Rowman & Littelfield.

Thurman, R. (1991). Tibetan psychology: Sophisticated software for the human brain. In Dalai Lama, H. Benson, R. Thurman, H. Gardner, D. Goleman, (Eds.), *Mind-science: An East-West dialogue* (pp. 51–73). Boston: Wisdom Publications.

Tianji, J. (1991). The Problem of Relativism. In E. Deutsch (Ed.), *Culture and modernity: East-West philosophical perspectives* (pp. 161–173). Honolulu: University of Hawaii Press.

Trungpa, C. (1987). *Cutting through spiritual materialism*. Boston: Shambhala.

Tuck, A. P. (1990). *Comparative philosophy and the philosophy of scholarship: On the Western interpretation of Nagarjuna.* New York: Oxford University Press.

Turner, D. (1995). *The darkness of God: Negativity in Christian mysticism.* Cambridge, UK: Cambridge University Press.

Underhill, E. (1955). *Mysticism.* New York: Meridian.

Valentine, E. (1997). The validation of knowledge: Private and public. In J. Pickering (Ed.), *The authority of experience: Essays on Buddhism and psychology* (pp. 208–218). Surrey, Great Britain: Curzon Press.

Valle, R. (1995). Towards a transpersonal-phenomenological psychology: On transcendent awareness, passion, and peace of mind. *Journal of East-West Psychology, 1*(1), 9–15.

Valle, R. S. (1989). The emergence of transpersonal psychology. In R. S. Valle & S. Halling (Eds.), *Existential-phenomenological perspectives in psychology* (pp. 257–268). New York: Plenum Press.

Van Der Steen, W. J. (1993). *A practical philosophy for the life sciences.* Albany: State University of New York Press.

Varela, F. J., Thompson, E., & Rosch, E. (1991). *The embodied mind: Cognitive science and human experience.* Cambridge: MIT Press.

Vaughan, F. (1979). *Awakening intuition.* Garden City, NY: Anchor Books.

Vaughan, F. (1982). The transpersonal perspective: A personal account. *Journal of Transpersonal Psychology, 14*(1), 37–45.

Vaughan, F. (1986). *The inward arc: Healing and wholeness in psychotherapy and spirituality.* Boston: Shambhala.

Vich, M. A. (1988). Some historical sources of the term "transpersonal." *Journal of Transpersonal Psychology, 20*(2), 107–110.

Vich, M. A. (1990). The origins and growth of transpersonal psychology. *Journal of Humanistic Psychology, 30*(2), 47–50.

von Brück, M. (1991). *The unity of reality: God, God-experience, and meditation in the Hindu-Christian dialogue.* New York: Paulist Press.

von Glasersfeld, E. (1984). An introduction to radical constructivism. In P. Watzlawick (Ed.), *The invented reality: How do we know what we believe we know? (Contributions to constructivism)* (pp. 17–40). New York: W. W. Norton.

von Wright, G. H. (1971). *Explanation and understanding.* London: Routledge & Kegan Paul.

Vroom, H. M. (1989). *Religions and the truth: Philosophical reflections and perspectives.* Grand Rapids, MI: William B. Eerdmans.

Wade, J. (1996). *Changes of mind: A holonomic theory of the evolution of consciousness.* Albany: State University of New York Press.

Wade, J. (1998). Meeting God in the flesh: Spirituality and sexual intimacy. *ReVision, 21*(2), 35–41.

Wade, J. (2000). The love that dares not speak its name. In T. Hart, P. Nelson, & K. Puhakka (Eds.), *Transpersonal knowing: Exploring the horizon of consciousness* (pp. 271–302). Albany: State University of New York Press.

Wainwright, W. J. (1981). *Mysticism: A study of its nature, cognitive value and moral implications*. Madison: University of Wisconsin Press.

Walsh, R. N. (1984). An evolutionary model of meditation research. In D. H. Shapiro, Jr. & R. N. Walsh (Eds.), *Meditation: Classic and contemporary perspectives* (pp. 24–32). New York: Aldine de Gruyter.

Walsh, R. N. (1990). *The spirit of shamanism*. Los Angeles: J. P. Tarcher.

Walsh, R. N. (1992). The search for synthesis: Transpersonal psychology and the meeting of East and West, psychology and religion, personal and transpersonal. *Journal of Humanistic Psychology, 32*(1), 19–45.

Walsh, R. N. (1993a). The transpersonal movement: A history and state of the art. *Journal of Transpersonal Psychology, 25*(3), 123–139.

Walsh, R. N. (1993b). Phenomenological mapping and comparison of shamanic, Buddhist, Yogic, and schizophrenic experiences. *Journal of the American Academy of Religion, 61*(4), 739–769.

Walsh, R. (1995). The spirit of evolution. *Noetic Sciences Review,* Summer, 16–21, 38–41.

Walsh, R. N., & Vaughan, F. (1993). On transpersonal definitions. *Journal of Transpersonal Psychology, 25*(2), 199–207.

Walsh, R. N., & Vaughan, F. (1994). The worldview of Ken Wilber. *Journal of Humanistic Psychology, 34*(2), 6–21.

Washburn, M. (1990). Two patterns of transcendence. *Journal of Humanistic Psychology, 30*(3), 84–112.

Washburn, M. (1994a). *Transpersonal psychology in psychoanalytic perspective*. Albany: State University of New York Press.

Washburn, M. (1994b). Stolorow and Atwood's psychoanalytic intersubjectivity theory: Its implications for transpersonal psychology. *Transpersonal Review, 1*(2), 3–8.

Washburn, M. (1995). *The ego and the dynamic ground: A transpersonal theory of human development* (2nd ed.). Albany: State University of New York Press.

Washburn, M. (1996a). The pre/trans fallacy reconsidered. *ReVision, 19*(1), 2–10.

Washburn, M. (1996b). Linearity, theoretical economy, and the pre/trans fallacy. *ReVision, 19*(2), 36–37.

Weber, M. (1978). *Economy and society*. (R. Wittich & C. Wittich, Eds.). Berkeley: University of California Press.

Weber, R. (1986). The search for unity. In R. Weber (Ed.), *Dialogues with scientists and sages: The search for unity* (pp. 1–19). London: Routledge & Kegan Paul.

Welwood, J., Capra, F., Ferguson, M., Needleman, J., Pribram, K., Smith, H., Vaughan, F., & Walsh, R. N. (1978). Psychology, science and spiritual paths: Contemporary issues. *Journal of Transpersonal Psychology, 10*(2), 93–111.

Whitehead, A. N. (1926). *Religion in the making*. New York: Macmillan.

Wiggins, J. B. (1996). *In praise of religious diversity*. New York: Routledge.

Wilber, K. (1975). Psychologia perennis: The spectrum of consciousness. *Journal of Transpersonal Psychology, 7*(2), 105–132.

Wilber, K. (1977). *The spectrum of consciousness*. Wheaton, IL: Quest.

Wilber, K. (1982). Odyssey: A personal inquiry into humanistic and transpersonal psychology. *Journal of Humanistic Psychology, 22*(1), 57–90.

Wilber, K. (1984). *A sociable God.* Boston: Shambhala.

Wilber, K. (1986). The spectrum of psychopathology. In K. Wilber, J. Engler, & D. Brown, *Transformations of consciousness: Conventional and contemplative perspectives on development* (pp. 107–126). Boston: Shambhala.

Wilber, K. (1987). The spectrum model. In D. Anthony, B. Ecker, & K. Wilber (Eds.), *Spiritual choices: The problem of recognizing authentic paths to inner transformation* (pp. 237–264). New York: Paragon House.

Wilber, K. (1990a). *Eye to eye: The quest for a new paradigm.* (Expanded ed.). Boston: Shambhala.

Wilber, K. (1990b). Death, rebirth, and meditation. In Doore, G. (Ed.), *What survives?: Contemporary explorations of life after death* (pp. 176–191). Los Angeles: J. P. Tarcher.

Wilber, K. (1990c). Two patterns of transcendence. A reply to Washburn. *Journal of Humanistic Psychology, 30*(3), 113–136.

Wilber, K. (1993a). Psychologia perennis: The spectrum of consciousness. In R. Walsh & F. Vaughan, (Eds.), *Paths beyond ego: The transpersonal vision* (pp. 21–33). Los Angeles: J. P. Tarcher.

Wilber, K. (1993b). The Great Chain of Being. In R. Walsh & F. Vaughan (Eds.), *Paths beyond ego: The transpersonal vision* 214–222. Los Angeles: J. P. Tarcher.

Wilber, K. (1994). Foreword. In J. E. Nelson, *Healing the split: Integrating spirit into our understanding of the mentally ill* (pp. viii–xii). Albany: State University of New York Press.

Wilber, K. (1995). *Sex, ecology and spirituality: The spirit of evolution.* Boston: Shambhala.

Wilber, K. (1996a). *A brief history of everything.* Berkeley: Shambhala.

Wilber, K. (1996b). *The Atman Project: A transpersonal view of human development* (2nd ed.). Wheaton, IL: Quest.

Wilber, K. (1996c). *Up from Eden: A transpersonal view of human evolution.* (2nd ed.). Wheaton, IL: Quest.

Wilber, K. (1996d). A more integral approach. A response to the *ReVision* authors. *ReVision, 19*(2), 10–34.

Wilber, K. (1997a). *The eye of the spirit: An integral vision for a world gone slightly mad.* Berkeley: Shambhala.

Wilber, K. (1997b). An integral theory of consciousness. *Journal of Consciousness Studies, 4*(1), 71–92.

Wilber, K. (1998a). *The marriage of sense and soul: Integrating science and religion.* New York: Random House.

Wilber, K. (1998b). Response to Jorge Ferrer's "Speak now or forever hold your peace: A review essay of Ken Wilber's *The marriage of sense and soul.*" *Journal of Transpersonal Psychology, 30*(1), 69–72.

Wilber, K. (1999a). *One taste: The journals of Ken Wilber.* Boston: Shambhala.

Wilber, K. (1999b). Spirituality and developmental lines: Are there stages? *Journal of Transpersonal Psychology, 31*(1), 1–10.

Wilber, K. (1999c). An approach to integral psychology. *Journal of Transpersonal Psychology, 31*(2), 109–136.

Wilber, K. (1999d). Introduction. *The collected works of Ken Wilber: Vol. 2*. Boston: Shambhala.

Wilber, K. (2000). Introduction. *The collected works of Ken Wilber: Vol. 7*. Boston: Shambhala.

Wild, J. (1940). The concept of *the given* in contemporary philosophy—Its origin and limitations. *Philosophy and Phenomenological Research, 1*(1), 70–82.

Williams, B. (1998). The end of explanation? *The New York Review of Books, XVL*(18), 40–44.

Williams, P. (1989). *Mahayana Buddhism: The doctrinal foundations*. New York: Routledge.

Wilson, B. (Ed.). (1970). *Rationality*. New York: Harper & Row.

Wittgenstein, L. (1968). *Philosophical investigations* (3rd ed.). (G. E. M. Anscombe, Trans.). New York: Macmillan.

Wittine, B. (1989). Basic postulates for a transpersonal psychotherapy. In R. S. Valle & S. Halling (Eds.), *Existential-phenomenological perspectives in psychology: Exploring the breadth of human experience* (pp. 269–287). New York: Plenum Press.

Woodroffe, J. G. (1919). *The serpent power*. Calcutta: Ganesh.

Wright, P. (1995). Bringing women's voices to transpersonal psychology. *ReVision, 17*(3), 3–10.

Yandell, K. E. (1993a). *The epistemology of religious experience*. New York: Cambridge University Press.

Yandell, K. E. (1993b). Some varieties of religious pluralism. In J. Kellenberger (Ed.), *Inter-religious models and criteria* (pp. 187–211). New York: St. Martin's Press.

Yensen, R., & Dryer, D. (1996). The consciousness research of Stanislav Grof. In B. W. Scotton, A. B. Chinen, & J. R. Battista (Eds.), *Textbook of transpersonal psychiatry and psychology* (pp. 75–84). New York: Basic Books.

Zaehner, R. C. (1957). *Mysticism sacred and profane: An inquiry into some varieties of preternatural experience*. New York: Oxford University Press.

Zaehner, R. C. (1960/1994). *Hindu and Muslim mysticism*. Rockport, MA: Oneworld.

Zaehner, R. C. (1970). *Concordant discord*. Oxford: Clarendon Press.

Zimmerman, M. (1998). A transpersonal diagnosis of the ecological crisis. In D. Rothberg & S. Kelly (Eds.), *Ken Wilber in dialogue: Conversations with leading transpersonal thinkers* (pp. 180–206). Wheaton, IL: Quest.

Zimmerman, R. L. (1987). The metaphysics of Claude Lévi-Strauss' structuralism: Two views. *International Philosophical Quarterly, 28*(2), 121–133.

Zinnbauer, B. J., Pargament, K. I., Cole, B., Rye, M. S., Butter, E. M., Belavich, T. G., Hipp, K. M., Scott, A. B., & Kadar, J. L. (1997). Religion and spirituality: Unfuzzying the fuzzy. *Journal for the Scientific Study of Religion, 36*(4), 549–564.

INDEX

Abhishiktananda, Swami, 105
The Absolute, 135
Absolute Consciousness, 81–82
Absolutism, 34, 87, 99, 188–189, 210n7;
   arguments for, 89; conflicting viewpoints
   and, 175; emptiness and, 102; exclusivist,
   178; inclusivist, 178; inconsistency with
   spiritual liberation, 176; nature of reality
   and, 103; pregiven spiritual ultimates in, 180;
   relativism and, 90; ultimate nature of, 93;
   untenability of, 176
Acts of the Apostles, 119
Adorno, Theodor W., 198n19, 210n7
Advaita Vedanta, 5, 6, 27, 74, 79fig, 89, 93, 102,
   103, 129, 145, 218n1; concept of
   experience in, 50–51; epistemology of, 48;
   experientialist emphasis in, 49;
   experimental basis of, 50–51; meditative
   practice and, 27
Agape, 128
Agnosticism, 45, 143
Ahumada, Jorge., 61
Alienation, 133; collective, xvii;
   epistemological, 213n17; existential, 127,
   213n17; individual, xvii; modern, 142;
   spiritual, 21, 127
Allah, 79fig
Almaas, A-Hammed Ali, 35, 198n20, 198n21
Almond, Philip C., 136
Alston, William P., 51
Amis, Robin, 125
Anarchy, 171; religious, xvii; spiritual, 152, 153,
   191
Anatman, 49, 63
Anderson, Rosemary, 44, 199n2
Anthony, Dick, 78, 203n17
Anthropocentrism, 28
Apophasis: mystical, 178, 223n9
Apophatic: language, 122, 180; modes of
   discourse, 206n2; mysticism, 220n17, 223n9
Armstrong, Karen, 209n1
Art, 52, 56
Asamprajñata samadhi, 74, 129
Asanga, 163
Asceticism, 214n23

Assagioli, Roberto, 6
Atman, 48, 103, 154, 201n12, 204n24
Augustine, M.J., 214n22
Aurobindo, Sri-, 6, 48, 82, 84
Avatar, 214n23
Avidya, 127
Awareness: of emptiness, 148; expanded, 11, 16;
   experiential, 51; liberated, 148; mystical, 91,
   171; phenomenal, 177, 212n12; selfless, 168;
   self-reflective, 173; of single spiritual
   ultimate, 177; spiritual, 65; transcendence of
   human and, 28
Ayahuasca, 120

Bache, Christopher M., 120, 178, 220-21n1
Bagger, Michael, 137
Bamford, G., 61
Barnard, G. William, 122, 146
Barnhart, J.E., 103
Barrett, S.R., 97
Barthes, Roland, 96
Barušs, Imants, 44
Baudrillard, Jean, 213n15
Bechtel, W., 61
Beck, D., 223n10
Beena, C., 170
Behaviorism, 212n8
Being: and-the-world, 64, 176; creativity of,
   157; degrees of, 103; Heidegger and, 6; in-
   the-world, 196n9; knowing and, 140;
   Mystery of, xiii, 134, 178; participation in
   spheres of, 28; self-disclosure of, 109; as self-
   presentation, 109; self-unfolding of, 166;
   source of, 143, 182; states of, 174;
   transpersonal, 116; unfolding of, 169
Belief(s): consensual, 166; diverse systems of,
   166; metaphysical, 200n13; mythical, 54, 55;
   mythical *vs.* dogmatic religious, 62; plurality
   of, 166; theistic, 51
Berman, Morris, 21
Bernard of Clairvaux, 209n17
Bernstein, Richard J., 21, 29, 97, 197n13,
   225–226n10
Between: ontological status of, 119; place of
   spiritual realization, 119; realm of, 119

Bhartrhari, 207n4, 218n1
Bhavanakrama, 163
Big Three, 24, 25, 52, 53, 55, 56; as
    Buddha/Dharma/Sangha, 26; as I/We/It, 26
Blavatsky, Madame, 74
Bodhisattvabhumi, 163
Bolle, Kees W., 127
Bordo, Susan, 21, 29
Borella, Jean, 74
Boucouvalas, Marcie, 43
Bouyer, Louis, 209n1
Bradley, F.H., 212n8
Bragdon, Emma, 37
Brahamasutrabhasya, 218n1
Brahmajñana, 103, 147
Brahman, 49, 77fig, 79fig, 81, 89, 102, 103, 127,
    129, 136, 145, 160, 201n12, 202n14
Brainard, F. Samuel, 194n2, 209n1
Braud, William, 44, 199n2
Bregman, L., 198n19
Brown, Daniel P., 137, 147, 163
Buber, Martin, 119, 218n4, 223n10
Buddha, 26, 137, 164; awakening of, 50;
    cosmic, 31
Buddhaghosa, B., 128, 147, 163
Buddhahood, 148
Buddha-nature, 49, 130, 148, 154
Buddhism, 77fig, 130, 178, 195n7, 218n1. See
    also Zen Buddhism; authority of claims in,
    49; counterculture influence of, 6; doctrine
    of no-self in, 63; egocentric perception in,
    214n22; focus on spiritual experience in, 17;
    grounding in universal experience, 17;
    hierarchies of spiritual insights in, 160; inner
    experience in, 129; liberation in, 130;
    Madhyamaka, 102, 220n17; Mahayana, 81,
    103, 104, 128, 145; meditative practice and,
    27, 30, 49; modernization of, 163; no-self
    doctrine, 102; peak-experiences and, 106;
    perfections in, 152; Shingon, 31; spiritual
    cocreation in, 154; Tantric, 147; Theravada,
    6, 63, 128, 129, 148, 161; Tibetan, 6, 49, 150,
    161, 199n23, 208n15; Vajrayana, 31;
    Westernized, 129, 163
Buddhist studies: attainment of liberation in, 50
Bullock, A., 18
Buswell, Robert E., 160, 161, 164, 165, 168
Byrne, Peter, 107, 176, 177

Caldwell, B.J., 61
Campbell, Joseph, 200n3
Candrakirti, 163
Caplan, Mariana, 35
Capra, Fritjof, 21, 29, 43

Caritas, 128
Carlson, T.A., 223n9
Carmody, Denise L. and John T., 135, 197n14
Carpenter, David, 109, 207n4
Carr, Karen L., 213n17
Cartesian: dualism, 21; ego, xviii, 11, 149;
    epistemology, 109; model of cognition, 33,
    109; model of knowledge, 11; philosophy of
    consciousness, 29; pseudoproblems, 2
Cartesian Anxiety, 2, 21, 29, 197n13
Cartesianism. See also Subtle Cartesianism;
    association with various maladies, 21;
    challenges to, 29; dismantling, 131; gap
    between subject and object in, 11;
    limitations of, 29; model of cognition, 122,
    131; model of knowledge, 29; modern focus
    on, ix; narcissism and, 36, 198n22;
    perennialism and, 90, 91, 138–140;
    perpetuation of, 33; subject/object gap, 142;
    subject-object model of cognition and, 28;
    transpersonal phenomena and, 33;
    transpersonal theory and, 28–34, 43, 109
Cartesian-Kantian paradigm, 151–155, 166,
    176
Catholicism, 21
Caws, Peter, 96, 97, 100, 203n17
Chakras, 85
Chalmers, Alan F., 56, 58
Chaudhuri, Haridas, 6, 48
Chinchore, M.R., 93
Chirban, John T., 121
Chittick, William C., 128, 209n17
Chomsky, Noam, 96, 97, 100–101, 102,
    201n12, 203n17, 203n20
Christian, W.A., 165
Christianity, 77fig, 79fig, 103, 130, 160;
    constrictions of, x; decline of, xvii;
    disengagement of self from, ix; dogmatic
    forms, 204n22; Eastern Orthodox, 121;
    egocentric perception in, 214n22;
    meditative practice and, 27; mysticism and,
    68, 69, 81, 104, 128; religious imagination
    and, ix; saintly virtues in, 152; spiritual
    events in, 119
Cioffi, F., 61
Clarke, J.J., 45, 48, 65, 74, 78, 107
Cobb, John, 219n10
Cocreation: of divine unfolding, 154; partici-
    patory, xv; spiritual, 154; visionary, 12, 121
Cocreative participation, xiii, 121, 127, 133, 177
Cognition, 173; Cartesian model of, 33, 109,
    122, 131, 187; contemplative models, 11;
    creative element of, 140; enactive paradigm
    of, 99, 123, 139; objects of, 34; represen-

tational paradigm of, 29, 59, 139; subject-object model, 28, 198n18; transconceptual, 146, 149; transpersonal, 34; vision-logic, 25, 197n12
Collins, J., 73
Comans, Michael, 105
Confucianism, 161; peak-experiences and, 106
Consciousness: altered states of, 20, 46–47, 199n1; Cartesian philosophy of, 29; consciousness of, 204n24; cosmological estrangement of, 142; creation and, 83; of emptiness, 146; evolution of, 31; expansion of, 9; exploration of, 51; extension of, 16; Great Holoarchy of Being and, 96; higher, 36; human, 32, 109; individual, 3, 9, 120; innermost, 32; interest in, 6; modification, 216n32; multilocal transpersonal events and, 3; narcissistic modes, 36; noetic, 209n17; nonordinary states of, 150; overcoming epistemological constraints in, 45; participation in transfiguration of world, 109; participatory account of research in, 149–151; powers of, 82; psychology of, 6; reality as, 48; research in, xii, 72, 210n4; science of, 69; special states, 80; spiritual, 37; states of, 15, 33; structures of, 96; technologies of, 149; traditional spiritual shores in, 149; transcendent ground of, 197n15; witness, 30, 196n9
Consciousness Force, 82
Constructivism, 84, 210n7; experiential, 212n13; genetic, 201n12; radical, 139
Contemplation: foundation for, 27
Contemplative knowing, 181
Contemplative traditions, 5, 6. See also Mystical traditions; common ground in, 136; consensus about the nature of reality in, 52; deep structures of, 99; empiricist readings of, 50–51; falsifiability and, 63; goals of, 127, 128, 145; homogeneity of message of, 74–75; ideals and, 6; impact of Western thought on, 50–51; inner empiricism and, 49; insights of, 64–65; issues debated, 93; mystical insight and, 49; participation in states of discernment in, 64; projection of Western notions on Eastern, 102; reality and, 75; spiritual goals of, 126; surface structures in, 85; transpersonal phenomena and, 126; universal spiritual reality and, 89
Contextualism, 134–144, 210n7; frameworks and, 165; mysticism and, 171; nature of spiritual knowledge and, 156; Neo-Kantian roots of, 140–144; partial truth of, 151, 156; perennialism and, 138–144

Coomaraswamy, Ananda K., 74, 88
Corless, Roger J., 65
Cortright, Brant, 105
Cosmology: involutionary, 75, 84; Jain, 83; perennialist, 93
Cosmos: foundation of, 75; understanding, 8
Cox, C., 129, 203n17
Crossan, J.D., 203n17
Cryptoamnesia, 216n32
Cupitt, Don, 140
Curd, M., 60
Cutsinger, James S., 87, 94

Dalai Lama, H.H., 65–66, 145, 147, 148, 161, 170
Damasio, A., 21
Davidson, Donald, 59, 139, 141–142, 213n15, 213n16
Davidson, L., 18
Dean, Thomas, 88, 107, 170
de Chardin, Teilhard, 84
Defense mechanisms: projection, 31
Deikman, Arthur, 137
Derrida, Jacques, 97, 102
de Saussure, Ferdinand, 96, 100, 201n12
Descartes, René, 21, 142, 143, 198n22
Deutsch, Elliot, 107
Devekut, 103, 153
Development: of compassion, 128; dynamics of, 30; personal, 30; psychospiritual, 196n9; scientific, 106; of transpersonal field, 107; transpersonal models, 162–165, 197n15
Dharana, 27
Dharma, 26, 147
Dharmakaya, 67, 81, 154, 202n14
Dharmakirti, 50, 163, 199n10
Dhyana, 27, 58
Dialogue. See also Interreligious dialogue; authentic, 175; monastic, 201n11
Dionysius the Areopagite, 217n37
Dissociation, 25
Diversity, 145–146; of spiritual claims, 147
Divine: becoming, 154; conventional view of, 153; human relationship with, 153; incarnation of, 214n23; nature of, 153; reality, 174; realization of, 171; self-expression, 153; theories about, 178
Divine Play, 82
Dogen, 148, 223n10
Dogmatism, 20, 54, 60, 64, 103, 109; in perennialism, 92–95
Doore, Gary, 51
Dualism: Cartesian, 21; epistemological, 181; reality and, 172

Dualism of Framework and Reality, 141, 143, 156, 157, 172, 213n15, 214n21
Duhem, Pierre, 61, 89
Duhem-Quine principle, 61, 89
Dumézil, Georges, 203n17
Dupré, Louis, 137, 153, 154, 204n23, 209n1, 215n29
Dzogchen, 148

Eastern traditions: interest in, x, xvii
Eckhart, Meister, 137, 223n9
Ego: Cartesian, xviii, 11, 149; defining, 196n9; inflation, 35; relation to Dynamic Ground, 197n15; sovereignty, 125
Egocentrism: truth and, 168
Eliade, Mircea, xviii, 78, 120, 203n17
Emanation: doctrine of, 207n4
Emotion: role in human inquiry, 59
Empiricism, 142; broad, 53, 54, 55; defining, 44; expanded, 27; experiential, 44; intra-subjective, xiii, 8; radical, 6, 50, 51, 221n4; religious, 199n5; sensory, 66–69; standards of, 42; stretched, 50; testing principles, x; total, 48; traditional, 29, 42; two dogmas of, 139; validation and, x, 29
Empowerment, 30
Emptiness, 74, 81, 102, 103, 130. See also Sunyata; achievement of, 148; of the aggregates, 148; awareness of, 148; consciousness of, 146; of emptiness, 148; incomplete, 161; of the person, 148; as preliminary, 161; transformation of, 102
Enaction(s): of a dynamic/indeterminate spiritual power, 150, 156; of a world, 122–123; of reality, 169, 177; of spiritual data, 64; of spiritual doctrines, 164; of spiritual insights, 147, 149; of spiritual shores, 149, 150–152, 160; of spiritual ultimates, 4, 147, 151, 157, 165; of spiritual universes, 148; of the world, 213n16; of transconceptual disclosures of reality, 149, 165; of transpersonal forms, 151; of ultimate reality, 216n30; validity of spiritual, 152, 169
Enactive: nature of spiritual knowing, 151; nature of spiritual truth, xiii; participatory knowing as, 122; transpersonal knowing as, 124; transpersonal phenomena as, 122, 123
Enactive codes: meditative maps as, 164–165
Enactive paradigm of cognition, 139, 202n12, 207n8; participatory vision and, 122; Wilber and, 99, 154–155, 207–208n9
Enlightenment, xiii, xv, 17, 143, 204n22; rationalism and, x; universal truth of objective reality and, x

Entheogens, 109, 149
Enthymesis, 30, 31, 197n14, 212n13
Epistemology: Advaita Vedanta, 48; Cartesian, 109; contemporary, 10; emancipatory, 182; experiential, 44–46; feminist, 139; hierarchical, 75, 76; indigenous, 139; modern, 156, 173; Neo-Kantian, 45, 140; objectivist, 90–91; participatory, 122, 139, 155, 173; perennialist, 90–91; postmodern, 156; pragmatist, 219n11; religious, 10; spiritual, 159; subjective, 20, 69; transpersonal, 8–9, 10; Western, 10
Epstein, Mark, 196n9, 198n20, 215n24
Eriugena, 180
Esotericism, 19; dogma and, 93; sapiential, 89; Western, 6, 130, 209n17
Essentialism, 100; perennialism and, 91–92, 137–138, 182
Ethics, 17
Evans, Donald, 34, 35, 36, 122, 136, 137, 143, 214n22
Evidence: falsifiable, 62; psychedelic, 217n34; sensory, 53, 56; underdetermination of theory by, 61, 89
Evolution, 54, 62, 83, 95, 99, 152; constraints on, 102; cosmic, 7; creative power of, 102; integral theory of, 207n9; spiritual, 82, 102, 155; teleological, 84, 155; tracing, 84
Exclusivism, 94, 218n7; dogmatic, 165
Existence: of God, 48, 51, 174; of God archetype, 45; human, 7; legitimating spiritual dimension of, ix; Mystery of, xiii, 145; psyche's commensurability with, 80; spiritual depths of, 7; transformation of, 214n22; transmigratory, 127; transpersonal dimensions of, 5–6
Existentialism, 91
Experiences: collection of, 38; core-religious, 19, 106, 109; direct, x; dualism with knowledge, 125; enlightened, 208n15; epistemological value of, 18; as foundation of all religions, 50; human, ix, viii, 28, 44, 46; immediate, 138, 200n13; individual, ix, xix, xviii, 1, 11, 12, 15, 16, 17, 22, 26, 34, 38, 39, 181; inner, xix, 1, 11, 12, 15, 17, 18, 20, 22, 26, 27, 34, 36, 42, 45, 143, 181, 195n8, 221n4; integration into everyday life, 15; interpretation of, 50, 137; intrasubjective, ix, 2, 8, 12, 15, 116, 118, 129; lived, 6; medita-tive, 127, 163; mental, 53, 54, 55; modern notion of, 116; monistic, 218n4; mono-logical, 198n17; mystical, xi, 45, 50–51, 74, 88, 127, 135, 136, 137, 141, 143, 154, 171–172, 197n15, 201n8, 204n23, 204n24,

206n2, 210n5; near-death, 125; nondual, 129; nonintentional, 206n2; numinous, 51; out-of-body, 85; paranormal, 50; peak, 19; personal, 50, 218n6; private, ix, 181, 187; psychedelic, ix; pure, 91, 210n5; pure consciousness, 136, 137; religious, 17, 200n13; sensory, 47, 53, 54, 55; spiritual, 89, 163, 208n16; spiritual realities beyond, 28; subjective, xviii, 1, 20, 22, 25, 52, 56; subjective/objective boundaries of, 31; transcendental, 51, 106; transient, 125; transpersonal, 9, 11, 43, 198n17; understanding, 194n1; unmediated, 171–172

Experiential: awareness, 51; epistemology, 44–46; events, 118; perennialism, 109

Experientialism, 1, 4, 181, 223n9; individual inner experiences and, 2; integral, 48; intrasubjective reductionism and, 181; narcissistic pitfalls of, 198n19; nature of knowledge in, 9; social reform and, 195n8; spiritual narcissism and, 181; Subtle Cartesianism and, 181

Experiential vision: fundamental problems of, 21–38; historical source of, 17–18; humanistic origins of transpersonal orientation and, 18–20; of human spirituality, 15–39; integrative arrestment and, 37–38, 125; limitations of, 21–38; methodological source of, 20–21; nature of, 15–16; origins of, 17–21; peak-experiences and, 195n6; perennial philosophy and, 106–110; philosophical source of, 18–20; relation to participatory vision, 186–188; roots in modern conceptualization of Western spirituality, 17; spiritual narcissism and, 36; transpersonal orientation and, 39; transpersonal phenomena and, 16, 28; validity of, 20–21, 187

Eye of the Heart, 87, 90

Faith: defining, 88; as "yes" to the One, 88

Faivre, Antoine, 74

Fallibilism, 68

Falsifiability, 42; contemplative traditions and, 63; current inapplicability of, 61; as demarcation between science and pseudoscience, 61–62; Duhem-Quine principle and, 61; as hallmark of knowledge, 60; implausibility in spiritual matters, 60; introduction of auxiliary hypotheses and, 60; of knowledge, 54; myth of, 62; Popper's principle of, 54, 60, 67, 68; refutation of theories and, 61; in religion, 62–65; in science, 60–62; shortcomings of, 60–62; spiritual experience and, 63; spiritual science

and, 57; as standard for knowledge, 27; structuralism and, 97; through direct contemplation, 48; of transpersonal knowledge, 43

Faure, Bernard, 130, 163

Fay, Brian, 61

Feminism, 29, 65, 139; inner empiricism and, 51

Fenton, John Y., 137, 146

Feyerabend, Paul, 60

Ficino, Marsilio, 73

Fontana, David, 49

Forman, Robert K.C., 136, 137, 172, 198n18, 204n24, 206n2, 209n1, 210n3

Fort, A.O., 50

Foucault, Michel, 96, 97, 100, 201n12

Four Quadrant Model, 24, 25, 26, 212n11

Frakenberry, Nancy, 51

Frank, M., 102

Freud, Sigmund, 6

Frohlich, Mary, 197n15

Fromm, Erich, 6

Funk, Joel, 7

Gadamer, Hans-Georg, 57, 58, 61, 67, 109, 139, 173, 207n4, 222n8

Gardner, Howard, 96, 97

Garfield, J., 103

Gatens-Robinson, E., 61

Gelpi, Donald L., 214n19

Gendlin, Eugene T., 198n19

Gill, Jerry H., 198n18

Gimello, Robert M., 137, 141, 160, 161, 164, 165, 168

Gnosis, 58, 74, 76, 87, 103, 125, 217n37

Gnosticism, 6, 209n17

God, 77fig, 135, 136, 202n14; belief in, 160; cleaving to, 153; communion with, 119, 166; existence of, 45, 48, 51, 174; in future, 84; I-Thou relationship with, 218n4; knowledge of, 45, 122, 128, 209n17; love for, 128, 153; loving presence of, 145; mystical insight of, 49; personal, 81; transformation of, 153; union of human soul with, 117

Godhead, 79fig, 82, 89, 103

Godlove, Terry, 213n15

Goldstein, Joseph, 6

Goleman, Daniel, 163

Goodman, Nelson, 59, 139, 210n7, 213n15

Graves, Clare, 223n10

Great Chain of Being, 52, 54, 62, 63, 65, 66, 72, 75, 95, 96, 97, 102, 103, 106, 202n13, 203n15, 203n19

Great Holoarchy of Being, 96

Griffiths, Paul J., 65, 75, 128, 165

Grinshpon, Y., 50

Grof, Stanislav, viii, xi, xv, 5, 6, 16, 18, 21, 29, 32, 37, 72, 78, 80–83, 88, 89, 120, 122, 149–151, 193n1, 194n2, 198n17, 201n8, 210n4, 216n32, 217n34

Ground of Being, 44, 74, 78, 81, 89, 135, 156

Guénon, René, 74, 88

Gyatso, Janet, 208n15

Haas, Alois M., 209n1

Habermas, Jürgen, 17, 22, 24, 25, 52, 57, 58, 97, 100, 123, 191, 197n10, 197n11, 210n7

Halbfass, Wilhelm, 18, 50, 160, 163

Hales, S.D., 210n7

Halifax, Joan, 120

Hanegraaff, Wouter J., 19, 92, 94

Hanh, Tich Nath, 223n10

Harland, Richard, 99

Harman, Willis, 29, 51, 72, 122

Harvey, Peter, 129

Hausman, D.M., 61

Hayes, Richard P., 50, 102, 163, 199n10

Hayward, Jeremy H., 49

Heard, Gerald, 48

Heidegger, Martin, 6

Heim, S. Mark, 65, 107, 166, 215n27, 218n7, 219n8

Hermeneutics, xii, 65, 139; cognition in, 140; of discovery, 173; East–West, 107; experience of truth and, 58; of the heart, 173; knowledge in, 140; perennialist, 88; spiritual, 166; structuralism and, 102–103; of suspicion, 173; transpersonal, 181

Hermeticism, 6, 209n17

Heron, John, 58, 102, 138, 151, 152–155, 172

Hick, John, 78, 135, 165, 212n12, 214n21, 214n22, 215n27, 215n29, 218n7

Hierarchical gradations, 160, 165

Hierarchy: construction of, 164; of deep structures, 78, 85; of forms of knowledge, 209n17; of levels of reality, 88, 96; of levels of spiritual insight, 78, 92, 160; of mystical experiences, xi, 161; of religious tradition, xi; transpersonal theory and, xi

Hillman, James, 220n1

Hinduism, 77fig, 79fig, 81, 82, 102, 130, 136, 216n32; concept of experience in, 50–51; counterculture influence of, 6; empirical foundations of, 48; experiential emphasis in, 17–18; experimental basis of, 50–51; four yogas of, 170; mysticism in, 105; personal experience and, 50; renaissance in, 163;

spiritual gradations in, 160; Western empiricism and, 18

Hoffman, Frank J., 50

Holdrege, Barbara, 207n6

Hollenback, Jess Byron, 30, 128, 137, 197n14, 212n13

Hollis, M., 61

Hopkins, T.J., 127

Hoy, David-Couzens, 222n7, 226n10

Hua-Yen, 148, 161

Humanism, ix; peak-experiences and, 106

Human nature: essential information on, 41; spirit as essence of, 7; spiritual tradition and, 7, 71; transpersonal dimensions of, 5–6; transpersonal theory and, 7; understanding, 8

Hunt, Harry T., 16

Hutchins, R., 71, 72

Huxley, Aldous, 48, 74, 76, 81, 135, 201n9, 214n23

Ibn al-'Arabi, 128

Idealism: absolute, 212n8; German, 53; ontological, 48

Ideals: contemplative, 6

Idel, Moshe, 153, 206n2, 217n37

Identity: collective, 178; conscious, 120; deep, xviii; extension of sense of, 16; of God's own life, 153; ontological, 146; personal, xviii, 196n9; phenomenological, 146; realization of, 171; self, 32, 196n9; subjective/objective, 90; transpersonal phenomena and, 16

Ihde, D., 29

Imagination: empowered, 197n14; of mystics, 31; psychological, 41; religious, ix

Impersonalism, 123

Inclusivism, 218n7; hierarchical, 165

Indich, W.M., 128

Individual: sovereignty of, ix; spirituality and, 28

Individualism: competitive, 34

Ingram, Paul O., 214n22

Inner empiricism, 2, 3, 20, 69, 70, 181; allusions to, 43; broad, 47–48; of Buddhism, 129; contemplative traditions and, 49; experiential epistemology, 44–46; fundamental problems of, 51–69; influence of, 43; nature of, 42–44; origins, 42–44; peak-experiences and, 46; spiritual insight and, 43; spirituality and, 119; spiritual knowledge and, 108; state-specific science and, 46–47; transpersonal phenomena and, 109; transpersonal psychology's commitment

to, ix; transpersonal theory and, 44; varieties of, 44–51
Insight: causal, 78; compassion-raising, 145; contemplative, 62, 64–65; into eternal self, 129; heretical, 137; mystical, 141; nondual, 78, 94; participation in spiritual states of, 129; psychic, 78; spiritual, 43, 63, 68, 125, 133, 146, 149, 150, 153, 160, 162, 208n15; subtle, 78; universal, 172
Integration, 25
Integrative arrestment, 36–38, 184; experiential vision and, 37–38
Intellect, 87, 88, 90
Intentionality, 25
Interiorization, 198n19
International Transpersonal Association, xi
Interreligious dialogue, xii, 10, 65, 87, 95, 107, 152, 170, 180, 201n11
Intrasubjective reductionism, 22–28, 33–34, 36, 131, 221n4; experientialism and, 181; participatory turn and, 124; participatory vision and, 117
Intuition: metaphysical, 87, 88, 93; of objective truth, 214n19; spiritual, 93; structuralism and, 97; universal, 87
Involution, 51, 75, 82, 83, 89, 95, 202n14
Irrationalism, 171
Irwin, Lee, 166, 170
Isherwood, Christopher, 48
Islam, 130, 160
Isolation, 128, 129; tanks, 20
I/We/It, 52, 53, 59

Jacoby, Russel, 35, 198n19
Jaggar, Alison M., 59
Jainism, 83
Jakobson, Roman, 96
James, William, viii, 6, 8, 51, 127, 146, 167, 199n5, 219n11, 221n4
Jantzen, Graze M., 138
Jaspers, Karl, 73
Jayatilleke, K.N., 50
Jesse, Robert, 216n32
Jhanas, 128
Jñana, 50
Johnston, William, 119
Jones, Richard H., 137, 198n18
Judaeo-Christian tradition: antagonism toward, x; Western legacy of, x
Judaism, 130, 145
Jujushin, 161
Jung, Carl Gustav, viii, 6, 19, 44–46, 78, 193n1, 195n7, 220n1

Justification: of spiritual claims, 27; of transpersonal knowledge, 10

Kabbalah, 6, 31, 81, 103, 150, 153, 217n37
Kaivalyam, 128, 129
Kalansuriya, A.D., 50
Kalupahana, David J., 50
Kamalasila, 163
Kant, Immanuel, 142, 143, 213n15
Kasulis, Thomas P., 31, 161
Katz, Steven, 136, 137, 138, 141, 172, 198n18, 210n3, 212n14
Keiji, Nishitani, 129
Keller, Evelyn Fox, 59
Kelly, Sean, 7, 203n19
Kieckhefer, R., 214n23
Kitaro, Nishida, 17, 129, 163
Kitcher, P., 61, 62
Klee, Robert, 60
Klein, Anne, 27, 49, 137, 199n23
Knitter, Paul F., 107
Knowledge/knowing, 55. See also Transpersonal knowledge; acquisition, 57; being and, 140; beyond ordinary time-space limitations, 16; of Brahman, 129; Buddhist theories, 199n10; Cartesian model, 11, 29; coherence with the Mystery, 169; contemplative, 181; dogmatic, 54, 68; dualism with experiences, 125; emotional, 121; empirical, 56, 76; essential, 76; experiential, 12, 44–45; genuine, 54, 68; of God, 122, 128, 209n17; of the heart, 121; of higher realms of hierarchical ontology, 76; intuitive, 87, 90, 209n17; liberation and, 128; matched with pregiven reality, 169; metaphysical, 209n17; of the mind, 121; moral dimensions of, 90; mystical, 127, 135, 172, 177, 197n14; of nature of self, 9; objective, 17, 52, 90, 91, 109; participatory, 143, 181, 186, 194n12; during peak-experiences, 46; by presence, 122; questions on claims of, 11; rational, 76; reduction to sensory evidence, 53, 56; relativist, 210n7; sacred, 63; sources of, 54; of Spirit, 76; state-specific, 46–47; subject-object model of, 28; tentativeness of, 68; testing, 47–48; three eyes of, 58–59; transcendental, 48; transpersonal, 8, 9, 10, 42; universal standards for, 56; valid, 17, 49, 53, 58, 65, 66–69, 109, 140; value of religion for, 195n3
Koran, 160
Kornfield, Jack, 6
Kosmos, 25, 53, 55; universal aspects of, 99

Krishnamurti, Jiddu, 157
Kuhn, Thomas, 52, 53, 57, 59, 60, 65, 68, 139, 199n8
Kukai, 31, 161
Kumarila,, 218n1
Kundalini, 85, 102
Kyoto school, 163

Lacan, Jacques, 96
Lajoie, D.H., 16
Lakatos, Imre, 61
Lakoff, George, 29, 34
Lam rim chen mo, 163
Lane, M., 102
Language: apophatic, 122, 180; of disontology, 180; experiential, 130; objectivist, 198n16; phenomenological, 198n16; structures of, 201n12; theories of, 201n12; translatability of, 141; universal organization of, 201n12
Lasch, Christopher, 34, 198n19
Laudan, Larry, 62
Laughlin, Charles D., 51, 78
Lawson, A.E., 61
Leach, E., 96, 97
Leder, D., 21
Levin, David Michael, 16, 21, 33, 198n16, 198n22
Lévi-Strauss, Claude, 96, 97, 201n12
Liberation, 27. See also Spiritual liberation; Buddhist, 50; knowledge and, 128
Lila, 82
Lindbeck, George A, 213n15
Linguistics, 29, 96, 97, 201n12
Loemker, L.E., 73
Logos, 125
Lopez, Donald S., 218n6
Loy, David, 215n26
Lukoff, David, 209n1
Luminous Presence, 148
Luria, Isaac, 137
Lynch, M.P., 210n7

McClintock, Barbara, 199n9
McGinn, Bernard, 27, 128, 153, 199n23
MacIntyre, Alasdair, 210n7, 222n8
Macy, Joanna, 11
Madhyamika, 161
Maharishi Mahesh Yogi, 6
Mahavakyas, 48
Margolis, Joseph, 210n7
Marsh, J.L., 21, 29
Maslow, Abraham, viii, xv, 5, 6, 18, 19, 20, 21, 28, 37, 46, 72, 106, 108, 109, 110, 193n1, 195n6, 195n8. See also Peak-experience

Materialism, 8; spiritual, 34, 35
Maturana, Humberto R., 123
Maya, 83
Mayeda, S., 129
Mediation: Dualism of Framework and Reality and, 172; epistemic, 2, 34, 198n18; mysticism and, 197n15; participation in self-disclosure of world and, 173; in spiritual knowledge, 159, 171–174; strong thesis of, 135, 141, 150, 210n4; between subject and object, 198n18; weak thesis of, 210n4
Meditation, 11, 20, 25; Buddhist, 30, 49; detached attitude in, 30; foundation for, 27; paths of, 147; as process of deautomatization, 136–137; scriptural foundation of manuals, 163; stages of, 164
Meditative maps, 162–165
Meditative practices, 64
Mendes-Flohr, Paul, 119
Merkur, Daniel, 217n34
Merton, Thomas, 200n3
Metamotivation, 6
Metaphysics, 6; Enlightenment critiques, 17, 143; issues debated, 93; modern deflation of, 197n10; monistic, 89–90, 94; narcissism and, 198n22; pluralist, 219n11
Metzner, Ralph, 216n32
Mill, John Stuart, 44
Miller, M.E., 16
Min, A.K., 107
Minism, 80
Mishra, K., 48
Mitchell, D.W., 66
Mizvot, 153
Modernity: alienation and, xvii; differentiations of, 52, 55; difficulties of, 57; features of, 17; focus on individual Cartesian subject, ix; fragmentation in, 24, 42, 56, 57, 70; Great Chain of Being and, 52; remediation of problems of, 25; scientific discourse of, xvii
Moksa, 27, 127, 129, 148, 218n4
Monasticism, 214n23
Monism, 56, 82, 94; methodological, 67; nondual, 160
Moore, Peter, 137, 150
Morality, 52, 56
Müller, Max, 78, 200n13
Murphy, Michael, 49, 51
Murti, T.R.V., 102
Mutkananda, Swami, 6
Mystery, 34, 170, 174, 182, 214n22; affirmation of, xiii; of Being, xiii, 134, 178; contact with, 169; of existence, xiii, 145; as source of all, xiv; from which all arises, 4

Mystical practices: Asian, x; encounter with, x
Mystical traditions, 5. *See also* Contemplative traditions
Mysticism, 6, 30, 85, 135–138, 194n2; apophatic, 180, 223n9; causal, 85; Christian, 6, 68, 69, 81, 104, 128, 130, 153, 199n23, 217n37; claims of, 171; cognitive value of, 75; comparative, xii, 10, 76–80, 107, 178, 181; conservatism of, 141; contextualism and, 171, 210n5; defining, 135; deity, 85; describing, 209n17; experiental, 53, 223n9; "family resemblance" in, 215n29; formless, 85; as form of presence-knowledge, 209n17; goals in, 78; Hindu, 105; interpretation of, 74; Islamic, 130; Jewish, 130, 217n37; knowledge and, 127; as "meaning event," 206n2; mediation and, 197n15; monastic, 199n23; nature, 32, 85, 102, 109; Neo-Hindu, 6; Neoplatonic, 217n37; nondual, 218n4; objectifying contents of subjective space in, 31; origin, 209n1; paths in, 78; Platonic, 103; postmodern, 140; psychic, 85; radical contextuality of, 137; of secondarieness, 140; structuralist accounts of, 78; subtle, 85; unity of, 109, 111, 138; universality of, 90, 217n34
Myth: unfalsifiable, 54
Myth of the Framework, 144, 157, 214n21, 217n34; defining, 156; participatory vision and, 141; in religious studies, 141
Myth of the Given, 151, 157, 212n8, 212n11, 213n15, 213n16, 214n21, 215n27; defining, 156; disposition of, 139; perennialism and, 138, 145; rejection of, 176; in religious studies, 138, 139, 142, 143, 162

Nagarjuna, 102, 103, 148, 178
Nagel, Thomas, 167
Nagy, Marilyn, 45
Narcissism. *See also* self-centeredness; Spiritual narcissism; appropriation of, 2; Cartesianism and, 36, 198n22; culture of, 52; egocentric, 24; experiential, 195n8; metaphysics and, 198n22; normal, 198n20; opposition to spirituality, 36; overcoming, 170; pathological, 198n19, 198n20; peak-experiences and, 195n8; self-realization and, 198n21; unnecessary, 198n20; withdrawal from responsibility and, 198n19
Naropa Institute, 6
Nasr, Seyyed Hossein, 75, 78, 88, 90, 92, 127
Needleman, Jacob, 43, 174
Negoita, C.V., 210n7
Nelson, Peter L., 44, 51

Neo-Advaitin philosophy, 72
Neo-Hinduism, 18, 50, 201n9, 204n22
Neo-Kantian, 45, 140–144
Neoperennialism, 72, 83–86, 95–105, 205n25
Neoplatonism, 6, 65, 73, 89, 103, 203n15, 207n4
Neo-Positivism of Vienna, 58
Neovedanta, 65
Newton, Isaac, 60–61
Nietzsche, Friedrich, 195n3
Nihilism, 53, 99; emptiness and, 102; existential, 213n17; modern, 213n17; nature of reality and, 103
Nirmanakaya, 67
Nirodhasamapatti, 128
Nirvana, 77fig, 79fig, 127, 129, 136, 147, 166
Nirvikalpa samadhi, 129
Niyama, 27
Nominalism, 214n19
Nondualism, 147, 201n12; insight into, 94; of Sankara, 92
Nonduality, 218n4
Non-violence, 27
Normativity: epistemic, 11
Nothingness, 33, 85
The Noumenal, 135, 203n17; reality, 162
Noumenon: phenomenon and, 88
Nuernberger, P., 48
Nyanaponika Thera, 30
Nyaya school, 160

Objective/objectivism, 210n7; becoming subjective, 30, 31, 32; demarcation from subjective/subjectivity, 33; myths of, 34; nature of, 90; pregiven spiritual ultimates in, 180; reality, 32; relativism and, 29; residual, 99; subtle, 98–99; transition to subjective, 30; transpersonal theory and, 2; truth and, 59
Observation: neutral nature of, 139
Ocean of Emancipation, 4, 144–149, 156; entry into, 146; many shores of, 147; trans-conceptual disclosure of reality and, 145
O'Donovan-Anderson, M., 21, 29
O'Hear, A., 60
Olds, Linda E., 51
O'Leary, J.S., 215n29
Olsen, W.S., 120
Ontology: hierarchical, 75; modern epistemology and, 173; participatory knowing and, 122; phemenology and, 177; pluralistic, 199n2; of spirituality, x, xi; valid, 170; Western dialectical, 171
Orange, D.M., 61

Otto, Rudolph, 80
Outhwaite, W., 61

Panikkar, Raimon, 157, 167, 171, 173, 174, 176, 210*n7*, 215*n30*, 218*n7*, 219*n11*
Paramitas, 152
Paranjpe, A.C., 48, 50
Parrinder, Geoffrey, 214*n23*
Participation: cocreative, 121, 133, 177; in self-disclosure of Spirit, 121
Participatory: account of consciousness research, 149–151; emancipation of spirituality, 178; epistemology, 155; knowledge/knowing, 181, 182; meanings of, 120–121; ontological predicament of human beings, 121; role of individual consciousness in, 121
Participatory events, 206*n2*; enaction and, 123; in epistemic terms, 12; in experiential terms, 12; transpersonal phenomena as, 2, 3
Participatory knowing: access to reality and, 3; enactive, 123; nature of, 121–124; presential, 122; spiritual quest and, 126–131; transformative, 123–124
Participatory turn, 181; emancipatory value of, 124–126; integrative arrestment and, 125; intrasubjective reductionism and, 124; religious rankings and, 159–162; spiritual narcissism and, 125; subtle Cartesianism and, 124–125
Participatory vision, 2, 151, 181, 215*n25*, 221*n4*; acceptability of, 175; accessibility of, 150; claims of, 180; egoic appropriation of spirituality, 125; epistemic features of, 115–131; honoring diversity of spiritual tradition, 180; of human spirituality, 182; interreligious dialogue and, 180–181; interreligious relations and, 159–181; intrasubjective dimension, 186; intrasubjective reductionism and, 117; of knowledge, 143; mystical claims and, 208*n11*; Myth of the Framework and, 141; origins of, 9–12; of reality, 143; recognition of creativity of spirit in, 180; relation to experiential vision, 186–188; self-contradictory nature of, 180; situating, 187; of spirituality, 156; spiritual universalism of, 189–191; tension with the mystical, 176; transpersonal world and, 194*n7*; validity of, 187
Patañjali, 27, 50, 74, 128, 129, 147, 160
Patriarchy, 59
Peak-experiences, 6, 18, 106, 109; cognitive element in, 46; core-religious experience and, 19, 106; experiential vision and, 195*n6*;

inner empiricism and, 46; knowledge gained during, 46; narcissism and, 195*n8*; nature of, 195*n6*; plateau-experiences and, 37; as secularized spiritual phenomena, 38; spiritual experiences as, 27; spiritual realizations and, 38; traps of seeking, 195*n8*; typological, 80
Peirce, Charles Sanders, 212*n8*
Penner, Hans H., 203n17
Pentecost, 119
Perennialism, 67, 68, 181; alternatives to, 134–138; as an a priori philosophical stance, 87–89; basic, 76, 77*fig*; Cartesianism and, 90, 91, 138–140; common core of spirituality and, 3, 107; common goal in all traditions, 76; contextualism and, 138–144; deep structures of, 78, 95–105; dogmatism in, 92–95; esotericist, 76–77, 81; essentialism and, 91–92, 137–138; evolutionary, 84; experiential, 109; Grof and, 80–83; intolerance in, 92–95; mysticism and, 74, 85, 135–138; Myth of the Given and, 145; Neo-Hindu, 204*n22*; Neo-Kantian, 212*n12*; New Age, 94; as objectivist epistemology, 86, 90–91; partial truth of, 151, 156; perspectivist, 78–79, 79*fig*, 81; popularity of, 200*n3*; privileging of nondual monistic metaphysic, 89–90; spiritual insights and, 133; spiritual universalism and, 71; structuralist, 78, 79*fig*; traditional, 76, 87–95; transpersonal theory and, 195*n6*, 201*n9*; ultimate nature of reality in, 74; universal values of, 2; validitation of, 201*n8*; varieties of, 76–80; Wilber and, 83–86
Perennial philosophy: articulations of, 73–76; assessing truth of, 88; association with transpersonal theory, 72; common core of spirituality in, 87, 107; conflicting information in, 94; defense of, 89, 95; defining, 73; doctrinal core of, 75; experiential vision and, 108–110; Eye of the Heart and, 87; mystical version of, 75; Neo-Advaitin, 32, 80–83; neoperennialism, 72, 83–86, 95–105; problems with, 86–110; psychological presentation of, 72; revisitation of, 71–80; roots of transpersonal perspective in, 72; single Truth of, 74; support for, 72; transpersonal theory and, x, 105–108; universalist vision of, x, 84
Perovich, Anthony N. Jr., 90, 135, 137, 172, 198*n18*
Perspectivism, 210*n7*
Phenomena: intrinsic nature of, 55
Phenomenology: challenges to Cartesianism, 29; ontology and, 177; transcendental, 6

Phillips, S.H., 48
Philo of Alexandria, 73
Philosophy of science, 10
Piaget, Jean, 25, 201n12, 203n20
Plato, 6, 210n7
Pluralism, 181, 189–191, 210n7, 218n7, 223n10; doctrinal, 74; ecumenical, 165, 177, 178, 218n7; epistemological, 58; radical, 140; relation to universalism, 191; religious, 66, 215n27; of spiritual claims, 140
Pneuma, 81
Polkinghorne, Donald, 57, 58
Popper, Karl, 52, 53, 54, 57, 60, 62, 65, 67, 68, 141
Positivism, viii, 8, 142; prejudices of, 59, 60; residual, 60, 67; valid knowledge in, 29, 56
Postempiricism, 29
Postmodernism, xii, 53
Poststructuralism, xii, 100; reintroduction of subject in, 97
Potter, Karl H., 127
Power: emancipatory, 64, 169; of spiritual insights, 125; transformative, 64, 65
Prabhu, Joseph, 65
Pragmatism, 212n8
Prajña, 127, 128
Prakṛti, 129
Projection, 31; of repressed feelings, 31
Proudfoot, Wayne, 17, 137, 143, 200n13
Psychedelics, 109, 149
Psychedelic tradition, 20; altered states and, 6; counterculture of, 5–6; research, 6
Psychology: of consciousness, 6; Fourth, 5; humanistic, 5, 19, 20; Jungian, 19; Western, 5, 6
Psychosynthesis, 6
Pure Consciousness, 33, 75, 81, 85, 102, 103, 204n24, 206n2, 215n26
Pure Mind, 148
Purusa, 128, 129
Putnam, Hilary, 59

Quine, Willard V., 59, 61, 89, 139, 142, 213n16

Rabinow, P., 57
Radhakrishnan, Sarvepalli, 18, 49, 50, 73, 163
Rajneesh, Bagwan, 6
Ramanuja, 93, 160, 161
Rambachan, Anantanand, 27, 50, 199n23
Raphael, Melissa, 138
Rationalism: Enlightenment, x
Rationality: aesthetic-expressive, 17, 22; devaluation of, 53; instrumental-technical, 17, 22, 52–53; moral-pragmatic, 17, 22

The Real, 135
Realism: naive, 142; valid knowledge of, 29
Reality: absolute, 32, 92, 102; access to, 3, 172; as consciousness, 48; cosmic confidence in, 174; descriptions of, 64; direct apprehension of, 109, 135; disclosure of, 176, 177; divine, 74, 87, 174; egocentric understanding of, 3; enacted, 169, 177; essential information on, 41; expanded universe of, viii; hierarchy of levels of, 52, 88, 96; independent of diversity of human interpretation, xi; inner, 32; intersubjectively shared, 7; intuitive understanding of, 74; mapping, 25; material, 83; misconceptions about, 127; multidimensional access to, 121, 194n12; nature of, 7, 165, 167, 219n8; nature's, 155; noumenal, 79, 162, 165, 212n12, 219n8; numinous depths of, 142; objective, ix, x, xi, 32, 74, 90; outer, 32; participatory vision of, 143; physical, 201n12; plural, 145–146; pregiven, xi, 85, 90, 99, 133, 151, 156, 165, 172, 207n9, 219n11; psychological, 45; self-disclosure of, 181; self-unfolding of, 155; spiritual, xv, 28, 45, 80, 89, 133; spiritual systems and, 37–38; subject's separation from, ix; supreme, ix; as supreme truth, ix; transcendental, 177, 194n8, 212n14; transconceptual disclosures of, 145, 147, 149; transpersonal, 7; ultimate nature of, 74, 93, 103, 135; understanding, 1, 37–38; uninterpreted, 139, 141, 142, 143; unity of, 87; universal, ix, xiv, 89; validation of, xi, 58; virtual, 83
Reason: human, 21; liberation of, 21
Reductionism, viii, 8, 141; of empiricism, 42; experiential, 186; of perennial philosophy, 182; of science, 54; secular, xii; sensory, 42, 56, 57, 58, 66–69, 67; transpersonal theory and, 22–28; Western, xix
Reincarnation, 48, 51
Relativism, xii, 34, 181, 188–189, 210n7; absolutism and, 90; integration with science, xii; mistaken, 210n7; moderated, 210n7; objectivism and, 29; pluralistic, 223n10; refutation of, 222n8; self-contradictory, 53; self-refuting, 197n13; spiritual, 152, 182; universalism and, 99
Religion(s): association with dogmatism, 20; common elements in, 4, 136, 145, 153; comparative, 200n13; conflicting truth-claims in, 159, 165–167; cross-cultural philosophy of, xii, 76–80, 107; differing contemplative goals in, 148; differing traditions of, 65–66; doctrinal ranking of,

Religion(s) *(continued)*
103–105; dogmatic, 55; ecumenical search
for common grounds, 66; empiricism and,
199n5; exoteric, 74, 81; experience as
foundation of, 50; falsifiability in, 62–65;
foundations for, 63; as immediate
experience, 200n13; integration with
science, 52, 56, 58; marginalization of, 52;
multicentered view of, 148; mythical beliefs
of, 54, 55; parallels among, 91–92;
premodern, 65; ranking, 159–162;
reconstruction of, xvii; root, xvii; sacred
places in, 120; schism with science, viii;
science and, 42, 52; structuralist accounts of,
78; transcendental unity of, 72, 87; world
views and, 10
Religious studies: modern, 48–51
Renaissance, ix; Spiritual, xvii
Replicability, 42; spiritual science and, 57
Representational paradigm, 29, 59, 139
Rescher, Nicholas, 210n7, 213n16
Revelations, 46, 50, 207n4
Richard of Saint Victor, 153
Richards, G., 102
Ricoeur, Paul, 96, 203n17
Ring, Kenneth, 125, 208n10
Robbins, R.H., 78
Robbins, Thomas, 203n17
Roberts, Bernadette, 104–105
Romanticism, 6, 53
Rorty, Richard, 29, 59, 123, 139, 213n15
Rothberg, Donald, 7, 17, 22, 23, 24, 26, 32,
37–38, 44, 57, 58, 71, 75, 106, 107, 137, 178,
198n18, 210n3, 210n7, 218n5
Rowan, John, 106
Roy, Rammohan, 18, 163
Rumi, 128
Runzo, Joseph, 213n15
Ruse, M., 61
Ryle, Gilbert, 212n8

Sacred: as "other," xviii; transpersonal
"hierophany" and, xviii
Sacred places, 120
Saguna Brahman, 160
St. Augustine, 73
St. Basil, 122
St. John of the Cross, 117, 130, 208n16,
209n17, 223n9
St. Teresa, 130, 208n16
Saivism, 48
Samadhi, 27
Sambhogakaya, 67, 85
Samkhya Yoga, 128, 129, 160, 218n1

Sanders, P.T., 62
Sangha, 26
Sankara, 89, 92, 127, 128, 129, 160, 218n1,
218n4
Sankhya-Yoga school, 50
Sartre, Jean-Paul, 33
Satcitananda, 148
Satori, 79*fig*, 103, 129
Schiebinger, L., 199n9
Schleiermacher, Friedrich D.E., 17, 200n13
Schmitt, Charles B., 73
Scholasticism, 73
Scholem, Gershom, 210n5
Schuon, Frithjof, 74, 75, 76, 81, 87, 88, 89, 90,
91, 92, 93, 135
Science: apprehension and, 62; artificial
reconstructions in, 65; bogus, 54; cognitive,
29, 139; confirmation and, 62; of
consciousness, 69; contradictions of, 55;
correspondence theory of truth for, 59; deep,
62, 63; empirical, x, xi, 17, 20, 21, 22, 27, 56,
199n9; empiricist, 69, 138; falsifiability and,
60–62, 61, 62; feminist, 59; human, 61; of
human experience, 20, 69; injunction and,
62; inner, 49; instrumental reason and, 57;
instrumental-technical rationality in, 52–53;
integration with religion, xii, 52, 56, 58;
liberation from Catholicism, 21;
monological, 56, 199n9; natural, 17, 42, 43,
52–53, 53, 56, 57, 59, 61; objective, 17, 56;
physical, 44; postempiricist philosophy of, 65;
post-Kuhnian philosophy of, xii;
pseudoscience and, 60, 61–62; reductionism
of, 54; of religion, 200n13; religion and, 42,
52; schism with religion, viii; similarity to
spirituality, 41; spiritual, 20, 43, 57, 69; state-
specific, 46–47; Tantra and, 48; Taoist, 20, 69;
transpersonal research and, 42; valid
knowledge of, 27; Vedantic thought and, 48
Scientific method: essential aspects of, 53;
human inquiry and, 57
Scientism, 66–69, 67; critique of, 59
Searle, John R., 139
Sefirots, 153
Self: beyond, 196n9; change in, 31; cognized,
145, 196n9; defining, ix; empty nature of,
49; estrangement of, 142; eternal, 129;
higher, 36; identification with body, 30;
identification with mind, 30; identity, 32;
individual, 5; knowledge of, 9; modern, ix,
xviii; nature of, 127; transformation, 24,
37–38, 122, 167; transpersonal, 30; ultimate
nature of, 93; understanding, 196n9;
Western, ix

Self-absorption, 15
Self-actualization, ix, 6, 18–19, 46, 106
Self-annihilation, 209n17
Self-centeredness, 4, 34, 36, 127, 144, 145, 168, 170, 175, 177, 193n6, 214n22, 214n23, 215n24
Self-contradiction, 210n7
Self-discipline, 27
Self-exploration, 81
Self-expression: divine, 153
Self-growth, 35
Self-identification, 196n9; with Absolute Consciousness, 82
Self-preoccupation, 34, 35
Self-realization, 198n21
Self-transcendence, 19
Sellars, Wilfrid, 139, 212n8
Sells, Michael A., 122, 178, 206n2
Sepher Yetzirah, 150
Shaivism, 154
Shaktism, 48
Shamanism, 79fig, 130, 145, 216n32; psychedelic, 147
Shanon, B., 29
Sharf, Robert H., 17, 50, 129, 130, 163
Sheldrake, Rupert, 120
Shepherd, L.J., 59, 199n9
Shingon Esoteric school, 161
Short, L., 198n18
Smart, Ninian, 76, 215n29
Smith, A.P., 51
Smith, Barbara Hernstein, 210n7
Smith, Huston, 75, 76, 81, 87, 88, 90, 167, 170, 201n9
Smith, J.E., 51
Smith, Jonathan Z., 213n15
Smith, Wilfred Cantwell, 215n27
Sophists, 210n7
Sorell, T., 56
Soul, 128; nondual, 82; union of with God, 117
Spirit: absolute, 84; creative power of, 182; dialectic of, 6; as end point of evolution, 84; as essence of human nature, 7; as foundation of Cosmos, 75; immanent, 75; involution of, 75; knowledge of, 76; manifestation of, 75; nature of, 187, 190; nondual, 103; recognition of, xviii–xix; self-disclosure of, 157, 191; transcending, 75
Spirit-in-action, 26
Spiritual: alienation, 21, 127; anarchy, 152, 153, 191; awareness, 65; claims, 64; cocreation, 154; consciousness, 37; creativity, 126; development, 76, 85, 103, 149, 152, 187, 196n9, 218n5, 221n3; diversity, 201n12;

dynamism, xv; eclecticism, xvii, 152; emancipation, 175; energy, 44; epistemology, 159; events, 28; evolution, 82, 102, 155; experiences, 53, 55, 89, 163, 208n16; hermeneutics, 166; inquiry, 146, 149, 157; insights, 1, 4, 43, 63, 68, 125, 146, 149, 150, 153, 160, 162, 167, 208n15, 221n3; intuition, 93; knowledge, 32, 41, 42, 46; materialism, 34, 35; nondual, 162; pathology, 37; paths, 147; perspectives, 1; phenomena, 2, 143; power, 4, 133, 150; pregivens, 154, 155; reality, xv, 28, 45, 80, 89, 133; realization, 119, 178, 206n3, 223n10; relativism, 152; science, 57; syncretism, xvii; theistic, 162; tradition, 144–149; transformation, 34; truth, 159; ultimates, 78, 81, 133, 138, 147, 148, 151, 160, 168, 174, 177, 178, 212n12; unity, 76; universalism, 4, 71, 189–191; worldspace, 154
Spiritual choices: privileged, xix, xx
Spiritual development, 76, 85, 103, 149, 152, 187, 196n9, 218n5, 221n3
Spiritual diversity: reductionistic nature of, xix
Spiritual events: Christian, 119; communal, 119; in locus of collective identity, 120; as self's experiences, 36
Spiritual experiences, 17, 20, 23, 26, 27, 35, 36, 37, 41, 43, 52, 53, 55; cognitive value of, 52; corroboration of, 64; doctrinal beliefs and, 137; falsifiability of, 63; integration into everyday life, 15; meaning of, 137; science of, 69; thirst for, 15; validity of, 108
Spiritual inquiry, 68; assimilation of in masculinized science, 59; claims and, 64; logic of, 3, 64, 65; normal, 68; revolutionary, 69; self-defeating account of, 60; spiritual insights and, 4; three strand model, 68, 69
Spirituality, x; authentic, 60, 62; cognitive dimensions of, 7, 53; confusion about, xvii; contemporary forms of, 55; devaluation of, 23, 56; ego-centered version, 35; emancipation of, 23; empiricist colonization of, 3, 41–70; epistemic value of, 1–12, 8; as epistemologically sterile, 8; as essential foundation of psychological health, viii; experiential vision of, 7, 15–39, 24; freeing from constraints of modern world view, 23; impoverishment of, 133; as individual inner experience, xix, 15; individuality and, 17, 28; individual subjective experience in, xviii; as inner experience, 18; integral approach to, 26; integrity of, 60; intrasubjective account, 199n23; legitimization of, xi, xvii, 3, 10, 55, 181; limitations of contextualism in, 150;

Spirituality (*continued*)
  marginalization of, 20, 23, 28, 55, 109;
  meaning of, 7; meeting the standards of
  natural science, 65; modern concepts of, 15,
  28; as multilocal epistemic event, 12;
  mystical conception of, 119; nature of, x,
  178; ontological status of, x, xi; participatory
  emancipation of, 178; as private, 124;
  psychological health and, 19; science and,
  41, 43; socially engaged, 24; standards of
  validity in, 3; structuralist account of, 96;
  understanding, 12, 15, 34, 55; universal, 78,
  85, 99; of women, 138
Spiritual knowledge/knowing, 32, 41, 42, 46;
  assumptions about, 133; cognition in, 140;
  conflicting claims of, 78; cultural factors in,
  140; emancipatory nature of, 127; as
  empirical, xix; enacting, 166; integrative
  arrestment and, 125; justification for, 108;
  legitimization of, 41, 55, 163; liberation and,
  128; mediation in, 159, 171–174;
  metaphysical status on, 182; nature of, 46,
  63, 133; ontological status of, 182;
  participatory nature of, 115–131;
  redemption of, 23; of spiritual experiences,
  15; spiritual liberation and, 130; universality
  of, 2; validation of, 3, 42, 65, 163, 168, 182,
  221*n4*
Spiritual liberation, xiii, 102, 129, 134, 159,
  174–178; centrality of, 182; differing, 4;
  diversity of, 156; epistemic nature of, 129;
  epistemological-ontological dimensions of,
  174, 175; multiplicity of, 175; ontological,
  177; participatory knowing and, 130;
  phenomenological, 177; soteriological-
  phenomenological dimensions of, 174, 175;
  "things-as-they-are/can be," 175, 176, 177;
  ultimate, 148; universality of, 2
Spiritual narcissism, 15, 34–36, 115, 131;
  defining, 35; ego-inflation and, 35; experientialism and, 181; participatory turn and,
  125; spirituality and, 34; symptoms of, 35;
  truth and, 168
Spiritual phenomenon: Cartesian account of,
  198*n18*
Spiritual pluralism, 208*n11*, 223*n10*. *See also*
  Pluralism; challenge of, 133–138;
  epistemological, 175; existence at
  metaphysical level, 167; metaphysical, 175;
  ontological implications, 175, 219*n11*;
  ultimate reality and, 167
Spiritual power, 133, 150
Spiritual practice: conservative management of,
  68

Spiritual tradition, 4, 64; authoritarian
  tendencies in, 151–152; Cartesian-Kantian
  notions in, 151–155, 166, 176; Christian
  mysticism, 6; conflicts in, 92; doctrinal
  ranking of, 103–105; dogmatism and,
  92–95; Gnosticism, 6; Hermeticism, 6;
  hierarchical gradations in, 160;
  incommensurability of, 149; intolerance
  and, 92–95; Kabbalah, 6; Neoplatonism, 6;
  participatory vision and, 180; privileged, xix,
  xx; ranking, 159–162; restrictive conditions
  in, 152; universal truth and, 71; visions of
  reality in, 71
Spiritual truth, xiii; validity of, 167–171
Spiritual ultimates: universality of, 2
Sravana, 199*n23*
Sruti, 50
Staal, Frits, 122
Stace, Walter T., 80, 209*n1*
Stamos, D.N., 61
Stenger, M.A., 170
Steuco, Agostino, 73
Stiver, D.R., 96, 97, 102, 203*n17*
Stoddart, W., 90
Stoeber, Michael, 161, 212*n13*
Streng, Frederick J., 102
Structuralism, 84; abstractive fallacies in, 100;
  biogenetic, 78; challenges to, 97;
  consciousness and, 96; deep structures in, 95,
  97–98; defense of, 203n17; doctrinal ranking
  of traditions in, 103–105; essentialism and,
  100; falsifiability and, 97; genetic, 201*n12*;
  hermeneutics and, 102–103; human
  behavior and, 96; linguistics and, 96; logic
  of, 201*n12*; self-criticism and, 97; self-
  refutation of, 100; subtle objectivism in,
  98–99; surface structures in, 95, 98–99;
  transformation and, 101, 102; universal
  structures and, 96; validity of, 100–101;
  verifiability and, 97
Subjective/subjectivism, 143; accusations of,
  109; becoming objective, 30, 31, 32;
  environment and, 32; falsity of, 91; human,
  30; individuality, xviii; innermost, 90; myths
  of, 34; of psychedelic experience, ix; self-
  delusion and, 198*n22*; structures of, 31,
  198*n18*; transition to objective, 30;
  transpersonal theory and, 2
Subtle Cartesianism, 28–34, 124–125, 181
Suchness of all Forms, 102
Suffering, 102; eradication of, 149; liberation
  from, 145; self-imposed, 145, 149
Sufism, 77*fig*, 79*fig*, 81, 103, 128, 147, 209*n17*,
  216*n32*; devotional, 154; Melveli, 120

Sunyata, 74, 77*fig*, 81, 102, 103, 147, 148, 178, 190, 201*n12*, 204*n24*
Sutich, Anthony, 5, 7, 18, 42
Suzuki, D.T., 6, 17, 129, 163, 200*n3*
Swan, Jim A., 120
Swinburne, Richard, 60
Synchronicity, 45

Tagore, Rabindranath, 18
Tantra, 48, 216*n32*
Tao, 77*fig*
Taoism, 5, 20, 28, 77*fig*, 79*fig*, 81, 161, 195*n7*, 202*n14*; counterculture influence of, 6; peak-experiences and, 106
Tarnas, Richard, 21, 139, 142, 143, 155, 172, 173, 194*n8*, 194*n11*, 204*n22*, 214*n18*
Tart, Charles, 16, 46–47
Tathagata, 102
Taylor, Eugene, 51
Teresa of Avila, 153
Theoria, 58
Theosophical Society, 74
Theosophy, 209*n17*
Theurgy, 217*n37*
Thibaut, G., 160
Thinking: global, 25; teleological, 155; Vedantic, 48
Thiselton, Anthony, 203*n17*
Thomism, 73
Thompson, Evans, 21, 29, 139, 152, 201*n12*
Thurman, Robert, 49
Tianji, 210*n7*
T'ien-t'ai, 161
Tradition: cultural, ix; humanistic, 18; Islamic, 209*n17*; metaphysical, 19; ranking, 159–162; spiritual, 144–149; tolerance among, 177; Western, ix, 18, 19
Transcendence: nondual, x; self, 19
Transcendentalism, 6, 214*n19*
Transconceptuality: cognition and, 146; disclosure of reality and, 145; equation of, 145; spiritual inquiry and, 146
Transformation, 101, 102; participatory knowing and, 123–124; personal, 123; self, 122, 167; willingness for, 122; of world, 122
Transpersonal: anthropology, xix; as "beyond ego," 196*n9*; as "beyond personal," xviii; claims, 198*n16*; defining, 5; derivation, xv; development, 197*n15*; disciplines, xix; ecology, xix; experiences, 9, 11, 43; hermeneutics, 181; hierarchical gradations of, 165; "hierophany," xviii; inquiry, 41, 181; knowledge, 9, 42; multidisciplinary orientation, xix; phenomena, 2; redefining, xv;

self, 30; understanding term, xviii; world, 194*n7*
Transpersonal development, 30; models, 159; nature of, 19
Transpersonal epistemology, 8–9, 10
Transpersonal experiences: causes of, 16; collective identities and, 120; constituting, 196*n9*; defining, 11, 16, 194*n2*, 196*n9*; as extension of consciousness, 16; facilitating, 206*n3*; knowledge accessed during, 10; leading to transpersonal knowledge, 16; as participatory event, 116; in psychedelic sessions, 120; in relation to objects of existence, 33
Transpersonal inquiry: empirical grounds for, 2
Transpersonalism, 6
Transpersonal knowledge/knowing: absolute/relative analysis, 10; criteria for claims of, 10; defining, 10; as empirical, 18; of human nature, 8; immediate/mediate analysis, 10; justification of, 10; nature of, 10; nebulousness of nature of, 10; objective/constructed analysis, 10; participatory nature of, 122, 128; transpersonal experiences and, 125–126; universal/contextual analysis, 10; validity of claims of, 20–21
Transpersonal movement: historical roots of, 106; lack of consensus on fundamental matters in, 7; as modern project, xviii; origin of, xvii, 5–6; religious anarchy and, xvii
Transpersonal phenomena: Cartesianism and, 28, 33; contradictions in revelations of, 9–10; defining, 11, 16, 196*n9*; as epistemic event, 3, 119–120; as epistemic events, 12; extension of sense of identity in, 16; integration into everyday life, 36; intrasubjective dimension of, 3; knowledge and, 8; as multilocal, 119–120, 124, 206*n1*; nature of, 194*n2*; nonintentional nature of, 116; optimization of, 109; as participatory, 120–121; perennialist disposition of, 106, 107; results of study of, 7; study through empiricist science, 3; subjective-objective structuration and, 30; subtle Cartesianism and, 124–125; understanding, 7, 109; witness-consciousness and, 196*n9*
Transpersonal psychology: addresses the schism between religion and science, viii; commitment to inner empiricism, ix; goals of, x, xi, 72; inclusion of spiritual dimension of experience, viii; inherited principles and; legitimization of, 108; liberating impulse in, viii; origins, viii; paradigm shift in, viii;

Transpersonal theory (*continued*)
  reaction against Western cultural tradition
  in, ix; to transpersonal theory, xix
Transpersonal studies, 76–80; centrality of
  knowledge in, 9; defining, 20; empiricist
  colonization of spirituality and, 3; epistemic
  validity of, 69; freeing from Cartesianism,
  12; independence from specific religious
  traditions, 71; legitimization of, 21;
  participatory turn and, 126, 127; peak-
  experiences and, 19; replication of claims in,
  3; on self-actualization, 18–19; Western
  humanist tradition and, 18–20
Transpersonal theory, 1–12; association with
  perennial philosophy, 72; Cartesianism and,
  43, 109; commitment to intrasubjective
  reductionism, 28; conceptualization of phenomena in experiential terms, 15; constraints on, xv; deep structures in, 95, 97–98;
  empiricist language and, 41; epistemology
  of, 10; hierarchical rankings in, xi; inner
  empiricism and, 44; inner experiences and,
  18; intrasubjective reductionism and, 22–28;
  metaphysical speculation and, 9; myths of
  subjectivism and, 2; objectivism and, 2;
  participatory turn in, 116–121; perennialism
  and, 195n6; perennial philosophy and, x,
  105–108; philosophical foundations, 71;
  rejection/affirmation of spiritual traditions
  by, xi; subtle Cartesianism and, 28–34;
  validity of knowledge of, 23
Transpersonal vision: bringing forth a transpersonal world by, 7; contrast with scientific
  paradigms, 8; diverse, 7, 166; in epistemic
  terms, 1, 8–9, 12, 194n10, n11; intention of,
  7; spiritual import of, 7–8; as way of
  thinking, 7
Trungpa, Chögyam, 6, 35
Truth: absolute, xi, 64; conflicting claims in
  religion, 165–167; consensual theory of,
  44–45; correspondence theory of, 59,
  212n11; cosmic, 174; degrees of, 103;
  emancipatory power of, 168; event, 139,
  207n4; as event of self-disclosure of Being,
  109; experience of, 109; impersonal, x;
  independent, x; nature's, 155; objective, 22,
  59, 74, 214n19; of objective reality, x;
  perennial, x, 83, 87, 88, 92, 140; psychospiritual, 45; single, 75; single absolute, ix;
  spiritual, 167–171; transcendent, ix; ultimate,
  71; universal, x, xi, 9, 71, 73, 181; for validity
  of spiritual experiences, 108
Tsong kha pa, 163
Tuck, A.P., 102

Tulku, Tarthang, 6
Turner, D., 208n16, 223n9

Udayana, 160
Ultimate reality, 32, 73, 78, 90, 133, 135, 147,
  151, 165, 167, 171, 175
Unconscious: collective, 6; Freud and, 6
Underhill, Evelyn, 135
Unity: metaphysical priority of, 191; mystical,
  109, 111, 138, 178; original, 83; of reality,
  87; spiritual, 76; transcendent, 72, 87, 171;
  undifferentiated, 82
Universalism, 210n7; abstract, 204n22; deep
  structure, 95; defense of, 205n25; as mark of
  what is True, 87; of numinous, 80; of
  perennial philosophy, 108; pregiven spiritual
  ultimates in, 180; problems with, 94; relation
  to pluralism, 191; relativism and, 99;
  spiritual, 4, 71, 183–191
Universal Mind, 75
Upadesasahasri, 127
Upanishads, 82, 89, 93
Upaya, 168

Vajragnana, Pandith, 150, 164
Valentine, Elizabeth, 49
Validation: empiricism and, x; of pregiven
  reality, xi
Validity: of claims of meditation, 49; of
  knowledge in science, 49; objective, 9; of
  spiritual truth, 167–171; of structuralism,
  100–101; of transpersonal knowledge, 42–43
Valle, Ron S., 16, 71
Van Der Steen, W.J., 61
Van Ruusbroec, Jan, 153
Varela, Francisco J., 21, 29, 85, 99, 123, 139,
  152, 201n12
Vaughan, Frances, xix, 16, 72, 194n2
Vedanta, 148
Verifiability, 42; communal confirmation and,
  47; instrumental injunction and, 47, 56;
  intuitive apprehension and, 47, 56; of
  knowledge gained in altered states, 46–47; as
  standard for knowledge, 27; structuralism
  and, 97; through direct contemplation, 48; of
  transpersonal knowledge, 43
Vich, Miles, 5
Vichara, 58
Vijñanabhioksu, 160
Vipassana, 6, 17, 129, 163
Vision-logic, 25
Visuddhimagga, 163
Vivekananda, Swami, 74
Voegelin, Erich, vii

The Void, 81, 85, 202*n14*
von Brück, Michael, 51
von Glasersfeld, Ernst, 139
von Wright, G.H., 56
Vroom, Hendrik M., 64, 65, 107, 148, 170, 218*n7*
Vyasa, 160

Wade, Jenny, 186, 207*n5*
Walsh, Roger N., xix, 16, 32, 51, 71, 83, 106, 163, 194*n2*
Washburn, Michael, xix, 19, 44, 186, 197*n15*, 214*n20*
Watts, Alan, 6, 200*n3*
Weber, Max, 17, 18, 52
Weber, Reneé, 42
Welwood, John, 43
Whirling Dervishes, 120
Whitehead, Alfred North, 17
Wiggins, J.B., 107, 176
Wilber, Kenneth, 16, 19, 23, 24, 25, 26, 27, 30, 31, 35, 36, 37, 42, 47–48, 51, 53, 54, 55, 56, 57, 58, 59, 61, 62, 63, 65, 66–69, 71, 72, 75, 78, 83–86, 89, 93, 106, 108, 126, 137, 147, 154, 155, 162, 163, 172, 178, 186, 196*n9*, 197*n12*, 198*n17*, 198*n20*, 201*n8*, 202*n13*, 202*n14*, 203*n17*, 203*n18*, 203*n19*, 205*n25*, 207*n9*, 215*n24*, 218*n3*, 223*n10*
Will: acts of, 46
Williams, Paul, 128
Wisdom: disclosure of, 128
Wittgenstein, Ludwig, 92
Wittine, Bryan, 72
Woodroffe, Sir John, 48

World: cognized, 145; decentered understanding of, 197*n11*; intrinsic features of, 139–140; making, 139; nature of, 194*n7*; pregiven, 139; sensoriomotor, 140; transpersonal, 194*n7*; visionary, 166
Worldspace, 31, 212*n11*; deep structures of, 95; enacted, 85, 86, 207*n9*; spiritual, 154; structural potentials for, 96
World views, 171, 194*n8*; Cartesian-Kantian, 214*n18*; clashes between, 10; cultural, 25; individual, 17, 22; intersubjective, 17, 22, 24; intolerance and, 92–95; natural, 17, 22; objective, 17, 22, 24; plurality of, 110; rational, 197*n10*; religious, 10; social, 17, 22; subjective, 17, 22, 24; unified religious-metaphysical, 22
Wright, Peggy, 138

Yama, 27
Yandell, Keith E., 51
Yazdi, Ha'iri, 209*n17*
Yoga, 74, 128, 160, 195*n7*, 218*n1*; ethical preparation for, 27
Yogachara, 148
Yogananda, Paramahansa, 6
Yoga Sutra, 129
Yogasutras, 50

Zaehner, Robert C., 80, 160, 218*n4*
Zen Buddhism, 5, 79*fig*, 103, 129, 130; Fromm and, 6; Kyoto school, 17; popularization of, 6
Zimmerman, Michael, 224–225*n10*
Zimmerman, R.L., 96
Zohar, 150, 207*n6*

Printed in the United States
18749LVS00003B/52-102